"A well-packed re-creation of the lives of star-crossed lovers through an era that would come to be defined in part by Nathanael West."
— *Publishers Weekly*

"*Lonelyhearts* lays bare the dark side of America's bicoastal 1930s glitterati. Meade has taken the contrasting stories and twisted them into a spiraling narrative that makes compulsive reading."
— Amanda Vaill, author of *Everybody Was So Young: Gerald and Sara Murphy: A Lost Generation Love Story*

"A literary page-turner, *Lonelyhearts* brings a fresh view to bookish New York and philistine Hollywood in the years leading up to the Second World War. Meade's exhaustive research yields some surprising new material. But her great triumph is to plumb the mind of one of America's strangest and most original authors."
— Diane Jacobs, author of *Christmas in July: The Life and Art of Preston Sturges*

PRAISE *for*

BOBBED HAIR AND BATHTUB GIN

"Intoxicating . . . Any reader even remotely interested in the 1920s or its literary figures will be hard-pressed to find a more scintillating and easily readable book."
— *Associated Press*

"[Meade's] writing is bright, her language charged with gritty details . . . gossipy tidbits . . . and accomplished one-liners."
— *San Francisco Chronicle*, Best Books of 2004

"Wonderful."
— *Washington Post Book World*, Best Books of 2004

"Dazzling. Fast living never felt like this on the page before."
— Stacy Schiff, Pulitzer Prize–winning author of *Vera (Mrs. Vladimir Nabokov)*

LONELYHEARTS

BOOKS BY MARION MEADE

Biographies

*Free Woman: The Life and Times
of Victoria Woodhull*

Eleanor of Aquitaine

*Madame Blavatsky: The Woman
Behind the Myth*

Dorothy Parker: What Fresh Hell Is This?

Buster Keaton: Cut to the Chase

The Unruly Life of Woody Allen

*Bobbed Hair and Bathtub Gin: Writers
Running Wild in the Twenties*

*Lonelyhearts: The Screwball World of
Nathanael West and Eileen McKenney*

Novels

*Stealing Heaven: The Love Story of
Heloise and Abelard*

Sybille

LONELYHEARTS

THE SCREWBALL WORLD

of

NATHANAEL WEST

and

EILEEN McKENNEY

MARION MEADE

MARINER BOOKS
HOUGHTON MIFFLIN HARCOURT
BOSTON NEW YORK

First Mariner Books edition 2011

Copyright © 2010 by Marion Meade

For information about permission to reproduce
selections from this book, write to Permissions,
Houghton Mifflin Harcourt Publishing Company,
215 Park Avenue South, New York, New York 10003.

www.hmhbooks.com

Library of Congress Cataloging-in-Publication Data
Meade, Marion, date.
  Lonelyhearts : the screwball world of Nathanael West
and Eileen McKenney / Marion Meade.
      p. cm.
  Includes bibliographical references.
  ISBN 978-0-15-101149-0   ISBN 978-0-547-38638-6 (pbk.)
  1. West, Nathanael, 1903–1940. 2. Authors, American—20th
century—Biography. 3. McKenney, Eileen, d. 1940. I. Title.
  PS3545.E8334Z822 2009
  813'.52—dc22
  [B]   2009013285

Book design by Melissa Lotfy
Map by Jeffrey Ward

Printed in the United States of America
DOC 10 9 8 7 6 5 4 3 2 1

Photo credits appear on page 367.

Once again for Alison, Ashley, and Katharine

Wildly funny, desperately sad, brutal and kind, furious and patient, there was no other like Nathanael West.

—DOROTHY PARKER

CONTENTS

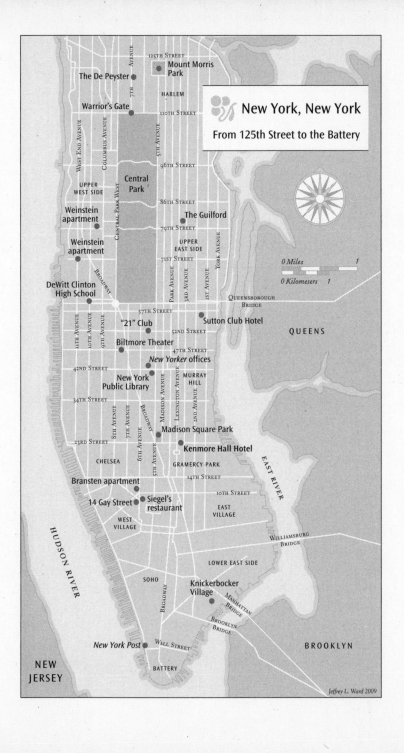

125TH STREET

Mount Morris
Park

The De Peyster

7TH AVENUE

HARLEM

Warrior's Gate

110TH STREET

New York, New York

From 125th Street to the Battery

WEST END AVENUE

COLUMBUS AVENUE

5TH AVENUE

96TH STREET

UPPER
WEST SIDE

Central
Park

CENTRAL PARK WEST

86TH STREET

Weinstein
apartment

The Guilford

79TH STREET

UPPER
EAST SIDE

Weinstein
apartment

71ST STREET

YORK AVENUE

1ST AVENUE

2ND AVENUE

3RD AVENUE

PARK AVENUE

0 Miles   1

0 Kilometers   1

BROADWAY

DeWitt Clinton
High School

QUEENSBOROUGH
BRIDGE

QUEENS

57TH STREET

11TH AVENUE

10TH AVENUE

9TH AVENUE

"21" Club

Sutton Club Hotel

52ND STREET

Biltmore Theater

47TH STREET

New Yorker offices

42ND STREET

MADISON AVENUE

LEXINGTON AVENUE

2ND AVENUE

MURRAY
HILL

New York
Public Library

34TH STREET

8TH AVENUE

7TH AVENUE

BROADWAY

Madison Square Park

23RD STREET

6TH AVENUE

5TH AVENUE

Kenmore Hall Hotel

CHELSEA

GRAMERCY PARK

EAST
RIVER

Bransten apartment

14TH STREET

10TH STREET

14 Gay Street

Siegel's
restaurant

EAST
VILLAGE

WEST
VILLAGE

WILLIAMSBURG
BRIDGE

HUDSON RIVER

LOWER EAST SIDE

SOHO

Knickerbocker
Village

BROADWAY

MANHATTAN
BRIDGE

BROOKLYN
BRIDGE

New York Post

WALL STREET

BROOKLYN

NEW
JERSEY

BATTERY

Jeffrey L. Ward 2009

THE ENSEMBLE

LEADS

NATHAN WEINSTEIN, AKA NATHANAEL WEST—high school dropout, candy maker, hotel manager, passionate hunter of doves, novelist who sets his stories in locations such as a horse's bowels and the Hollywood "dream dump"

EILEEN MCKENNEY—one of two Ohio sisters who move to Manhattan and live in a basement apartment; accidental muse known to the public as "my sister Eileen"

SIDNEY J. PERELMAN—son of a failed chicken farmer, now writer-cartoonist, one of Nat's college friends and later brother-in-law

RUTH MCKENNEY—sister of Eileen, whose humorous stories about her Cleveland family draw an enthusiastic response from Depression-era audiences

SUPPORTING PLAYERS

JULIAN SHAPIRO, AKA JOHN SANFORD—Nat's boyhood friend from Harlem, later a lawyer-writer

QUENTIN REYNOLDS—a sometime lovelorn columnist, war correspondent, Nat's classmate at Brown

KATHARINE SERGEANT ANGELL WHITE—*New Yorker* fiction editor, also the person responsible for discovering Ruth McKenney

ST. CLAIR MCKELWAY—charming *New Yorker* writer-editor and Eileen's companion

LORRAINE (LAURA) WEINSTEIN—Nat's youngest sister who marries Sidney Perelman

JOSEPHINE HERBST—kind-hearted novelist who introduces Nat to Bucks County

WALK-ONS

STANLEY ROSE—bookseller

BENNETT CERF—publisher

DANNY, JULIE, GURKE, AND ASTA—animals

BEATRICE MATHIEU AND ALICE SHEPARD—fiancées

MORRIS JACOBS AND RICHARD BRANSTEN—husbands

EDMUND WILSON, LILLIAN HELLMAN, JOHN O'HARA, JOSEPH SCHRANK, F. SCOTT FITZGERALD, ROBERT COATES, DASHIELL HAMMETT, BUDD SCHULBERG, JEROME CHODOROV, JOSEPH FIELDS—literati

OTHERS—a corps of neurotics

INTRODUCTION

IN THE WANING DAYS of the Depression, on the evening of December 26, 1940, a comedy premiering at the Biltmore Theater in New York earned unanimous raves, exploding it into the Broadway firmament. Few of the glowing reviews for *My Sister Eileen* mentioned that the show's true-life heroine had been killed with her husband in a car crash four days earlier. Eileen McKenney had achieved a certain stardom in her sister's *New Yorker* tales, whereas her husband, the author of four slender novels and a score of B movies, was relatively unknown to the general public; none of his books had sold well. A writer ahead of his time, Nathanael West created psychologically complex antiheroes and violent, pitch-dark fictions that he (but few others) called comic novels. His rude message—*guess what, folks, the American Dream is a scam*—wasn't too popular either. A provocateur at heart, he was happiest swimming against the tide.

Not until after the Second World War, in that post-A-bomb, Dr. Strangelove era, did West's brand of nightmare humor find an appreciative audience. His novels were first collected in 1957 by Farrar, Straus & Cudahy, and the Library of America would follow some forty years later by adding his complete works to its canon of classic American literature. As Number 93, he was the first Jewish writer enshrined in an elite pantheon that includes Mark Twain and Nathaniel Hawthorne. *Miss Lonelyhearts* now is recognized as one of the significant

American novels of the twentieth century while *The Day of the Locust* is credited as the most trenchant book ever written about Hollywood moviemaking.

The story of Nathanael West and Eileen McKenney has never been told, although their individual portraits have been presented in earlier biographies and memoirs. At first glance, it is hard to see any logical connection. They met in the fall of 1939, married the following spring, and wound up dead on the highway on December 22, 1940, when she was just twenty-seven and he was thirty-seven. What does a high-strung New York intellectual have to do with a nonintellectual darling from Ohio? And when is fifteen months enough time to become friends and spouses, much less enjoy the pleasures of a good fight? Only in the turmoil of the 1930s, with its attendant rainbows and banana peels, could two people complement each other so precisely.

Their short lives necessarily leave open the question of what else they might have done. McKenney missed turning forty in the year 1953 and seeing one of the all-time marvelous musicals, *Wonderful Town*, based on her own story. She never had the opportunity to watch Rosalind Russell belting out "Why, oh why, oh why, oh—why did I ever leave Ohio?" Today, McKenney remains a symbol of all the fabled heroines and their real counterparts who migrate to the bright lights in quest of their destinies. West never got to enjoy the rewards that fall to renowned writers. Had his life continued another thirty years, would he have overcome his disillusionment with fiction writing? Would he have found a more satisfying career as a movie and television director or producer?

Their marriage has been called a romance by romantics, a tragedy by those who dote on reasonably happy endings. As we shall see, it was both—and neither. Mr. and Mrs. West were not a Bonnie-and-Clyde jalopy couple although, to a man with West's outlaw personality, anybody on a crime spree could not be all bad. In Westian parlance, their story had a twisteroo punch line, proving that anything can happen, and sometimes does.

LONELYHEARTS

1

IN THE HOTEL

THE LOBBY OF the Kenmore Hall Hotel was deserted at three in the morning. Its skylit lounge was shrouded in pearl shadows, the passenger lift stood wearily at attention, the night porter dozed in the vestibule. Sitting behind the front desk was the assistant manager, a long-legged youth of twenty-six in a Brooks Brothers, three-button wool suit. On this night he bent over the keyboard of a typewriter, pounding out a letter to his girlfriend, Beatrice, in Paris and puffing on a cigarette. "Nothing happens," he wrote.

Kenmore Hall, a pretty redbrick residence hotel not yet two years old, was home to hundreds of young professionals who booked by the week or month. Prized for its desirable address near Gramercy Park, its reasonable rates, and amenities such as a pool and roof garden, the place always had a waiting list for vacancies, sometimes a long one. Nat was supposed to remember guests' names, but he happened to know a great deal more, and not just gossip either. He knew exactly when they awoke and when they left for their offices, who got mail and from whom, what time they went to bed, and which ones couldn't sleep, because the bleary-eyed were known to shuffle down to the lobby and fret about it, as if he could do anything. There were friendly women who found pretexts for inviting him to their rooms. To all proposals he would beg off with an easy smile and a general refusal worded to give no offense. He took fewer pains with the prostitutes, alone or in pairs, who constantly tried to sneak past the desk on their way to the elevator. Hookers—and stolen bath towels—were his biggest aggravations.

Otherwise, the position of assistant manager was not terribly taxing. Aside from charming everyone, the main requirements on the graveyard shift were staying awake and issuing orders in emergencies. Even at the best hotels, the worst things were liable to happen after midnight, and Nat had trained himself to take in stride noisy parties, fires, heart attacks, failed suicides, occasional corpses, and unscheduled checkouts of guests trying to jump their bills. As some anonymous hotelier once said, "Listen to everything and say nothing." And so Nat had diligently learned to comport himself with a silky mixture of servility and severity.

But typically nights at Kenmore Hall were serene. From the tiled spa and pool below his feet rose the steady slapping of brilliant sapphire-colored water. Stacked on top of his head stretched the hushed building, seven hundred rooms, twenty-two stories, its long carpeted hallways mouse-quiet. He kept a room there and when nothing required his special attention he could, if he wished, slip upstairs to 207 for a short rest (but he could never close his eyes). Occasionally he invited people to drop by for a nocturnal swim. Alone, he was rarely in the mood to bother changing clothes and showering, returning to the desk with wet hair and the faint perfume of chlorine still in his nose. For a year now, he'd been saving his free time for his book.

Last winter, something like March—or maybe February—he had gone to eat at Siegel's, a deli nestled under the Sixth Avenue elevated tracks in the Village. It was a friendly place smelling of pickles and pastrami, and Nat liked stopping there before work to meet two former classmates, Quentin Reynolds and Sidney Perelman, both of them writers and the latter his sister's fiancé. One day Quent showed up with a handful of letters from readers of the newspaper where he was employed. Like most big papers, the *Brooklyn Daily Times* published an advice column, "Susan Chester Heart-to-Heart Letters," which appeared on the women's page, hemmed in by meat-loaf recipes and Modish Mitzi fashion cartoons. Signing theatrical pseudonyms ("Puzzled," "Heart-broken and Blue"), the letter writers typically sought guidance on un-requited love or how to attract husbands sure to bring them lifetimes of misery.

Whether there ever had been a person named Susan Chester scarcely mattered; the Susan beat was rotated throughout the news-room, to female and male staff alike. The only qualification for doling out advice was reasonable good sense. Not surprisingly, the assignment was viewed as an irritation, something to be endured without com-plaint, accompanied by prayers for speedy deliverance. Quent, keen to cover sports or straight news, was stuck with Susan for the moment. To Siegel's he brought six letters the paper had discarded as too disturbing for its readers, thinking Sid might be inspired to do a satire on advice columns.

Midway through dinner the letters were passed around the table, but Sid handed them back with a shrug. A few showed "comic super-ficialities," he told Quent, but where were the laughs? For that matter, were they true? It was hard to tell if the writers were real people. Some impressed Sid as stock characters, your average New York crackpot. What he needed were subjects lending themselves to subtle ridicule, like his lampoon of dental magazines, in which he offered a guide to performing one's own extractions. The Dear Susan letters were quickly forgotten when the conversation shifted to more pressing matters. In recent months he and Quent had been collaborating on a humorous novel but had yet to agree on a suitable title, something catchy that might sell a million copies. *Through the Fallopian Tubes on a Bicycle*?

Nat, who had remained silent, began to look at the letters out of cu-riosity. One of them came from a woman identifying herself as Broad Shoulders, who claimed that her husband beat her and infected her with gonorrhea before abandoning her with a brood of kids. Another writer was a crippled sixteen-year-old who feared never being asked for a date. Still others described problems having to do with the evils of gin. To be sure, the situations sounded pitiful, but after a point it was really hard not to giggle.

Immediately Nat was intrigued by these freaky people who, claiming to be cheated of a normal life, kept busy reporting their sagas to anonymous editors, and to strangers who might bear witness to the unfairness of their plights. How in the world did they manage to keep going, let alone write about it? Of course Sid could be right in suspecting the letters to be stunts. For all Nat knew, they came from aspiring writers in disguise, although there had to be easier ways to get published.

As the men were leaving the restaurant, Nat decided to stick the letters in his pocket. It was possible that the material was wrong for satire but useful fodder for fiction. To begin with, the idea of Quent, a big guy who'd played varsity football at Brown, being shoved onto the lovelorn beat and forced to pretend he was Susan Chester, was good for a few laughs. With the addition of the crazed letter writers—a regular mulligan stew of loons, cripples, permanent deadbeats, and retards—the story became even more tempting. Imagine what complications might follow if the poor guy had to meet one of these screwy dames.

For weeks on end, Nat pondered the letters. Maybe something unpredictable could be done, perhaps a kicky cartoon story about a male advice columnist. Such an original concept would surely provide a lot of fun.

A whole year had passed since that evening at Siegel's and he had made little progress on his story about a columnist he was calling Thomas. Later, of course, the columnist wouldn't be called Thomas and Nat would forget he ever had writer's block, even try to repress how he got the letters in the first place. But now he was bogged down in details like whether to use first- or third-person narration. He couldn't tell who was the hero and who the villain. Were they the same person? And did it really matter? After reading several chapters, Sid said the manuscript resembled something out of *Beowulf*. It was too epic, too professorial, too ridiculously intellectual. Get rid of the Dostoyevsky stuff, he suggested; forget about playing amateur psychologist and start describing "people and things," like other writers. Nat said that was "just what I was trying to avoid." He didn't want to be like anybody else.

He had already completed a first novel deemed absolutely, positively unpublishable by all who had seen it. A published author in his daydreams, he imagined himself living on some little street in the heart of the Latin Quarter, lounging on the sand beaches of the Côte d'Azur, and writing whenever the mood took him. Planning to join his girlfriend in June and get married, he had memorized ship schedules but now he knew he wasn't going anywhere. He couldn't. Quitting his job was too scary. When Beatrice found out, she would kill him.

With the appearance of daylight on that Sunday morning in March, Nat's shift was drawing to a close. Beyond the lobby the early morning smell of baking bread floated in from the kitchen; above stairs, there were polished shoes and folded newspapers lying outside doors and laundry baskets that would soon be overflowing with crumpled sheets; and so another day was about to dawn for the dreaming ladies and gentlemen of Kenmore Hall. In a rush to finish his letter, Nat ignored the spelling errors and ended gracefully something he hadn't wished to write in the first place. He typed, "You are a swell girl," which was true, followed by "and I love you," which was open to some doubt.

When his night-duty report had been turned over to the manager, it was time to weave his way uptown, past Madison Square Park, toward Times Square and Columbus Circle, into the quiet streets of the Upper West Side, where he lived with his parents in a cramped apartment, its four rooms a melancholy reminder of all that had gone wrong lately. Five months after the stock market crash, upheavals in residential construction had left developers like Nat's father feeling powerless and his wife of thirty years terrified. Consumed with worry, Anna Weinstein could not be bothered with her son's Gentile girl or his ambition to become a writer—and as she liked to say, everybody knew that writers were good-for-nothing bums.

His mother didn't believe in him. The trouble was, neither did anybody else. But he was going to be writer anyhow; it was something he had known since he was eight, reading *Anna Karenina* on his roof in Harlem. If writing meant becoming a bum, that's what he would be.

2

DUSTY ESKY IN HARLEM

IN 1912, A PAIR of eight-year-olds stood side by side on a strip of grassy island in the middle of Seventh Avenue in Harlem. A bus lumbered by and one of them, a jug-eared boy, began pointing excitedly. "Dion-Bouton," he shouted, naming the French manufacturer. Nathan Weinstein hopped up and down on his spindly legs. Another behemoth came shimmying toward them. "Métallurgique," he called out.

His companion, a boy named Julian Shapiro, looked at him with awe. How did he know that?

"The red car's a Stanley Steamer, and the green one's a Winton," he said. An avid lover of all kinds of motor vehicles, he excelled at the game and could easily identify the spectacular vehicles a block away, the Loziers, the Chalmerses, the racy Apperson Jack Rabbits. It was his greatest talent, the only one with any real street value.

The background music of his childhood had nothing at all to do with cars. What the young Nathan Weinstein heard were the furious birth pangs of buildings being born: the thunderous bulldozing and jack-hammering, the riveting of steel girders, the snorting of gargantuan machines hauling soil, cement, timbers, bricks. On a construction site, it is impossible to hear yourself think, there is no peace from dawn to dusk, and unlucky neighbors longing to kill go quietly mad instead.

Harlem commonly calls to mind the storied capital of black America, a three-square-mile section of upper Manhattan that is almost a city within a city. But prior to the turn of the twentieth century, before African Americans arrived, Harlem was a rustic village of high-stooped, chocolate-brown houses next to older frame buildings, weed-choked empty lots, here and there a handful of surviving farmhouses under the open blue skies. Within a decade or so, around the time Nathan Weinstein was growing up there, the placid village had been supplanted by a luxurious suburb. Developers like Nat's father had boldly transformed Harlem into a leafy oasis full of twittering birds for New Yorkers seeking an alternative to the southern part of Manhattan, which had been settled by waves of immigrants.

This residential district looked like a toy town tumbled out of the sky. Near Fifth Avenue, stately private houses and apartments towering six stories high edged Mount Morris Park. Just beyond the park, along the boulevards streaming north and south through the heart of Harlem, spread block after block of solid apartments, modestly priced but still imposing. Lured by the modern housing were German, Irish, and Jewish families of means, as well as upwardly mobile strivers who clustered there to provide their youngsters with superior educations in an experimental teaching program at P.S. 81. Endowing the neighborhood with a cultural cachet were such establishments as Hammerstein's Opera House on West 125th Street and the Regent a few blocks south, a motion picture theater modeled after a Venetian doge's palace.

There was no poverty in Harlem, no pushcarts or crowded tenements, no suggestion of disease, hardly any crime. From this sanctuary Harlem fathers set out for their offices downtown six mornings a week, and between Decoration and Labor days, entire households made the ritual trip to Brooklyn for roller-coaster rides and hot dogs at Coney Island, but otherwise there were few good reasons to venture below 110th Street. Looking back some eighty years later, Julian Shapiro (renamed John Sanford by then) held tight to memories of this lost paradise. Past the age of ninety, the old gent could still rattle off the merchants' names: Nick Stano's shoe repair, Pop Schorrs doing a brisk business in soda water and Mary Janes for the children of P.S. 81, Kuck's saloon at the northeast corner of Seventh Avenue and 119th Street with its lithograph of Custer's Last Stand behind the bar and the fragrant smell of beer streaming through the swinging doors. The pace of life back then, he wrote, was "sedate."

Sedate, yes, but already beginning to unspool at lightning speed. When Woodrow Wilson was elected president in 1912, vast social and cultural changes were under way, and Harlem reflected the aspirations of the country. Practically everybody believed in the importance of progress—progress and of course patriotism—which would spark a future of brighter electric lights, heavier flying machines, and faster and faster Stanley Steamers.

Nat Weinstein, a youngster who kept to himself, stood alone outside the doorway of 1980 Seventh Avenue. The real estate developers of the new Harlem were prompted by pretension and civic pride to name their properties after notable New Yorkers. Nat lived in the De Peyster, so called for one of the city's oldest families. In the heart of Harlem, the De Peyster and the neighboring Kortright stretched a full city block on the west side of Seventh Avenue between 119th and 120th Streets. Attached like Siamese twins, the matching pair of six-story fireproof buildings of rose- and oatmeal-colored brick resting on limestone bases were built at a cost of $350,000 (equivalent to $8 million in today's currency). Together they presented an impressive façade embellished with sculpted stone ornaments and wrought-iron fences accented by fleur-de-lis finials. Plush, dark red carpeting adorned the tiled lobbies; each of the six-to-eight-room units had sliding doors and tall ceilings with decorative molding, parquet floors, state-of-the-art bathrooms, steam heat, mail chutes, intercom systems, and wall safes. The *New York Times* real estate section called this type of structure a "high-class elevator building."

Like a crown prince monitoring his personal fiefdom, Nat stood guard at the regal doorway as if he owned the block, which in a sense he did because both fortresses had been put up by his father. Indeed, his entire life had been passed in buildings erected by Max Weinstein, in the desirable top-floor apartments reserved for the family.

In the heat of summer, the Harlem streets were filled with ice wagons and shrieking children playing hopscotch, tag, Red Rover, kickball, pickup sticks, and jump rope. On Nat's block, boys with dirty knees were always shooting marbles under a row of shady elms outside the De Peyster. Stationed on a patch of dirt between the sidewalk and the gutter, they hunkered over their glassies, singsonging dubs and knucks down tight. They ignored the kid with the jutting ears, the one on the steps who watched their games through half-closed eyelids, who never worked up a sweat and always looked dreamy. His family teasingly nicknamed him Sleepy, even though other Weinsteins had inherited the same droopy gaze.

He sometimes took a book up to the De Peyster rooftop, where he was liable to come upon Julian with a Frank Merriwell thriller, whose formulaic plots featured Indians and poison knives. An apple-cheeked boy with a helmet of Buster Brown bangs, Julie was the son of a lawyer who came from the same Lithuanian town in the Pale of Settlement as Max Weinstein. (The Pale, the only area of the Russian Empire where Jews were legally permitted to live, was a 386,000-square-mile swath, roughly the size of Texas and New Mexico, between the Baltic and the Black Sea.) The two families had become acquainted at a Catskills resort in the summer of 1905. Nat didn't really want to see Julie, but the Shapiros lived around the corner on St. Nicholas Avenue and Julie used to slip over to the De Peyster to visit his cousin Jasper Perlman.

He pointed to Nat's book. Was that a new Merriwell?

The suggestion that he might be reading a dime novel irked him. "Merriwell! This is *Anna Karenina*. A Russian writer wrote it."

Julie was not conversant with Russian writers. "What's it about?"

"A lady that throws herself under a train," Nat said.

To get his goat, Julie once had declared that he knew Nat's nickname: "It's Natchie." If there was one thing Nat hated, it was being called Natchie, his mother's pet name for him. And as if Natchie wasn't bad enough, he also disliked his given name, so mundane that several of his cousins were also called Nathan.

Nat's greatest happiness was holing up alone in his bedroom with a book and his miniature bulldog. Shutting the door, he discouraged interruptions from his sister Hinda and the baby, Lorraine, by training the pet to growl at anyone who tried to barge in. Sometimes he steam-rolled through "two books alternately," Hinda recalled. The double-door cases in the parlor were stuffed with the usual classics, works by Dickens, Balzac, and Thackeray. Hooked on Flaubert, he decided that French novelists must be the best and scribbled "no good Americans" in his copy of *Madame Bovary*. But in the end, it was the Russians who made the biggest impression. Developing a bottomless appetite for the novels of Dostoyevsky, his all-time favorite, he was gripped by Mother Russia and its ice-blanketed villages pickled in subzero darkness, the images of snow, samovars, and Siberian desolation that he would re-member ever afterward.

Julie, who wanted to be tough like the marble shooters and could often be found kneeling under the elm trees, tried to make sense of Nat's odd behavior. Was he a sissy, or just a coddled kid who thought himself smarter than everybody else? In Julie's theory, he was "one badly-made boy" whose parts didn't match. Anybody could see he was hopelessly clumsy from the way his arms dangled, "as if his sleeves were stuffed." Of course he was "real smart"—he used big words—but what good was that when your wires were crossed?

When Julian got on his nerves, which was often, Nat lost patience and took him to task. There were great books, he said, and there was trash. Julian was reading trash. When he held forth on his revered Dos-toyevsky—he boasted of having read all his books—it was a waste of breath. Julie, a compulsive reader of the Motor Boys books, had never heard of the man. Julie couldn't even pronounce the name. "Dasty Evsko, or Dusty Esky, something like that," just another of Natchie's Russians, he thought. It was "a dumb kind of book to waste time on."

Julie usually found a way to get under Nat's skin. They were con-stantly bickering.

The following year Nat moved away, and that seemed to be the end of Julie. From the upper floor of the De Peyster, Max Weinstein transported his family four blocks south to another high-class elevator building he had just completed at 1884 Seventh Avenue. Julie's family left for West 117th Street after the death of his mother and setbacks in Philip Shapiro's law practice. The boys could have stayed friends, but they didn't. A chance meeting would bring them together again a dozen years later.

Harlem's luxury elevator buildings did not yet exist when the Weinsteins arrived from Russia in the 1880s. With the opening of three elevated rail lines running as far north as 129th street, though, the building boom that was turning so much of Manhattan into a vertical city could finally surge uptown to Harlem. The Weinsteins were not far behind the trains.

Max Weinstein had been born in Kovno (now Kaunas), Lithuania, in 1873, one of five brothers, Charles, Julius, Jacob, Max, and Abraham, and two sisters, Mollie and Rosel. In the building trades, Nathan Weinstein, Nat's grandfather, was a skilled laborer whose sons expected to follow in their father's footsteps.

Like so many others, however, the Weinstein boys had to leave Kovno in order to avoid serving in the military under Russia's harsh conscription laws. Although the city lay hundreds of miles from St. Petersburg, the army regularly rounded up Kovno's young men and marched them away for five or ten and sometimes twenty-five years. Throughout the 1880s, the Weinstein sons straggled to New York City in ones and twos, and their parents and sisters eventually followed. First to make the journey across the Atlantic was Charles, in his late teens; sixteen-year-old Max, a carpenter according to his naturalization petition, arrived on November 21, 1889. Max was a soft-spoken, slightly built boy with delicate features and sad, droopy eyes. Dreamy and sweet-tempered, he had a habit of seizing a person's hands with both of his, and easily won people's affection with his friendliness. Yet he was also given to feelings of sadness. As an adult, his personality, the mild manner so attractive in a youth, came across as ineffectual and lacking in virility. Try as he might to conceal it, Max's natural state would always be deeply melancholic.

In New York's frenzied economy, the city was climbing geographically uptown until it reached the northern end of Manhattan Island, while at the same time it soared higher and higher into the air. It was this phenomenal growth accompanied by a ravenous appetite for housing that became the Weinstein brothers' bread and butter. Hired carpenters and masons in the old country, the brothers found themselves in a strange new land with the right professional skills. They set up their own companies, first developing modest commercial projects on the Lower East Side and what is now the East Village, before specializing in six-story residential buildings with ground-floor stores. By 1900, they had come a long way from Kovno.

Nat's mother, Anna Wallenstein, was also born in Kovno, where her father owned a lucrative company constructing railroad stations along the St. Petersburg–Hamburg line. Shortly after her birth, in March 1878, the family moved some hundred miles to Dvinsk (now Daugavpils), a commercial and manufacturing center in Latvia. Bringing with them a successful business and a patrician lifestyle, the Wallensteins continued to thrive; Anna's early childhood was passed in upper-middle-class comfort, with servants and summer holidays on the Baltic Coast and all the luxuries befitting people of prominence. She was a middle child among nine, her sisters Maria, Pauline, Sophia, Susana, and Fanny, and three brothers. At the Gymnasium, she did not stand out, certainly not compared to her elder sister Pauline, an accomplished linguist fluent in six languages. Nor was she blessed with the high intelligence and butterfly charm of her younger sister Susana, or the artistic talent of her brothers Saul and Samuel. In most respects Anna tended to be average.

Despite their wealth, the Wallensteins had to scramble for stability and security by the 1890s. Misery was gobbling up Dvinsk's Jewish community. If not unemployment or conscription into the czar's army, it was treacherous cholera epidemics that decimated entire families.

A third of the city's Jews were forced to apply for charity and rely on soup kitchens. In 1891, Pauline and Saul Wallenstein, little more than adolescents, were packed off to New York by themselves, followed the next year by their oldest sister, Maria, and her husband, Jacob Wimpie, a buying agent for the Russian government, and five years after that by eighteen-year-old Anna. Finally, in the summer of 1899 the rest of the family arrived: the sixty-year-old patriarch with his wife, Ethel, and their youngest children, Sophia, Susana, Sidney, Samuel, and Fanny. Bypassing the Lower East Side and its warrens of filthy tenements, Lazar settled his household uptown in East Harlem, at 248 East 115th Street, where they were apparently the only Jewish tenants. In typical fashion, Lazar swung into action. No sooner had he landed than he applied for a permit to construct a forty-thousand-dollar apartment house on Sullivan Street in Greenwich Village.

Of all his daughters Lazar had always doted on Pauline. Taking great pride in her academic accomplishments, he encouraged further studies, perhaps envisioning her marriage to a wealthy merchant or some distinguished scholar. Instead, three years after he sent her to New York, his highminded, pioneering daughter had wed a man whom he considered hopelessly inferior: Charles Weinstein. Because Charles's father, Nathan, had once been an employee of his in Kovno, Lazar was acquainted with the family and knew them to be inconsequential manual laborers unsuitable for his special child. In the Pale of Settlement, where no mingling took place between working-class and middle-class Jews except at the synagogue, a girl would never disgrace her family by marrying a man of lower status. This was not a union that Lazar could bless. Afterward, he fumed that he regretted overeducating a daughter, and would never do so again. But he had not seen the last of the Weinsteins.

Eager to embrace the American way of life, Lazar enrolled his younger children in free public schools, while Susana had no trouble gaining admission to the prestigious Lydia F. Wadleigh High School for Girls on West 114th Street. Anna had already completed her education in Dvinsk. At the age of twenty, attractive but no beauty, she was an efficient young woman with brown hair and eyes and a round face. She tended to be headstrong, even domineering. Living with Pauline and Charles, she could not avoid getting to know Charles's brother Max, but familiarity failed to breed intimacy. Initially she seems to have shown little interest in her sister's brother-in-law, who, aside from his bland temperament, looked nothing like his handsome brother, a six footer with blond hair and twinkling blue eyes.

By then twenty-four, Max was physically slight. His quiet, withdrawn manner seemed more suited to a clerical job than to workdays spent in sweaty shirtsleeves, surrounded by hod carriers and bricklayers. After more than a decade in America, he was no longer struggling financially but seemed to lack the entrepreneurial drive of his self-made brothers. To a girl like Anna, in a position to be choosy, Max was not a particularly good catch. She had no wish to marry a man with no formal schooling, and the fact that he was a Weinstein would be sure to displease her father.

In the end, Anna changed her mind about Max. In the four years since she moved to New York, suitors came calling but Anna had not found a husband to her liking, and the prospect of spinsterhood loomed. Braving Lazar Wallenstein's displeasure, she announced her intention of marrying Charles Weinstein's younger brother, whose ambition, relative to that of his brothers, seemed limited to building stables and warehouses. Two months after her twenty-third birthday, they married at a Lower East Side hall with the Weinsteins and the Wallensteins in attendance. The day of the wedding, May 7, 1901, was cool and showery; the leaves had just burst and the trees sprayed silvery droplets. A year later, when twenty-nine-year-old Saul Wallenstein married the Weinsteins' little sister Rosel, the families became even more entwined despite Lazar's disapproval. As the years passed, he would make peace with his children's choices of mates and live to see eleven Weinstein grandchildren, but one thing never changed: the Wallensteins would always look down their noses at the steerage-class Weinsteins.

In the fall of 1903, shortly before the Wright brothers' first flight, Anna Weinstein gave birth to a son in an apartment building constructed by her husband, a clear sign that Max intended to make something of himself after all. The boy, born on October 17, was named Nathan after his paternal grandfather. A formal family portrait taken when he was around ten months old shows a robust infant being dandled on his mother's lap. At the photographer's studio, where Anna and Max are seated side by side in a wagon with a steering column, neither one of their blank expressions suggests any clue to how their marriage was faring. The only feelings being expressed come from little Natchie, who leans impatiently toward his father to grab for the driving wheel.

The house where Nat first lived was the Guilford, double-fronted redbrick-and-limestone apartments at 151 East Eighty-first Street, between Lexington and Third Avenues in a blue-blooded section of town recognized for its elaborate dwellings. An advertisement in the *New York Times* promised prospective renters in the seven-story elevator building "refined surroundings." Each floor had three flats of six and seven rooms, some of them with fireplaces and bay windows. The Weinsteins occupied the best suite, on the airy top floor. Such an elegant setting suited the tastes of Anna Weinstein, even though her husband was not the owner but only the contractor. He built the Guilford for his older brother Jacob's father-in-law, Morris Monsky, a contractor and wholesale liquor dealer who had been having financial difficulties. For Max, it marked both a turning point and a beginning. His first solo project, started the year after Nat's birth, was the ambitious development of the De Peyster and Kortright, for which he employed George Frederick Pelham, one of the city's most prolific designers of residential edifices. It was an astonishing leap forward for a person previously content to erect warehouses in the East Village. The following year his firm undertook—simultaneously—five apartment houses east of Fifth Avenue, and he continued to prosper in Manhattan's cutthroat real estate market for the next decade.

Three years after Nat's birth, the Weinsteins had a daughter, named Hinda after Max's mother, but always called Sis because little Nat was unable to pronounce her name. And when Nat was seven, there came another sister, Lorraine.

In the early years of the marriage, Anna placed value on living at the best addresses, decorating her home expensively, owning a grand piano. For the cooking and housework she employed high-status German domestics. She prized smart clothes and seats at the opera. Her husband, while himself indifferent to the trappings of culture in any form, let Anna do whatever she liked. He appeared, in the description of one observer, "gentle to the limit of the word's meaning."

But despite Max's devotion, personality differences kept intruding in their relationship. Max's chronic depression, and a marshmallow meekness that continued to soften with age, sparked Anna's frustration and led to fits of anger. What initially had seemed to be a suitable match, presumably a happy, loving one, would ultimately turn out to be volatile.

By 1910, the Weinstein-Wallenstein clan had expanded enormously in size as well as prosperity. Nat had twenty-four aunts and uncles and thirty-five first cousins, including four Leonards (or Leons), three Hildas and a Hinda, and two Mortimers. The clan was packed with four Nathans (usually Americanized to Nathaniel), who were distinguished within the family by babyish nicknames—Ninny, Nutsy, Nissy, and Natchie. In the crowd of Nathans, Nat, aka Natchie, failed to stand out. Small for his age, he tended to stumble around like a sleepwalker.

Hinda Weinstein described her brother as "a timid shy boy." A snapshot of them together when Hinda was a toddler shows two very different children, one a delicate, shrimpy little boy with grave expression and squiggly ears, the other a chunky terrier of a girl, her jaw thrust forward, who looks as if she could eat him as a snack. His timidity did not prevent Natchie from being constantly at odds with his mother, who would not countenance disobedience. By the age of three or four, he had learned to bottle up his feelings, retreating into silence so that she would not know what he was thinking, in effect throwing up a wall between them. As an adult, he would always find it difficult to deal directly with women.

The parent he idolized was his father, who seldom made demands, either passively giving in or otherwise coming to his rescue by pleading his case with Anna. People who saw the two of them together, struck by their unusually close bond, remembered that the boy was "plainly wild about him" and called him by his first name in place of the usual Papa, as if he were a beloved friend. With his controlling mother, though, he clashed to the end of his life. No doubt Anna was a conventional immigrant mother, fiercely committed to the success of her children, but to Nat her love cut like jagged knives. In a revealing portrait written when he was a grown man, he called her "preposterous," "crazy," emotionally "disordered." Even the remembered smell of her garments had the power to oppress him.

As a toddler, he exhibited a mixture of physical problems: clumsiness, poor coordination, manifested in difficulties using a knife and fork and dressing himself, and an abnormally slow gait. In addition, he suffered from congenital hand tremors that he would always refer to as "the shakes."

In the fall of 1908, Nat started first grade at P.S. 81, the highly regarded teachers' training facility. Viewed by the neighborhood as a mini-Sorbonne, the Model School was around the corner from the De Peyster, but its proximity and reputation were meaningless because he had to be practically dragged there. As an adult, he described his years at the school as a time of discovering "ideas of American history, the world, or what is worthwhile." More to the point, he hated P.S. 81. He was the type of extremely withdrawn child forever prone to be picked on by schoolyard bullies. Inside the classroom, his mind drifted. He mangled the spelling of words and had trouble grasping numbers. His shaky hands resulted in poor handwriting, with spidery penmanship that lurched between script and print, the "gaunt caps and lank descenders" wobbling downhill across the page.

Scolded by his embarrassed parents, he continued to fail despite his superior reading skills and the school demoted him from the advanced section to average. He began suffering comparison to his "gold star" cousins—the sons of Charles and Pauline and Saul and Rosel, the Jarcho boys of his Aunt Susana and her husband Julius, an eminent doctor—who were forever outshining him, skipping grades while

Nat passed by the skin of his teeth. At puberty, his school phobia was exacerbated by emotional problems—possibly including an inherited disposition to depression. It was only through Anna's efforts, her emergency invitations to Natchie's teachers, tea on her best china at her high-class elevator building, that he was never required to repeat a grade. It was not until junior high school at P.S. 186, aided by considerable tutoring and perhaps his mother's nagging, that his work perked up. Occasionally he brought home satisfactory marks. Encouraged, his parents had reason to hope that their problem child had turned an academic corner at last.

In the Weinstein household, it was Anna who took responsibility for both making the big decisions and attending to the smallest details. She put her two little girls in matching tartan outfits, supervised the housemaids, Emma and Rose, organized healthful summers on a Connecticut farm or repaired to the Jersey Shore (at the upper-crust Jewish resort of Deal). In her midthirties, still young but growing stout, she began to lose some of her attractiveness, in part due to her sweet tooth, and became increasingly combative with her husband. Having cast herself as a person of gentility, her sharp corners polished, she focused her efforts on raising her children as well-mannered ladies and gentlemen. In the case of her less-than-perfect boy, who seldom passed up an opportunity to provoke her, she had not given up. Whatever else he might be, Natchie was "The Son," entitled to all the respect accompanying that position. One way or another, he would succeed. She would see to it.

3

MISHAWAKA

CCORDING TO ROMANTIC legend, Mishawaka, Indiana, was named for a Shawnee princess who lost her heart to an enterprising trapper named Deadshot. Settled after the discovery of bog iron deposits in the 1820s, the lovers' trysting place grew into a small but thriving industrial town known for its blast furnaces and manufacturing plants. Lying about ten miles south of the Michigan-Indiana state line, tucked between South Bend and Elkhart, Mishawaka has always been conscious of its image. At one time billing itself the Peppermint Capital of the World, it now claims to be the Best Hometown in America. None of this begins to suggest what may be the city's grandest attraction today, its colossal assemblage of shopping malls that lure motorists off the highway.

Eileen McKenney was born in Mishawaka in the spring of 1913. Her father, John Sydney McKenney, an engineer employed by one of the town's leading companies, was hoping to make his way up the corporate ladder. Eileen's mother, Marguerite Adelaide Flynn, a former schoolteacher, felt confident that her husband was destined for great things. Neither was a native. Shortly after their wedding the young couple had moved there from Cleveland with the intention of getting started in a fresh setting and living a long, happy life. If good fortune could be had anywhere, it was bound to be in some pleasant spot like Mishawaka.

. . .

As no Flynn girl had ever married a college man, Syd McKenney was greeted as a novelty, perhaps not quite a Sir Galahad but at least a special suitor. When they met at a dance in 1908, Marguerite was an impetuous nineteen-year-old; Syd, twenty-three, was a serious, straight-arrow young man, five feet seven, with brown hair and glasses. At the dance, dashing in white cotton gloves, he asked for a waltz, and then another, before politely requesting permission to come calling on Marguerite. Pleased to have caught the eye of a proper gentleman with refined manners, she invited him to dinner. Beforehand, she warned her family not to embarrass her. Remember, he was a mechanical engineer. No yelling, no scrapping, no singing.

For almost two years, Syd rode the streetcar every Tuesday evening to Marguerite's house on Woodland Avenue. Aside from their attraction for each other, they had very little in common. Swept off his feet by her black curls, blue eyes, and sense of mischief, Syd could overlook the fact the shanty-Irish Flynns ranked pretty much at the bottom of the social ladder, in addition to being Democrats. This was a problem because Syd's Republican father had been heard to announce that "no McKenney ever was, or ever will be, a Democrat."

Although Marguerite found the perfectionist Syd a bit of a sad sack compared to the Flynns, he was highly intelligent and well educated despite having left Ohio State before graduation. Her refined gentleman was a white-collar professional, as impressive as any doctor or lawyer. The wedding took place in the Flynns' front parlor on December 27, 1910.

The Logan Street Bridge fell into the St. Joseph River. Otherwise, the winter of 1911, the McKenneys' first year in Mishawaka, was uneventful. For weeks on end, South Main Street lay buried under snow, impassable to buggies, and those who needed supplies from Morse Hardware had to pick their way through the drifts on foot. It was a scene evoking a Currier & Ives lithograph of skating ponds and sleigh rides and cozy parlors with blazing hearths.

Mishawaka was a small industrial city whose population had

swelled to fourteen thousand, whose prosperity rested on manufacturing companies like Mishawaka Woolen, Perkins Wind Mill, and Simplex Motor Car, in addition to factories turning out furniture, flour, and beer. One of the town's leading businesses was Dodge Manufacturing, a thirty-two-year-old company that had grown from production of wooden hardware to a complete line of power transmission equipment. The profits of companies like Dodge resulted in quite a few rich people living in stately homes, and accounted for the fact that haute cuisine was served in the dining rooms of the brand-new, four-story, eighty-room Hotel Mishawaka.

On November 18, Marguerite gave birth to her first child, a girl she named Ruth for her seventeen-year-old sister. The next summer she became pregnant again, and Eileen was born on the morning of April 3, 1913.

Throughout the next several years, the McKenneys seemed on the outside to be an average couple, contentedly swaddled in the demands of parenthood, good mixers who led an active social life and enjoyed, in the words of the *Enterprise*, Mishawaka's paper of record, "a wide circle of friends." At Dodge, Syd was well liked and received regular promotions. Their comfortable brick house had front and back porches and a commodious yard. The McKenney children were adorable. A studio portrait from around 1915 shows a pair of solemn tykes dressed in white eyelet dresses, their locks cropped into the Dutch-boy bangs then in vogue for youngsters.

The girls did not look much like sisters. Eileen, said to resemble her mother, was exceptionally pretty. Her eyes were blue-green and she had long, dark lashes. With her elfin nose, small, elegant chin, and creamy complexion, she looked like a storybook princess, the type of child that caused strangers to coo. Ruth, however, was not so blessed. She had a pug nose, and her most notable features were freckles and a toothy grin. "I was homely as a mud fence," she would insist, homely and fat. From early on, food was snatched from her plate, diets and exercise were imposed, clothes made with elastic waists. Nothing worked. Stealing food and sneaking away to eat kept her plump as a partridge. Her mother, a slender woman with a bird's appetite, was deeply ashamed of Ruth's appearance.

In an attempt to rectify nature's inequities, Marguerite began assigning roles to her girls: Sister Eileen, she told them, was the pretty one, and Sister Ruth was the smart one. As a result of insistent repetition throughout their childhood—maternal love gone awry—the sisters came to accept the ideas as gospel. For the rest of her life, Eileen doubted her intelligence while Ruth, who would still have large buttocks and double chins at twelve, yearned to be thin and pretty.

If outwardly there seemed to be little resemblance, the two of them did share a medical defect: speech impediments. Ruth, a high-strung child, was three before she talked at all. Both stuttered, and Eileen, in addition to repeating and holding sounds, developed a slight lisp. Since the causes of these conditions were unknown, there was really nothing to do except hope that they would be outgrown eventually. For Ruth this turned out to be true; her stammer disappeared except in moments of stress. Eileen continued to stutter throughout her life, most noticeably when she spoke on the telephone. To compensate for her difficulties, she sometimes spelled out words that she was unable to articulate.

By the sixth year of their marriage, Marguerite and Syd's petty disagreements had a way of turning into ugly battles. Most evident was Marguerite's chronic unhappiness, in which marital conflict, homesickness, depression, and immaturity all played parts. In her loneliness, she began to consolidate her various dissatisfactions and then to project them onto a single target, bucolic Mishawaka. She disparaged it as a dreary, one-horse hamlet whose dry goods emporium was a "wigwam trading post" alongside Halle Brothers, Cleveland's nicest department store. She even scorned the new electric streetcar into South Bend, the nearest big town, which she mocked as a "Toonerville Trolley." Neither was she impressed by gala events—the new Carnegie public library going up on North Hill Street, the reopening of the old Century Theater with an orchestra and four-act vaudeville shows. What she could foresee of her future in "gross, primeval, backwood" Indiana—cut off from her family, with a husband who had proved to be narrow and pig-headed—looked unbeautiful.

Today, a wife as unhappy as Marguerite would have found a way out of her marriage in no time. In the early twentieth century, when divorce was frowned on, it was customary for the woman to stick with the man, not because of the children but largely because she had no resources. Devising her own solution, Marguerite proposed that the family return to Cleveland. If she and Syd had to make the best of it and remain together, she wanted at least to live near her family, whom she missed terribly. He resisted for fear of setting back his career.

Increasingly careless about camouflaging her discontent, Marguerite began indulging in childish fits of temper. For some reason, she had taken a dislike to one of Syd's bosses, a Dodge overlord who liked to recite the inspirational Hoosier verse of his favorite poet, James Whitcomb Riley. Marguerite seemed bent on treating the man disrespectfully. Knowing him to be nearsighted, she cut him dead on the street, badly frightening Syd with her recklessness.

The McKenney children found themselves drawn into their parents' battles as Marguerite raved about the wonders of her hometown. There was no place on earth like Cleveland, an exotic city to which they would return one day, she promised. In addition to descriptions of the city, she exalted the Flynns in a rainbow of near-mythological terms. Since she was an excellent storyteller, and because summer visits to Grandpa and Grandma Flynn had left powerful impressions, the girls listened eagerly. At the same time, they felt distressed because neither Eileen nor Ruth had any desire to leave Mishawaka. That, their mother told them, was only because they didn't know any better.

Marguerite eventually succeeded in wearing down her husband. Persuaded to test the waters in Cleveland, he quit his job and they left town in 1916. But America's involvement in World War I left the country facing uncertain times in the spring of 1917. While family men like Syd were in no danger of being called up for service—Syd's brother William, a second lieutenant in the Quartermaster Corps, would see action in France—the war effort on the home front depended on companies like Dodge and their skilled technical staffs. The McKenneys remained in Cleveland only a few months before quickly trooping back to Mishawaka, where Marguerite had no choice but to wait for the end of the war. Not long after the armistice, the McKenneys moved for good.

Hunkered on the shore of Lake Erie, the city of Cleveland had never managed to produce a Riley or a Sandburg or a Whitman to sing its praises in verse, a bit of bad luck for the biggest city in Ohio and the sixth largest in the nation. Owing to steel and ore production and a huge foreign-born population, it had spiraled in size to almost six hundred thousand. The city boasted a symphony orchestra, an art museum, exceptional schools of science and technology, three daily newspapers, affluent suburbs like Cleveland Heights, and unique real estate developments like Shaker Heights. Cleveland's downtown offered department stores such as Halle Brothers, Higbee's, the May Company, and Sterling-Lindner-Davis, and the skylit Arcade was the country's first indoor shopping mall. And of course it had the Cleveland Indians, the American League ball club that in 1920 would take the World Series against Brooklyn.

Arriving the summer of 1919, the McKenneys were obliged to live with Marguerite's family on Kinsman Road due to the postwar housing shortage. In the congested household, Grandpa Flynn's colorful, domineering presence hovered over the children, even after they grew up and married. Tom Flynn was a hothead, blustering over the Democratic Party and the Sinn Fein rebellion, melodramatically brandishing a carving knife at meals and daring God to strike him dead, bathing only once a week. The first to leave was Anna, whose husband, Raymond Brooker, clerked at a railway supply company, followed by Walter, who worked for an auto repair shop and lived with his in-laws on Merl Avenue. Lyda, the eldest daughter still at home, was a public school teacher who had passed the age for marriage, but Ruth, twenty-five and also a teacher, still held out hope of finding a mate. The youngest, Mildred, a clerk at the public library, was disfigured by scoliosis and considered unlikely to marry. Flynn women of all ages regarded men, other than their father, as nonentities. As a result, their spouses would be compliant men treated as "pale, unimportant fringe people," appendages who wrung their hands and got in the way during crises.

The role of doormat was abhorrent to Syd McKenney. Squeezing in with the Flynns for even a few months while he looked for a suitable house made him "nervous," because his father-in-law remained every bit as maddening as he had been a decade earlier. Hard-pressed to conceal his sarcasm, he derided his wife's kin as low-class people who didn't amount to much. By foolishly throwing their money around, they would end up dependent on prudent people, people of good judgment like himself, who had saved for a rainy day. In years to come, he would identify shortcomings in his daughters as a legacy from the crackpot Flynns. Anxious to get away from them, he put a down payment on a small house at 14916 Shaw Place in East Cleveland, six miles from the Flynns.

In the summer of 1919, Syd obtained a position with Apex Electrical Manufacturing Co., a major producer of consumer appliances such as washing machines and vacuum cleaners, while Marguerite sharpened her pencils and went back to teaching in September. Their pair of charming girls—one smart and the other a beauty—were enrolled at nearby Prospect Elementary School. Their new home was too far away from the Flynns to suit Marguerite, but it was better than living in the Indiana boondocks. Constantly making excuses to visit, she dropped in at least once and sometimes twice a day. At thirty, against all odds, she had managed to turn back the clock.

4

SAN JUAN HILL, NEW YORK

To show that he was a grown-up boy who read the classics, Nat would put on his knickers suit and knee stockings in the mornings and leave the house clutching a translation of Aristotle's *Ars Poetica* under his arm. He boarded the elevated train downtown to DeWitt Clinton High School. The Ninth Avenue El had the reputation of being the most dangerous line in the city because its tracks skimmed across a high iron bridge just before looping a bend called Suicide Curve at West 110th Street. Although Suicide Curve failed to live up to its name—almost no riders seemed eager to kill themselves—the chance of somebody plummeting to his death could never be ruled out. When the train pulled into the station at West Fifty-ninth Street, Nat descended a flight of iron stairs and started off in the direction of San Juan Hill.

Unlike Harlem, San Juan Hill was uninviting. This section of town—the West Sixties between Ninth and Eleventh Avenues—was named for the Spanish-American War battle made famous by Theodore Roosevelt and his Rough Riders. Charging up San Juan Hill, Cuba, a unit of black soldiers had performed heroically. San Juan Hill, Manhattan, was a black neighborhood as impoverished as it was unsightly. The exception was DeWitt Clinton, a voluptuous structure built in the Flemish Renaissance Revival style, its façade festooned with towers and gables. If not for the view from the fifth-floor windows—a hodgepodge of ferry slips along the Hudson waterfront and the rickety houses of Weehawken, New Jersey, moored on the opposite bank — it might have been sixteenth-century Brussels.

Clinton pridefully called itself the finest secondary school not only in New York but in the entire country. Neither claim was true. Probably the city's most prestigious public high school was Townsend Harris Hall, an uptown prep school for the Ivy League, whose rigorous program accepted brainy boys and graduated them in three years. It was not a suitable place for a boy like Nat, whose promotion in lower school had often depended on his mother's talent for currying favor with teachers. Getting into Clinton, rated close behind Townsend Harris, was pure luck. With an enrollment of eight thousand and a staff of around two hundred teachers, Clinton was far bigger than most colleges. Its cavernous gymnasium reflected the school's powerhouse athletics program and the titles it regularly captured in football and track. Its fancy pipe organ cost ten thousand dollars.

In the fall of 1917, Nat had been in school only a few days when five hundred disgruntled students organized a strike and walked out of classes to protest the new longer school day instituted by the administration. When a free-for-all broke out on Tenth Avenue, the rampaging strikers began chanting for their classmates to join in. Finally the insurrection was put down by Clinton's truant officers, but not until they had summoned the aid of the local station house.

The insanity that greeted Nat those first days at school evaporated, alas, and he soon discovered that Clinton without catcalls and violence was just as boring as the Model School or P.S. 186. The place reeked of hypocrisy: the teachers were jerks, his classmates phonies. While his grades the first semester showed a good start, he eventually stopped applying himself and failed to turn in papers. By the end of the year, in June 1918, his attendance had become halfhearted; he avoided the pressure of exams by skipping them. He had failing marks in all subjects except biology, elocution, and algebra, which he barely passed with 60s.

Around this time, he began to develop interests far more stimulating than algebra. He was learning to operate a car, which turned out to be difficult for him. He drove badly, as if there were no other motorists on the road; his hands and feet didn't always do what he intended, so there were a fair number of bent fenders. He had also become addicted to sporting magazines, reading *Field & Stream* instead of doing homework. Suddenly obsessed with the outdoors, about which he knew little firsthand, he sat in the middle of Harlem studying advertisements offering the latest camping knickknacks, like "Ever-Ready" flashlights ("$3.50 postpaid, complete with battery").

In the fiercely ambitious Weinstein-Wallenstein family, failure was the most grievous offense. Top grades were crucial, because graduation from elite public schools like Townsend Harris and Clinton meant boarding an express train to New Haven, Cambridge, or Princeton Junction. And if not to those Ivy League campuses, then to Columbia up in Morningside Heights. As word of his misdeeds spread throughout the family, Nat concealed his anxiety by cultivating a defiant attitude, alternately pretending not to care and promising to do better. Despite bouts of guilt he seemed unable to take the warnings from his family to heart and instead adopted a strategy for dealing with crises: inaction. By ignoring unpleasantness there was always the chance it would go away, and sometimes it actually did.

When Nat returned to Clinton in the fall, as pressures continued to mount, he panicked and ran away. Accompanying him in this caper was his cousin Wally—Nathaniel Wallenstein, who had just earned the highest grade ever recorded on the Columbia entrance examinations, a kid who should have known better. Pooling their allowances, they loaded their bags with camping gear ordered from *Field & Stream* and got as far as Grand Central Terminal. The same day, the renegades were marched back home in disgrace, after Max Weinstein and Saul Wallenstein got wind of the escapade. Given a dressing-down, they manufactured goofy excuses and professed eagerness to travel out west, where maybe they could pass for older than fifteen and enlist in the armed services.

Soon afterward the war ended. With flags fluttering in the November air, Clinton dismissed classes and the whole school streamed out of the building to join the shrieking crowds heading for Forty-second Street. The armistice put an end to Nat's romance of military service, although not to urges to run away.

One of the boys in Nat's class was Julian Shapiro, his playmate from the De Peyster, but Julie later would claim to have no memory of seeing him. The reason was simple: Nat was an Olympian truant. One semester he racked up thirty-eight absences, and that figure did not include the days he reported for class and then fled the building. Lost among the herds of stampeding boys, he would skitter along the corridors, down the glassed-encased stairwell, past the trophy cases full of dusty footballs, and do a victory sprint out the door. On Tenth Avenue he kept going. No wonder Julian never ran into him.

With freedom to walk the city, he soon discovered the New York Public Library on Fifth Avenue at Forty-second Street, where he set about educating himself. Unlike Clinton, the Beaux Arts marble building contained everything he had ever wanted. Just the sight of the pair of majestic marble lions looming over its entrance thrilled him. On the third floor, he bounded down a marble hallway to the main reading room and scribbled his requests on call slips that were magically whisked away by pneumatic tubes to the stacks. In the vast chamber of chandeliers, heavy with silence, he waited for his number to flash on the electric call-board and then plopped himself at one of the long, shiny tables, near a brass lamp with the books stacked near his elbow. Their touch and smell, "bright and clean and new," made him imagine a pristine mountain stream. As an honor student in his high school of one, he proceeded to pursue a vast number of subjects. While still besotted by his Russian heroes Tolstoy and Dostoyevsky, he worked his way through Conrad, Cabell, Proust, Pater, Coleridge, Thackeray, and Montaigne and also pored over books on Christianity, Jewish mysticism, Islam, witchcraft, and the supernatural. The library was, he thought, "a storehouse" of adventure: "Walled cities to be stormed. Ferocious natives to be outwitted. Heaving decks on which to swing a cutlass." Without teachers to distract him, he found the reading room "a continuous delight" where he lost track of time.

Library regulations were inflexible but not unreasonable: no smoking or spitting, no smiling or laughing or social chitchat, no eating, no talking except to librarians, a whispery atmosphere as solemn as a funeral parlor. Keeping quiet was never a problem for him, and smoking the cigarettes to which he already had become addicted only required stepping outside to the broad stairs descending to Fifth Avenue. To circumvent the ban on food, he came prepared with a stash of candy bars. (Like his mother, he was partial to sweets.) Making sure to avoid observation by the librarians, he would break off a piece at a time and squirrel the sweet into his cheek, sucking and chewing quietly. Sequestered in truant heaven, anesthetized with candy and books, his attendance record was exemplary.

The Weinsteins had moved to Central Park North by 1918, and Nat for the first time in his life was living in a building that had not been constructed by his father. Facing the park, near Warrior's Gate, 225 West 110th Street was a nondescript building of coffee-colored brick whose entrance was inset in a narrow cement courtyard. Its façade was sheathed from street to roof with a grid of black fire escapes. While the building was homely, Nat was overwhelmed by the beauty of the park, with its dingy pergolas and inky hills and flocks of wild ducks streaming over the lake. The park, right across the street, quickly became his personal property, a miraculous extension of *Field & Stream* for Nat and his cousins. In the Harlem Meer they bobbed for fish by baiting a bent pin with balls of dough. From studying their Boy Scout manuals, they learned how to snare squirrels—and an occasional rabbit—how to skin them with razor blades, and how to cook and eat them, all illegal activities. To avoid the park police they ferreted out unused trails. When the novelty of trapping and fishing wore off, intimate knowledge of the park and its isolated hiding places led to unexpected new adventures.

Once darkness settled in, the boys discovered, the bird watchers and baby nurses were replaced by individuals visiting for different purposes. Since the turn of the century, homosexual men had been using the park as a popular trysting place, particularly the secluded jumble known as the Ramble and the open lawn at its north end nicknamed the "Fruited Plain." By this time, the entire park had become a nocturnal love pad for both homosexuals and heterosexuals. There were various combinations of twosomes and threesomes, women and men, men and men, women and women—lovers, acquaintances, strangers exposing their privates—and a considerable variety of sexual activities. Whatever they were doing, Nat wanted to do the same. The sight of women masturbating or boy-boy kissing was endlessly fascinating to him and his companions. They stalked the lovers by scuttling through the underbrush and sitting absolutely still, staring for hours at a time if necessary. "We would wait until they were at the height of their excitement," he remembered, "then suddenly shout foul names and run, yelling wildly." Invariably the loud voices sent the lovers scrambling.

Suddenly the playground beyond Warrior's Gate had become a voyeur's paradise. Crouched in secret little thickets, surrounded by chirping birds, Nat peeked out at the sexual activities of grown-up women and men. Sexual arousal and hunting—the silent, motionless ogling of the prey—were to remain associated in his mind ever after. On a Clinton lunchroom wall was scribbled "Poor Alice, she gave away two hundred dollars worth before she knew she could sell it." Nat just wished he could meet Alice or someone like her. Unfortunately, none of the girls of his acquaintance was in the mood to give anything away. Not content to remain a silent observer, he began seeking out the prostitutes who plied their regular beats in and around the park.

When Nat was sixteen the Weinsteins left Central Park North for a new home at 24-25 Mount Morris Park West, a handsome building on the corner of West 122nd Street. Mount Morris Park, a tiny enclave of sweet gum and linden trees and pipe-railed lawns, didn't interest Nat, despite its charm. For one thing, it never seemed to attract the same sort of dirty lovebirds—or the prostitutes—that Central Park did, and it was uncomfortably close to home, both his own and the brownstone owned by Pauline and Charles Weinstein on West 120th Street. For his secret life he was obliged to make special expeditions downtown. He didn't mind.

In 1917, Nat began spending his summers at camp in the Adirondack Mountains. Long known for sublime scenery, the area once had been a high-class tourist destination, but by this time it was overrun by guest hostels, fleabag rustic cabins, and a profusion of children's camps offering programs to foster self-reliance. Camp Paradox, on Route 73 between Schroon Lake and the hamlet of Ticonderoga, had become a favorite of monied Jewish families like the Weinsteins (several of Nat's older cousins were regulars). The season cost $250 ($4,800 in today's money), laundry included. The owner, a New York teacher named Edward Goldwater, provided a handsome illustrated brochure that showed a spacious clubhouse, a hillside of orderly tents on raised wooden platforms, swarms of canoes and rafts docked on the icy lake, a baseball diamond, and tennis courts against a background of mountain peaks. To parents Dr. Goldwater directed a serious message reminding them of the "harmful influences of the usual summer resort"—meaning sex books and jerking off—and offered an image of Paradox as a wholesome alternative.

There was nothing particularly paradoxical about Paradox. Like all the mountain camps, it was centered around sports. Edward Goldwater's brochure listed a dozen different athletics, including hare-and-hound chases. Determined to appear fit, Nat immediately began volunteering for three-day canoe expeditions and brisk hikes. He was careful never to complain but his body sometimes betrayed him, and he had particular difficulty waking up in the mornings. After an arduous climb up Mount Marcy, he tumbled on his cot like a pile of dirty laundry and slept the whole next day. He continued to flop around in a zombie-like state of physical exhaustion, until some of the boys began snickering and calling him "Pep." In Nat's case the name Pep was derogatory; "pep" was exactly what a sleepy boy like Nat did not have. To show he was a good sport, he concealed his resentment by calling himself Pep Weinstein, a nickname that would stick to him for the remainder of his life.

Camp Paradox did not turn out to be the utopia Nat had envisioned. Somebody was always telling him what to do. Each day was regimented from dawn to lights-out. Despite his efforts to fit in, one of the counselors noticed his discomfort and would later describe him as "a quiet chap and not much of a mixer."

One afternoon the Paradox baseball team was playing rival Pine Tree Camp. By the fifth inning, Nat was standing in the outfield thinking about a million and one things and wishing the game was over. In the bright sunlight, the field had turned fiery and he "felt like going home." He had almost lapsed into a stupor when the batter walloped a ball that swatted him in the chest and rolled away. Panicked, he began groping in the brown grass. On all sides people let loose with the wildest whooping and yelling, but he was too groggy to find the ball and somebody fielded it for him. When Nat looked up, his cousin Ned was sprinting toward him with a bat, his expression murderous. Nat wheeled around and fled into the woods, where he trembled as his cousin beat the bushes to find him. After the game ended he crept out, hoping everybody had calmed down, but the boys greeted him with sneers, and his cousin, still put out, refused to allow him on the bus back to camp.

Nat, tottering in his baseball cleats, thumbed a ride back that afternoon. Long afterward, he would remember the shame washing over him as he stood in the outfield. He had not imagined how easily life could smack a person around. Anything could happen. The ball, he decided, represented the flattening hand of fate, all too happy to mop the floor with him, whereas his cousin with the bat and a heart of stone stood for friends ready to kill him.

Nat was stoical about Camp Paradox. Whining was thought to be unmanly, and he may have regarded his experiences as typical for boys of his age. Over the course of four summers, he improved his paddling skills and won a second-place award in canoeing and rowing. At the same time, he learned how to crack jokes at his own expense when people laughed at his pratfalls. In a bid to make friends, he learned to play the banjo. His last year, he was art editor of the camp magazine, creating snappy cartoons despite his shaky fingers and signing them "PEP." His cartoons reveal a sharpening of his drawing skills and the first hints of his talent for satire, with illustrations making fun of camp activities, his fellow campers, and the staff. Some things never changed, though; his fellow campers presented him with a box labeled Ingersoll Alarm, containing not a clock but a live chipmunk supposedly trained to wake him in the mornings.

All the while, things at Clinton were going from bad to worse. After two years of tutoring to coax his grades above passing, Nat had barely managed to slink into his junior year. Once more, there were predictions he would tote bricks for a living. His report cards showed failing marks in every subject except music, physical education, elocution, and hygiene, in each of which he earned a mess of zeros, reflecting his perfect lack of attendance. Anna and Max were dumbfounded by this latest batch of extremely poor grades—and by his blasé reaction. In contrast to his cousins, who skipped grades and went to college early, their boy was incorrigible. Saul Jarcho, the precocious son of Anna's sister Susana, had been accepted to Harvard at fourteen, although he planned to first take a year's breather and study Sanskrit. Nathaniel "Wally" Wallenstein was going to Columbia. Others were studying to become doctors and dentists. But what college was desperate enough to accept Nat?

In the midst of his troubles at Clinton, his double life as an unregistered student at the public library unexpectedly ended. "If anyone can be snug in the main reading room I was," he wrote, but now he had begun looking closely at his neighbors, the loyal regulars he had been accustomed to seeing, and decided it was time to leave. He had assumed them to be scholars, sincerely seeking wisdom, older than himself but otherwise not much different. Now it occurred to him that the ones always thumbing through dusty medical journals were fetishists chasing down details of loathsome diseases, that some of those nice duffers were no doubt dirty old men digging for pornographic treasures, that the place was overrun with professional contestants clawing furiously into just about any subject to extract information for their entries, hoping to see a Pierce-Arrow Phaeton or ten thousand dollars in cash appear at their doors. His refuge was also a gigantic, rent-free office for plagiarists, mainly frustrated cartoonists or burnt-out writers poring over old magazines for ideas to recycle.

Eventually he felt sickened by the reading room subculture, a "twitching crowd" of strangers. After his bastion of safety became "a monstrous place," he found it impossible to go there. Having to abandon the library meant losing a pillar of his existence, the only part of his life that made him truly happy. Betrayed, he began to hate the readers around him for defiling the holy books that now smelled to him like "a closet full of old shoes" when they did not give off the awful aroma of "death and decay." The phony library readers deserved punishment, but what kind? Rounding them up would present an impossible task, he thought; rehabilitation would be useless, genocide too messy, and banning them hard to enforce. A better solution, he decided, was to get rid of his sanctuary altogether, and he started flirting with the idea of deliberately burning it down. The venerable New York Public Library going up in smoke was a shocking but deeply thrilling vision.

All hope of a normal education was gone. On the verge of flunking once and for all, Nat emancipated himself. Five months shy of sixteen, he dropped out of school in June 1919.

5

THE STENOGRAPHER
FROM CANTON

L IKE A THANKFUL exile returned from a foreign country, Eileen's mother tried to make up for the lost years in Indiana. Settled in Shaw Place, reunited with her family, Marguerite went back to teaching and threw herself into an exhausting schedule in order to expose the children to "refinement," a favorite word of hers that signified Great Books, Grand Opera, and selection of the right utensil at table.

Bringing in extra income from her teacher's wages, she felt justified in spending some of it on refinement. No home, she believed, could be called stylish without classical music, and therefore her family must have a player piano. Knowing her husband would never agree, she decided to purchase it secretly. Presented with a fait accompli, he would have no choice but to acquiesce, or so she persuaded herself. When, at last, she had saved enough money for a down payment, she happily ordered the piano, a bench, and several music rolls; the store threw in a bonus, a free roll of Liszt's Hungarian Rhapsody no. 2. On the day of the delivery, Marguerite rehearsed the girls. Shoulder to shoulder, the three of them would sit waiting at the piano. When Syd returned home from work, Marguerite would begin pumping with dramatic fanfare as the piano burst into the "Blue Danube" waltz.

That evening, as their father stepped through the door, Eileen and Ruth greeted him with cries of "Surprise!" but before the piano could finish the waltz he was yelling at Marguerite. How dare she ignore their important financial responsibilities, for example, their life insurance premiums? Learning that the piano was to be paid off in installments of one dollar a week simply fueled his anger, as he hated buying anything on credit. He refused to give in and the following day telephoned the music store to report that the instrument had been purchased by mistake. Without delay, a truck pulled up and movers carried out the piano, the bench, and the music rolls, including the free Hungarian Rhapsody. For weeks afterward, Marguerite and her abject daughters trooped to the store to beg for a return of the deposit. Unfortunately, she had signed an agreement forfeiting the down payment should the instrument be returned.

If Marguerite thought she could outsmart her tightfisted husband, she was mistaken.

In September 1918, the Spanish flu struck swiftly and viciously. Over the course of six months, it rampaged around the globe killing tens of millions, including at least a half million in the United States, where it claimed the lives of more soldiers than the war. There was no cure, no effective escape short of complete quarantine. Nobody was immune. Although the onset of the illness was unremarkable—aches, fever, and cough similar to an ordinary cold—most victims went on to develop high fevers and hemorrhaging of the lungs, followed in short order by pneumonia, delirium, and unconsciousness. The end could come in a few days or a few hours.

Never had so many people died so quickly. As the bodies continued to pile up, funeral parlors fell behind and were forced to operate overtime. In the end, even Marguerite's father, Tom Flynn, then in his sixth decade and retired from the iron works, went back to working as an embalmer at the Flynn-Froelk Funeral Home owned by his relatives. Ultimately, as eerily as it had arrived, the plague retreated.

By the time the McKenneys returned from Indiana in the summer of 1919, the deadly nightmare seemed to be over and even those who had lost loved ones were getting back to normal. The flu had disappeared from the headlines, replaced by more pressing topics, like the national prohibition of alcohol that would begin in January. Then, without warning, after New Year's, a fresh outbreak came roaring through Cleveland like a perverse apparition—seven hundred died during January—and it was clear that the flu was back. As in numerous other households, some of the Flynns were ailing, and possibly more than one of them suffered a mild case, but the family member most severely affected was twenty-one-year-old Mildred. It was Marguerite, a daily visitor—young, healthy, and unconcerned about her own safety—who threw herself into nursing her sister.

In the first week of February, just as Mildred was beginning to recover, Marguerite came down with the disease. Several days later, on Sunday, February 8, she died. She was thirty years old. The funeral took place the following Wednesday afternoon, at Windermere Presbyterian Church on Euclid Avenue. For her devastated daughters, it was the major trauma of their lives. One moment their mercurial mother was there, the next she was not.

In the aftermath of their mother's death, when it seemed as if nothing as terrible could happen again, it did. At the end of March, Tom Flynn developed a cold and high fever; he too succumbed in a matter of days. Furthermore, the flu had left Mildred brain damaged and partly blind so that she required constant care. With Tom gone, Lyda became the head of the household. A highly capable woman, she took charge of the family much as she did the students in her classes, and prevented it from falling into complete disarray.

Never would Eileen get over the loss of her mother and she would not discuss the death, but the hidden fissures would crack and recrack for the rest of her life. In the case of her combative grandfather, she had only really known him during the brief period following their return from Mishawaka. But she would hear an endless stream of stories about him from Ruth, to whom he was a tragic hero who succumbed not to the flu but to "a broken heart" after watching his children "abandon everything he thought of as good, and dear, and beautiful for an empty and ignoble American middle class life." Ruth mined the lives of both Marguerite and Tom for fictional material, sometimes even making light of the double tragedy. She once said that anything "a normal family does once ours does six times."

Certainly there was nothing normal about the situation facing Syd, left to bring up two children alone amid thinly veiled animosities between him and his in-laws. After ten years, the Flynns viewed him as more of an outsider than ever. Decades later, there were Flynns painting him as a scoundrel who had somehow mistreated his wife. Always conscientious, Syd worried about his six- and eight-year-old daughters falling under the influence of his dead wife's relatives. He hurried to provide them with a new mother, which was the last thing Eileen and Ruth wanted.

Syd's secretary at Apex Electrical was a petite, dark-haired, twenty-one-year-old girl from Canton. Ethel Weirich was the firstborn of three children with a hard-driving father and a mother who married the wrong man. After the union ended in divorce, Clarence Weirich remarried and went on to become a successful business executive. Lydia Weirich was compelled to follow the frugal path customarily trod by genteel ex-wives and rent rooms. Ethel and her brother and sister shared the boardinghouse with a succession of carefully screened young stockbrokers and clerks. After high school, living at home and contributing a portion of her earnings as a stenographer to the family income, she couldn't wait to leave Canton. "She was a rebel," one of her children says. "Coming to Cleveland by herself at twenty-one and finding a job was pretty brave." At Apex, Ethel started out working for a man some fourteen years her senior, a married father of two children. The influenza virus changed everything overnight and she was soon calling her boss Mac.

On June 16, 1921, seventeen months after Marguerite's death, Syd and Ethel married at Windermere Presbyterian Church, where Syd and Marguerite had been parishioners. The Flynns were offended by

Syd's haste. It seemed to confirm their suspicions that he regretted his first marriage and wished to waste no time pushing Marguerite out of his life. If for no other reason than the sake of his girls, he should have waited awhile before bringing another woman into his home.

To Ethel, who had grown up without a father in the house, the difference in ages was no drawback. At thirty-five, Syd remained an attractive, still-youthful man, a successful professional with a good job, a savings account, and a charming home. His self-assurance, strong work ethic, and apparent lack of bad habits seemed to promise he would make an ideal husband. The only flies in the ointment were those two children.

While Syd felt ready to put his first marriage behind him, his thrift would not allow him to purchase a new home. Ethel found herself installed on Shaw Place, sleeping in the bed of another woman, surrounded by her predecessor's furniture, dishes, and personal possessions, and, worst of all, caring for stepchildren too old to tuck in, too hostile to woo. "She was unprepared to take on children the caliber of Eileen and Ruth," says their cousin Richard Selvey. "They opposed her at every turn." The ghost wife seemed to be lurking in the house too, because sometimes Syd forgot himself and called Eileen by Marguerite's name.

In the mornings, the girls walked to Prospect Elementary; at noon, they came home for lunch, spoke hardly a word to the stranger who did not belong there, then walked back to school. It was clear that winning their acceptance was going to be an uphill battle. But Ethel, young, restive, eager to get on with her life, simply made an end run around the problem. (Family members describe her as "in one word, stubborn.") Three months after the wedding she was pregnant with John Sydney, Jr., born April 14, 1922. For the girls the appearance of John, Jr., called Jackie, whom Ethel always put first, would be the final straw. Mother had "a hell of a time" with Syd's daughters, Jack McKenney says. His recollections are echoed by his much younger brother, Bob: "I always heard that Ruth was a rebel from the word go. If you said white she'd say black. She gave my mom a lot of hell."

In fact, Eileen could dish out hell too. Sassy, withering in her scorn, reluctant to accept discipline, she treated the second wife as little more than a housekeeper. By the time she was ten, Eileen had become adept at bouncing between Syd and Ethel, coming and going as she liked, hard to keep track of.

Meanwhile, Eileen's memories of her mother and the years they had spent in Mishawaka were beginning to blur, replaced by recollections from the Flynns, whose exaggerated tales turned Marguerite into an Irish saint. One of Marguerite's notions, continually reiterated, was the idea of a pretty sister and a smart sister. Ruth, envious, nonetheless ceaselessly praised Eileen's looks. Eileen protested that Chubb—her nickname for Ruth—looked average for a fat girl. But Ruth never appeared to listen because she believed being fat was "terrible," and how would somebody like Eileen ever understand that.

Eileen did not question that Ruth was more intelligent, because their mother had said so. Ruth was an indefatigable reader with a gift for composition; what Eileen wrote never sounded as good as Ruth's work. When a local bank sponsored an essay contest for a description of its new headquarters, Ruth won the twenty-five-dollar prize. Her relatives found this hilarious, not because she had produced the best essay but because, as Syd marveled, "she did it without ever having seen the inside of the building." Events like the essay contest helped to reinforce the family gospel that Ruth was exceptionally clever—and Eileen just average.

If her relationship with her sister was complicated, it became deeply confusing as well. Without a mother, the girls naturally turned to each other for support and affection. As the older sister, Ruth assumed the role of mother and teacher, but at other times she wanted to be Eileen's best friend. In her mind, they were locked together like a pair of twins, able to "read each other's minds," so close that "we hardly needed speech to communicate." The symbiosis could get too claustrophobic for comfort, though; Ruth was capable of speeding from cuddly to vicious in a split second. One of these shifts regularly occurred each year on Valentine's Day.

At Prospect Elementary, Eileen received more cards than any of her classmates, both the store-bought kind and the homemade cards sticky with paste. Ruth was hurt and jealous. There were years when she failed to receive any cards at all, or she got chintzy duty cards from pitying teachers. Valentine's Day, she scornfully told Eileen, was a lot of "mush." In junior high school, Valentine's Day was all about boys. Eileen, Ruth recalled, would start to "lick her chops" as the day approached. "I used to spend Valentine's night listening to my sister, flushed with triumph, recite her terrific victories." One year, Eileen made a record haul: four heart-shaped boxes of chocolates, a box of bonbons with pineapple centers, and three bottles of Coty's cologne in special Cupid packages, in addition to a motley assortment of cards. That was the year Chubb had a crush on the president of the high-school literary society, a pimply boy Eileen would never look at twice. For the first time, Ruth got a box of chocolates, with a poem copied from the works of John Keats.

The odes of an English Romantic poet seemed tame stuff to Eileen, whose subteen literary taste ran to stories that would have made Keats's readers swoon in embarrassment. In the *Cleveland Press* at the time was a serialized novel that had managed to thrill the city—the whole country, in fact—with its scandalous details. The Elenore Meherin novel related the ups and downs of a stenographer named Helena "Chickie" Bryce, a heart-of-gold girl who is determined to be a Zelda Fitzgerald–type flapper and snap her fingers at convention. Virginal Chickie, "as dumb as she was pure," Ruth decided, is seduced and abandoned by a raffish millionaire heel. Finally came the most daring installment, with all of Cleveland holding its breath: Chickie looks in the mirror and falls on the bed sobbing because she is pregnant. Exactly how such a thing could happen confused Eileen, but Ruth explained it as "horrid." When *Chickie* was released as a movie, Eileen and Ruth sat through countless viewings. It was only a story, to be sure, but "it put a mark on us," Ruth would admit.

Eileen at twelve spent every cent she could get her hands on for clothes and cosmetics. Dying to appear sophisticated, she swished around in slinky outfits that made her look twenty. Shaving and penciling in eyebrows, she applied purple eye shadow, painted her mouth a fiery-red Cupid's bow, and slathered herself with the scent of Evening in Paris. With minimal supervision at home, she ran around with older boys. By the standards of the day, this was shocking behavior. She was not so reckless as to give up her virginity, however. How could she forget the story of Chickie?

Ruth never said she was going to kill herself. But at the movies one Sunday afternoon, Eileen began to feel nervous after the lights dimmed. Even though the ticket had cost nearly all of her weekly allowance, she left the theater and rushed back to Shaw Place. The house was empty, her father playing golf and Ethel and three-year-old Jackie away somewhere. Eileen heard suspicious noises coming from the basement. As she made her way down the steps, a slight movement was visible. On the floor of the cramped coal cellar she found Ruth half-conscious, with a rope crudely knotted around her neck and a note pinned to her dress.

To hang yourself by means of a clothesline and stepladder is not the most foolproof method, but it can be adequate if done correctly. Ruth's attempt terrified Eileen. "You make me sick and tired," she screamed. "People will think you're queer." She was "furious," Ruth recalled. Behind the terror of another abandonment lay Eileen's own deep insecurity. Taking into consideration that Aunt Mildred was kept out of sight in the state hospital for the insane in Garfield Heights, madness could be her fate and Chubb's as well.

Frightened or not, Eileen was a stubborn twelve-year-old who spent much of her time trying to wriggle from under her father's thumb. Uncertain how to handle her, he blustered and lectured before finally looking the other way. She usually did as she pleased. But however difficult she may have been at times, she was a model child compared to her sister. Increasingly unmanageable, Ruth perpetually bristled with rage, and waged guerrilla warfare against her father until everyone became affected by the poisonous atmosphere in the household. By her own account, she was "a problem child," but her behavior was not simple adolescent angst. There is little doubt that she suffered from a psychiatric illness: her moods alternated between euphoria and depression, symptoms that are consistent with bipolar disorder. Some of her conduct seems an extreme form of behaviors exhibited by Tom Flynn, while traces of the disorder were evident in her mother as well. In manic periods, marked by excessive energy and excitement, Ruth spooled off pages at a time of fiction that was largely incomprehensible. The elation never lasted, and then she would slip into alarming dark moods, her body debilitated by arthritic pains. During these phases of severe depression, she would be unable to carry on everyday activities.

Eager to forget the suicide attempt, Ruth denied any intention to harm herself. There was nothing seriously wrong, she argued, as if trying to hang yourself in the coal cellar was an everyday occurrence. By her own account "the homeliest girl in East Cleveland," she firmly believed that her unhappiness stemmed from a "beastly fat" body and the curse of freckles.

A year went by, and then it happened again. She jumped out a second-story window of their house and broke her ankle. Once more, the family had no idea what to do. Complicating the situation was Ruth's quick intellect; as she was obviously a bright child, the bewildered family must have been reluctant to draw any conclusions about her mental state. Neither did they know how to deal with the suicidal feelings of, as Ruth would describe herself, "a serious, too sensitive child." There was no successful treatment for manic-depressive illness, only stigma. The vast majority of cases went undiagnosed, and for those who did receive a diagnosis, medical care commonly consisted of water therapies using wet packs and prolonged baths. Insulin coma, Metrazol convulsive therapy, and electroshock did not appear until the 1930s; the first effective mood stabilizers, like lithium carbonate, lay decades in the future.

Throughout her life Ruth suffered recurring breakdowns that she tried to pass off as garden-variety depression. "Tiring of suicide, I took to drink, stud poker, and evil companions," she joked, using humor to sugarcoat these periodic relapses. Hospitalization would be necessary more than once in years to come.

Ruth, fourteen, made no effort to hide her contempt for Ethel, who could be plenty obnoxious herself, and animosity toward her father intensified until it bordered on the phobic. Much later, she would still describe his face as "infinitely despicable." Occasionally she would think of him with pity, but mostly she reviled him and his like as "primeval beasts" deserving of obliteration. This savaging of her father was partly political, reflecting her Communist beliefs, but the bile was genuine and extremely personal.

The solution to Ruth's adolescent difficulties came from Lyda Flynn, Marguerite's eldest sister. As much as Syd disliked the Flynns, he made an exception in the case of Lyda, who treated Ethel kindly. At thirty-seven, having advanced to a good position in the public school system, Lyda finally married a widower ten years her senior, the owner of a printing shop. When she and Otto Thomas offered to take charge of Ruth, Syd accepted with relief. If he had reached the end of his rope, so had his wife. Devoted to her son Jackie, Ethel was "not at all sad to see her go," says another of her sons. Ruth's move to the Thomas home on Chalfant Road in Shaker Heights was a tacit acknowledgment that she and her father could no longer live in the same house. For Lyda, childless but a veteran teacher of twenty-five years, dealing with adolescent mayhem was all in a day's work.

Over the next few years, life improved for Ruth. At Shaw High School, she joined the debate team and showed herself to be a talented public speaker. When Otto Thomas put her to work in the evenings in his print shop, she learned how to set type and proofread. After school she and Eileen fell into the habit of meeting at a snack shop. In a back booth of Joe's Hamburg Eaterie they sipped sodas and puffed on cork-tipped Turkish cigarettes. Ruth once announced she was writing a novel about two sisters, one of them a hunchback who goes insane, and explained to Eileen that her "bitter" tale symbolized the timeless oppression of women. To emphasize her new independence—and the wages she received from Otto—Ruth proudly insisted on picking up the check.

6

CRIMES AND MISDEMEANORS

IN HER DIARY, Hinda Weinstein made a list of important events:

"Hair permanently waved, Sept. 26, 1921."
"My first real evening dress wedding, Sept. 29, 1921."

Entries about her brother tended to be sparse. However, there was one occasion that fifteen-year-old Sis recorded—a day nobody had ever expected to see:

"Nat left for college, Friday, Sept. 30, 1921."

As a high school dropout, Nat appeared to have bungled his opportunities for a proper university education. Nonetheless, suddenly and mysteriously, he was accepted by Tufts College as a candidate for the Bachelor of Science degree.

His admission was supposedly based on a high school transcript confirming that Nathaniel (*sic*) Weinstein had earned the required fifteen college entrance credits, plus an extra half credit. In subsequent years, inquiries would fail to produce evidence of DeWitt Clinton's submission of any such record. Much later his family told biographers that Nat himself manufactured the academic report with the encouragement of his cousin Nathaniel "Wally" Wallenstein. Transforming an old Clinton transcript by means of ink and ink eradicator, he had awarded himself four years of passing grades and modified his given name from Nathan to Nathaniel.

The idea that a fumble-fingers like Nat could possibly counterfeit any document, much less a transcript, is not convincing. A modest talent for drawing cartoons was outweighed by his hand tremors and poor manual dexterity. A pencil between his fingers "became a sixth finger hostile to the other five, a stiff and sullen balking thing," Julian Shapiro would say. Even picking up change could be tricky because the coins sometimes dribbled downward like water.

There was little that money could not buy, however, and in fact colleges did not routinely request official transcripts but rather required applicants to prove graduation with high school diplomas. Procuring a diploma could be easily done. At the New York State Education Department in Albany, cash-strapped clerks regularly trafficked in such documents. For those in a position to pay—and it wouldn't have been the first, or last, time determined parents like the Weinsteins bought a hot diploma—it was money well spent.

Tufts was a small liberal arts college known for a first-rate medical school, as well as fraternity hazing parties and a lamentable football team. Located in the working-class town of Medford, six miles from Boston, the school was a fallback choice for rejects from Harvard and Yale. In honor of Tufts's major donor, P. T. Barnum, the school mascot was Jumbo the circus elephant, whose taxidermied hide was on permanent display in the bowels of a campus building. Compared to DeWitt Clinton, Tufts, with only a few hundred students, was tiny.

Had Nat applied to Tufts or to an Ivy League school three or four years later, he would have found entry much tougher, if not impossible. When he made his application, these institutions had no formal admissions offices. Those youngsters with secondary school diplomas or high scores on written entrance exams—proving competency in core subjects like languages and math—were generally admitted, along with those offering athletic skills and family connections. Standard practice was changing, though, as leading universities discreetly altered their admissions policies in order to restrict the number of Jews. Columbia, for instance, made extensive cuts in the proportion of its Jewish students, to 22 percent from 40 percent, between 1920 and 1922. Under the new policies, character and leadership qualities trumped academic qualifications. Schools began requiring interviews and closely examining last names, photographs, social status, and WASP recommendations, creating an informal quota system that screened out Jews. Luckily for him, Nat was able to squeeze in under the wire.

That autumn everybody was crossing their fingers. Anna and Max hoped they had seen the end of their son's academic problems, and Nat, who had spent the two years since leaving Clinton working on his father's construction sites, wanted nothing more than to be a regular college student. Arriving on campus with his banjo, a member of the class of 1925, he lacked proper high school credentials but otherwise resembled the boys immortalized by F. Scott Fitzgerald's *This Side of Paradise*, published the previous year, whose blueprint for college life he knew by heart. A month short of his eighteenth birthday, he weighed an underfed 130 pounds and had not reached his final height of six feet. He was sometimes mistaken for younger than he was. Although lank and slightly stoop-shouldered, he was learning how to carry his beanpole physique. Like his fastidious cousin Sam Weinstein, then employed by the august Wall Street investment bank of L. F. Rothschild, Nat shopped at Brooks Brothers, where merchandise was stacked on oak tables, the air smelled of wool and leather, and a salesman approached a customer only when summoned.

After pledging the Jewish fraternity Phi Epsilon Pi, Nat moved into the frat house at 19 University Avenue and immediately got distracted by his new life of fraternity parties and football games. Fitting in was serious business for a self-conscious boy who'd always been an indifferent conversationalist at best.

If he seemed to be adjusting nicely in his social life, he was far less successful academically. Often he missed morning classes because he could not drag himself out of bed. He had to struggle for consciousness until he could keep his eyes open, and even then continued to feel exhausted. To get moving, he splashed his face with icy water until he was gasping, a routine repeated several times. Although this generally worked, he sometimes would be shuffling around an hour later, still woozy. Before long, he was having trouble showing up to classes no matter what hour they convened, and then further problems developed when he slipped into the habit of showing up only when he felt like it.

In November, after Phi Epsilon Pi's Thanksgiving dance, a formal affair with full orchestra and buffet at the Copley Plaza Hotel in Boston, Nat decamped for home. An ice storm delayed his return to campus and when Nat finally got back to the Phi Epsilon Pi house, he was summoned to a faculty meeting. In his absence, the promotions committee had reviewed scholastic records for the first half of the term to determine how students were faring—and who should be shown the door. Among the freshmen who appeared to be unprepared for college-level work was Nathaniel Weinstein. One of the worst—possibly the very worst—students in his class, he had partied his way into failure in every course. His French grade was a pathetic double F. The physical education department claimed to have never seen the phantom student. In spite of his protests and promises to get down to business, the committee sent him packing, offering to mark his official record as "withdrew" so that there would be no evidence of his failing grades. In years to come, the only trace of his enrollment would be the Freshmen Register, in which he is listed as "Weinstein, Nathaniel, bs., New York, N.Y., Phi Epsilon Pi House," along with a stray biology report noting "Left Before Christmas" and a grade of FF ("discreditable").

Nat found himself back on Mount Morris Park West with his trunk of Brooks Brothers suits. "Poor kid," Sis wrote in her diary, "I'm sorry for him & wonder what'll happen to him." In an attempt to reframe an unpalatable calamity, he characterized his dismissal as unfair. As he saw it, he was just trying to have a good time like his classmates. Still, he felt worthless. By then he was always conscious of being an embarrassment to his long-suffering parents, his misdeeds the subject of perpetual disapproval within the family. To save face he smudged the facts. Since Tufts had not officially recorded his marks, there was no way to prove how miserably he had done, and drawing attention to details would cause Anna and Max too much pain.

During the holidays the relatives crowded as usual into their uptown parlors, where little had changed in twenty-five years: the real estate deals, the garrulous Wallenstein aunt, the penny-pinching uncle opposed to private schools, the supersmart boy cousins, his sister modeling her first fur coat. A cold snap hit the city on New Year's Eve but downtown, the sex dens were doing brisk business in holiday customers. His future turned upside down, Nat crept off. If sexual adventures once had been special treats, they were a necessity by this time as a way to feel a bit of masculine pride. Sometimes he got into trouble, though. On New Year's morning, after being out all night, he returned home at eight-thirty with his face "all smashed up," Sis noted in horror. She got no answers to her questions about "where and what really happened."

At the ripe age of eighteen Nat was down and out, again, with no way to get back on his feet. Should he resume working for his father as a hod carrier, ten hours a day in mud-caked boots, which in the eyes of his cousins was like death? Should he wait until next year and apply to another school, or try a midyear switch as a transfer student? That had happened to his brainy cousin Wally, who, after being expelled from Columbia, had bounced around to Haverford and finally to Tulane. But Nat could hardly claim to be a transfer when he had earned no official grades at Tufts.

Quickly, the family conceived a plan for Nat to resume his education. That the scheme might not be strictly legal, or moral, or even sensible, was the last thing on their minds. To a family fiercely committed to winning, there was only one question. Would the mission succeed?

Weinstein is a common Jewish surname. It so happened that among the students registered at Tufts were several Weinsteins, one of them coincidentally named Nathan. Soon after the start of the term, Nat heard about the other Nathan Weinstein from his frat brothers. Four years older, he came from nearby suburban Dorchester and graduated from the English School in Boston before enrolling at Harvard dental school. He transferred in 1920 from Harvard to Tufts, where he earned Bs and Cs in German, physics, psychology, and biology, the standard subjects for a science or medicine major. Never had Nat crossed paths with his namesake; just as he got to Medford, the other boy transferred to the Tufts medical school in downtown Boston. All this meant nothing to Nat until December, when the coincidence became useful information in the Weinsteins' determined efforts to rescue Nat. The other Nathan Weinstein didn't know it but he was going to transfer again, this time to an Ivy League college more prestigious than Tufts.

At once, Nat submitted an application to Brown University in Providence. Presenting himself as Nathan Weinstein, he requested admission as a transfer student from Tufts and arranged for the usual transmission of records. (He added a year to his age by giving his birth date as 1902.) The audacious idea's success hinged on the Tufts registrar submitting the med school Weinstein's academic credits as Nat's own—and on Brown's accepting the stolen information.

The hoax unfolded exactly as planned. Shortly after Christmas, Brown notified Nat of his acceptance for the second term, pending a review of his transcript to determine the exact number of semester hours. When the tally became official, he was awarded fifty-seven credits, more than half of them from physics and other science courses, never his strengths. He was, in short, no longer a freshman in the class of 1925 but a sophomore in the class of 1924. That he had done nothing to earn those miraculous fifty-seven credits hardly mattered to Nat, or to his family, who masterminded the trickery.

Identity theft one day would become a crime. Even though the concept did not exist in 1921, the tort of fraud or misrepresentation had a long history. Yet issues of right or wrong—the morality of stealing another's personal data—did not matter greatly to the Weinsteins. American business history had a rich tradition of foreign-born entrepreneurs achieving their goals by any means necessary in a dog-eat-dog world. In their minds, no malice was involved—they meant no harm to Nathan Weinstein—and Nat was merely borrowing grades to get back into col-

lege and continue his education. All that counted was a degree from
an Ivy League school.

The unexplained detail is the unknown accomplice in the Tufts
registrar's office who made it possible. Although Nat never revealed
the insider's identity, it is almost certain that the conspirator was a university employee who did the dirty work of mailing out the wrong transcripts. Whatever the particulars, the Brown admissions office seems to
have been exceptionally poor at smelling rats.

The counterfeit Nathan Weinstein rolled into Providence in early
February 1922. With him he lugged a trunk crammed with brand-
name clothing, a banjo, twelve volumes of Tolstoy, and the knowledge
that this was his last stop if he wanted a college education. To his new
classmates he introduced himself as Pep, a sophomore from Tufts. He
claimed to have served at sea with the U.S. Navy, an unconvincing tale
given that he looked to be about twelve years old. Not so silly was his
fat weekly allowance of twenty-two dollars, twice that of the average
student. In Room 28 at University Hall he unpacked his trunk and got
acquainted with his roommate, another transferring sophomore. Both
of them came from affluent New York City families, but Philip Lukin
was a legitimate transfer student from City College.

Soon after Nat arrived at Brown, he noticed that his testicles were swollen, and a creamy discharge was oozing from the tip of his penis. The
stinging pain soon became impossible to ignore. It was gonorrhea—
the stealthy gonococcus organism, the dreaded "g.c.," the clap. Never
would he forget his shock: "Coming from the bathroom, you discover
that you have gonorrhea." The infection, he learned, was highly conta-
gious, as dangerous as diphtheria or smallpox, and could cause sterility
and bladder or eye trouble. Should the inflammation go untreated and
reach the deep urethra, it could become chronic. On the other hand,
gonorrhea was quite common—eight times more prevalent than syphilis, a life sentence that could lead to madness.

Over the next weeks, he underwent the standard pre-antibiotic-
era treatment of urethral irrigations and instillations along with pros-

tatic massage, which turned out to be horribly traumatic. Ordered to forgo sex and alcohol, he needed no encouragement to stay away from whorehouses. Now that he had learned his lesson, he would be a monk. As the symptoms subsided, he believed himself cured. But he did not keep his vow of celibacy: the symptoms would recur the following year.

During the gonorrhea treatments Nat got beat up in one of downtown Providence's collegiate drinking holes. It was an unfriendly Texan, all bone and muscle, who savagely blacked both his eyes and broke his nose. He had nothing personal against Nat—he was drunk and Nat was only shooting the breeze—but Nat came away from the encounter looking like "a bloody wreck."

Back on his feet again, he played it cool. "I've challenged this guy to a fair fight," he announced. "He and I will have it out." Asked when the fight was going to take place, Nat replied, poker-faced, "As soon as he gets down to my weight." This retort won him respect for his sensible handling of an awkward situation, and even the Texan apologized. After that, he was judged to be a good sport, who "couldn't fight his way out of a charlotte russe," but could take a bludgeoning without getting sore and still demonstrate an admirable sense of humor. In fact, Nat was learning to make himself agreeable as an exotic outsider, a 130-pound Russian-Jewish impostor.

From the outset, Nat ran headlong against anti-Semitism, then rampant in Ivy League colleges. Brown, a Baptist school requiring chapel attendance three mornings a week, was no exception. Its enrollment included a handful of Jews, but Nat avoided them and shunned membership in their Menorah Society. He was hoping to blend in.

This was the first time Nat had lived among Christians. Other than haughty German Jews who scorned their Russian coreligionists as lower-class money-grubbers, he had never been forced to confront classic anti-Semitism. Rejection was familiar to him, but that was for reasons other than his heritage. He always insisted there was no difference, after all, between a Jewish American and, say, an Irish American.

When, in the fall of 1922, he tried desperately to join a fraternity he found out differently. Aware that Brown had no Jewish fraternities, and that none of the nineteen Christian houses accepted Jews, he decided the restrictions did not apply to him and dived into fall rush. After all, the Greeks every now and then did recruit a Jew, usually an athlete.

He failed to receive a single bid. Just as he had reacted stoically when the Paradox campers named him Pep, he tried to give the impression of indifference. He proceeded to make himself at home in the Delta Tau Delta house, when he was not mingling with the blue bloods of exclusive Psi Upsilon, which was known as the most anti-Semitic fraternity on the campus. One of his friends in Psi Upsilon remembered waking in the morning "to find him snoring beside me in my absent roommate's bed." Later a Christian classmate was to say of him, "Nobody ever thought of Pep as being Jewish anyhow." But Nat was about as white Anglo-Saxon Protestant as matzo ball soup, and Jewish students at Brown were Jews first, called "kikes" behind their backs. There was no way to blend in, not even by switching the obviously Jewish Nathan to Nathaniel, and adding a middle name— vonWallenstein—to create an aristocratic Germanic ring.

Being Jewish turned out to be only one of his difficulties. Another was immaturity. In his dormitory room, strewn with waste paper and dirty laundry, he took for granted that the obliging Philip Lukin would clean up. He chain-smoked a thousand cigarettes a day and flicked his ashes wherever. To one of his classmates he seemed "very young, hardly more than a child really," but extremely curious. Drawing further attention was his hesitant demeanor and slow speech. He looked out of it. Although Brown was notorious as one of the Ivy League's drunkest campuses, his trancelike states caught the notice of the administration. "Tell me something, Mr. Lukin," a dean said to Nat's roommate. "Does Mr. Weinstein take dope?"

At Brown Nat made two lifelong friends, one of them a sophomore from Providence who lived at home and commuted to College Hill. Sidney Joseph Perelman was undeniably odd looking. Dish faced, with steel-rimmed eyeglasses, he had elephant ears even more prominent than Nat's. His suits were cheap and frumpy. The only child of Russian-Jewish immigrants, he was born in Brooklyn in 1904 but grew up in Providence, where his father worked as a laborer in a tool factory. Joseph Perelman, a survivor of several mismanaged businesses, had failed as a poultry farmer and dry goods merchant. The story of the Perelman family was hard living, five thousand white leghorns, and poor egg sales. In order to pay his Brown tuition, Sid worked jobs electroplating car radiators or clerking at a cigar store.

Nat admired the poultry farmer's son, not only his talent for cartooning but also his droll writing with its odd words. His sense of humor was demented—as unconventional and irreverent as Nat's own. In Nat, Sid recognized a person with "warm and fanciful humor and great erudition" that almost made him seem juvenile. Unquestionably, some of his values were nutty, like his fixation on fraternities, for which Sid had no use. He did not see eye to eye with Nat on Russian novels either, in particular not *Crime and Punishment*, "a most depressing book," he believed, "and that goes for all of Dostoievsky."

Nat's other affectionate friend was Quentin Reynolds, one of the most popular boys in his class. Born into a large middle-class family, his father a high school principal in Brooklyn, Quent took for granted the necessity of working part-time jobs (dance hall bouncer, hatcheck boy at a Masonic temple). He and Nat seemed an unlikely pair, a Catholic and a Jew, a towering redheaded tackle on the varsity squad and a bookworm, a jovial optimist and a suspicious cynic. But Nat's adolescent behavior didn't faze Quent, who found nothing wrong with being "proudly lazy" if you were the soul of gentleness. Nat, he thought, was an amazingly nice kid, "warm, sympathetic and sentimental, and my bet is that he never made an enemy."

With Quent, Nat went out of his way to offer favors. When Quent needed a job one summer, Max Weinstein hired him as a hod carrier; when he got caught selling illegal rotgut in the Green Lantern Tea Room in Providence, Nat created a first-class defense featuring terminally ill parents and failure to attend Mass, plus instructions to inform the dean that "you want a degree from Brown so badly that you'd lie, cheat, steal, even sell bootleg liquor to get it." Another time, Nat composed Quent's Senior Class Day speech: a compendium of puns, classical allusions, kooky words, and obscene jokes that mixed Greek and Latin double-talk. The people in the audience, clueless about what Quent was saying, laughed their heads off.

That Class Day speech was memorable for another reason. It introduced two fictional characters who would reappear in Nat's adult work: a saint—St. Puce, Nat called him—a flea who once lived in the armpit of Jesus Christ, where he sipped the Savior's blood and snacked on his flesh. The other was St. Puce's biographer, Maloney the Areopagite, who while trying to interest a publisher passed the time crucifying himself with thumbtacks. With St. Puce and Maloney, closer to Bugs Bunny and Mr. Magoo than Raskolnikov, Nat gave serious thought to writing for the first time.

One of Nat's strategies for getting along was to make his classmates laugh. His first published efforts appeared in the school's literary and humor magazine. What appeared to be an intellectual essay—"Euripides—A Playwright"—was actually an orgy of nonsensical scholarship, name-dropping references on everything from Tiresias to Thomas Hardy and *Uncle Tom's Cabin*. The essay, originally a term paper for a course in Greek drama, blended the lecture hall with vaudeville slapstick. He also composed two poems: "Death" relied on a jumble of styles modeled on English aesthetes, and the cartoonish "Rondeau" frankly mocked poets (Ernest Dowson among them) associated with the fluttery artifice of the Decadent movement. Nat got a kick out of archaic words like "mayhap" and "witchery," and he routinely lifted bits and pieces from other writers to patch into something funny.

None of Nat's friends took his writing aspirations seriously. Not only did he have trouble with the fundamentals of composition, his attempts to produce decent term papers involved "self-torture," his roommate said. On the other hand, he had amassed an impressive collection of books, probably the largest library of any student, and was said to be the first person on campus to read James Branch Cabell's banned novel *Jurgen*. Quentin Reynolds always thought he "became a writer by reading."

Nat barely squeaked through three years at Brown. There were only three subjects—French culture, Greek drama, and music appreciation—in which he excelled, and he also passed a required swimming test. Otherwise, he regularly overslept. He forgot to study. In a pinch, he submitted term papers written by his cousin Nathaniel Wallenstein. Attendance was halfhearted, borderline cheating the norm. In a poetry exam, he was caught copying answers from his roommate, an A student, who rescued him: "Pep was on college discipline for over cutting and would have been dismissed for this infraction and I assumed the blame," Philip Lukin reported.

Twice more he dodged a bullet: In May of 1922, disciplined for excessive cutting, he was unceremoniously chucked out but let back in. The following February, he landed on probation. After a party in New York, he had picked up another dose of the clap and was too busy with his penis, a possibly damaged prostate, and fending off a couple of haberdashery-bill collectors to worry about his marks. In the spring of his senior year, protesting a modern drama course that failed to include twentieth-century authors, he refused to complete assignments. After receiving a flunking grade of E, he had to go to the teacher and put on a tearful show of contrition, including heartrending references to his parents and how his failure to graduate would surely kill them. His grade was raised to a D.

After two and a half years in Brown's doghouse, it looked as if Nat would manage to get a diploma. He had learned a lot—some of it so odious that exacting the appropriate revenge would take a lifetime— but it was nevertheless important to leave behind a lovely footprint. His yearbook picture, artistically sidelighted, gave him the classic WASP nose he had always wanted. For good measure, the White Studio doctored his ears and cleaned up his skin. The write-up accompanying the photograph turned out to be a work of art as well.

Editors of the *Liber Brunensis* faced the delicate task of judging Nathaniel vonWallenstein Weinstein, who, unlike the majority of the class of 1924, had not a single campus activity to his credit. "To predict his future would indeed be a hard task, so we'll leave the answer to the crystal and the astrologer." They commended him for being "an easy going genial fellow" who "passed his time in drawing exotic pictures, quoting strange and fanciful poetry." They gave him credit for being "a bit eccentric at times, a characteristic of all geniuses," before slyly quoting a motto associated with the English Order of the Garter: *Honi soit qui mal y pense* ("Shame on him who thinks this evil"). The cryptic saying might have referred to any number of misdeeds: cheating, compulsive lying, those admission rumors, or possibly the cardinal sin of skipping out on bills owed to local clothing stores. Nathan the impostor could not get worked up over the snotty people at *Liber Brunensis*. All he wanted was the degree. Never would he regret his years at Brown, but neither would he forget the humiliation of being an inconsequential Jew named Weinstein.

7

BECOMING "NATHANAEL WEST"

O N THE MORNING of June 18, 1924, the day of his commencement at Brown, Nat overslept after a night of drinking and awoke with a hangover. He ran half-dressed to catch up with the processional march to College Green and heard flowery speeches as the school president conferred an honorary degree on the Japanese ambassador. Afterward, in keeping with a solemn college tradition, he lined up with his 184 classmates to file through the open Van Wickle Gates. In the crowd of onlookers none were more overjoyed than Max and Anna Weinstein, whose golden boy, for all his repeated setbacks, had earned a degree from an Ivy League college. That evening the family celebrated with a gala party at the Biltmore, the city's new luxury hotel.

From Providence, Nat lugged home his life's possessions, crates of books and a wardrobe largely bought on credit from Brooks and other exclusive menswear shops. The books meant everything to him, the unpaid bills nothing at all. After making it through the years of school torment, he was ready to begin living his life. It was the summer of the Democratic Convention at Madison Square Garden, and Fifth Avenue was strung with so many blinking yellow lightbulbs that it felt like Coney Island. The weather steamed up, the stink of speakeasy beer choked the air, and the throngs of sticky conventioneers, weary of milling around holding little American flags and applauding patriotic speeches, began to look flattened. People listened on the infant gadget called radio to Franklin D. Roosevelt make a rousing nominating speech for New York's own "Happy Warrior" governor, Alfred E. Smith. Nat, pretty much indifferent to politics in any form, basked in his own triumph.

No one offered to hire him because he had graduated from Brown. In fact, he didn't waste his time looking for work. Fortunately, he had a well-off father, unlike his closest friends, who were obliged to make their way in the world. Sid Perelman aspired to become a writer. After leaving school without his degree (he could never pass trigonometry), he lived in the Village and did cartooning for the humor magazine *Judge*. Quentin Reynolds took a job on the *Brooklyn Daily Times*, planning to enroll in law school at night. But Nat did not believe himself to be the kind of person cut out for a job, at least not in the real estate business. He wanted to accomplish grand things with his life, he announced. Henceforth he intended to occupy himself with "lit-rachoor" and foreign travel, making his home in a romantic country like France. Scorning journalism or advertising as hack work, he imagined himself as a son of Dostoyevsky, a true artist who would dedicate himself to the kind of pure literature that guaranteed a life of unemployment.

The slightest mention of literature sparked fierce arguments with Anna, who in her eagerness to put him on the right track was constantly finding fault. In these free-for-alls, his father took no part, characteristically relying upon his wife to play the heavy. To prove he meant business, Nat decided to try his hand at a novel, but his efforts were half-hearted. In the end, he mooched through the summer, figuring there was plenty of time to make decisions.

His aimless life came to an abrupt end shortly after his twenty-first birthday, in October, when his father was injured in an automobile collision. Jerked forward on impact and pinned against the steering wheel, Max sustained internal injuries and his recovery was slow. Then Nat's cousin Nathaniel Weinstein injured himself playing football. What appeared to be an ordinary accident, an innocuous heel infection, turned out to be serious. Ned died in November at the age of twenty-two. This was the second death of a child for Charles and Pauline Weinstein, who had earlier lost their twelve-year-old daughter Hilda to complications from a mastoid operation.

Nat looked for meaning. It seemed inconceivable that his cousin, with all his life before him, had been cheated of his existence by an injury seemingly no worse than a skinned knee. Fate was undeserved and random, Nat decided; barbarity ruled. An unlucky person could be minding his own business, idly daydreaming of happiness in some paradise of sugary sunshine and oranges, when suddenly the lights go out. Always an uncertain pessimist, he now began to focus his gaze obsessively on the dark side, until one day his cynicism would advance "to the point where it colored his whole outlook on life," said the writer Robert Coates, who knew him well a decade later.

While his cousin's death was devastating, it was Max's accident and his debilitation afterward that would settle matters for Nat. His company recently had committed to three new buildings, and Nat was needed to work as a superintendent. Nat's worst fear had come to pass, and there was nothing he could do about it: he was going into the construction business he so loathed. Even more depressing, his father was making fewer and fewer big deals. Instead, his company was putting up utilitarian brick cubes on properties in the unfashionable Inwood section of upper Manhattan, a hilly backwater where names instead of numbers identified the streets. Nat, barely able to tolerate minor emergencies, suddenly had to face a new reality in which acts of God become regular events. He was not prepared.

Harlem had become a different place from the gentrified enclave of Nat's childhood. After the war, a wave of black immigration had repopulated the neighborhood with working-class families, and by the twenties, many white householders, Jewish and Christian alike, were in retreat to Riverside Drive and West End Avenue. Among them were Charles and Pauline Weinstein, who gave up their family home near Mount Morris Park.

After twenty years in Harlem, Max and Anna also relocated to the

Upper West Side, where they first rented an apartment at Broadway and Ninety-seventh Street, then a nicer place near the American Museum of Natural History at 164 West Seventy-ninth Street. They brought their stylish new dining room set, the baby grand, the rose-quartz lamps, the petit-point love seat and armchairs, the satin draperies, so that the new flat did not look much different from the old one. Still, exiled from the place where she had raised her children, Anna had a hard time adjusting to the unfamiliar neighborhood. Sis mentioned fits of moodiness that she described as "Ma's hysteria." To cheer herself up, Anna decided to take a vacation in Europe and asked Sis to accompany her. "Oh, gosh, I'm lucky," Sis wrote in her diary. "I'm thrilled to the marrow." In March, Anna and Sis drove downtown to the passport office to file an application, a procedure that annoyed Sis because she was too young for her own passport and had to be included on her mother's. Thomas Cook and Son made the arrangements for them to sail July 8 and return September 15, the standard two-month excursion.

During their absence Nat was to mind the store and look after his father and Lorraine, then fourteen, known in the family as Baby. Tall and rail thin, she was more interesting-looking than conventionally beautiful. With her brown hair pulled back, her head resembled that of an exotic Egyptian bird. Her most striking feature was her large, deep-blue eyes. Baby, a moody child who bottled up her feelings, warmed to people slowly. Reluctant to assert herself except by puckish observations similar to her brother's, she attempted to imitate his mannerisms, until some who knew them thought she might have been his twin. Troubled by her slowness to make friends, Baby was emphatic in her belief that she and Nat shared some pathological lethargy causing them to depend on others for social contact. Lorraine, even as a teenager, exhibited signs of the clinical depression that colored much of her later life. "We are a strange family," she wrote in her diary. "Soft and all of us without friends."

"All of us" did not include her gregarious sister, whose diary is full of colorful descriptions: a St. Patrick's Day party, the Junior Council dance, bridge afternoons ("my partner was a big baby"), double dates to roadhouses ("first time I've ever been drunk"), a great New Year's Eve in Times Square. No sooner did Sis get her driver's license than Max and Anna bought a Stutz and she began taking friends for a spin. On an outing to New Jersey, she once got pulled over for not having a local license. From a station house she summoned Nat to run her home. "He came in our other car and was promptly arrested and fined for the same reason," she recalled. "He was a bit absent minded."

While Nat got along well with Sis, he would always remain closest to Baby. There was no finer girl on earth, he declared, and never would he marry unless he found someone of her caliber. A brother so obviously smitten with a sister struck some people as odd.

Nat was finally learning to be organized. His Brooks Brothers suits hung meticulously in the closet, his Brooks underwear and pajamas lay folded in his bureau drawer, even his tasteful shoelaces were purchased from Brooks. All summer and fall of 1925, he made the daily trip uptown to a pair of five-story brick apartment houses on Thayer Street in upper Manhattan, where his hours were spent with crews of carpenters, electricians, painters, and plumbers, largely dirt-cheap Italian immigrant labor. In his crisp khakis, he left for work when it was still dark, a far cry from the student unable to shake himself awake. In the evenings he read or tried to write, and on weekends he decamped for the beach, either Long Island or New Jersey. Once there was a brief romance, something he described as "an attempt to love," but it fizzled and the individual quickly disappeared from his life. The relationship left him afraid that "experiencing a genuine emotion" might never be possible.

That summer, along with the rest of the country, he took up the game of golf and equipped himself with expensive paraphernalia and the latest knickerbocker trousers and tan-and-white argyle sweaters. On slow days at his job, he slacked off and headed to the Jersey Shore, where there were good public links and he felt comfortable playing by himself.

The beach resort of Asbury Park was a mirage of seaside dwellings designed to look like Swiss chalets and Italian villas. In keeping with the odd architecture, the boardwalk teemed with bathers gorging on saltwater taffy, butter-drizzled popcorn, and five-cent franks that they slathered in mustard from a sloppy communal bowl by means of a wooden trowel. It was all so awful that Nat could not help feeling entertained.

He was on the second nine holes one afternoon when another solo player came behind him. He motioned him to pass, but the fellow stepped toward him instead.

"Aren't you Nat Weinstein?" he asked. "From Harlem?"

The young man with the fair hair and pale skin appeared around his age, but did not look familiar. Nat took his time replying. His name was not Nat, he finally said as he singed his hair lighting a cigarette, it was Nathaniel.

Didn't he remember when they used to see each other at the De Peyster? It was Julian Shapiro. People usually called him Scotty now. He lived in Brooklyn, but his folks were renting a summer cottage several miles away, in West End.

Continuing together over the rest of the course, they exchanged meaningless patter about mashies and downhill lies until the conversation took a personal turn. "I'm studying law at Fordham," Scotty said, without explaining that he had dropped out of three colleges before enrolling in Fordham Law School with a fraudulent diploma obtained by bribing a New York State official. Not to be outdone, Nat offered a heavily edited version of his personal life in which he failed to reveal working for his father, his card in the bricklayers' union, or his proficiency as a plumber. Neither did he mention that, still shackled to his parents, he was living at home. Finally he dragged out his alma mater. "I went to Brown," he said. Not satisfied, he cast about for an impressive punch line. "I'm writing a book," he announced.

Scotty later remembered thinking that his legal career was turning to "yellow leaf" right there on the golf course. His future, always in doubt, suddenly appeared clear. What he really wanted, without knowing it, was to be a writer. Never would he forget Nat's voice: "I went to

Brown. I'm writing a book—and thereafter nothing remains of the day, not the rolling ground, the greens, the flight of a dimpled ball." Collecting himself, he wondered out loud, "What kind of book?"

Hesitating, Nat replied that he supposed it was a novel but couldn't say exactly. It was about a poet who is traveling in Turkey, in an area said to be the site of ancient Troy, when he notices in the tall grass a military landmark: the fabled wooden horse of the Greeks. The story was set inside—that's right, inside—the Trojan horse and involved a biographer writing the life of a flea who had taken up residence in the armpit of Jesus Christ.

The flea struck Scotty as highly comical.

After meeting at Asbury Park, Nat and Scotty quickly reestablished their relationship. The camaraderie flourished because both of them were lonely, especially Nat, who, often by himself, hungered for somebody to confide in. Neither did it hurt that Scotty seemed awed that he was writing a book. Nat's parents, relieved he had settled down to a job, viewed writing as a hobby, at best; there was no respect from the aunts and uncles and cousins, and not even college friends like Quentin Reynolds considered him a writer. So whenever Nat spoke about books or writing, nobody paid attention except Scotty.

On warm nights they met on the Upper West Side and strolled along Broadway to Seventy-second Street before boarding a bus and continuing downtown to Washington Square. In an expansive mood, Nat could go on and on about writers. "Ah, the names he launched on the nighttime air," Scotty remembered: Joyce and Eliot, Pound and Pater, starring in "tales of high living and of wild and wasted lives." Taking blatant swipes at his cherished geniuses, he unreeled stories "of failure and madness and suicide, of who was serious and who was killing time," not that Nat had any firsthand knowledge of the literati.

Even though Nat could go on dropping names all night, he avoided details of his own life, and neither did Scotty seem eager to discuss personal facts about himself. Nat secretly regarded Scotty as a Mister Goody Two-Shoes, too nervous, clean-cut, and insecure to get sexually involved with women, and it occurred to him that Scotty might be a homosexual. He certainly did not talk like a homosexual, neither did he behave like one, but his intense admiration made Nat wonder if he could be attracted sexually. Nat was right about one thing: his sexual experience was limited. Knowing the truth about Nat—the promiscuity, prostitutes, and heavy price from gonorrhea—would have shocked Scotty, who was terrified by venereal disease.

"Here's a story for you, Scotty," Nat said one night. This American tourist hiking through Turkey is hoping to look up a certain famous sage by the name of Apollonius. One day Balso comes across a rare sight, unlisted in the guidebooks: a snake that seems to be slithering into a man's anus. It must be some secret local custom, he decides.

So this tourist goes up to the man and tries to strike up a friendly conversation. He says, "Pardon me, my good fellow." Is he aware that a reptile has just entered his backside?

The man, a philosopher, is not accustomed to such impolite strangers. He finally says to the tourist, "Yes, sir, he lives there."

What a lucky break. Turns out it's Apollonius of Tyana, just the sage he's looking for. He says to him, "Here's a letter of introduction from my brother George. May I see the snake?"

Apollonius is not hesitant about displaying his snake, but the tourist isn't satisfied. He doesn't want to miss anything. He points and says, "Now the rectum."

It was, Nat told Scotty, a passage from his novel. How funny was that?

Scotty thought it was funny.

But it didn't sound as if he really got it. "The tourist, you understand, always armed with credentials."

"I get the point," Scotty insisted. "I understand."

Nat remained doubtful. "Just as the snake is in the rectum of Apollonius, Balso is in the rectum of the Wooden Horse of Troy. A rectum within a rectum, so to speak."

"That makes it twice as funny," Scotty agreed.

But did Scotty understand that Balso's problem was which crevice to enter: the mouth (out of reach), the navel (a cul-de-sac), or the rectum? His only choice, of course, is to use the last.

But there are four openings, Scotty said.

"What do you mean—four? How do you get four?"

What about the trap door of the Greeks?

Nat blew up. "Jesus Christ, you're killing the joke!"

Well, Scotty suggested, why don't you nail up the door?

When it came to comedy Scotty was tone-deaf, Nat decided.

If nobody but Scotty thought of Nat as a writer, Nat himself also felt unsure. Scotty's impression that Nat must be exceptional was based on faith alone; he had yet to read a single word. To be sure, Nat talked about the novel as if it existed, calling it "The Journal of Balso Snell." Balso, his poet protagonist, was named for Walter Snell, the head baseball coach at Brown, a heroic tough-guy sort of fellow, much admired on campus because he had been a reserve catcher for the 1913 Boston Red Sox. And perhaps Nat just liked the sound of the words. Balls of Snell. Smelly balls. Balso. Balso Snell. Balso's initials were B. S., and the idea of naming his main character Bull Shit would have tickled Nat.

Far less enjoyable was the actual writing, which he had discovered to be tedious, especially when he hated what he had accomplished. On days when he did not feel like a writer, he rationalized his pokiness. He was "a Sunday writer" who worked in his free time. But even had that not been the case, he still would have been a dawdler, cautiously tiptoeing forward, forever erasing, rewriting, fussing.

The day he ran into Scotty at Asbury Park, the manuscript mostly consisted of shards jotted on scraps of butcher's paper, laundry cardboards, whatever materials came to hand. Tentatively shifting gears, he decided to use real paper, yellow, blue, and white foolscap, on which he painstakingly typed or scribbled. He noticed that white paper "acts as a laxative" with the result being "a diarrhoea of words." Almost everything really stank.

If composition was excruciating, revisions were worse. Unlike authors who effortlessly corrected troublesome sentences by hand, he found himself unable to edit his prose in an efficient manner. His drafts resembled scrambled eggs. He was forced to adjust and readjust by speaking the sentences aloud, line by line, over and over. He claimed to be writing the voices that his characters talked—and insisted he was incapable of working in any other fashion. To those in the vicinity, his incessant mumbling was so annoying that people felt like throttling him.

Through Scotty, Nat met George Brounoff, a bond salesman whose Russian-born father, Platon, had been a composer and whose sister, Olga, worked as a chorus girl while studying for an operatic career. On Sunday afternoons, George's coterie of friends, all erudite Jewish intellectuals, would crowd into the Brounoff apartment on Central Park West, its drawing room dominated by the grand piano, the Bakst prints, the scores of Schubert and Brahms tucked on the music rack, overshadowed by a portrait of the deceased Platon. They discussed philosophy and Russian literature, and George might play Chopin—setting a European tone that appealed greatly to Nat. When they were not browsing the Gotham Book Mart for experimental literature, the Brounoff crowd was in the habit of reading foreign magazines and attending Russian art films. Frequently Nat accompanied them to concerts at Carnegie Hall. Afterward everyone gathered for discussion at the posh Russian Tea Room or the not-so-posh Fifty-seventh Street Childs cafeteria, where they pushed tables together, drank coffee, and smoked a lot of cigarettes. For all their idealism, Nat found them charming, at least for a while. Within a few years, tired of their pretensions, he would mock George as a modern version of Dostoyevsky's idiot, Prince Myshkin.

If he had Scotty to thank for these contacts, Scotty received something valuable in return: the courage to run amok. Until their reunion, he had been planning to become a lawyer like his father. Although continuing his studies at Fordham—in time graduating, passing the bar, practicing from a room in Philip Shapiro's suite of offices—he decided that he would rather be a writer. As he was to insist over the next seven decades, during which he published numerous novels, histories, and autobiographies, it was through Nat that he had discovered his true calling. Not that Nat had ever offered him a word of encouragement. But "he set an example," Scotty said in retrospect. "He was writing, and I followed suit."

Nat had no interest in being a muse, and Scotty's air of gratitude eventually began to make him uncomfortable. He preferred to regard him as an unimaginative law student, or the boy on the De Peyster roof reading Frank Merriwell novels, the kid who had never heard of Dostoyevsky. That Scotty might actually possess talent for writing never occurred to him. So when he began talking about abandoning law and devoting himself to a career in fiction as if he were the next Hemingway, Nat reacted with indifference and hoped Scotty would shut up about it.

He didn't. Once, while they were on a bus, Scotty brought up their meeting in Asbury Park. "That day was my birthday," he remarked: a random encounter had led to discovery of his true vocation. In response to this expression of feelings, Nat immediately lurched to his feet and jumped off the bus at the next stop.

At twenty-two, after working for his father for almost two years, Nat desperately wanted to escape. Always unhappy, he thought that nothing good would happen to him until he got away from home. Convinced that living with his parents had stymied his attempts to write, he imagined a place where he might be able to concentrate on his novel—definitely foreign soil, ideally the terrace of a Parisian café—and he beseeched his father for financial support. But Max balked. Bankrolling a kid's grandiose schemes so he could bum around Paris seemed senseless when cash was increasingly hard to come by.

If Nat was unable to refute his father's views, neither could he shake the bewitching example of, say, F. Scott Fitzgerald. Against all odds, he had managed to spin royalty gold from the exploits of gin-soaked college boys sporting Brooks wardrobes and driving Stutz Bearcats (coincidentally, a page from Nat's own playbook). Living the frothy expatriate life in France, Fitzgerald had recently published his third novel,

The Great Gatsby, eagerly awaited by readers who had made *This Side of Paradise* a bestseller. As it turned out, *Gatsby* received disappointing reviews, but aspiring writers like Nat continued to idolize its writer.

Over the winter and spring of 1926, frustration drove Nat to consider dubious strategies for earning extra money. One of his ideas was to scavenge issues of *Field & Stream* and patch together their formula articles into pieces that looked new. But common sense suggested that regurgitating old magazine pieces was not worth the effort: payment was negligible. He also discussed with his Brown buddy Brae Rafferty a plan to obtain a bank loan on his father's credit. Surely Max would not be held accountable. The impulse to defraud passed, but he would allude to it in a story called "The Impostor," writing "I was very busy trying to swindle my mother out of some money."

As scams seemed to come naturally to him, he thought of keeping a crime journal to list his crimes, real and imaginary. Knowing himself, however, he probably would just wind up writing lies. There was no point in a diary if you lied to yourself.

Mortimer Weinstein, Nat's cousin and brother of the dead Ned, had begun to suffer mysterious aches and twitches, muscle cramps at first scarcely noticeable in a young man in apparent good health. In time, he became increasingly unsteady on his feet, so that he tripped and fell on his face. The paralyzing weakness in his arms and legs was subsequently diagnosed as amyotrophic lateral sclerosis, a rare fatal neuromuscular disorder (named in the 1940s "Lou Gehrig's disease," for the New York Yankees baseball player) that destroys the ability to control movement.

The diagnosis crushed Pauline and Charles. Life had not been kind to them as parents. After the deaths of Ned and Hilda, three children remained: Sam, married and working on Wall Street; Susanne, living with her husband in Mississippi; and Mortimer, a construction supervisor, unmarried, living at home, and now stricken with a fatal disorder. Their household on Claremont Avenue revolved around caring for Morty, whom doctors predicted would be dead in a year or two, once the atrophied muscles of his respiratory system made breathing impossible. No cure existed; the only treatment was physical therapy. As the disease continued to advance, he became unable to stand, walk, or swallow. Finally, helpless, only his brain continued to function. His deterioration was "slow and painful to watch," says his niece.

Accepting that his desperately ill son would never recover, Charles offered Nat a trip to Europe, in a sense designating him a surrogate for his own boy. Anna's brother Saul Wallenstein also contributed to the expenses. Some years later, Nat liked to give the impression of having lived in France as long as a year or more. In fact, he was a lucky kid whose relatives underwrote a standard tour.

In September 1926, Nat telephoned Scotty at his father's office near City Hall Park one morning. Could Scotty get away to meet him at the passport office? He had just learned that a witness was required for the application. It would only take a few minutes.

On the application, he described himself as a male Caucasian, six feet tall with brown eyes and brown hair, residing at 164 West Seventy-ninth Street, New York City. Date of birth: October 17, 1903. Occupation: student. He planned to remain abroad one year in order to pursue his studies in Italy, France, Switzerland, and Belgium. Nathan Weinstein was gone, replaced by a name that sounded like a writer's. Nathanael West had been his new legal name for only four weeks, since August 16, and he still signed it like a child, crafting the letters with self-conscious delight. To complete the form he submitted a photo, the same boyish portrait, nose airbrushed and droopy eyelids perked up, that he'd had taken for the Brown yearbook. He had changed little, except that close up, his hair seemed to be thinning slightly.

The news of Nat's new name flabbergasted Scotty, who had the desire but not the nerve to do something similar. When he eventually did anglicize his name from Julian Shapiro to John Sanford, rejecting Nat's suggestion for "Starbuck" as a fine, American-sounding surname, he apologized to his father. There was no intention to hurt his feelings, he insisted.

In response, Philip Shapiro posed a question. "Did Pep hurt Max?"

"I never asked," Scotty admitted. With Nat you didn't pry.

Nobody in the Weinstein family seemed to care, actually. A precedent for Americanizing the name had already been established when Samuel Weinstein began his career on Wall Street and renamed himself Sam West, even though Rothschild was a Jewish banking firm. The name became so popular that two of Jacob Weinstein's sons, Leon and Sydney, followed suit. Sydney, a dentist, always claimed it was a perfect name for his career because of the popular Dr. West's brand of toothbrushes. Nat was eager to emulate his much-loved cousin Sam in every way possible. Eventually Nat's sister Lorraine would call herself Laura West, and even Anna favored the change, leaving instructions that her tombstone should read Anna West.

West was a pleasing surname, short, crisp, and it did not sound Jewish, while Nathanael spelled with an *ael* had a certain seafaring flavor, like a character in one of Herman Melville's novels. In the future, Nat would see no reason to explain his actions or analyze his refusal to be categorized as a Jew. To those vulgar enough to question his motives for becoming Nathanael West, he cited the advice attributed to the *New York Tribune* editor Horace Greeley: "Go west, young man." Nathanael with an *ael* went east. Setting sail for France on October 13, 1926, the grateful voyager was halfway across the Atlantic when he turned twenty-three.

8

BALSO SNELL'S BOOK OF
DIRTY LITTLE SECRETS

I N PARIS IT WAS GRAY and chilly, and some cafés had already put braziers on their terraces. From the boat train Nat had gone directly to the Lutetia, a luxury Art Deco–style hotel on boulevard Raspail close to all the famous cafés. Several days later, he decided it was too expensive and moved to a side street off boulevard du Montparnasse. At the Liberia, a romantic little hotel in rue de la Grande Chaumière, he would be able to live economically and have money left over for shopping. Just up the street were two important art academies, the Grande Chaumière and the Colorossi, where there was always something going on. From his window, he could look down on the small, cheap cafés and the students squealing and swirling along a street so stagy it cried out for replication in fiction.

Each evening he joined the night crawlers thronging the hot spots — le Dôme, le Select, the famous Deux Magots on boulevard Saint-Germain, la Closerie des Lilas, where Hemingway wrote in his blue notebooks with a pencil, la Brasserie Lipp, the all-night Dingo Bar, the fashionable la Tour d'Argent, with its haughty ducks. Sitting alone, he was surrounded by tables of drinkers, women in slinky, ankle-length dresses, men in open-neck shirts and corduroy trousers, some wearing sandals. In a bid for attention, he started dressing in "hard collars and carefully pressed suits of formal, stylish cut" and carried a tightly rolled English umbrella. He would claim that this costume was so impressive that "I was asked to all the parties," but in fact he was asked nowhere. With his homburg and yellow gloves, he looked like a baby bond salesman.

Paris was the ultimate sleepaway camp for American writers wishing to escape bourgeois lives in St. Paul and Oak Park, or on West Seventy-ninth Street. ("1000 parties and no work," F. Scott Fitzgerald had once remarked.) If Nat sometimes took pleasure in making sneering comments about the creators of "lit-rachoor," it was to cover his obsession. Down deep inside he revered these individuals as holy beings, the embodiment of all he hoped to become. He was prepared to fall at their feet, if he could find them.

In Paris it stayed gloomy and cold. He made frequent visits to Shakespeare and Company, Sylvia Beach's lively bookshop and rental library on rue de l'Odéon, where he purchased several copies of James Joyce's *Ulysses* (banned in America) and introduced himself to Djuna Barnes, still a decade away from publishing her novel *Nightwood*. While cordial, Barnes did not encourage any social contact. Nat would have felt thrilled to rub shoulders with Ernest Hemingway or Scott Fitzgerald, to take tea with Gertrude Stein, and perhaps stop by Les Trianons to gawk at James Joyce eating supper with his family. At the very least he hoped to run into Sherwood Anderson, who was supposed to be in town for Christmas. After a while, he would have settled for a glimpse of any celebrity writer in a café or on the street. As it happened, he probably would have met more stars on West Seventy-ninth Street.

The famous writers were completely unapproachable, and half of them were leaving. Still living on the Côte d'Azur, but soured on France, Scott and Zelda were planning to go home. Hemingway, whose first novel, *The Sun Also Rises*, had been published on October 22, was frantically seeking a divorce so that he could remarry as quickly as possible. Dorothy Parker had been at the Lutetia, but a fight with her wealthy boyfriend had caused her to fling his gift of a Cartier diamond watch from the window and book passage home immediately. James Joyce was nowhere to be seen—he in fact was spending the week of November 4 on his sofa at 2, square de Robiac reading Anita Loos's new novel *Gentlemen Prefer Blondes*—but Nat did spy André Gide and Jean Cocteau at a distance.

It had not occurred to Nat how little interest the professionals would take in an awestruck boy who had published a few things in his college magazine and worked for his father as a construction supervisor. Neither did he realize how many of them were anti-Semites, unremarkable at a time when anti-Semitism was both prevalent and acceptable. In those days there were practically no Jews among the expatriate writers, with the possible exception of Gertrude Stein. In the expatriate fiction being published, the most prominent Jewish characters were either criminals (Meyer Wolfsheim in *The Great Gatsby*) or weaklings (Robert Cohn in *The Sun Also Rises*).

The fiction business had long been monopolized by Gentile writers, just as American publishing itself was traditionally white Anglo-Saxon Protestant. In recent years, the mainstream houses had been joined by Jewish upstarts like Knopf and Liveright. Still, there were very few Jewish novelists, nor would there be until writers such as Norman Mailer, Saul Bellow, and Philip Roth emerged after the Second World War.

In mid-November, gusts of freezing rain swept winter into the city. Wet chestnut leaves smeared the sidewalks, the trees grew bare, and on St. Catherine's Day (Thanksgiving Day back home), fog darkening the sky at noon brought traffic to a halt. Wrapped in his plaid Brooks overcoat, Nat kept warm in steamy cafés heated by potbellied stoves, not much caring if they were clean. Had he come upon similar places in New York he would have hurried by, disgusted, but everything was fun in Paris, he reminded himself.

After a time, he discovered the rue Saint-Denis red-light district. At the city's most famous brothel, Aux Belles Poules, prostitutes performed various exotic acts—customer requests accepted—which included lesbian love and the art of the dildo. Nat later claimed he visited so many whorehouses that he could have compiled a glossary of the amusing slang used by French prostitutes.

He managed to make a friend after all, an American who called himself Hilaire Hiler—his real name was Hiler Harzberg—who had come to Paris to paint but wound up bartending and playing jazz piano in Left Bank clubs like Le Jockey, where he also sang and did Yiddish recitations. A tall, fat man a few years older than Nat, the welcoming American from Minnesota was a popular figure on the Left Bank. Meeting Hiler was the lucky highlight of a trip that was turning out to be disappointing.

The most sociable people, he discovered, were avant-garde artists like Max Ernst, the controversial German associated with Dada and Surrealism. The pioneering techniques of Ernst, along with those of Marcel Duchamp and Francis Picabia—their hallucinatory montages and collages using borrowed materials, their junk sculptures—were exactly the kind of art that attracted Nat. He appreciated paintings like Duchamp's Mona Lisa with the mustache on her upper lip because it made him laugh and thus was automatically valuable. Although Dada by then had been absorbed into Surrealism, Nat saw the possibilities of experimenting with Dada devices to create collages of words. He bought several of Max Ernst's prints.

Over the course of the autumn, Nat made periodic efforts to continue writing *Balso Snell*, the ostensible reason for his trip. Although failing to make noticeable progress on the novel, he would incorporate his surroundings into the narrative. The pregnant hunchback Janey Davenport, in the imagination of her seducer and betrayer Beagle Darwin, is living on the rue de la Grande Chaumière when she throws herself from a window of the Liberia. Paris would also serve as background for a short story, "The Fake" (published for the first time in 1997 as "The Impostor"), about an American visitor falling under the spell of a deranged man impersonating a sculptor, whose stunts include purchasing a cadaver from the morgue. Beano Walsh ends up institutionalized for the rest of his life, but the naive narrator wonders if Beano might be faking insanity. Nat was fond of Beano—who, like himself, he had to admit, "never finished anything."

Even though his few months abroad produced only a minuscule amount of writing, it was not a waste. Nat was able to make good use of certain firsthand insights into the stupidities of Americans traveling abroad. Most of all, he picked up practical ideas about how to present and position his material. Slowly he was learning to become a writer, not a conventional storyteller—nobody like a Fyodor Dostoyevsky—but a writer who was strange and not easily classified.

Mortimer Weinstein was dying. Nat rushed home, but it was too late. When the *De Grasse* docked in New York on February 11, 1927, he had been dead nine days, buried next to his brother Ned and sister Hilda at Mount Zion Cemetery in Queens. After a two-year struggle with amyotrophic lateral sclerosis, he succumbed to respiratory failure on his twenty-ninth birthday. His last days had been passed in appalling agony.

In the aftermath of Morty's death, Nat struggled to overcome his horror and reconnect with his interrupted life. Although he had neglected to write Scotty from Paris, he telephoned with an invitation to visit the Weinstein apartment. He had a gift for him, he said. In the past they had always met on street corners because of his reluctance to bring friends home; this included everybody, not just Scotty. ("First time ever had a friend of Nat's to dinner," Sis recorded in her diary on December 31, 1923, at which time Nat was twenty.) On this particular evening, however, he felt eager to show off his collection of travel souvenirs.

"God, what you can buy over there!" Nat said. He pointed to a bookcase full of volumes with foreign titles and costly fine bindings: Walter Pater's *Marius the Epicurean*, Ezra Pound's memoir of the Cubist sculptor Henri Gaudier-Brzeska, familiar authors like Coleridge along with the obscure G. S. Street, wedged in among oversized art books containing reproductions of Max Beerbohm caricatures and Man Ray photographs. Scotty could only conclude that Nat must have spent a fortune. His gift was a sketchbook of Leonardo da Vinci's sepia drawings that showed skinny old men and odd-looking machines. Scotty doubted if so unsuitable a gift had been specifically chosen for him.

Waiting for Nat to change his clothing, he made conversation with the Weinsteins. Nat's mother impressed him as a "typical *Yiddische hausfrau*, kindly enough and devoted to her family but dominating." The father, introduced by his first name, was "a quiet, sunken-eyed man, consumptive-thin and mild." Max looked older than his fifty-three years. With his wispy, soft voice, he was birdlike beside his "thick-bodied" spouse. Mention of Nat's novel drew no comment from Max, but triggered a scorching tirade from Anna, who announced that "Natchie" had to "quit the nonsense." Even after her son emerged from his bedroom, she continued to rant. Nat showed no emotion.

Although it was uncomfortable weather for lingering outdoors, Nat and Scotty set off on foot to Columbus Circle before turning east on Fifty-seventh Street. Near Fifth Avenue, they were blocked by a woman who stepped out of a doorway and reached for Nat's sleeve.

Scotty kept going, but Nat stopped short. "How much?"

"Ten dollars."

By a glance at the prostitute's face, he could see she had syphilis. He suddenly began shouting. "It's a syphilitic lesion, and it's mine for ten dollars." His voice rose: Don't come any closer, don't tell me it's a cold sore.

Silently the woman retreated to the doorway, and Nat caught up with Scotty, who knew nothing about venereal disease. "You didn't have to piss on her," Scotty scolded as they walked rapidly toward Fifth Avenue. "You could have walked away."

"I should have punched her in the face!"

Unaware of Nat's history of gonorrhea, Scotty decided that his anger was too theatrical to be genuine. What was the point of vilifying a whore?

Upon returning to New York, Nat pushed himself to complete a respectable first draft of *Balso Snell*, or as he now referred to it, *The Journal*. He had written six versions, he told Scotty. But this wasn't true. His reluctance to show his work to others more likely reflected fear of criticism and embarrassment over flawed usage ("to" for "too") and countless spelling errors.

"And it still isn't right," he said. "I want it to be lean." There were a lot of bloated passages that made the book "fat." Scotty had never heard of "fat writing."

"Read Tolstoy. There's plenty of lard in Tolstoy."

Having recently got around to tackling *War and Peace,* Scotty felt qualified to offer an opinion. "I didn't see any."

Nat replied that Tolstoy "should've left out every other page."

Nat knew there was something wrong with his novel, but he didn't know what to do about it. He was always losing sight of "the broad sweep, the big canvas, the shot-gun adjectives, the important people, the significant ideas, the lessons to be taught." For someone who practically teethed on the sweeping narratives of nineteenth-century Russian literature, it was depressing to find himself incapable of writing panoramic scenes or in a linear fashion. Instead, he seemed to compose vertically, as if compressing an onion bulb. Pretty soon layer was tightly stacked upon layer, which meant that anybody interested in reading his story would be obliged to peel the skins away.

Balso Snell starts with a middle-aged American poet who encounters a cast of eccentric *Reader's Digest* characters while touring Turkey. With its fragmented narrative and highbrow allusions, the plot can be difficult to follow. Think of it as a raunchy Monty Python sketch combined with the famous Lenny Bruce routine peppered with all the dirty words Bruce could dredge up. Using the techniques of collage, Nat disemboweled the works of Euripides, Shakespeare, Dostoyevsky, Marlowe, Joyce, Proust, Rabelais, Suetonius, Baudelaire, Gertrude Stein, and countless others, without attribution, of course. Eager to test the limits of vulgarity, he spiked this rich brew with potty humor, religious bigotry, classic misogyny, and gross behaviors.

"*While walking in the tall grass that has sprung up around the city of Troy, Balso Snell came upon the famous wooden horse of the Greeks,*" Nat wrote. After crawling inside the Trojan horse, Balso meets a dimwitted tour guide, presumably representing the local chamber of commerce, who offers to pilot him around. Soon the two of them are at odds. In his eagerness to promote tourist attractions, the guide begins crowing over a pile of feces, a "Doric prostate gland," he claims, while shrilly attacking Americans as a backward people who had produced nothing more memorable than the flush toilet. Balso, irked, lets his feelings be known. "You call this dump grand and glorious, do you?" Had he ever seen Grand Central Station? How about the Holland Tunnel or Madison Square Garden? Balso boldly goes on to denounce the guide as a "stinker," then mischievously sneaks in an anti-Semitic remark. "I am a Jew!" cries the tour guide, offended. Imagine that, Balso replies, pretending not to understand. "I'm a Jew! A Jew!" Say no more, says Balso, "some of my best friends are Jews."

Turning on his heel, Balso manages to escape the thin-skinned tour guide and continue his journey, only to discover that the inhabitants of the horse's bowels are primarily dabblers, unpublished writers in search of an audience, chronic masturbators, and irritating boobs. What a disappointment, when he had been expecting sages, scholars, or stray descendants of Homer. At one point he meets a naked biographer crucifying himself with thumbtacks, Maloney the Areopagite, who is writing the saga of St. Puce, a flea famous for living in Christ's armpit. The next character to appear is John Raskolnikov Gilson, a hot-blooded twelve-year-old, whose professional accomplishments include a crime journal in the style of Dostoyevsky and a confessional pamphlet of transvestite fantasies involving fornication with Central Park whores and flirtation with a couple of horny sailors; and finally, Mary McGeeney, who looks like a truck driver in drag, strenuously trying to trade up her stupid job as a P.S. 186 English teacher for a more rewarding career as a biographer. Miss McGeeney volunteers that she is writing the life of Samuel Perkins, "the man who wrote the biography of the man wrote the biography of the man who wrote the biography of Boswell." In other words, Balso notes, she has her head up her ass.

When the place gets on his nerves, Balso tries unsuccessfully to trace his way back to the exit, finally falling asleep in a café over a beer and dreaming of a beautiful hunchback, Janey Davenport, and her abusive lover, Beagle Darwin. Awakening, he again finds himself face to face with the creepy Miss McGeeney, who discloses herself to be a childhood sweetheart, and the story concludes happily in a clump of bushes.

Working sporadically, Nat would continue to write—and rewrite— *The Journal of Balso Snell* for another two years.

A frequent visitor to the Weinstein apartment in 1927 was Sid Perelman. For eighteen months he had been living on Staten Island, which he loathed: not a single decent delicatessen, pastrami sandwiches that were a mockery of the real thing. Shortly after his return to Manhattan, he and Quentin Reynolds found a seventy-dollar sublet on West Eleventh Street and the three former Brown students resumed their old friendship.

By this time Nat was the only Weinstein child living at home. Once Sis graduated from Hunter and found a position as a public school teacher, she married her boyfriend, Isaac "Ike" Rosenthal, who worked in the clothing business. Lorraine, sixteen, almost six feet tall and calling herself Laura, was a freshman at Pembroke, the women's division of Brown, where she felt like a misfit. Compared to the other students, who impressed her as shallow New England rubes, she viewed herself as a sophisticated New Yorker. While home from Providence over the Christmas break, she caught the interest of Sid Perelman. She liked "Perel" very much. It was hard not to like him, because he was entertaining, and his homely bespectacled face notwithstanding, physically attractive.

Seven years her senior, and three inches shorter, Sid lost no time in establishing his domination over her. He was a natural controller, and Laura was seeking someone to take charge of her life. In contrast to her reserve, he knew how to keep people laughing. An irrepressible wisecracker, he needed to be the life of the party, and if he sometimes came across as a bit of a smart aleck nobody minded.

Enthusiastic from the first, Nat encouraged the relationship, referring to the pair as "the kids." Since graduation Sid had been struggling with the death of his father and a relatively dead-end job producing cartoons and short comic essays—feuilletons, he called them—for *Judge* magazine. But even though his earnings remained fairly modest, he had begun building a reputation as a clever satirist. The future of S. J. Perelman, as he signed his byline, looked bright.

Before long the flirtation developed into a serious romance. Sid made regular trips to Providence, and Laura would race from her Saturday morning classes to the train station for a weekend in the Village at the Brevoort Hotel, without revealing the trysts to her parents. Judging by their letters to each other, any mention of other women made Laura jealous. She ought to have more faith in him, he chided. He could happily be with her seven nights a week and wish there were an eighth. "If you haven't been told, Perelman and West, Sidney and Laura, are in love." The pairing of his little sister and one of his close friends pleased Nat enormously.

9

CLEVELAND HEIGHTS PRINCESS

SYD McKENNEY BOUGHT a brand-new two-story white Colonial (three bedrooms, one bath, and a detached garage out back) at 3372 Silsby Road in Cleveland Heights. While not upper-crust Shaker Heights, the suburb was solidly middle class, known for its concentration of business and professional residents. Moving from East Cleveland to the Heights was fitting for a work-obsessed executive like Syd, who continued to rise through the ranks at Apex Electrical, eventually becoming purchasing director. In 1925, at forty, he was a spectacles-wearing Republican, an occasional churchgoer, and a conservative in most matters. Opposed to credit, he paid cash for the cheapest model Chevys. To his second set of children, he was a man of methodical, predictable habits. As one of them recalled, "He worked from six in the morning until six at night, came home, ate dinner with his necktie on, fell asleep between seven and nine o'clock, then he'd get up and go to bed. Saturdays and Sundays he played golf. Mom was a golf widow." Summer vacations were spent at Big Bear Lake in north-central Michigan, where the family spent their time fishing and boating while Syd played more golf.

With the surging stock market of the twenties, with chickens in every pot and cars in every garage—and every other person smashed on bootleg booze—the country was enjoying unprecedented prosperity. For Syd, life revolved around vacuum cleaners and washing machines, his regular golf and bridge games, and the weekly *Saturday Evening Post*, which he read religiously from cover to cover. But his was not really a Norman Rockwell existence, certainly not a life completely devoid of heartbreak, because his offspring from the first marriage continued to cause worries. The rift with Ruth had never healed. For that matter, it was a struggle to understand either of his daughters. Alarmingly irresponsible, and an expert emotional blackmailer, Eileen spent considerable energy wasting his money. As he couldn't imagine what he had done wrong, it was tempting to blame the Flynns.

In the fall of 1928, Eileen entered Cleveland Heights High School, a prized public school that had opened two years earlier a few blocks from the McKenney home. The baronial building featured a clock tower and turreted windows, two gymnasiums, an auditorium seating two thousand, and a swimming pool. The pool in particular excited Eileen, an excellent swimmer who competed in Cleveland's All-City Junior Diving Contest. Nearly 100 percent of the student body was white, and a significant portion was Jewish, the children of doctors and business executives. Few students had after-school jobs. Typically they had allowances, cars, and nice clothing. The emphasis was on conformity.

"Eileen was no shrinking violet," says the novelist Ruth Beebe Hill, a classmate and one of Eileen's best friends. "She was a big girl, standing maybe five-eight or more, with a stocky physique, not exactly heavy-set but not slender either. Everybody commented on the exceptional color of her eyes and her eyelashes, thick, black, and long enough that she could have put them up in bobby pins." Eileen never developed a strong appetite for books, but she earned average grades and did well in sports (swimming and diving, golf, tennis, and horseback riding). She also participated in extracurriculars such as operetta and dramatics and joined a number of after-school clubs (friendship, boosters, lifesaving, golf). Enlisted for the *Black and Gold* student newspaper, she is remembered by Ruth Beebe, one of its editors, as "a good but not a great writer." Her outgoing personality made her popular with both sexes, but she was particularly appealing to boys. Eileen was "quite a gal," remembers her classmate Bob Rippner. "She used to kid the boys about '8009.' That was a house of ill repute at 8009 Carnegie Avenue. It was all in fun of course."

Ruth noticed that boys seemed to turn into zombies around Eileen: "They looked paralyzed. Their Adam's apples worked feverishly, and their eyes took on a fishy, helpless gaze." She became obsessed with the idea of fevered frat boys and football players chasing her sister, the ones who "courted her austere favors, laughed uneasily at her speared wit, and pleaded for a chance to squander their patrimony on buying her Black-Eyed Susans." Eileen could not get worked up about forty-cent banana splits topped by chocolate and never really understood why Chubb's idea of success was attracting the attention of some dopey jock. "I suppose you think I'm planning on marrying a basketball player," she once snapped. Her husband, she told Ruth, would not be an athlete. She was going to marry a man with lots of money.

Ruth did not talk about matrimony. Gum disease would eventually lead to all her teeth being pulled. The originals, she said, were "ugly tusks that stuck out in front at a spectacular angle," but the dazzling white false teeth were "a hideous mistake" too. There had never been a real beau, and she got her information on sex from books. Her extravagant fantasies about Eileen bore little relationship to reality; Heights High boys were anything but gentleman zombies who kept their hands in their pockets. For practically any female student at Heights High— especially the pretty ones—school meant four years of power struggles. A girl tried to retain her virginity by walking a tightrope, going far enough but not all the way. Some were tempted, others succumbed, but Eileen was not inclined to venture down that dangerous road. How could she forget Chickie's reckless conduct?

The sisters' relationship continued to be fraught with difficulties. To be sure, Ruth seemed Eileen's biggest fan. While she could be counted on for admiration and compliments, she was hard to get along with and tone-deaf about people, a self-absorbed girl wrapped up with her own problems. At Shaw High School in East Cleveland, one of

Heights High's archrivals, she excelled as a champion debater and the class brain. Teachers loved her, and she was chosen valedictorian of the 1928 graduating class. But she was a social "pariah" who never saw the inside of the local teen hangout, a dine-and-dance chop-suey parlor familiar to Eileen since eighth grade. Sometimes Ruth would ask if Eileen had read this or that book, but Eileen usually didn't know what she was talking about. Ruth's reading tastes ran to Galsworthy, Shelley, and Norman Douglas, and to any work upholding the innocence of the executed anarchists Sacco and Vanzetti. A nimble writer, she could effortlessly dash off hundreds of pages in a few days, a Niagara Falls of words spilling from her typewriter. Once she wrote "a gruesome novel of several hundred thousand words" about blind, hunchbacked, insane Aunt Mildred and how Grandpa Flynn succumbed to heartbreak. In light of her psychiatric history, these spurts of demonic energy were always ominous signs of her illness.

Because competing with Ruth was impossible, Eileen didn't even try.

The summer of 1930, when Eileen was seventeen, her father insisted she apply for a vacation job. This had nothing to do with Eileen, who was entering her senior year at Heights High, and everything to do with the collapse of the stock market the previous fall. While Syd's position at Apex was in no particular danger, the condition of the economy worried him. The idea of another summer with his daughter loafing around the house when she was not busy assaulting Halle Brothers with his charge plate must have seemed un-American.

But Eileen had no interest in a job. On her agenda was a summer of sleeping late, swimming, and recreational shopping. In August she was planning a trip to Cape Cod with some of her friends. Already she had her eye on a drop-dead white satin bathing suit, one of the new two-piece styles that were all the rage. Her father, however, was insistent: no bathing suits unless she paid for them.

Finally, under pressure, Eileen decided to look for a waitress job. As it happened, the face of downtown Cleveland was about to change with the opening of Terminal Tower, the fifty-two-story skyscraper that would be the tallest building between New York and Chicago. The food franchise had been assigned to the Harvey restaurant chain and comprised a half-dozen eateries ranging from snack bars to first-class dining rooms. When Eileen showed up at the Harvey tearoom, an upscale luncheon operation catering to suburban shoppers, getting hired was no problem. Harvey's was quick to welcome a youngster with wholesome, well-scrubbed looks who assured them she was an experienced waitress. (Ruth got hired too.) That the job might take skill never crossed Eileen's mind. Everybody knew that waitresses wrote down orders and carried back food. How much of a brain did that take? In a fluffy little cap she looked so fetching that the restaurant assigned her to the most prominent station in the dining room.

On her first day she came to grief over a tray of chicken-patty lunches. Carrying it with outstretched arms, she staggered through the maze of tables until reaching the middle of the dining room. Unable to keep the tray in the air another instant, she jerked to a halt, wobbled, and yelled for help. Patrons leaped out of their seats to rescue the hot platters before they crashed. Eileen was immediately reassigned to a station at the rear of the restaurant.

She was just getting the hang of things when a boisterous party of Flynns showed up unexpectedly. Like hayseeds, they had packed their own lunches—baloney-and-onion sandwiches—and someone began passing around hard-boiled eggs. Then some joker, as if she had never heard of Prohibition, ordered a beer. For a tip they left Confederate currency. Eileen soon discovered that waitressing was a demanding job. And back in the kitchen, she had to fend off gropings from the overly friendly male help.

One day she dropped orders of creamed mushrooms on toast, another time bowls of fruit salad with whipped cream, then a chocolate cake. To Eileen, the cake looked only slightly squished, but the pastry chef, in a frenzy, claimed it could not be fed to customers, and so she promptly ate it herself. She was not being paid to eat cake, Harvey's angrily told her. At the end of two weeks, when friends of hers stopped by to say hello, she walked off the job in the middle of serving a table of diners their creamed chicken.

Her father lost his temper. Only two weeks! Unless she married a son of a millionaire, something he very much doubted in spite of her taste for the good life, she was going to wind up in the poorhouse. Eileen was not, obviously, cut out to be a waitress. What is surprising is not her departure but her sticking it out two weeks. After Harvey's, she spent the rest of the summer as a golf bum, inviting her girlfriends to Syd's club, where she charged everybody's lunch to his account. These acts of defiance provoked scoldings. "How in the name of God could five little high school girls eat $17.80 worth of lunch?" he sputtered.

Eileen graduated from Heights High in January 1931. Her senior-class entry in the Cauldron yearbook shows a healthy, self-confident young woman. The photogenic face in the snapshot has a sparkle of mischief around the eyes and a spunky expression. She is wearing a demure turn-of-the-century, high-collared blouse (an unconventional choice for 1931) and the latest hairdo, a scrupulously arranged finger wave. Athletics topped the list of her extracurricular activities, along with an interest in writing and dramatics.

Eileen's friend Ruth Beebe was going to Oberlin College to study geology, but the typical female graduate of Heights High would turn directly to marriage, motherhood, domesticity. Some of Eileen's classmates were already engaged or arranging their weddings, while others planned to use an obligatory college year to get pinned or engaged. Eileen was eager for marriage too, but not before she had shopped around, met the right person, and fallen madly in love. What was the big hurry? She wanted to have a career first. Her mother and aunts, typical of their generation, had attended normal school in preparation for teaching, before moving on to more traditional roles. But the idea of being cooped up all day with a bunch of rowdy eight-year-olds held no appeal for Eileen. She decided to enroll in business school and train to become a secretary.

In 1931, there was no more exciting place for a woman to work than a business office. Traditionally all-male domains, offices were all of a sudden ruled by armies of experts trained to use new technologies that radically altered mass communications: typewriters, telephones, Dictaphones, duplicators, adding machines, vertical filing systems, and card indexes. At the center of these new systems stood the all-important, all-knowing secretary, the epitome of modern womanhood, the indispensable "gal Friday" glorified in film and fiction. The suggestion of freedom, empowerment, and meaningful wages brought millions of women into the job market for the first time. Having no objection to making coffee for the boss, they passionately embraced duties that a later generation would call demeaning. But at the time there was nothing second class about entering the business profession.

Eileen enrolled in commercial courses to study shorthand and touch-typing (seventy words a minute was considered good), the basics for a position in the corporate world. Like most women, she was aware that the best place to explore the marriage market was an office and hoped to join a company employing a slew of unmarried men about to make good, perhaps even become executives one day. Didn't her father marry his secretary?

Technically Eileen was a virgin. For six years, she had been fending off schoolboys trying to go all the way, younger kids who pulled down girls' underpants in weedy backyards, and packs of teenagers ganging up to force a girl to touch their genitals. At Cleveland Heights High, everyone understood the consequences of sex. Pregnancy was the worst thing that could happen. A pregnant girl—who had to hide somewhere to give birth, then give up the baby for adoption—might as well have shot herself. No man would marry her. The disturbing story of Chickie, who in the movie version of the novel had a baby and lived happily ever after, was twisted into a fairy tale. In reality, a girl's reputation would be compromised beyond redemption. All this was harrowing but not unusual. Shoved somewhere to the backs of girls' minds lurked the subject too terrible to talk about, the horror story of rape.

At some point around the time of her graduation from Heights

High, Eileen appears to have been raped, although she took care never to use that disturbing word. *Practically* raped, she was to say, which somehow allowed her to pretend that it hadn't really happened. While on a date, she was involved in an automobile accident and wound up on a porch bruised and bleeding, disoriented but not hurt seriously enough for hospitalization. She was overpowered by somebody she knew, perhaps her date or another passenger in the car. Whether or not she tried to fight the man off, the experience left her terrified. At home afterward, she could not decide what had happened but knew better than to tell her father.

This traumatic event planted feelings of shame and unbearable memories that would linger in the years to come. As alcohol may have confused the details, it seems likely that she herself remained uncertain exactly how it came about.

10

RING OUT, WILD BALLS

NEW YORK CITY was still raw in the 1880s when the Weinstein brothers had arrived. It took ten years of hardship and hustling to make good, but in the bountiful years following the turn of the century they reaped the fruits. Although their fortunes were modest compared with those of the Rothschilds or the Guggenheims, they had done extremely well. After forty good years in America, the Weinsteins were not expecting bad things to happen. And when trouble did come it crept in so quietly that nobody noticed.

In the middle of the flourishing twenties, the torrent of apartment construction that had begun in the 1890s began to subside. There were still announcements of projects like the forty-five-story Majestic on Central Park West, with developers feeling confident of the continued demand for luxury housing—but this prediction would prove wrong. The population of the metropolis had grown to nearly five million, making it the biggest city in the world, but Manhattan in particular had become saturated with the classic multiple-family towers that were the Weinsteins' livelihood.

Economic slowdown coupled with illnesses and advancing years began to take their toll on the self-made Weinstein brothers. For Max, suddenly faced with uncertain profits and delicate health, life had grown precarious. His Sirwein Realty Corporation nonetheless continued to develop properties, like the fifty-seven-unit, $450,000 building on Sickles Street in upper Manhattan, begun in 1926. Two years later, Max filed a permit for a six-story bank-and-office building at 72 Second Avenue, at an estimated cost of $105,000, his final independent undertaking. Thereafter, he would operate as a subcontractor on hospitals and other institutional projects, taking whatever work he could get.

Nat was often heard to bemoan how working for his father was ruining his life. His negative feelings about the construction business were shared with many of his cousins. Looking beyond real estate, the assimilated second generation of Weinsteins and Wallensteins had been educated for professional careers as lawyers and investment bankers. One exception was Nathaniel "Wally" Wallenstein, Nat's boyhood comrade in mischief, who would erect some splendid buildings on Lexington Avenue. Another was Jacob Weinstein's oldest son, Leon West, who was vacationing in Los Angeles when he noticed vacant lots and began putting up New York–style apartment houses on Sunset Boulevard.

With Sirwein Realty hip-deep in red ink and his still uncompleted novel consigned to a drawer, Nat understood that he must figure out a way to earn a living, and so he decided to go into business for himself. Not real estate. Candy. Judging by the instant mass appeal of Milky Way and Three Musketeers, it seemed obvious that candy could be a very profitable retail business, and certainly a more sensible undertaking than writing. His parents were quick to offer encouragement, perhaps supposing that candy making would end his literary ambitions. With a few backers (no doubt relatives) Nat came up with a confection that would use the exotic pulp and juice of cactus as a sweetener.

He had no idea how to develop a consumer product, but he spent the next two years working harder on the candy recipe than he had ever worked on anything. Test samples turned out to be tasty but disappointing. The problem was not the flavor, because the sweet prickly pear cactus would later be used successfully as an ingredient in jellies and syrups. The basic weakness was appearance: the bars resembled cakes of soap. Even though he continued to make improvements, it became clear that cactus candy was never going to reach the market. Admitting failure as a confectioner in 1930, he sold his interest in the product for sixty-five dollars and "a two volume edition of Chapman's plays—very nice, printed in England." (The new owner never made the sweet either.) Shortly after Nat abandoned his candy, a new product made of nougat, roasted peanuts, caramel, and milk chocolate was introduced to the public. Snickers would become the best-selling candy bar of all time. It did not contain cactus.

Reluctant to waste his hard-earned knowledge about the food business, Nat looked around for another promising product. Everybody liked chili. "I'll probably make a million dollars," he said. On the other hand, he didn't want to make a fool of himself twice. Maybe stenography? Everybody needed a stenographer.

Meanwhile, he was performing his duties in a perfunctory fashion on Sickles Street, watching the clock and sneaking out after lunch whenever he could. He regularly spent evenings on the town with Sid Perelman, who was still dating Laura. They would take in a first-run movie in Times Square, followed by a show at the Parody, a comedy club on West Forty-eighth Street, often headlined by their favorite comedian Jimmy Durante, and a late meal at Childs cafeteria. Other nights they met at the Weinstein apartment, where Sid had got into the habit of making himself at home.

By 1929, Nat had finally completed *The Journal of Balso Snell*. One night he corralled Sid into listening while he read aloud the entire seven chapters, but Sid's reaction was unenthusiastic. He smiled, even tittered occasionally, although not as frequently as Nat would have liked, and to make matters worse kept rolling his eyes at the profusion of obscenities. Although Nat was willing to acknowledge that his jokes at the expense of intellectuals, women, and Jews might offend people, he dismissed Sid's criticism. No group was exempt from ridicule, he protested. Still, being a huge admirer of Sid's judgment, he found his friend's lack of approval discouraging. Sid, for his part, considered him naive and confided to Laura that "these litry guys at Boni and Knopf are so pure they make one retch, but after all, they hold the reins." Sure, her brother might fancy himself an exception, but the chance of a publisher letting him get away with puerile dirty jokes was nil. It was clear that the book would never be published.

Sid's presence served as a welcome firewall in the Weinstein apartment, where Nat tangled with his mother over another escape to Paris. He had to get down to business with a real job, she insisted. In these nightly battles, she held the upper hand because Nat could go nowhere without the Weinstein money. And so it went, week after week.

Out of desperation, Anna consulted the family. Surely a position might be found for a clever Ivy-educated boy. Her sister Susana had married an obstetrician, Julius Jarcho, whose brother Morris owned a plumbing business that Max Weinstein had helped to finance. Over the years, despite problems with antitrust violations, Morris Jarcho had done very well and the fifty-five-year-old businessman now sat on the Jewish Real Estate Board. His company was the plumbing contractor for a twenty-two-story hotel scheduled to open soon at 145 East Twenty-third Street. Under pressure from his parents, Nat agreed to apply for a job.

Kenmore Hall was one of the innovative "club hotels" going up all over town that catered to single businessmen and -women. The residences hoped to attract young professionals earning modest salaries who would appreciate clubby living quarters combined with regular housekeeping, and communal socializing in lounges just an elevator ride away, almost like a small town or a college dormitory. They included an array of expensive amenities such as gymnasiums and swimming pools, umbrella-shaded rooftop terraces, libraries, and restaurants.

Club hotels were so popular that they filled up overnight and then had to open waiting lists.

The former cactus-candy man was twenty-five when he began working at Kenmore Hall that fall. Totally ignorant of hotel operations, he appeared to be unqualified for executive employment. Nonetheless, family connections got him the position of assistant manager and a salary of thirty-five dollars a week—a pittance by his standards—plus meals

Nathan Weinstein in 1913, when he was living in Harlem and attending P.S. 81, "the Model School."

Eileen McKenney with her sister, Ruth, in Mishawaka, Indiana, 1915. Their mother was homesick for Cleveland.

To see more photographs of Nathanael West and Eileen McKenney, visit www.lonelyheartsthebook.com, www.nathanaelwest.com, and www.eileenmckenney.com.

Although a precocious reader, Nat fared poorly in school and dropped out at the age of fifteen.

Anna Weinstein dressed her daughters, Hinda (Sis) and Lorraine, in identical outfits.

Nat graduated from Brown University by the skin of his teeth. While there he made two close friends, Sidney Perelman and Quentin Reynolds, but otherwise college was not a happy experience.

EILEEN McKENNEY
Life Saving Club (2);
Friendship Club (2); Boosters' Club (2, 3, 4); Operetta (3); Black and Gold Staff News Editor (4); Golf Club (2, 3); Sophomore Dramatics (2).

Popular and pretty, Eileen studied shorthand after her graduation from Cleveland Heights High School in 1931.

Tiny Gay Street in Greenwich Village would become famous after the success of Ruth's book *My Sister Eileen*. The sisters lived in the basement of number 14, the first white house on the left.

KENMORE HALL
145 East 23rd St., New York City

The Kenmore Hall Hotel in New York. Nat began writing *Miss Lonelyhearts* when he worked there on the graveyard shift.

Sid and Laura Perelman depart on a French honeymoon, 1929.

Nat and John Sanford spent the summer of 1931 in the Adirondacks, where Nat worked on *Miss Lonelyhearts*.

Nat dedicated *The Dream Life of Balso Snell* to Alice Shepard, a stunning fashion model, but their romance did not work out.

The novelist Josephine Herbst encouraged Nat to complete *Miss Lonelyhearts*. She was his most enthusiastic booster and closest female friend.

Nat and a borrowed dog on Josie Herbst's porch in Erwinna, Pennsylvania, 1932. He and the Perelmans split the cost of a nearby farm.

Visiting the newly purchased farm in Bucks County. From left: Robert Coates, Dashiell Hammett, Nat, and Laura and Sid Perelman. Lillian Hellman snapped the picture.

Ruth McKenney holding her nephew Tommy, after wedding the coffee heir Richard Bransten and writing a bestseller.

Morris Jacobs, Eileen's first husband, with their son, Tommy. The marriage was short-lived.

and a free room. If inexperienced, he did bring certain useful qualities to the job. Not only was he of a similar age to the residents, but he was beautifully groomed, comported himself like a gentleman, and had a pleasant speaking voice. Even the loss of his boyish looks—his receding hairline, a hint of age around his eyes—was not a handicap because it made him seem mature.

Showing up six nights a week was an adjustment, but the work was more interesting than at Sirwein and he performed his duties with ease. He liked the quiet middle-of-the-night hours, when nothing was happening and he was free to work on his writing. The neighborhood was pleasant too. The hotel was two blocks from Madison Square Park, a six-acre strip of green on the north side of Twenty-third Street between Fifth and Madison Avenues that Nat liked to walk through on his way to and from work. In the daytime it was full of children at play and the twittering of secretaries, but at night it turned into a pickup site, which, along with Bryant Park on Forty-second Street, was popular with homosexual men. Frequently he stopped to sit on a bench facing Fifth Avenue near the Mexican War obelisk and grew so fond of the little park that he chose it as a setting for several of the scenes in a new novel. If he had to work, Kenmore Hall was not so bad.

Even though Nat rejected Sid's reservations about *Balso Snell*, he had given up hope of its publication for the simple reason that no publisher showed any interest. Needing to console himself, he had begun saying that he didn't "really care about *The Journal* very much" because he was concentrating on his next book, about the lovelorn columnist. To friends he periodically reported "working pretty hard on the opus, here puss, what a puss." In fact, it was embarrassing to admit how little he had done since that night in 1929 when Quent showed him the Susan Chester letters at Siegel's. In the interim, Quent left the paper, Sid married Laura, the stock market crashed. While he continued to believe the letters were good sources, he also realized that the correspondence alone, however juicy, was inadequate. The lives of the letter writers fragmented the story instead of moving it forward.

Finally, however, something was happening. During the graveyard shifts at Kenmore Hall he managed to sink the rough foundations of his book: a protagonist, Thomas Matlock, a newspaper columnist who goes off the deep end; a comic-strip structure, consisting of a prologue and fourteen panels; and a name—the same name—for Matlock's column and the book's title. Both would be called *Miss Lonelyhearts*.

At the *New York Post-Dispatch*, a reporter whose ambition is to write a syndicated gossip column is instead called upon to edit the daily advice column, a job that required selecting two or three letters and composing plausible answers. The main difficulty is to vary replies to the same old subjects without mocking anybody's anguish.

Miss Lonelyhearts begins with Thomas Matlock at his desk trying to write a lead. His deadline fifteen minutes away, he has written one sentence ("Life *is* worthwhile . . ."). It isn't punchy and offers no plan of action, but he can think of nothing else to say. "He found it impossible to continue. The letters were no longer funny."

To people in and out of the office, Thomas appears to be an ordinary young man, harmless, polite, soft. He wears an innocent expression, "the smile of an anarchist sitting in the movies with a bomb in his pocket." In fact, Thomas is an extravagantly unhappy individual perched on the edge of a breakdown. Steaming over the slightest little thing, he is at odds with his girlfriend and even picks fights with cigarettes. At work, the trouble starts when Thomas, depressed to begin with, can't stop obsessing over the unusable letters. The son of a Baptist minister, he comes to believe that the column is his true calling, an opportunity to offer genuine consolation to troubled souls. In fact, he is in worse shape than the misfits who, at least, are able to acknowledge their troubles. If his first mistake is to imagine he can really help people, his second is to make unprofessional personal contact with a reader wishing to relate her grievances about a crippled husband. With little thought for the consequences, Thomas makes an appointment to meet in the little park near the Mexican War obelisk, then hustles her to his rooming house for a tryst, even though Fay Doyle, despite her short plaid skirt and tam-o'-shanter, resembles a police captain.

Surely, Thomas's qualifications for counseling women are nonexistent, because he is utterly confused about his own sexual identity, but the particulars of whether he is bisexual or a repressed homosexual are never explored. Attempting to cure what ails him, he gets engaged to a young woman while simultaneously trying to seduce his editor's wife. But as a result of his involvement with Fay Doyle and her husband, Thomas eventually spirals into madness. When he attempts to embrace Fay's husband, the puzzled man accidentally shoots him to death.

Among Nat's principal characters is a sadistic editor, Willie Shrike, so named for a vicious bird of prey that impales small birds on thorns and tears them into bite-size pieces. A man whose wife avoids sleeping with him, Shrike flaps about in pursuit of women with mannish haircuts and dysfunctional young men like Thomas, whom he torments about his masculinity. Shrike's cruelty is reprised in the man-eating Fay Doyle, a rough draft for another character named Faye that Nat would create later on.

Thomas's fiancée is a conventional, patient, forgiving young woman who traffics in loving-kindness and boiled chicken and treats his obnoxious outbursts with the clinical concern of a mother controlling a hysterical six-year-old. What's the matter? Betty asks. Does he feel sick?

"What a kind bitch you are," he explodes. "As soon as anyone acts viciously, you say he's sick." No, he is not sick.

To lift his spirits, Betty (labeled Betty the Buddha by Thomas) prescribes such diversions as a walk in the zoo—she believes in the restorative power of animals—and a weekend in the country, but her well-meaning efforts result in teardrops, pregnancy, and abortion.

In April, after writing four chapters, Nat sat back and counted the words—only fifteen thousand. Obviously the narrative could use padding. But he didn't do it.

When Laura and Sid married, in June 1929, Max Weinstein provided a two-month European honeymoon, a gift he could ill afford considering the state of his business affairs. Recently it had become necessary for the family to move to a smaller, cheaper apartment at 235 West End Avenue. Sid and Laura often talked about living abroad permanently if only they had the means to do so, but of course they did not. Instead, Sid regretted to say, he was forced to return home from Paris and "bake my nuts in Sodom."

Back in New York, Laura and Sid raved about a new friend, Beatrice Mathieu, an American writer who had relocated to France a few years earlier and reported on haute couture for a number of magazines. After a seaside holiday together on the French Riviera, the Perelmans decided their new pal would make an ideal subject for a play about Americans in Paris, a sophisticated comedy of love and loneliness on the Left Bank. Inspired, they had already begun drafting a script featuring a fashion journalist, in love with an unemployed barfly but tempted to go to the other extreme and marry a dull fellow from the New York suburb of New Rochelle if the drunk doesn't reform.

Before long, the Perelmans were not only dramatizing Beatrice Mathieu but also playing matchmaker. Enamored themselves, they assumed Beatrice and Nat would also click. She would be perfect for him, they insisted, and Nat could not help feeling flattered. She was clearly an emancipated career woman, perhaps even one of those terrifying female-warrior writers who used three names, whom he found unappealing. But he trusted the kids and was eager to meet their "swell girl friend," who would soon be coming home for a visit. When she arrived on the *Leviathan* at the end of October, accompanied by her mother, he was relieved to meet a solid, no-nonsense person. She was everything the kids had said: vivacious, friendly, irreverent, and well educated (she had studied at the University of Chicago and the Sorbonne). Her sophistication, French accent, and presumably intellectual background dazzled Nat. In fact, as the youngest of five children in a working-class family of French-Canadian immigrants, she came from humble beginnings. Her father, Michael, was a barber in Seattle.

Beatrice was not beautiful, but her looks were pleasing. She had dark hair and a heart-shaped face. She appeared to be around twenty-five, though she was actually thirty-four. She understood how to dress elegantly and to make the most of herself. Spending time around stick-figure fashion models had made her sensitive to her body weight, and she tended to worry about putting on pounds. In her personal habits, she was capable, self-sufficient, at times opinionated, traits that crossed over to her work. As a competent professional, she could easily transform a few inconsequential facts into an entertaining story and later would use these skills as a contributor to *The New Yorker*. She and Nat made an attractive couple, the sophisticate trailing Parisian glamour and perfume, the urbane young gentleman with old-fashioned manners and casually elegant suits. While she treated Nat's writing ambitions with respect, the fact remained that she was experienced and he was an unpublished amateur in the hotel business. Sometimes he struggled not to feel intimidated. Whenever she threatened to outshine him, he felt obliged to cut her down to size with an affectionate threat to "take a stick to her."

The week prior to Beatrice's arrival, the stock market had crashed. The rest of the year, the economy would be beaten into mashed potatoes as one of the rockiest decades in the nation's history got under way. Nat, oblivious to the extent of the wreckage, was caught up in the excitement of getting to know Beatrice. The romance quickly grew sufficiently serious—without being sexual—that he proposed marriage. He could envision a life in Paris that would center around his novels, her fashion shows, their family dogs, idyllic summers on the Cote d'Azur, all the blessings of a golden expatriate world. Beatrice was his salvation, the ticket to France that his mother had withheld. The responsibilities of being a husband never occurred to him, but he did love the idea of playing engaged to be married. This delightful fairy tale did not sit well with his relatives.

Over the years the Weinstein household had become nonobservant, with Max and Anna attending synagogue twice a year (and Nat unwilling to be even a part-time Jew, refusing to go at all). But their daughters married inside the faith, and Anna expected the same of her son. When news of his whirlwind courtship with a Christian reached her ears, she raised hell, as he knew she would. He had no intention of marrying a bagel—his belittling name for Jewish girls—just to please her, he announced. Beatrice seemed at a loss about how to react. "His mother was offended," she recalled. In an attempt to navigate the religious issues and cut loose the apron strings, she tried a light touch. Maybe she could pass for a Jew. Didn't her nose look "sort of Jewish"? Soon Nat began calling her Beazel or Beazeleh.

By the time Beazel booked passage in March, their plans were set. When he joined her in June, they would go south to Bandol for a vacation, and then he would remain in Paris, writing for as long as his savings lasted. What would happen then, he could not foresee. In the meantime he promised to write to her three times a week.

In fact, he was desperately frightened and his love letters to "darling Beazel" bristled with ambivalence. Shying away from making a definite commitment, he insisted their plans be kept secret. She should not tell "anyone" about the marriage until he saw her in Paris, he instructed. Even his going-away gifts suggested reluctance: an impersonal alarm clock and a black male Scottish terrier, for which Beatrice chipped in. When she named the dog Coco, for the designer Gabrielle "Coco" Chanel, he apparently had no sense of the couturier's fame and kept misspelling the dog's name as Koko, a clue that Beazel's world of hairdos, hats, and hemlines held little interest for him. A picture was beginning to emerge, but Beatrice did not—or could not—see it.

Over the course of four months, he struggled to write amusing letters, but there was not much to say except that he missed her. He remained silent about his job, which required him to work among hordes of people coming and going at all hours, and spoke instead about his buddy Quent and their swell times downstairs in the pool or playing handball for a quart of whiskey. He ordered an omelet for lunch, he reported; he went to the movies eight times; he decided to grow a mustache.

Throughout that spring, as Nat completed drafts of four chapters of *Miss Lonelyhearts*, the narrative began taking on weight and the story underwent some unexpected twists. Suddenly his characters became real personalities with priorities and convoluted feelings—surprisingly brutish feelings—not the anemic cartoon figures of *The Journal of Balso Snell*. There were nightmarish spectacles of extreme cruelty—blood-soaked college boys torturing a lamb, homophobes deliberately tormenting an elderly homosexual man—and misogynist fantasies of sexual perversion and gang rapes. "Violent images are used to illustrate commonplace events," Nat would explain. "Violent acts are left almost bald." Violence was baked into the text. The story shifted between the all-male newspaper city room, the public toilet in Madison Square Park, a brownstone speakeasy modeled on Nat's favorite, Delaney's, and the smelly rooms with sinks full of dirty dishes lived in by men without cleaning women. (Miss Lonelyhearts climbs into bed with his Dostoyevskian security blanket, a copy of *The Brothers Karamazov*.) Into the story had found their way an assortment of boorish voyeurs in pajama tops, cripples who rolled on the floor growling like dogs, and fifty-seven varieties of hairy-chested woman-haters. Marching in step with the guys trooped Nat's female characters: women with masculine haircuts and hearty handshakes and the world's lustiest man-eater.

Unfortunately Nat's protagonist was causing problems. Was the homophobic Thomas Matlock a closeted homosexual? Might he be bisexual? Did he ever do it with other men for kicks? And why did he imagine snakes and doorknobs? Nat shared none of this with Beatrice.

Hoping that the four chapters might bring him an advance against royalties, he made an appointment in April at Simon and Schuster, or, as he gleefully named them, Semen and Schuster. (Sid called the publisher Simon and Shoestore.) The editor who glided out to the receptionist impressed Nat as a "smug bastard." Although they'd never before met, Clifton Fadiman adopted a peculiar air of intimacy.

"Oh yes, yes, Mr. West, of course I remember you," he said cheerily as he escorted Nat back to his office. How nice that Mr. West had brought them something. He had been thinking they had surely lost him. Of course, it should have his immediate attention.

"Fat arse Fadiman" was the one who ought to get lost, Nat said to himself as he was hustled out. But Fadiman had already retreated to his office, and the elevator door was closing on Nat. Sick of being the outsider with his nose always pressed to the glass, he had come to detest publishers, editors, and writers, all the smug, blackballing phonies who lunched at their private clubs.

A few weeks later, Clifton Fadiman gave him the bum's rush for a second time. Sid Perelman agreed with Fadiman: the book was boring. Nat vehemently disagreed.

Meanwhile, he was keeping his normal routines. He attended a concert at Carnegie Hall and occasionally showed up at Sid and Laura's Village apartment on Grove Street. Following publication of *Dawn Ginsbergh's Revenge,* a collection of comic essays, Sid had been freelancing for *College Humor* magazine and working on a screenplay for a Marx Brothers movie. The kids were in the habit of entertaining various writer friends on Saturday nights. Sometimes these gatherings were fun, but too often the guests were windbags, Nat thought; the air smelled of literature. Surrounded by professional writers, he struggled to suppress feelings of inferiority. E. E. Cummings, known to sit on the floor of Siegel's and bark dirty words, was "crazy," he decided, "not funny but very loud" and very infantile. Edmund Wilson, the critic and *New Republic* editor, was "a great writer" with unfortunate tics ("peculiar sounds, sudden gestures, and violent faces"). Before long, he had devised a variety of ways to misspell Philip Wylie's name ("Whylie," "Whyle," "Whiley").

When he and Beatrice were together, he had not felt the least uncomfortable, but his letters were tongue-tied and awkward. Somehow he could never seem to please her. Worse, at some point she began to turn into a shrew, exasperated that he did not write often enough and making him feel guilty. "We'll get drunk my first night in Paris," he promised. Her letters were "not very nice," he thought.

Evidently something was happening to the relationship. In Paris, his wife-to-be was busy making plans for their reunion and reported she had found a cheap place for him to stay when he arrived, but most of the time she was bawling him out.

Did he book his passage yet?

"No SCOLDING," he replied sulkily.

When did he intend to book his passage?

Here was another side of Darling Beazel, who underneath was as relentless as his mother. When she mailed him a photograph of herself sitting in a café, he commented, "My God you have grown fat." Beatrice in the meantime had begun using his letters as scrap paper while scribbling notes at fashion shows ("pink faille shoes for evening").

Emotionally on the edge, he went on a bender with Quent, starting to drink in the early afternoon, and by eleven he was slobbery "crying." Soon his letters were buzzing with whoppers and half-whoppers. He lied about his passage on the *Bremen* for June 28, but told himself it was not a deliberate falsehood, because he knew it was what she wanted to hear. He also fibbed when he said he could hardly wait to see her, and when he described his tummy as "pendulous" when it was only average. On the other hand, he did shop for a white linen suit to wear at the seashore, which he thought made him look like a British colonial, and bought her a half-dozen pairs of silk stockings.

By the end of May, his nerves shot, he was working overtime to manufacture problems. Kenmore Hall had not yet hired his replacement, he informed Beatrice. How could he leave the hotel in the lurch when it had treated him so decently? Did he mention they had offered to make him manager at a fatter salary? His friend Scotty wanted to sail with him, an upsetting development; he was "a fat white slug—very womanly too." Oh, by the way, had he ever told her that Scotty was a queer? While he had never made an "overt act, I know that he has all the makings of a homo. He's just afraid, I think—Paris may break down his inhibitions." Did Beatrice sense what he was talking about? She might have.

His pussyfooting finally ended in late June. With a display of sackcloth and ashes, he cabled: "SAILING POSTPONED NEW SAILING DATE SOON PLEASE FORGIVE IM NOT THE LOUSE I APPEAR." He hoped she would not be angry.

A ladylike young woman, like Betty in *Miss Lonelyhearts*, would have been sweet about an eleventh-hour change of plans and waited politely for another sailing date, but Beatrice wiped the floor with him. He was "an awful bastard," she said before returning his correspondence by the very next mail.

He mailed them back. "SENT LETTERS BACK POSITIVELY COME IN THE FALL PLEASE FORGIVE." Scrambling to eat humble pie, he told her he felt "desolate" and called himself—what bad names could he use?—"phoney," "louse," and "yellow." He was afraid. Didn't she understand that "times are indeed hard"? He'd "rather work in a hotel" than try to earn a living as a writer and wind up—*boo hoo*—an apple seller. Beatrice wanted nothing more to do with him. For all she cared he could rattle a tin cup.

Morris Jarcho—Nat's benefactor, who had his fingers in numerous pies—had become a stockholder in a Jarcho family company developing a new hotel in the exclusive East Side waterfront neighborhood known as Sutton Place. Extending from Fifty-third to Fifty-ninth Streets, the district had been originally centered on a white-glove co-op apartment building at One Sutton Place South, but palatial townhouses were going up all the time and plans were also under way for construction of a motor concourse along the river (the future FDR Drive). Already a synonym for wealth, the Sutton enclave seemed to be a premier location for an upscale residence hotel.

Grandly designating itself "The Sutton, a Club Hotel," the building initially opened its doors at the end of 1930 as a women's residence but quickly repositioned itself for a mixed clientele, similar to Kenmore Hall only more pretentious. (Its sea-foam-green stationery glinted with gold lettering.) The seventeen-story hotel, at 330 East Fifty-sixth Street, just a few doors in from First Avenue, was the tallest building in the vicinity. Completed at a cost of $750,000 (more than $10 million in today's currency), it had 322 rooms, many looking out on the river or the rooftops of the East Side and the soaring spires of the new Chrysler Building in the distance. Rates were $12 a week for a single, $22.50 for a suite. The lobby was tastefully decorated with chintz-upholstered divans and potted palms. Adjacent to the lounge was a restaurant and a

350-seat theater for concerts and private entertainments. A luxurious white-tiled spa was tucked away in the basement.

That fall Nat was appointed manager of the Sutton, with a salary of fifty dollars a week and a spacious, light-flooded apartment on the top floor. Equally impressive was his office, off to one side of the lobby, where the brass doorplate announced, MR. WEST, MGR.

By his calculation, Nat was capable of whipping out five pages a month on average, an effort that, in the case of the ill-fated *Journal of Balso Snell*, had yielded a typescript of a mere fifty or so pages over five years. Discouraged but never completely losing hope, he continued trying to sell the *Journal* and submitted it to Brewer & Warren, a small general-interest house run by the poet William Rose Benét. Unbeknownst to Nat, the firm was teetering financially. It would have been corporate suicide to accept a scatological, blasphemous, anti-Semitic, misogynistic project, with its readership likely limited to a few of the author's friends. Brewer & Warren hoped he would "find a home for this mss somewhere."

But, alas, where?

Nat often browsed at Moss & Kamin Booksellers in the Barbizon-Plaza Hotel. While chatting with the owners one day, he casually mentioned that he had written a novel. Would they care to read his funny, dirty book? In addition to their store, David Moss and Martin Kamin owned a small publishing company, formerly the Paris-based Contact Editions, founded by the American writer Robert McAlmon. In the 1920s, Contact had introduced exciting new works, including Ernest Hemingway's first book (*Three Stories and Ten Poems*) and Robert Coates's Dadaist novel *The Eater of Darkness*. But this type of expatriate press, at one time handling books too experimental for mainstream houses, was quickly disappearing. Contact Editions, consisting of little more than its name and an elite history, was one of the last survivors of this dying breed.

Nat's manuscript impressed Martin Kamin, who offered to consider it for publication. For a second opinion he decided to show it to

William Carlos Williams, a preeminent figure of the Modernist movement whose work had been influenced by Dada and surrealism. The forty-seven-year-old poet, a pediatrician living in Rutherford, New Jersey, expressed interest. It was obvious that Nathanael West knew how to write, indeed he had "a fine feeling for language." The work was sufficiently fresh to warrant publication. He later would reject suggestions that the text was sordid, saying "Good God" it wasn't perfect—"few first books are"—but it certainly wasn't obscene. Based on Williams's approval, Kamin and Moss accepted the manuscript. There was no possibility of payment—the booksellers had no money—and the print run would be 500 copies if Nat agreed to purchase 150. The deal was about as close to vanity publishing as an author could get, but Nat did not hesitate for a minute. Neither did he quibble when Kamin and Moss changed the title from *The Journal of Balso Snell* to *The Dream Life of Balso Snell*, as if calling the story a dream might sanitize the content.

Throughout the fall of 1930 and into January of 1931, he divided his time between managing the Sutton and writing *Miss Lonelyhearts*. Upon receipt of the *Balso Snell* galleys, he enlisted Scotty to help with the proofreading. To ensure privacy for making corrections, he rented a one-room apartment on Bank Street in the Village and spent ten dollars on a secondhand kitchen table and two chairs.

Scotty knew nothing about proofreading. "How do we go about this?" he wondered.

"You read," Nat said, without preliminaries.

In the temple of proofreading, snow was falling on the windowsill. Between them on the table lay a set of two dozen galleys, which Scotty began reading aloud. Over the next weeks they would repeat the corrections process several times: revised galleys, page proofs, and revised proofs, four readings altogether. Scotty thought it odd that Nat avoided discussion of the book, nor did he show any great interest in Scotty's opinion. He could hardly fail to notice the striking similarity between the Trojan-horse characters and their author. Seated across the table, he wanted to say, "They're all *you* in there, Pep, every one of them," but tactfully held his tongue. After hearing about the novel for five years, ever since the golf course at Asbury Park, he was naturally curious to read it. What he saw both startled and disturbed him. There were sly, real-life vignettes, such as the Carnegie Hall scene in which George Brounoff–like concertgoers, "sensitive young Jews" seeking culture, are buried under buckets of excrement. It was funny, to be sure, but it also went too far, and in years to come he blamed Nat for humiliating his friends by mocking their simple pleasures. ("Pep writes of cripples, and he does not weep for them; he kicks them in the face.") At the Bank Street apartment, he said nothing.

When *The Dream Life of Balso Snell* finally appeared, in August 1931, priced at $3 with a handsomely designed paper jacket, it was a skimpy 95 pages that barely qualified as a novel. (By contrast, *The Great Gatsby* came to 218 pages, *Main Street* to 451.) To give it a boost, Nat composed a promotional leaflet in which he billed himself as "vicious, mean, ugly, obscene, and insane." Despite this provocative hype, the book found few devotees of vulgarity and even fewer reviewers. One of them was the ever-loyal Scotty, who insisted in the *New Review* that the book was a joke, "a good sort of literary fooling," misunderstood by the stodgy old critics because of the "handfuls of dung" that West was flinging in their faces. Actually, there was only one other review, in another "little magazine." *Contempo* called *Balso Snell* "a distinguished performance in sophisticated writing."

Nat hoped to pass off the book as a second cousin to *Alice's Adventures in Wonderland*, but he did not succeed. Reviewing *The Dream Life of Balso Snell* in 1957, Malcolm Cowley wrote it off as "an elaborate joke" that fell flat. Usually dismissed by present-day critics as juvenile junk, the novel remains important as a blueprint for Nat's work. It revealed his attitudes and preoccupations and foreshadowed the themes he developed in later works: the moral indignation, the ferocious hatred of organized religion and hypocritical intellectuals, the homoerotic fantasies. Its character types would also reappear: Balso the seeker of truth, Maloney the holy fool, naive Janey Davenport the vapid castrator, Mary McGeeney the dim female intellectual, Beagle Darwin the mocking sadistic torturer, followed by a crowd of dreamers, losers, scapegoats, and wolfish destroyers in walk-on roles.

Not surprisingly, the most disappointed reaction came from Nat's mother, who refused to show *Balso Snell* to her friends because it was filth: "all it says is 'stink stink stink.'" If the book made Anna squirm, other relatives honestly did not know what to think either. A cousin tried to be tolerant. Was it a joke? Taking the high road, Nat assured him the novel was art, a serious experiment with various literary styles.

One afternoon in late 1930, around the time he began running the Sutton Club, Nat bumped into his sister, shopping with one of her Pembroke friends on East Fifty-seventh Street. As they stood there making small talk on the sidewalk, he realized he was staring. Laura's friend was a knockout.

Alice Shepard lived in New Rochelle, an elegant suburb favored by the wealthy and socially prominent. Her father, Frederick Shepard, Harvard '03, was the general manager of Socony-Vacuum Oil Co., her mother, Pauline, active in the Junior League, her brother Herbert, Yale class of '33, often mentioned in the sports pages as an important member of the school's championship rowing team. Alice and her two siblings had a conventional upbringing that included attendance at the local Congregational church. Like Laura, she attended but dropped out of Pembroke. Following a European tour, she returned home hungry for a challenge. A leggy girl with light brown hair, slim-hipped and loose-limbed, she had no trouble signing as a model with a leading couturier. As it happened, Elizabeth Hawes's recent collections, showing free-form, corsetless frocks and gowns in a bedroomish mood, had catapulted her into the spotlight, creating so much buzz that literary and theatrical notables flocked to her showings. Alice became one of her favorite models.

Nat soon began keeping company with Alice, who, at twenty-three, was not only classically beautiful but funny and vivacious. She had a good head on her shoulders, a "very grounded person," says one of her daughters.

In the matter of life's pleasures, Nat had gradually evolved an attitude of self-preservation — "what I can't have I don't want," a step toward maturity for a boy who had grown up assuming he was entitled to everything. Pursuit of the impossible, whether publishing fame or Aryan fraternities, was "self-torture," but Alice was crazy about him from the start. Whether it was the stimulation of being around writers, or Nat's promise to dedicate his new book to her, or the fun of hobnobbing with Sid and Laura and their theatrical circle, Alice was taken with all three of them. They frequently socialized together, and when Laura needed formal gowns for special occasions, Alice made sure she got them on loan, or gratis.

Nat took such great pride in Alice and her Junior League background that people like Scotty got the impression that she belonged to the Standard Oil family, an exaggeration, because her father was only an employee of the company. In light of Nat's boasting, it is not surprising that Scotty found Alice to be average, "tall and good looking" but only "conventionally so as are five million American girls of any generation." To Edmund Wilson, there was nothing average about Nat's thoroughbred sweetheart. At a showing of Elizabeth Hawes's collection, he sat in the front row goggling so outrageously that Alice winked at him as she marched down the runway.

By Christmas, Nat was having a hard time remembering why he had wanted to marry Beatrice Mathieu. While Beatrice had remained close to Laura and Sid, she continued to harbor bitter feelings about her ex-fiancé. Writing to the Perelmans about a job offer from *Vogue*, she cautioned against mentioning her personal business to "that little flower, M. Wallenstein West." In no time her ball-busting smear got back to the little flower. So she wanted to talk about balls, did she? He retaliated with a cable: "RING OUT WILD BALLS AND MERRY CHRISTMAS AND HAPPY NEW YEAR AND LOVE." The next day, sheepish, he wired a corrected greeting: "RING OUT WILD BELLS." Neither of his sallies amused her.

11

THE BIG STEAL

A T A LOT ON West 125th Street, Nat and Scotty were pricing secondhand cars. When the dealer offered them the keys for a Ford Model A roadster, Scotty hit the gas pedal and they sped up Riverside Drive to Grant's Tomb. "Son of a bitch runs like a scalded dog," Scotty declared. Back at the lot, pleased to learn the price was only $195, they decided to take it.

When Scotty asked for a receipt, the car-lot guy grabbed the keys. "I don't give no bill of sale," he snapped, and began walking away.

But they needed proof of ownership, Scotty said. What if it was a stolen car?

"Pay him," Nat hissed, then announced out loud that the man obviously had to be an honest fellow.

"You got sense," the man said to Nat. "Your friend here is a schmuck."

A moment later Nat and Scotty were cruising downtown in their stolen roadster. "You know something, Scotty," Nat said. "You *are* a schmuck."

After three years in the hotel business, Nat had developed into a capable executive. His complaints to the contrary, he excelled at overseeing a sizable staff and assuming responsibility for the multitudes of guests coming and going, steady employment that proved gratifying and bolstered his self-respect. But sometimes the Sutton became suffocating. The phone kept ringing in his penthouse to summon him downstairs to tidy up one mess or another. There was no privacy at all.

"There's always some fucking deadbeat I have to throw out on his ass," he grumbled to Scotty one day. It would be exciting, he thought, to get away for a while. In fact, both of them could benefit from "a summer of writing." Scotty, inspired by Nat's example, had completed three hundred pages of a first novel. After admission to the bar in 1928, he worked in his father's office but now spent a good part of his time writing. He jumped at Nat's proposition. What was more, he even knew of a cheap cabin for rent in the Adirondacks.

Picturing a disgusting little one-room shack, Nat began to get nervous. "How would I shut myself off from you?" he wondered.

"Go outside."

At six A.M., Nat stood under the Sutton's striped awning surrounded by fishing poles, piles of camping equipment, and a case of whiskey. Among his special purchases were red flannel Brooks Brothers pajamas, a cookbook by Horace Kephart—the Fannie Farmer of camp cookery—and a five-foot-long, cowhide safari bag. A cigarette dangling from his fingers, he wore a three-piece suit and sporty alpine hat adorned with a feather. Scotty, pulling up in the Ford, began hooting. He would never be caught dead in an alpine hat. "We're supposed to be heading for the wild," he teased.

Nat had standards. "One never lets down," he said.

Renting for a mere twenty-five dollars a month, the cabin was 220 miles north of Manhattan, in the Hudson Valley on a dirt back road half a dozen miles from the nearest village. The six-room house was furnished with iron beds, old Morris chairs, and bookcases piled with *Smart Set* magazines dating back to 1907. There was no electricity or indoor plumbing, only coal-oil lamps and a two-hole privy at the rear, but a small dock sat on a pond jumping with trout.

For two months the trip unfolded like pages from a Boy Scout handbook: towering green trees, campfires, fresh-killed birds and rabbits, and for Nat a return to the field-and-stream fantasies of his childhood. Their routine was a morning of writing, with the rest of the day spent tramping the woods or rowing Viele Pond and keeping warm around the woodstove in the freezing evenings. The meals were fried birds or gooey stews that they dug into like "swine." Three times a day they boiled fresh coffee; they smoked butts when they ran out of cigarettes. One afternoon, while trying to bag partridges for their supper, Nat absent-mindedly jabbed Scotty's back with his shotgun. When Scotty discovered the gun was not just loaded but the hammer cocked as well, he sat down because he was trembling so badly, and then he began cursing. He was overreacting, Nat said casually. By this time Scotty had quietly taken charge of the Ford because Nat was a thoroughly incompetent driver. He forgot to pay attention. Or "he'd signal for the brake and tread on the gas." How on earth had he passed a driving test? In fact, he was "bloody fumble-fingered" about operating anything mechanical.

There was no discussion of either driving or writing, but one night Nat mentioned Scotty's book. "You mind if I read it?" he asked.

The next morning he returned the pages, taking Scotty to task for modeling one of the female characters on George Brounoff's dead sister, Olga, with whom Scotty had been in love. Readers, Nat warned, would easily be able to identify Olga. It was very bad form.

Why did he say that? Scotty replied in disbelief. It was his own life story. Practically all the characters were real. But Nat refused to back down. "It simply isn't done," he repeated, falling back on literary chivalry that he himself ignored. Listening to Nat's lecture on good manners angered Scotty. At Viele Pond, however, the ladylike Olga Brounoff wasn't the issue. What rankled Scotty most was Nat's lack of appreciation for his novel (*The Water Wheel*, published in 1933).

Two months went by. Apart from the argument over Scotty's novel, they got along well. In photographs taken by Scotty's sister, Ruth, one of their few visitors, they relaxed companionably on the side of the Ford. On Saturday nights they wandered over to nearby Green Mansions, a chichi adult camp that Nat dubbed "an adultery camp" restricted to "Yiddische cowboys and their *schones*" from West End Avenue. In fact they had fun dancing and necking in the woods with cute girls in pastel silk party pajamas.

The relationship between Nat and Alice was withering, but he was uncertain how to end it. For two years he had been calling her his fiancée, although Alice would describe their courtship—in all probability unconsummated—as an understanding. There was never an official engagement, and in fact Nat had neither visited her home in New Rochelle nor met her family. People who knew them could hardly imagine a young woman of her background walking down the aisle with Nat. It was assumed that her Protestant parents would not be keen to have a Jewish son-in-law. He could not bring himself to break up with her, though. Nor did a summer apart seem to bother Alice.

What marred the Adirondacks summer for Nat were deerflies, whose bites at times caused his eyes to swell nearly shut. Worse, he failed to produce a first draft. As he wrote and rewrote, he realized the book didn't work. All he could see were insoluble difficulties.

Over the course of the next year, as he published five of the chapters piecemeal in literary magazines, the slowness of his progress became agonizing. The prominence of the Susan Chester letters gradually diminished, and with the exception of Fay and her husband, the lives of the letter writers began fading into the background. Originally his lovelorn columnist narrated the story in the first person. Next, Nat tried third person, but then switched back to first. He changed the name of Thomas's paper from the *New York Evening Hawk* to the *New York Post-Dispatch*. Aging Thomas from twenty to twenty-six strengthened the seriousness of his sexual confusion. Fay's husband, Martin, became Peter Doyle. Willie Shrike's invention of a new church, "The First Church of Christ Dentist," along with a new Trinity, "the Father, Son, and Wire-haired Fox Terrier," was junked. Not until the fall of 1932 would Nat make the radical decision to strip his protagonist of a name, obliterating Thomas Matlock as decisively as he had effaced Nathan Weinstein. By this ingenious gimmick, the hero-columnist would be henceforth identified only as Miss Lonelyhearts. And Nat decided once and for all to resume a third-person narrative.

Life in the woods would inspire a new chapter later on. In "Miss Lonelyhearts in the Country," Betty attempts to lift Thomas's spirits with a restorative camping trip. Bubbling with optimism, she borrows a Ford touring car and drives them to her family's farm in Connecticut. Thomas is enchanted by the clean, cool air and the spring leaves. The days pass euphorically—Betty cooks fried eggs and apples, launders clothing, and finally administers recuperative sex—but his happiness is short-lived. Driving back to the city, he knows by the time they reach the Bronx that Betty's cure has failed. Amidst the dark offices, apartments, and basement speakeasies of *Miss Lonelyhearts*, this chapter would stand out as the single bright scene.

Shortly after their return from Viele Pond, Nat invited Scotty, who was barely earning a living, to stay rent free at the Sutton. In the roof garden his friend struck up a chaste friendship with one of the guests, a small, plump woman with freckles and red hair. Noticing her absence one day, Scotty questioned the desk clerk but got no satisfactory answer. Finally Nat informed him that she had been evicted because she was a hooker. "Anyone can have her for fifty bucks, and just about everyone has."

But Scotty didn't believe him. The freckled woman—"she's my friend," he cried—was not bothering anybody at the hotel. What did she do wrong?

He would know if he'd ever had the clap, answered Nat.

If Morris Jarcho had turned out to be one of Nat's Good Samaritans, the other was William Carlos Williams. Nat appreciated the poet-pediatrician's help in the publication of *The Dream Life of Balso Snell*, which was released that summer by Moss & Kamin, but the two had never met. Suddenly, Williams offered him the opportunity to become an editor of a literary quarterly.

From time to time during the past decade, Williams and Robert McAlmon had issued a magazine called *Contact*, but McAlmon was not interested in reviving the publication, and Williams, involved in a similar journal, *Pagany*, felt unable to swing it alone. At the suggestion of Martin Kamin and David Moss, who were backing *Contact*, Williams invited Nat to serve as his unpaid assistant. He was happy to work for nothing. On a Friday night in early October, the pediatrician drove into the city from his home in New Jersey to meet Nat for the first time, but a few minutes after arriving at the Sutton, a telephone call from his wife summoned him back to Rutherford to deliver a baby. In certain ways, that night established the tone for their association, Williams acting as elder statesman and figurehead, Nat as the underling who held his coat and sloshed through submissions and managed production and proofreading. On occasion Williams would venture into New York for a face-to-face editorial meeting but mostly he stayed in New Jersey, busy working on his roof or attending his son's soccer games at Rutherford High School when he was not delivering babies.

While Williams respected Nat's writing and acknowledged his enthusiasm for the magazine, he was ambivalent about him personally. In patronizing remarks made to friends, he called Nat "a very curious type," and called attention to his being a Jew. Nat reminded him of an uncle who "died of cerebral syphilis contracted in the West Indies from a nigger when he was fourteen." This odd association did not bode well for their relationship. Fortunately for the magazine, though, they were in agreement on what to publish: American writing that emphasized the colloquial, the violent, and the surrealistic, what Nat dubbed "American super-realism." As for the division of labor, it was Bill who edited the manuscripts that Nat had acquired. Determined to bag some big game, Nat drew up a wish list that included Ernest Hemingway, John Dos Passos ("non-political prose—the big city stuff"), Archibald MacLeish, Hart Crane, and Edmund Wilson.

"I suppose most of this stuff is impossible to get," he told Bill. Not out of the question, it turned out, but not simple either. He scrambled to pry contributions from Erskine Caldwell, James T. Farrell, E. E. Cummings, Nathan Asch, Robert McAlmon, and Nancy Cunard, in addition to a few friends like Sid and Scotty. (*Contact* did not pay contributors.) The first issue of the reborn *Contact: An American Quarterly Review* appeared late, in February instead of January 1932. It found no praise from Bill Williams, who told people that he felt embarrassed by the flat-footed quality of the contributions and blamed his assistant, implying he wasn't up to the job.

Nat, hackles raised, felt obliged to defend himself. Most of the submissions were "really lousy," he reminded Bill. It was cream-puff writing, "lyric, lyric crap."

A few months later, physically exhausted and feeling unappreciated, Nat told Bill that the Sutton's "business is lousy and my company is close to bankruptcy." By spring he was quarreling with Kamin and Moss about their plans for an issue devoted to Communist writing. He had no sympathy with the party—its notion that politics could save the world was frightfully delusional, he believed—but he also bristled at being told what to do. *Contact* should print avant-garde writing, not ideology. Even his funders' taste in jacket design—the "stinkiest fake moderne" art he had ever seen—offended him, and finally he was "forced to do the cover myself." By the third and final issue, in October 1932, he had called it quits.

But the *Contact* position paid off. For one thing, the magazine published early versions of four chapters of the still-unfinished *Miss Lonelyhearts*. A comparison of these drafts with the published novel reveal how Nat painstakingly experimented with first- and third-person narration, revised the structure, and simplified and clarified the plot. In a few spots, he chose to tone down an incident—for example, making Fay's seduction of Thomas slightly less lascivious, and the homosexuality of the old man in the park less salacious. And in another respect, *Contact* legitimized him. As assistant editor of a high-toned journal—in association with a poet of Bill Williams's stature—he had climbed into the literary major leagues.

Max Weinstein clung to old-fashioned habits. He wore his derby in the house and refused to buy a radio set. Late in the afternoons he would sit quietly in his favorite petit-point chair, facing the front door, and read the newspaper. After supper, he went back to the paper until it was time for bed. More remote and sadder than ever, he seemed to his children older than his fifty-nine years.

In the Bronx, he was working on an extension to Fordham Hospital but lately he complained of fatigue. Despite chronic pulmonary disease, he insisted there was nothing wrong. For the better part of fifty years his life had been dominated by work, and he knew nothing else. One Friday morning in June he left home as usual but never came back. He collapsed with a pulmonary hemorrhage and was taken to the tool-storage building, where he lay lifeless surrounded by his crew.

On the morning of Max's funeral, services in Hebrew and English took place at the Riverside Memorial Chapel on Amsterdam Avenue. The sight of Max in his coffin horrified Nat, who kept thinking he looked like a window mannequin. His shaggy eyebrows had been shaved, his cheeks rouged, and looped around his neck was a large white tie he had never worn while alive. Not only did the embalmers do an atrocious job, but adding to Nat's distress was his own neck, "so swollen that I couldn't button my collar" due to black-fly bites from a recent visit to the Adirondacks with Scotty.

Max was laid to rest in the Weinstein family plot at Mount Zion Cemetery. The weather that Sunday was unseasonably cool, with temperatures in the fifties. Nat got "an awful jolt" when he threw the first spadeful of earth on the coffin. He could not help thinking of the catchphrase "from shirt sleeves to shirt sleeves in three generations," which in Max's case had turned out to be one generation. His whole life, Nat had loved nobody as much as his father, but he had not admired him for a long time. A lifetime of toil had hammered Max into a man without property, savings, or bequests for a son who had developed the Champagne tastes of a trust-fund baby. Max had traveled a complete circle, ending up, in the twilight of his career, almost as insignificant as when he had arrived in America. One of his final commissions had been a two-story garage in the East Nineties, a sad comedown from his days of building stylish apartment houses. If life had cheated the father, it had also cheated the son, who believed he was entitled to more.

Yet he knew that he had disappointed his father. If *Miss Lonelyhearts* managed to get published, he meant to dedicate it "To Max." It would be the only thing he ever did for him, he told himself.

In a flare of candor, Nat admitted to Bill Williams that he was "heartsick" over his father's passing: "My whole family-life destroyed." The task of trying to "straighten things" fell on him, and not until July 4 did he begin to "find myself," he wrote a friend. Then he was knee-deep in preparations of the hotel's newspaper ads and direct-mail brochures for the coming fall season. Still, these business worries paled next to the problem of his mother. Depressed and fiercely needy, she was a heavy burden, although more for her daughter than Nat. Laura's family made Sid claustrophobic—"no more of that snug-rug-bug-Mamma-Nat-and-the-kids stuff for me," he once warned—and he made himself scarce. More and more, he took pains to avoid "the old lady," who sometimes heard voices. In need of Laura's companionship, she suffered the common handicaps facing new widows and created problems for her children. Now she could not bear being alone, nor did she have the money to live on her own. She decided to put her belongings in storage and move from West End Avenue to the Sutton Club.

Two years into the Depression, the homeless were sleeping in subway stations and public toilets, the hungry nosing into restaurant garbage cans, and sixteen hundred New Yorkers killed themselves. Although still new and physically resplendent, the Sutton had begun feeling the chill from the economic downturn: the number of bookings kept falling, and the business of managing the hotel became particularly complicated. Nat kept two sets of books. He skipped tax payments and was prepared to bribe the Bowery Savings Bank to keep quiet about it. He cheerfully explained to Edmund Wilson that manipulating the law had become business as usual for New York hoteliers and that if the Sutton ever got into trouble he'd just "burn the books." The Sutton restaurant was instructed to serve beef liver, soaked in milk, as calf's liver, and to innovate a chicken salad made with veal and lots of celery.

Although the hotel could not afford to give away rooms, Nat wanted it to look full and began offering accommodations at no charge or reduced rates. Both his mother and the Perelmans, when not in Hollywood, became permanent nonpaying guests. James T. Farrell, awaiting publication of his first novel, *Young Lonigan,* moved in with his wife after being evicted from their Union Square apartment. He said later that Nat offered them the room "simply and unobtrusively as though it were a matter of course." Living there at various times were Erskine Caldwell, Robert Coates, and Edmund Wilson, and Quentin Reynolds, covering sports for the International News Service, came and went whenever he liked.

Among those to whom Nat offered a free suite was a famous writer who had made an abrupt departure from the Pierre Hotel wearing all his clothes after running up a tab of a thousand dollars. Dashiell Hammett, creator of the hard-boiled private detective Sam Spade, was not exactly a charity case, but he was broke and desperate. At thirty-eight, suffering from chronic tuberculosis, gonorrhea, depression, burnout, and booze — especially booze — Dash was going on the wagon in order to write his new novel, *The Thin Man.* He moved into the Sutton, a stay that would last until the following spring, with a girlfriend named Lillian Hellman. Whereas he was distinguished-looking, tall and elegant with a mane of prematurely gray hair, Lillian was a short, heavy-breasted woman with a large nose and rust-colored hair, not pretty despite her stylish clothes. Already an acquired taste, she was at twenty-seven feisty and very funny, brimming with ambition to write plays and depending on Hammett for a push onto the road to success. In Dash's new book, she was the inspiration for Nora Charles, the devilishly witty wife. There is nothing ordinary about Nick and Nora Charles, married charmers who solve crimes, are always drunk, and love each other and their dog madly. (The couple's dog would be named Asta after one of Laura's schnauzers.)

The Sutton had inadvertently become a literary hotel, not the Algonquin with its Round Table sophisticates but a refuge that provided writers with basic needs like a roof over their heads. Sid was tickled.

There were so many literary types cluttering up the lobby that the place looked like "a book and author luncheon," he said.

One afternoon in early October, Josephine Herbst and her husband, John Herrmann, friends of Bill Williams's, stopped in at the hotel to introduce themselves. Nat was delighted. Under the striped awning he welcomed the couple with smiles and outstretched hands, then conducted them upstairs to his penthouse, where they dutifully admired the magnificent views. Josie decided he was terribly attractive, with marvelous eyes and a sweet, witty manner; his manners were exquisite. She recalled that he handed her a drink with "the grace of someone offering you a rose." He immediately began bemoaning the fact that he had to work for a living managing a hotel, how he was a pitiful bird imprisoned in a beautiful cage, telling her that he put in grueling hours and always felt wrung out. It was a touching lament, even partly true, that made Josie determined to rescue him from the awful Sutton Club.

Josephine Herbst was a well-praised novelist who had published two books (*Nothing Is Sacred* and *Money for Love*). Nat was an admirer of her work and also thought highly of her husband, author of the banned novel *What Happens* and a contributor to *Contact*. In Paris in 1924, they had been among the first wave of American expatriates, but unlike John's close friend Ernest Hemingway, they had decided to return home. In 1928, embracing what was romantically known as the writer's life, the couple put down roots in eastern Pennsylvania, seventy-five miles from New York, in a plain stone house in Tinicum Township, built by poor farmers. Scratching out a bare living, they had learned to do without niceties like indoor plumbing and electricity. A spartan existence ensured plenty of leisure for reading and reflection. According to their philosophy, the simple life was a matter of principle and therefore writers should be prepared to make sacrifices, because writing was a state of mind. (While Nat endorsed this gospel, he himself was not prepared to forgo Brooks Brothers, nor did he wish to make his own bed, which was the reason God created room service.)

The afternoon he met Josie, he knew she was going to become a very good friend. Stay for dinner, he urged; stay overnight. As befitted a hotelier, he was the perfect host and refused to allow her and John to leave. If not for his job, with its constant interruptions, his novel would have been completed long ago, he explained. To his surprise, Josie invited him to visit them in Pennsylvania; disruptions were unknown in the restful village of Erwinna, consisting of a general store and a gasoline pump. It took little to persuade him. When they departed for home the next morning, Nat was in the rumble seat. Dressed in an old suit (his notion of casual), he carried a gun and an expensive leather suitcase in which he had carefully tucked a bottle of Scotch and an extra pair of polished shoes. Ah, said Josie to herself, he was "a dandy."

When Nat saw Bucks County for the first time, it was still warm and October light was flecking the foliage into lush shades of copper and crimson; he fell in love. During the next three days on Upper Tinicum Church Road, he and the Herrmanns hiked through fields rustling with tall weeds and red sumac and at night they emptied bottles of rotgut rye and some very nice homemade red wine. In Josie's little stone house, they recited poetry by the light of flickering oil lamps, noisily argued about Pushkin and Dostoyevsky, and talked shop about the publishing business. Harcourt was bringing out Josie's new novel in the spring, and Nat was excited to hear about her editor, Charles Pearce, and her literary agent, Maxim Lieber. "We barely slept," Josie remembered.

Josie, bossy, stroked his ego as she ruthlessly peeled apart his life. His problem, she said, was that he had stopped moving the book forward. He was becalmed, paralyzed with fixing and polishing, the favorite refuge of the fearful writer. Unfinished, the book would dangle forever in his consciousness like, as she put it, some decomposing corpse whose "deathly presence would putrefy his entire life."

Nat knew she was right. By the time he boarded the Lehigh train at Flemington Junction for the trip to Penn Station, his mind was made up to return. The hotel owed him six weeks of vacation.

• • •

Frenchtown, in Hunterdon County, New Jersey, was a two-block-long hamlet where most of the residents were on relief, trying to get on relief, or drunk because they couldn't, but was one of the few places in the area where a traveler might find lodgings. On October 12, Nat took up residence in the Warford House, built in 1805 on the banks of the Delaware River. The four-story, white-pillared, redbrick inn on Bridge Street was hardly the Sutton Club, but Nat's spirits were buoyed by the country atmosphere, the whiffs of crisp air, the fog-shrouded brown river, the friendly dog named Tim who belonged to the hotel owner.

In his quiet room he settled down with a pile of manuscript and a wad of pencils and got to work on a final edit. He was exploding with newfound energy, the stamina he had always been seeking. At dusk, after working steadily all day, he strolled across the trestle bridge to Bucks County on the Pennsylvania side of the river, then walked south on River Road, west on Uhlerstown Hill Road, south to 53 Upper Tinicum Church Road. Two miles there and two miles back under the stars. The evening of his twenty-ninth birthday—Monday, October 17—found him with John and Josie, a nightly habit. "They are swell people," he wrote to Bill Williams, not only for finding him a place to stay but "they feed me while I am working."

One weekend in early November, Nat borrowed a friend's car to take his sister and Lillian Hellman on a tour of Bucks County, followed by lunch at Josie's. On their way back to Frenchtown, his speeding on the winding country roads gave the women a scare. Lily took the wheel after dropping him at the Warford, but minutes later she smashed into a telephone pole and the windshield shattered. Although the damage turned out to be considerable, Lillian refused to take responsibility for the accident. Nat was furious that he had to pay for the repairs.

At Warford House, his only interruptions came from moonshining drunks on the main street and his mother's threatening phone calls and telegrams. To corral him home she enlisted the support of uncles and cousins, until finally he went into the city for the express purpose of confronting her: he would not come back before Thanksgiving, he announced, unless it was on a stretcher. When she began crying, he stormed out and left her with Laura.

It was a relief to be back in Frenchtown and Erwinna, where he had become friendly with some of the locals. These were country people who had continued to farm, hunt, attend church, and live in houses without plumbing or electricity for generations. For supplies they crossed the river to Frenchtown, hoping to buy on credit because the Depression had devastated an already-stagnant economy. There was usually a gang of old-timers and their dogs milling around outside the hotel smoking, boozing, and gabbing about hunting. These were not the sort of people who sent their children to Brown. Many had never learned to read or write.

Nat, who sometimes joined them, had always felt most at ease in the company of males (Laura excepted) but now he turned to a woman for friendship. With Josie, the childless benevolent mother figure, he felt safe in letting his hair down, and she, in turn, treated him like a beloved brother. "You could say anything to him," she wrote. "There was nothing you had to fence in." True, it disappointed her that his finicky tastes and lamentable addiction to financial security and "snappy suits" effectively ruled out a writerly life. Likewise, his savage fictional portrayals of women upset her. Still, she could forgive him practically anything.

She and John made an odd couple. Josie, forty and dowdy, looked older than her age, whereas John, eight years her junior and exceptionally good-looking, seemed a great deal younger. Although John's drinking was edging out of control, the Herrmanns appeared to have a rock-solid marriage. Nat had no way of knowing about their difficulties; nor did he realize until later that Josie was passionately involved with a painter named Marion Greenwood.

Although Josie would always be quick to say that she loved Nat, she denied the existence of sexual feelings on either side. "Not at all," she insisted in *Hunter of Doves*, her roman à clef about him. She was married to a man she "adored"—and for that matter she would have been surprised if Nat "didn't adore him too." Nevertheless, it was hard to account for the dream in which Nat crept up from behind and embraced her.

At the end of November, only six weeks after the Herrmanns appeared at the Sutton, *Miss Lonelyhearts* was finished. "The corpse came to life and walked," Josie joked. To celebrate his big achievement, she decided to cook a feast. That afternoon, Nat was so elated that he borrowed a gun and an old dog from the hotel and shot a pheasant in the woods. When the roasted bird emerged from Josie's oven it looked spectacular. Only one thing went wrong: the pheasant would have been better had they not had to spit out buckshot. Nat, an amazing writer, was a poor hunter.

While Nat was in Pennsylvania finishing his book, Sid was preparing for the opening of *Walk a Little Faster,* a new revue starring Beatrice Lillie and featuring some of his sketches. With screen credits on two Marx Brothers films (*Monkey Business* and *Horse Feathers*), three books, and steady contributions to *The New Yorker,* he was becoming known as one of those rare writers who easily straddled movies, stage, and publishing. But professional successes combined with a growing reputation as an avid skirt chaser kept his marriage at a nasty simmer.

Laura's life centered on her husband, whose own life in turn centered on himself. She was unable to get along without him, and so she told herself that Jewish men who feel ugly need to keep proving their masculinity with Christian women. After one year at Pembroke, she was unequipped for any sort of steady job, nor did she want one. Her ambition was a writing career like her husband's. But aside from a poem, "Even Stephen," which had appeared in the Pembroke literary magazine, her writing was limited to filling brown-covered school composition books with ideas for stories. In notes for a play titled "West End Avenue," she painted unflattering portraits of a family of well-off Russian Jews, the Ratkowskys, living at 224 West End Avenue on the Upper West Side: the worrying, Yiddish-speaking father, "a pig-headed old kike," whose big escape was reading the newspaper in his favorite chair; the well-fed, well-dressed mother who had worked on her accent; a brainless boy-crazy daughter; and a coddled son who quit school at the age of thirteen, changed his name, and "spends his time buying tailor-made clothes that are too fancy for him." This "Anglo-Saxon Jew" is an "absolute dope," tolerated by his father because he is "The Son."

Although Nat refused to acknowledge it, Laura's behavior was becoming self-destructive. She was obsessed with her schnauzer Gurke. She worried about her alcohol consumption—even posting reminders to eat before drinking—but Nat believed she was all right because she held her liquor well and never appeared drunk. What scared him more than Laura's drinking was her erratic behavior, including an impetuous habit of vanishing and refusing to say where she had been. Although New York was well policed, he feared she might come to harm and sometimes combed the streets in search of her. In the meantime, he continued to feel affection for Sid and tried to avoid taking sides in the Sid and Laura Civil War.

The Boston opening of *Walk a Little Faster* right after Thanksgiving precipitated another crisis for the Perelmans. The show required extensive rewrites, and Sid had no time for Laura, who had brought Alice Shepard along for company. Laura, wearing a designer gown that Alice had borrowed from Elizabeth Hawes, felt humiliated by her husband's behavior with showgirls in the cast, and each day ended in scenes and tears and sudden disappearances. One morning after being gone all night, she knocked on the door of Alice's hotel room only to learn that Sid had been fondling her in a taxi the previous evening, caresses that Alice primly referred to as "love pats." Laura could never be sure which of her friends he had tried to sleep with.

Nat spent Thanksgiving at the Sutton. He was in a hurry to have his manuscript professionally typed and to get in touch with Josie's literary representative, whose client list included John Steinbeck, Jack Conroy, Erskine Caldwell, James T. Farrell, and Robert Coates. In New York publishing, Maxim Lieber was known for handling polemical, "proletarian" fiction and also had become something of a legend for his swashbuckling style. He felt confident strolling into an editor's office and pitching a manuscript in person. On the other hand, he had been known to drop crybaby writers in need of nursemaids, as he called novelist John Fante. Lieber was sympathetic to liberal writers, the more left-wing the better, because he wore two hats: literary agent and Communist Party apparatchik. An oft-told story had him bouncing into the Knopf offices with a load of manuscripts and an editor shouting, "Are you bringing me another communist!" He was eventually alleged to be a Soviet agent, his literary agency a front for espionage. In 1932, however, he was a catch for an unknown writer like Nat. Lieber, who did not handle junk, responded eagerly to *Miss Lonelyhearts*. This signified a high likelihood of commercial success.

At the close of 1932, as Nat was about to sign with Boni & Liveright, the storied house of hits, it looked as if he was on his way.

Late one night in December, at a Childs restaurant on Thirty-fourth Street, he was drinking coffee after attending a concert with Scotty and other members of the George Brounoff crowd. They were joined by an attorney who had lived two years in China and considered himself an authority, one of those real blowhards who didn't know when to shut up. Listening to "the Chinaman," Nat became annoyed and began to bait him with queries about calligraphy and the various dynasties. Scotty finally lost his temper.

"Let him alone, Pep," he said. Why didn't he pick on someone his own size?

"Someone like you?" Nat shot back. Matching wits would be terrifying, he added, because, no doubt, Scotty could show him up for what he was.

"What you are, Pep, is a sheeny in Brooks clothing."

At this outburst, Nat never batted an eye. Scotty, far from offering an apology, seemed determined to pick a quarrel.

"A sheeny in Brooks clothing, Mr. West," he repeated. "I knew you when your name had two syllables."

Nat remained silent. Why was Scotty turning on him? His vulgarity, his childish lack of manners, calling him names in public, was shocking. Quickly everyone at their table got up and trickled out of the restaurant.

The next morning, Scotty took his leave of the Sutton. Ducking into Nat's office, he said that he would drop the key at the front desk.

"You shouldn't have spoken as you did," Nat chided. "It was unseemly."

Further riled by the reference to his manners, Scotty replied that he couldn't help it. Some people were naturally coarse, he guessed. Not everybody could be a gentleman like Nat.

The sheeny remark made Nat curious. Was it spontaneous?

No, Scotty admitted, he had been saving it.

"See you sometime, Scotty," Nat said.

"Same thing, Natchie," said Scotty, calling him by the hated childhood nickname. They would not speak to each other for four years.

That December, after Scotty left, Nat finally split up with Alice Shepard. The notion of an engagement either formal or informal had become a farce. Alice expected to become a traditional wife and mother, for which he didn't blame her, but connubial bliss was not for him, regardless of his affection for her. And so, much as his fictitious hero of *Miss Lonelyhearts* withheld affection from the vacuous Betty, he gradually began to pull back from Alice.

Leaving a party with her and Lillian Hellman one night, he first dropped Alice at Grand Central so she would catch her train to New Rochelle. Then he continued uptown with Lily, who was still living at the Sutton with Hammett. Sometime later that evening Alice phoned but got no answer. Throughout the night she made further calls, growing increasingly upset and suspicious.

The next day they met for coffee at a Longchamps restaurant, and Alice demanded an explanation. The most obvious answer would have been some hotel emergency—or a dozen other excuses—but instead Nat said that he had spent the night with Lillian. Whether this was true is questionable, but Alice believed him. He evidently gave a convincing impression of a man caught with his hand in the cookie jar. More surprising than his cheating on her was his choice of a partner. While

Lillian was certainly not without allure, and had notched up plenty of sexual conquests, compared to a professional beauty like Alice she was an ugly duckling. Nat proceeded to place the blame on Lily, who, he said, had invited him. It was the first time a woman had asked him for sex, which was so startling that he automatically agreed, thereby quaintly casting himself as a Boy Scout who helped little old ladies to cross the street.

Alice later wondered if she had been naive to believe his Lillian story. Possibly it was a lie, but Nat didn't have "a devious nature" and his "regret and remorse" seemed genuine. Besides, she thought, had he truly wished to break up he could have "by just doing it, harsh as it might have been." But Nat was incapable of just doing it. To sweep Alice out of his life, he had to use Hellman as a broom.

Afterward, Nat would say the problem was family disapproval of his marrying out of the faith, but he would not have been the first Weinstein to marry a Christian. His cousin Sylvia, Uncle Julius's girl, had recently wed an Irish-Catholic reporter at the *Daily News* (and a future television icon) named Ed Sullivan. He also repeated the story about sleeping with Lillian. According to Hellman, the incident never took place, and thirty years later she still emphatically denied her involvement.

After Alice, doing some bed-hopping, Nat began seeing a well-known theatrical publicist whose show-business career belied her Southern socialite origins. His affair with another Gentile triggered a volley of wisecracks from Sid. Had she met Anna? Because he didn't want to be around when "the old lady gets wind of it." What they should do, he chortled, is "buy him a Jewish girl made out of rubber whom he can lay and put back in the closet." Instead of cuddling with an inflatable sex doll, Nat was hit by a rush of ecstasy—a thrill called real estate.

While living at the Warford House, Nat had noticed a flyer advertising a farm for sale in Erwinna. The property sounded made-to-order for country squires, the sort of people who read *Field & Stream* and shopped at Abercrombie & Fitch. The real estate was eighty-three acres of tillable land, including a brook, fruit and nut trees, and woods crackling with game birds. There was a large house, a stone barn, and several sheds. Nearby, the Delaware River offered opportunities for swimming, fishing, and canoeing, and across the river in Frenchtown were plenty of retail stores selling bargain goods. The price: six thousand dollars.

As it turned out, the owner was Michael Gold, famous for his best-selling novel *Jews Without Money*, a gripping story of immigrant poverty on the Lower East Side. The book earned sufficiently handsome royalties that Gold was able to purchase the farm in Pennsylvania as an investment, but now he wanted to sell, not an easy matter in the third year of the Depression when numerous farms were on the market, some for as little as $1,500. Nat went to look at 160 Geigel Hill Road, on a dirt road about a half mile from Josie's house, and decided he wanted it.

Unfortunately, he did not have six grand, much less a down payment, and the stone house squatting on a hillside would need major renovations to make it livable. Josie advised against the purchase. Gold's house was a poor choice, she warned him; there were much handsomer houses available for less. He argued that Gold's came with electricity, a bathroom, and a pretty good furnace. Shortly thereafter, on an autumn day before the leaves fell off the aspens, he invited the Perelmans to drive out to Bucks County. At the farmstead, they trudged around the barn, the piggery, the corn crib, and the stream running through the property, by which point, Sid recalled, "the poison was circulating in our veins." Laura was swooning and Sid, who had come reluctantly, declared that the Gold farm was "the biggest steal since the theft of the Mona Lisa from the Louvre." He envisioned "sleigh rides, Hallowe'en parties, sugaring off, sugaring on, and bringing in the Yule log." The barn alone, "larger than the cathedral at Chartres," was simply magnificent. Love-struck, the three of them decided to pool their money and buy the property together.

On December 19, at the county courthouse in Doylestown, they made a $500 down payment, partly raised by selling the Weinsteins' grand piano, in storage since Max died, to the Sutton. (Nat recommended that a musical instrument might add a touch of class to the lobby.) Throughout the next few months, house repairs would become an endless drain on their cash. "We call the place Eight Ball," Nat wrote jokingly to Josie and John, who were wintering in Mexico. But it was no joke, because when the next property payment came due in January, they were broke and tried to put off Mike Gold with an IOU. Gold promptly threatened legal action, and Nat, having run out of pianos, had to scurry up a $150 loan from the Corn Exchange Bank.

12

MAROONED ON SILSBY ROAD

IN THE MORNINGS, Eileen headed for the corner of Lee and Cedar, where she caught a streetcar full of office workers for a twenty-minute ride downtown to the business district. On Sundays, she read the *Plain Dealer* society pages before beginning her preparations for the workweek ahead, the usual washing and ironing of dresses, freshening up her hats with brightly colored bows and ribbons. It was her hair that took the most time: a perfect finger wave, pinching the sharp ridges and flat ringlets, required as much precision as a soufflé. This was not vanity either. Her job depended as much on presentation—pretty frocks, finger waves, false eyelashes, and perfectly filed nails—as it did on taking dictation, maybe more.

Things could have been better, but she didn't complain. She was lucky to have a good job in the insurance business. What more could an unmarried young woman want? In 1932, one in four Americans was unemployed, and companies were more apt to lay off than hire; it was against these facts of life that she measured her accomplishments. For her employer, the Cleveland branch of a national company that ran credit investigations of people applying for policies, she operated the switchboard and typed up the reports between answering phone calls. That she had gotten the position was somewhat of a miracle because her stutter made her a less than ideal employee. But as the stutter was

most obvious when she had to converse on the phone, the office manager hiring her must not have noticed. Or perhaps his decision was
influenced by her looks—because a check of references would have
revealed how many times she had resigned, or gotten the boot.

When it came to her spotty employment record, her most severe
critic was her father. A major subscriber to the nursery mythology that
Ruth was smart, Eileen thick-witted, Syd McKenney scoffed at her
abilities and vocally patronized her as a scatterbrain. When she came
home fired up over the credit bureau, he questioned the judgment of
her new employer. "Don't they ever ask you for references?" he wanted
to know. Was it a reputable outfit? "I wouldn't any more hire you!" he
declared, thoughtless but honest.

As it turned out, this was her best job yet. Credit intrigued her because she could so easily identify it with the branches of her own family, which held diametrically opposing philosophies. The no-nonsense
McKenneys regarded a good rating as close to godliness, while the
Flynns tended to pay bills only when threatened by a collection agency.
As she discovered, investigating fraud sometimes involved high drama.
Soon she became an expert on the schemes by which people tried to
swindle insurance companies. Misbehaving husbands—always bad
risks for life insurance—were delightful, but nothing beat a spouse
murder for pure thrills.

At the dining table she kept the family entertained with stories from
the company, especially its handling of phony disability cases by inves-
tigators who used movie cameras to trail suspected wrongdoers. Her favorite case involved a supposedly disabled Greek storekeeper intent on
bilking his insurance company out of two hundred dollars a week for
life. (Secretly she was rooting for the able-bodied Greek.)

With such absorbing work she bent over backward to avoid mistakes. For a while she succeeded, but disaster struck when incriminat-
ing surveillance film on the cheating Greek storekeeper mysteriously
disappeared one day. Without the film, which had been stored for safe-
keeping in Eileen's desk, the credit bureau had no case. All the clues
led to Eileen, who—unable to admit the film burned up when she lit a

cigarette—said that it "just got lost." She felt terrible, but they fired her anyway.

Ruth was working as a feature writer and general-assignment reporter on the *Akron Beacon Journal* after three years as a journalism student at Ohio State. When she first arrived in Columbus, accompanied by her grandmother Celia McKenney, they had rented a furnished apartment off campus. Ruth explained this unusual situation by referring to Celia as her chaperone and claiming she was there "to keep house for me." Freshman girls in 1928 did not matriculate in the company of chaperones, certainly not with grandmothers; probably her history of mental instability made the presence of a companion prudent. Once Ruth adjusted to the university, Celia McKenney left to live with daughter Margery Pearce in Akron.

Ruth plunged into college life. Popular with her peers for the first time, she became known as one of the most intrepid students writing for the *Lantern*, the student newspaper, a go-getter of confidence and boundless energy who earned top grades. After learning that Winston Churchill's nineteen-year-old son, Randolph, was visiting Columbus on a speaking tour, she boldly marched up to his hotel room and knocked on the door. The result was an unexpected invitation to help him hunt for his lost socks under the bed. "I wrote my interview that night, and it was a big success," she recalled. Such scoops landed her stringer assignments from the *Columbus Dispatch*.

Ruth's mood swings seemed to be under control. Then, at the end of her junior year, she slid into a depression that could not be masked and threw her education into turmoil. Possibly, this involved another attempted suicide, because her problems came to the attention of the school administration. The dean of women advised that her illness was psychological—"unadjusted," as Ruth recalled her saying—but Ruth could not accept the warning. In an article written in 1944, she claimed that OSU denied her a degree for failing to comply with the university's physical-education requirement, but psychiatric illness seems a more likely cause for her departure.

The summer of 1931, after traveling around Europe with a college roommate, she landed a fine job on the *Akron Beacon Journal*. Already working there was a friend of hers from the *Lantern*, Harvey Earl Wilson, a farmer's son from Rockford, whose father expected him to become a farmer. A skinny kid with big ears and a bashful air, he was so taciturn that he seemed to be measuring out his words with a teaspoon. But underneath his shyness, he was as ferociously ambitious as Ruth, who liked to say that Ohio was only "an anteroom, a training ground, the Minor Leagues." They were always boiling with schemes, just biding their time until they could make a getaway to the center of the universe. Years later, after he had become a Broadway columnist, someone asked him, "Mr. Wilson, when did you first decide to come to New York?" and he replied, "The minute I heard about it."

At the *Beacon Journal*, Ruth wrote as if her life depended on it, sometimes whipping out seven columns a day. Denied assignments covering politics and labor (Akron was a bloody battleground of strife between the rubber companies and their workers), she got stuck doing human-interest stories about women ("Governor's Daughter to Marry This Afternoon"), and so she was continually fighting management. Her stridency made staffers roll their eyes. Yes, she was fast, but she made too many mistakes in fact and spelling. The editor who had hired her, John S. Knight, "sweated over her copy" and another employee recalled that her edited pieces "looked like the map of New Zealand." Still, everybody acknowledged that she had potentially formidable gifts, if she cared to develop them.

On leafy Silsby Road, eleven-year-old Jack McKenney sat on his front porch, mesmerized. He watched a Cord L-29 convertible glide up to their house, the breath of its front engine screaming under the long, sleek hood. The car was outfitted with wire wheels and fender-mounted spares, the silver grille flanked by a pair of bowl headlights; its $3,200 price tag was worn proudly, like a phantom diamond tiara. That one of his sister's boyfriends actually owned such a luxurious vehicle was thrilling, and he remembers that Eileen "would run out and jump into the car, and away they'd go."

From Jack's perspective, his sister lived a glamorous life. The driver of the Cord could have been Sterling Hubbard, whose family owned Cowell and Hubbard, the most prominent jewelry store in Cleveland. Of all her romances, this one was the most serious, the one most impressive to the Flynns and McKenneys. In *All About Eileen*, written twenty years later, Ruth claims Eileen was a social butterfly tooling around in the cars of polo players before hooking a large diamond from "Robert (Bidgie) Thomaston III, Princeton '31, steel scion and man about Cleveland." Given Ruth's habit of altering names, it seems possible that Bidgie was Sterling and that it was the Hubbard family who promised the engaged couple a completely furnished new home with four bathrooms. But the engagement broke off, just like that. Eileen, Ruth would later write, put her freedom ahead of a dull marriage, turning her back on the scion without so much as a tear for the four-bathroom house. But in truth Ruth couldn't explain why Eileen returned to her ordinary existence as a secretary and girl about town. So quietly did the breakup take place that her high school classmate Ruth Beebe, away at college and out of touch, would assume that the engagement had ended in marriage. If anyone was the type of man Eileen was meant to marry, it was Sterling Hubbard, Ruth Beebe says. But for Eileen, nothing had gone according to plan.

Just about every girl she knew had managed to assemble a normal life. After the race to the altar, they had their husbands, first babies, houses with two bathrooms, and time to be active in their local chapter of the pious Epworth League. On the second floor of 3372 Silsby Road, Eileen slept in her childhood room, at the front of the house, right next door to Jack and Ethel and Syd and the mutt, Skippy. In spite of the rape, it was hard to give up her Cleveland Heights fairy tale: she had always pictured herself the pampered wife of a grateful husband who would always want to look after her. The man would keep busy with his career while she devoted herself to their home and children. There would be no need to develop larger interests, to teach school or work at a job, no reason to think of money at all. Forever and ever she would remain beautiful, drive her own car, and use an unlimited charge account to shop in the enchanted forest of Halle Brothers.

In reality she was twenty and unmarried, which by Cleveland Heights standards meant her time had run out; she was a spinster, a marked-down dress that nobody was going to buy, who had yet to experience ordinary romantic love. It was embarrassing still to be living in her parents' home, where she increasingly felt like an outsider. "She expected more from her father," says her cousin Dick Selvey, "but I don't think it ever happened." Syd's marriage to Ethel, in its thirteenth year, had proved far more successful than his relationship with his first wife. Despite her secretarial background, Ethel had no interest in working outside the home. Her life revolved around keeping house, cooking meals, and mothering twelve-year-old Jack, a student at Roosevelt Junior High School. At thirty-four she was still a young woman who could have more children if she wished, and eventually she would.

An affectionate sister to Jack, Eileen felt no particular allegiance to Ethel, who never managed to replace her own mother. Bad feelings were, in this case, a two-way street. In years to come, neither sister could be mentioned in the house.

On Ruth's trip to Germany, her passport listed a home address at 3372 Silsby Road, but that had never been her home. Before the move to Cleveland Heights, she was already living with Lyda and Otto Thomas. Her dislike of Ethel remained undimmed, and except for a reference to a "mean old stepmother," there is not a single hint of Ethel's existence anywhere in her writings. In re-creating her family (sainted mother, flinty father, luminous sister) she chopped out Ethel. Less contentious than her sister, Eileen had managed, more or less, to get along. Ethel ruled the house, the kitchen being her special domain. Pots and pans did not interest Eileen, who never learned to "boil an egg or fry a strip of bacon," Ruth insisted, let alone put up tomato relish or concoct a Yorkshire pudding. Her only culinary skill was bread, baked from scratch, a recipe learned from her grandmother Mary Flynn.

By 1934, the idea of leaving Cleveland had become increasingly attractive, but whenever she mentioned relocating, possibly making a fresh start in some place like New York, her father got upset. "What's wrong with Ohio?" he wanted to know. There was something essentially un-American about New York. California at least made sense, because pushing west was the American way, but he couldn't imagine anybody wanting to live in a sorry place like New York. That was where immigrants landed before having the good sense to go elsewhere. The Flynns offered no support either. They thought she was bright but lacked any "intellectual gifts or creative streaks like her sister," one of her cousins says. Besides, nobody on that side of her family had ever moved out of state, except Aunt Ruth, whose husband dragged her to the backwater of West Virginia, and Marguerite Flynn, whose husband had carried her off to Indiana. The idea of an unmarried girl moving to New York had never crossed anybody's mind.

By this point her aunts and uncles were getting on. Lyda and Otto, then in their fifties, had no children. Aunt Ruth, forty but claiming to be younger, had married Forrest Selvey, an accountant who had been boarding in the Flynn household, and they had a son, Richard. Poor Mildred had been committed. Laura, the wife of Walter Flynn, died in 1932 after being electrocuted by a heater, followed shortly by her daughter Marguerite's near-fatal fall from a second-floor porch and the death of her son Thomas, eleven, shot in the head by a friend. Poor Uncle Walter had sunk into alcoholism (and died of a heart attack in 1936). As Ruth sometimes would say in jest, the Flynns never did things by halves.

Eileen and Ruth agreed on one thing: the Flynn women, for all their spunk and beauty and brains, offered little inspiration. It was sickening to see their "wretched marriages," thought Ruth, who vowed always to be her own woman and "NEVER to sink to this prison of life." This was not exactly the way Eileen would have put it, but under no circumstances was she willing to embrace her aunts' fates. "I'm just marking time," she said, realizing that she had to get out.

There were farm teams and there were the major leagues, and Ruth knew the difference. After being honored by the Ohio Newspaper Women's Association with four top writing prizes, including the prestigious Amelia Earhart Award (thirty-five dollars cash) for the best aviation story, she decided it was time to leave Ohio. She knew that if a writer could achieve fame in New York City, she would be famous everywhere. In the late fall of 1934, she jumped but landed on the wrong side of the Hudson River, in New Jersey.

Newark in 1934 was the biggest city in the state, with a population approaching half a million. A gritty metropolis known for insurance companies and stolen cars, the city supported four dailies to record its political wars and gang shootings. The one that gave Ruth her break was the *Newark Ledger*, a semitabloid morning daily partly owned by Samuel I. Newhouse. She arrived at 80 Bank Street full of enthusiasm to start her job, only to learn that the newsroom had just walked out on strike. At issue was the dismissal of eight employees, for reasons of economy, said management, but the American Newspaper Guild insisted otherwise. Because this was the year-old Guild's first major action against a large-circulation daily, the strike received a good deal of national coverage. Management blustered and dug in its heels, but after two intense weeks of incriminations both sides began to act ugly. Crossing the picket line never occurred to Ruth, caught in the crossfire but siding wholeheartedly with the Guild.

Having come this far, she had no intention of returning to Ohio. In the weeks before Christmas, she headed to New York and began making the rounds with her book of clips. The city's nine daily papers were all struggling, and the odds were stacked against newcomers like Ruth. This was the big time, where seasoned reporters snarled over openings on the *Times* and the *Daily News* and three years at Ohio State journalism school meant nothing, but her chief disability was her sex. With few exceptions, papers restricted female writers to the women's departments, carrying news of engagements and weddings and features devoted to fashion, cooking, and child care. To Ruth, who wanted to cover labor and local politics, this sort of journalism was fluff, but she was willing to take anything. After being turned away at every paper, whose busy editors had no time to see her, she faced the choice of going home or starting all over. One of the papers she tried a second time was the *New York Evening Post*.

The paper's headquarters at 75 West Street was a seventeen-story, Art Deco building in lower Manhattan, facing the waterfront where the oceangoing passenger liners were berthed. Ornamented with geometric blue-and-gold-glazed terracotta tiles, it looked more like a giant Turkish bath than an office building. It housed one of the nation's oldest newspapers, founded in 1801 by Alexander Hamilton.

"Be brief," the *Post* city editor said to Ruth. "Just give me one good reason why I should hire a twenty-one-year-old girl who came to New York on Monday." He went on sternly, "Keep to the point." King of the clamorous city room, his presence dominating the racket of typewriters, Teletypes, and cries for copyboys, was Walter Lister, Brown class of 1920, playwright, incessant bridge player, and stereotypical editor out of *The Front Page*. At thirty-six, famous for his cold stare, Lister had already worked for a number of metropolitan papers, including the *Houston Post* and the *Cleveland Press*.

If Lister meant to get rid of Ruth as fast as possible—had he known her at all—he would not have asked why he should hire her. Because, she informed him, she was Ohio's best newspaperwoman—the cream of the crop.

"Mr. Bixbee," as she named him in her sketch "Scattered by Such Winds," began laughing, and he continued to laugh so hard that he "had to wipe the tears from his eyes." Well, he couldn't hire her, he finally said, because she was a useless greenhorn. She knew nothing about New York. He bet she didn't even know how to get to Brooklyn.

"I could look it up on a map," she countered. She had "a strut and a swagger," Lister thought, qualities that made her "infectious and persuasive even when she's wrong." He decided to send her on a trial assignment. If she returned with a publishable story, he would put her on the staff, but if she failed, he warned, "you make me a promise you'll take the next train back to Ohio." She stayed, and not in the women's department but as a metro feature writer. She had typically expected that male editors were prejudiced. But the *Post*, of all the New York papers, was known to give women a slice of the pie occasionally, hiring writers like Edith Evans Asbury and financial editor Sylvia Porter.

Lister was not without reservations about Ruth. In her clips it was easy to spot a host of weaknesses: emotionalism, gullibility, a tendency to embroider facts. But Lister recognized that she had the potential to develop into a first-class reporter.

Everything Eileen knew about New York came from the movies: Warner Baxter in *42nd Street*, the Empire State Building in *King Kong*. It really didn't seem to be the happiest place in the world. The pretty chorus girl from Allentown chasing her Broadway dream, Fay Wray falling for a giant gorilla—nobody seemed relaxed, and even the ape wound up beating his chest on a tall building. To stay alive in that jungle a woman needed toughness of mind, the sort of cockiness that Chubb possessed, and lots of luck.

Eileen spent New Year's 1934 in Cleveland. Shortly after the first of the year, three months before her twenty-second birthday, she boarded a Greyhound bus bound for New York and new opportunities. Ruth had gone east to build her career, but what could Eileen do? Not writing, not even reading, for she had never got the hang of enjoying books. She could type, and she could meet someone. Somewhere in that big city of possibilities must live a man just waiting for her. And if nothing worked out, she could always go home.

13

SCREWBALLS AND SCREWBOXES

A BLOOD-RED HEART, a single eyeball, a portable typewriter. That was how *Miss Lonelyhearts* looked when it appeared in bookstores the first week of April 1933. Priced at two dollars and dedicated to Nat's father, it was praised in an early *New York Times* review as a "hard, brilliant, and very funny" novel certain to be one of the popular and critical "hits of the year." With the sweet prospect of royalty checks burning a hole in his pocket, Nat had acted like any writer who's having a great big success: he rushed out to buy himself a new car.

Several weeks later, he heard unpleasant gossip about his publisher. If Liveright owed him money, he was warned, it would be a good idea to get it while he could. This tip made him nervous, but his book had already hit Macy's bestseller list and he decided to put it out of his head. The next week, under the headline LIVERIGHT INC. PUT INTO BANKRUPTCY, the *Times* reported trouble with some of the company's creditors, but Nat still could not believe it. Could a prestigious company, the home of Dreiser and O'Neill, be utterly ruined? Liveright's chief executive swiftly responded that bankruptcy was "news to us." It was a mistake, said Arthur Pell.

The press, meanwhile, continued to sing Nat's praises. *The New Yorker* was all abuzz over "the sheer brilliance of the writing," promising that Nat's "gift for fantastic metaphor . . . will have you so dazzled you won't be able to think of anyone else to compare him to." The reviewer was Robert Coates, a novelist and the magazine's art critic, who anointed Nat a rising star and *Miss Lonelyhearts* "a book you'll simply have to read." His novel was saluted by the influential *Saturday Review of Literature* ("brilliant") and by the *Nation* ("exceptional"). One critic pointed out a resemblance to James Thurber's *New Yorker* cartoons. From the *New Republic*, on the other hand, came a notice slamming it as a repugnant psychodrama "patched together by lovelorn letters quite horrible enough to be actual facsimiles." All in all, though, the book brought forth "a really swell press," Nat thought proudly. So swell that Scotty, who had been as close to the writing of the book as anyone, concluded that Pep was "made."

The reviews were still coming in when Liveright filed for bankruptcy protection. Just when Nat had made his name, as he was conjuring the sale of fifteen thousand copies and his farewell to the Sutton, he learned that Arthur Pell had not paid his office staff in weeks; salesmen had walked out, and creditors were lined up to take legal action.

Horace Liveright was the third Jew to enter the book business, after Alfred Knopf and Ben Huebsch. Unafraid of the new and daring, he shoved aside fusty, nineteenth-century patricians like Charles Scribner's Sons to embrace writers they wouldn't touch. Horace's cocky personality set the tone for the house: the grand piano and private shower in his office, the daily cocktail party and the waiting room full of bootleggers. It was a "wacky joint," recalled Lillian Hellman, who once worked there as a manuscript reader, a job she described fondly as a "bag of plums." Over the years, from its brownstone on West Forty-eighth Street, Liveright launched T. S. Eliot, Theodore Dreiser, Sherwood Anderson, William Faulkner, Ernest Hemingway, Hart Crane, E. E. Cummings, Ezra Pound, Dorothy Parker, and Eugene O'Neill. But after investing heavily in the entertainment business and selling his Modern Library line of inexpensive classics to Bennett Cerf at Random House, Horace left the company with no cash reserves to weather hard times. Leadership had passed to Arthur Pell, the company treasurer, but he could not produce miracles.

For *Miss Lonelyhearts*, the end came quickly. Although Liveright printed 2,200 copies, only 800 had been shipped to bookstores. The remaining 1,400 remained in possession of the Van Rees Press, which refused to make deliveries until it was paid. Confusing matters, Liveright's author contracts contained no bankruptcy clauses providing for reversion of rights, so Nat's hands were tied. In a note to a friend, he admitted being "about half crazy." It looked as if "the book will go dead before I can get a release. I'm really heart-broken." His nightmarish situation attracted media attention. "Pity the poor author," wrote the *Hollywood Reporter*. "Take the case of Nathanael West, who has just written a best seller that he can't sell. It's that grand book MISS LONELYHEARTS and anyone who owns a copy has what practically amounts to a collector's item."

Nat needed help, not pity, and again his relatives came through. Cousin Sidney Jarcho, an attorney, arranged for the Liveright bankruptcy trustees to release the rights and assign the copyright to Nat for the sum of one dollar. Maxim Lieber then took the novel to Harcourt, Brace & Co., Nat signed a contract on May 26, and Harcourt purchased the plates on June 6. *Miss Lonelyhearts* was released under the new imprint almost at once.

Harcourt, Brace was a top-flight house, whose lists throughout the twenties had been studded with both serious books (the works of Carl Jung and John Maynard Keynes) and popular bestsellers like Sinclair Lewis's *Main Street*. To a great degree, its reputation for publishing quality fiction rested on Lewis, a heavy hitter who in 1930 had become the first American to win the Nobel Prize in Literature. At Harcourt, *Miss Lonelyhearts* was assigned to Charles A. Pearce (coincidentally, Josie Herbst's editor). Cap Pearce, only twenty-six, had worked for the company four years. Having demonstrated a flair for both the business and editorial ends, he was earmarked as a brainy kid destined to go places. He also happened to be a fastidious dresser, sporting Brooks Brothers suits. Even so, none of this was much consolation to Nat.

Beginning a letter to Josie with the words "A long story and a terrible one," he listed the particulars of his plight as if filing an accident report, citing book sales, legal strategies, and "swell offers" from Knopf and Harrison Smith. In fact, he was panicked. By the time Harcourt took over, only a few weeks had passed, but those hectic weeks were critical. Momentum lost, the title never got a toehold in stores and sales never materialized.

Scotty, whose novel *The Water Wheel* had just come out to unkind reviews and a "good quick burial," learned of Nat's woes from mutual friends. "If a heart can be broken, broken his was," Scotty thought.

Aside from besieging his writer friends with requests for blurbs or reviews, Nat continued to hustle publicity for *Miss Lonelyhearts*, but this was not going smoothly. Unable to decide on his audience, he felt obliged to lard his pronouncements with whatever he thought people wanted to hear. This meant wavering between pegging the novel as entertainment and pushing it as serious, edifying literature. He was angered by the *New York Evening Post's* pan, which said that he wrote with "his head in a sewer," but the sharpest knife of all belonged to the *Los Angeles Times*, which, detecting the gay subtext, called the story "dull and dirty" and mauled its hero as "a person of indeterminate sex."

Because religion and philosophy generally commanded respect, he decided to promote his main character as a modern-day priest undergoing "a religious experience." One of the sources he cited for the book's psychology was William James's *The Varieties of Religious Experience*. But these snippets of literary high-mindedness, afterthoughts designed to impress cultured friends like Edmund Wilson, were not only misleading but quite a bit different from his real sources.

To his alarm, one of those sources—the author of an original Susan Chester letter—danced out of nowhere like a malicious family ghost. This reader, displeased to find one of her personal letters in a novel, warned of her intention to sue. When a second woman fired off a similar objection, the International News Service broke the story to papers all over the country. WOMEN THREATEN TO SUE LOVE-LORN LETTERS AUTHOR. Eventually, although the story was good publicity for the book, Nat managed to put a stop to it by insisting that the complaints lacked merit because the letters were products of his imagination.

By this point it was easy to forget that the *Brooklyn Times* letters were written by real people. A shameless borrower of other writers' work, he was inclined to do minimal, and sometimes no, paraphrasing.

From the original letter to Susan Chester: *"Susan, don't think I am broad shouldered. But that is just the way I feel about life and me."*

In Nat's retelling: *"Dear Miss Lonelyhearts don't think I am broad shouldered but that is the way I feel about life and me I mean."*

Never would he disclose the novel's true inspiration, and so the identity of Quentin Reynolds, known within his family, would remain concealed. In revisionist explanations to Josie Herbst and others, he suggested that some of the letter writers might be modeled on guests at Kenmore Hall, no-account deadbeats whose harrowing stories had stirred his sympathy. Considering the fun-loving, after-work crowds of junior executives and bachelor girls splashing in the Kenmore Hall pool, this was quite an outrageous stretch.

There was nothing funny about the fate of *Miss Lonelyhearts*, which had flopped because of circumstances beyond his control. When it came to human nature, he always assumed the worst. "People like to see people take a fall," he figured. It was the reason we laugh at "the banana-peel. The mud-hole. Laurel and Hardy." The Liveright bankruptcy was a cosmic banana peel.

Nat found some solace in an unexpected development. Four movie studios—Universal, Paramount, MGM, and Twentieth Century—wanted to option rights to *Miss Lonelyhearts*. At the same time, he somehow came to the attention of a Hollywood producer, Samuel Goldwyn, who was hoping to make a star out of a Russian beauty named Anna Sten. Seeking a suitable story to launch her American debut, the famously uneducated Goldwyn first selected *The Brothers Karamazov*, but after failing to obtain the rights he decided on another classic, Zola's *Nana*. While continuing to scout properties for Sten, he approached Nat with a three-hundred-dollar advance to write an original synopsis. "Give me another *Morocco*, my boy," Goldwyn told him. Nat, who had no idea that a herd of writers had been working on the *Nana* shooting script for months, hatched a yarn bearing a vague resemblance to the children's horse story *Black Beauty*. "Don't worry about clichés," Sid advised. Remember to spice it up with "action, glamour," make it fantastic but don't go too far. Predictably, Nat's eight-page scenario failed to resemble *Morocco*.

But Nat had contracted the fatal movie-writing disease. No longer a nonentity, he had received a massive film-rights offer for his novel and faced the prospect of money galore. When Twentieth Century Pictures suggested three thousand dollars, a generous sum in 1933, Nat haggled for more. The studio agreed to his terms and shelled out four thousand dollars, which was more than Nat made at the Sutton in a year. He started counting the days until he could resign from the hotel and take up the simple life in Erwinna while writing another novel. Armed with his movie windfall, he paid a stack of bills from the Gotham Book Mart and the St. Regis Garage, settled a lawsuit with Brooks Brothers (Nat liked buying better than paying), even volunteered to loan the Perelmans money if they ever needed it, which was "god-damned sweet of him," Sid thought.

Every weekend that spring, eager to begin the farmhouse renovations, he drove his new Ford to Pennsylvania, usually with Laura for company. Even though the house was in terrible shape, he knew it would be "swell when I'm finished with it." Heading his list of gentrification projects was a white paint job for the exterior and the installation of a new bathroom. He bought a good stove and upgraded the Delco generator for lighting the house and pumping water. A new septic system would have to wait. Soon, he hoped, they could supplement their furniture with pieces thrift-shopped at the Sutton.

After the movie option of *Miss Lonelyhearts*, he was impatient to leave the Sutton. Even though the Goldwyn job had fizzled, he had grown obsessive about writing for the pictures. Everybody knew there were no free lunches and the Hollywood piñata had its price, but writers kept going to the Coast anyway, and Nat too was eager to try his luck. Twentieth Century would not be hiring him to write the screenplay for his novel—studios never trusted such assignments to a property's original author—but what about another studio? His newly acquired Hollywood agent at William Morris, James Geller, began pushing him as an up-and-coming writer.

Since early May, Sid had been in Hollywood, broke and looking for work after the financial failure of *Walk a Little Faster*. He was living with Lillian Hellman's ex-husband, the screenwriter Arthur Kober, and waiting for something to "pop," but felt almost ready to throw in the towel. He doubted if a babe in the woods like Nat would be happy in Hollywood, a place that made Sid froth at the mouth. It was nothing but "a gigantic rat-fuck," where holding a job was "a series of hysterical genuflexions and convulsive ass-kissings," and the loudest, most boorish person wins. In such an awful place, "gentility, manners, consideration, and worldliness are hindrances."

Gigantic rat-fuck! It sounded really wonderful to Nat. If Sid was to be believed, Hollywood was thick with characters in search of a comic novelist. It had been "a tough winter for this little group of artists and dreamers," he acknowledged to Josie. How bad could Hollywood be?

Very quickly, James Geller's efforts paid off. Columbia Pictures responded with a standard deal, a four-week contract including first-class traveling expenses on the Twentieth Century Limited to Chicago and the Santa Fe Super Chief to Los Angeles. Of course Nat knew that eastern writers were always hoping the four weeks would stretch into months if not years. In fact, this did not often happen, because writers knew nothing about the craft of screenwriting and its need for realistic dialogue, and few bothered to learn. Fearful of burning his bridges —and to pacify his mother—he decided to hold on to his job and take a leave of absence. In the first week of July, armed with a new Brooks Brothers valise, he happily trotted down the majestic red carpet for Twentieth Century Limited passengers at Grand Central.

At Union Station he was met by Sid, who drove him to the Knickerbocker, one of the big tourist hotels in downtown Hollywood. As they cruised along the palm-lined streets, Nat stared at the unfamiliar homes, the replicas of Samoan huts and Swiss chalets, the pretend Japanese temples and Rhine castles garnished with tar-paper turrets, each one more ridiculous than the next. The world-famous movie city looked remarkably like an architectural amusement park, not at all what he had expected—in fact, it brought back memories of summers at the Jersey Shore. It was like driving through "a desert got up to look like Asbury Park." On that July morning, the sky was perfectly blue, the air quivering with the smell of jasmine and orange blossoms, the heat swaddling him in a narcotic fog. In self-defense, he was obliged to purchase a pair of strong sunglasses.

Friday, July 7, he presented himself at 1438 North Gower Street, the headquarters of Columbia Pictures. Founded in 1920 by Harry and Jack Cohn, the company was originally called CBC Film Sales but adopted a more dignified name after jokesters dubbed it Corned Beef and Cabbage. Although Gower Street once had been home to a fleet of fly-by-night operations grinding out low-budget Westerns—and continued to be known as Poverty Row—Columbia had become its success story. The studio was developing into a major player, although it still trailed MGM and Paramount.

Ten minutes after walking in, Nat had an office and an assignment. Very quickly he reported to Edmund Wilson that everything he'd heard about movie writing was "all wrong." In a paramilitary setting, squads of writers toiled nine hours a day, with a full day on Saturday. They sat in rows of cell-like offices, and every hour or so, more often if anybody stopped typing, a supervisor would poke his head in the door to find out how he was doing. There was no fooling around, no staring at the ceiling. Nat and his fellow writers were treated like factory workers.

A rookie, Nat was in over his head, but Sid had helped him prepare a list of technical terms. His first week was spent bluffing his way through one of the company's ideas, a story set in a beauty parlor. He furiously stitched together a treatment, an eleven-page synopsis describing the characters and scenes, and by the end of two weeks completed the first draft of a shooting script. It was amazing to discover himself capable of producing four thousand words a day under pressure. In his first screenplay, the heroine is a manicurist at the swank DuBarry salon, a temple of sensuality where customers sip cocktails to the accompaniment of a tango orchestra. Carole, a hard-boiled Katharine Hepburn type, can't stand rich, snotty big shots lording it over her. On a blind date, she falls for a simple working-class stiff, a chauffeur, a good guy named Stephen, but Stephen is actually a no-good guy because he's filthy rich and only pretending to be a chauffeur. From there, Nat fearlessly proceeded to pile on complications: white lies (Stephen's wife), whoppers (Stephen's promise to get a divorce), and finally catastrophic bad news (Carole's pregnancy). Determined to give the studio plenty of drama, Nat poured twists and turns into the script. In the end, *Beauty Parlor* contained enough questionable material to ensure it would never pass the censor, let alone be produced.

Meanwhile, after they had been separated for six weeks, Laura joined Sid, and the three of them rented a Mexican adobe–style house at 5734 Cazaux Drive in the Hollywood Hills. In the mornings, Laura would chauffeur Nat to Columbia and Sid to Paramount, where he had finally landed a berth on a Ginger Rogers comedy. After two years in the business, Sid was vocal in his loathing for the "misbegotten flea-pit" where movies were assembled like jigsaw puzzles and writers treated like conscripts in a glorified labor camp. He kept returning for the big lump of cash he could earn, enough in four or five weeks to support himself for months. In addition to his hatred of the Marx Brothers—"I am fucking sick and tired of my endless identification with these clowns"—he had little respect for the screenwriting trade and disliked the California lifestyle. He relentlessly vilified the studio executives as vulgar, ignorant hoodlums.

The hoodlums tickled Nat. In exchanging pleasantries, he feigned collegiality by singing out Yiddish words, whether he understood them or not, and went out of his way to be adaptable. Buddying up to Abe Lastfogel, the stone-faced head of William Morris's Hollywood office, he slyly remarked, "And the Lastfogel shall be Firstfogel?" To which "Uncle Abe" did not crack a smile. Still, the exotic surnames in a practically all-Jewish business continued to amuse him. While the picture business did not seem to be a place where a person like him could comfortably fit in, he had no trouble taking things in stride, turning a blind eye to practices that repelled Sid. The movie business was a lot like the hotel business, he insisted charitably.

When Nat and Sid returned from the grind each day, they spent

the evenings talking shop and gossiping. Around nine Nat began doz-
ing off, and by eleven he was usually in bed. It was disappointing to discover that the weather was sapping the strength out of him. No matter how religiously he wore smoked glasses, he developed atrocious
headaches that he attributed to sunshine and the smell of bougainvillea. Actually, Hollywood was a big letdown in many respects. There
was little to do except golf, tennis, and movies, and how much orange
juice could a person drink? One Sunday he went fishing and caught
a twenty-five-pound yellowtail, and another time, having joined the
newly organized Screen Writers Guild, he attended a union meeting.

After two weeks at the studio, he was given a chance to develop an
original screenplay. His second script, *The Return to the Soil*, was a retelling of the old country-mouse/city-mouse story, in which a farm boy
takes a bank job in the city. Years later, an unemployed widower, with
two grown children and no prospects, John Anderson has learned his
lesson and buys a rundown farm in Maine. As Nat was completing the
sixty-three-page script, picket lines had gone up outside the studio: the
sound union had walked out on strike. One morning, he was greeted
with overexcited strikers chanting "A writer!" and aiming a round of
"lip-farts" at him. When cameramen and electricians joined the walk-
out, the studio "closed up as tight as a cow's arse in fly time," he wrote
Josie. Columbia let him go on August 25, after submission of his third
draft, his employment having extended two weeks beyond the original
agreement.

He was in no hurry to leave Hollywood. His sister Hinda was visiting, and the kids were busy revising their play about Americans in
Paris, inspired by Beatrice Mathieu, which was scheduled to open on
Broadway in December. Nat wrote two stories about the movie business. In one, a punk kid two years out of Columbia College manages to
outsmart his boss, a cigar-chomping, bicarbonate-swilling studio shark.
The disgusting ease with which young Charlie Baer manipulates Eugene Klingspiel into doubling his writer's salary suggests he will likely
be running Gargantual Pictures one day. In the other yarn, an Eskimo
family is imported for a picture about Alaska, but refuses to go home af-

terward because they're crazy about Hollywood. The narrator has been given the dirty job of babysitting the four disgusting "pus-pockets," an assignment complicated when the father contracts the clap, which he transmits to his wife. Sid didn't like the stories, claiming they sounded too much like Ernest Hemingway. "Business Deal" would be accepted by *Americana* magazine; the unfinished "Three Eskimos" would be reworked and incorporated into a novel. Both stories sounded nothing at all like Hemingway.

Although full of ideas for another novel, the one he had already begun calling his Horatio Alger book, Nat could not help recognizing rich fodder in the movie colony, an archaeological dig of exhibitionists and crackpots. The garishness of the place enchanted him. What was it about Hollywood that attracted so many "screwballs and screwboxes," he wondered. Collecting a gang of these cartoonish creatures and transporting them by yacht to an island in the South Pacific could form the premise for a very funny novel. His emphasis on prostitutes, thieves, dwarfs, and particularly homosexuals made Josie Herbst uncomfortable, because within a few years her emotional and sexual relationships would be exclusively with women. She would remember one of the freaks as being "a horrible great big lesbian. Every time he talked about lesbians or homosexuals I was scared."

As a newcomer in July, Nat had complained that Southern California was boring. "Phooey on Cal," he told Josie. But he had changed his mind by September. Los Angeles deserved more careful examination.

14

SHIRTSLEEVES
TO SHIRTSLEEVES

I N THE HEAT and dust of September, the woods on Geigel Hill crackled and the amber pastures dried to a duncolored brown. Cool nights in his stone house, Nat planned a new post-hotel life of tranquillity as he awaited October's frost. He was going to have a hunting dog and a shotgun, because this was Pennsylvania, where people went out and killed things to eat. He would be a gentleman farmer who worked on his books and tended his home and hearth. With these seductive thoughts in mind, he had taken the first step before leaving the Coast when, high on writerly exhilaration, he had mailed his resignation to the hotel. As he told Josie Herbst, he was a bit nervous because dollars did not grow on trees, but he was "going to take a chance."

By quitting his job, he raised the blood pressure of his entire family, including his devoted benefactor, Morris Jarcho, who warned that he was making a terrible mistake. Everyone issued predictions of disaster. Untroubled, Nat bought a dog.

He had finally been noticed as a writer, and *Miss Lonelyhearts* continued to gain attention. Just opening on September 30 was Irving Berlin and Moss Hart's new musical revue, *As Thousands Cheer*, with Marilyn Miller and great songs like "Heat Wave" and "Easter Parade." For one of the sketches, inspired by *Miss Lonelyhearts*, Berlin had composed a splendid ballad, "Lonely Heart." It was a nice surprise for Nat, who hoped the song would put the book in the spotlight and result in big sales. (It didn't.) Still, his confidence high, he felt eager to move ahead on his new novel.

In 1933, no telephone lines reached Geigel Hill Road, because residents refused to pay for rigging up poles, but emergency communications did manage to get through. The only way to contact Nat quickly was by telegram, which had to be phoned to the American Stores grocery in Frenchtown, where the butcher wrote down messages and his assistant delivered them by bicycle. It was an efficient system for people like Maxim Lieber and Cap Pearce, and of course there was regular mail service for those who did not believe in wasting money on telegrams.

For a few months, Nat settled down on Eight Ball Farm with his writing muse and his new white pointer, named Danny, but the quiet didn't last. After his break with the Sutton, another arrangement had to be made for his mother. He did not want her living with him, and, mercifully, she was not overly fond of the rural lifestyle. The Embassy Hotel, on Broadway and Seventieth Street, became a base of operations that allowed frequent visitations to the farm, where she enjoyed ministering to her unemployed son's care and feeding. The huge platters of fried foods appearing on the table were expected to be eaten, and Nat did his best to cooperate. Whenever he happened to be away from the house, he would check his watch to make sure of not being late for meals. In Sid's repertoire of biting comments on his mother-in-law, he needled her as a tiresome busybody who was always "baking, frying, and frying." Being overloved and overfed by a compulsive fryer wrought so much havoc with Nat's weight that he had to go on a diet.

Backward Erwinna presented certain inconveniences for Anna, who was accustomed to modern equipment and grumbled about the ancient kitchen sink, which kept stopping up. But she quickly grew fond of Nat's new dog—all the Weinsteins were ardent dog lovers— while fussing about Danny's hair on the sofa. She was decidedly less thrilled with Josie, whose neighborly visits were liable to set her teeth on edge. Whenever Josie defended Nat's decision to quit the hotel, Anna grew testy and contradicted her at every turn.

"How's he going to eat?" said Anna, hands folded, rocking in her chair.

Josie ventured that she ought to take pride in her son. He was an uncommonly gifted writer.

But Anna was determined to hear nothing she said. "How's he going to eat," she stonily repeated. At the Sutton he had been a person of consequence, and now he was stoking the furnace and hauling out ashes. Did she raise her son to be a janitor?

When, years afterward, Josie attempted to describe Nat in a scabrous roman à clef that spilled the beans on his whole family, she didn't mince words. Anna was a kind of Lewis Carroll character from *Through the Looking Glass*: "A large White Queen with a sweet tooth who longed to stuff her adored boy into acquiescence, but acquiescence for what?" She was a certain kind of mother: uninformed, opinionated, desperate to control an adored boy's life. In her possessiveness, she was guilty of loving her son "too much to take another woman's estimate of him."

Nat felt comfortable sharing the farm with the kids, who would camp there whenever they were not in Hollywood or at their New York apartment. As they continued to make improvements, Nat came up with a plan for damming up the brook. It would be nice to have a swimming pool. The Perelmans were agreeable, the natives skeptical but unprepared to offer advice to city slickers. After weeks of chopping trees for logs, the project was finished and they waited for the lake to fill up. Much to their dismay, a drought came along and turned the spot into a bed of slime. Forced to admit failure, Nat and Sid demolished the dam. A neighbor on Geigel Hill had been watching the operation from start to finish. "Coulda told you it wouldn't hold water," he said.

"Why didn't you?" Sid demanded.

"You never asked me," the man answered.

• • •

In the midst of his agony over the Liveright bankruptcy, Nat had read Josie's new novel, *Pity Is Not Enough*. The first title in a planned trilogy, it was set in the South after the Civil War, involving a carpetbagger who makes and loses a fortune and the effect on several generations of his family. But it was autobiographical as well; Josie wove in the lives of her own family. The theme was an American success story gone wrong, the insubstantiality of the famous so-called work ethic. What a coincidence, Nat wrote Josie, because she was telling "the story that I intended to do in my new book. The breakdown of the American Success Dream." It was a lie that hard work and discipline always led to a happy ending, he said.

The resemblance between the two books was hardly a coincidence. When they had first met in the fall of 1932, she was completing the novel and he had heard plenty about it since. Certainly the plot was familiar to him, just as her characters and their lives crystallized ideas of his own. There would be no duplication between the books, he reassured her, because his was a comedy. "I'm doing it satirically of course." He could hardly wait to talk to her. "I'm re-writing the Horatio Alger myths—from Barge Boy to President, or from Shirt Sleeves to Shirt Sleeves in One Generation." She should think of it as the hard-luck version of the American Dream hocus-pocus.

Shirtsleeves to shirtsleeves, words he connected with his father, brought back the bitter thoughts running through his head as he had spaded clumps of earth on his father's coffin at Mount Zion Cemetery. Since then, those morbid words had continued to resonate, and he would sometimes repeat them to certain friends as a sorrowful comment on the eventual futility of his father's life. What was Max—and indeed what were all the uncles—if not Horatio Alger characters, avid believers in the gospel that hard work was a sure thing, always promising prosperity. And yet the American fairy tale had tricked Max. Whose fault was that? He was thinking of titling his new novel *America, America*. It could just as easily have been called *The Max Weinstein Story*. Before he had a title, the new project was referred to as "my Horatio Alger book," shorthand that required no explanation. In the end, Nat called his story *A Cool Million*.

A homosexual Unitarian minister, Horatio Alger, Jr., lost his pulpit after charges of "the abominable and revolting crime of unnatural familiarity with *boys*," according to his Brewster, Massachusetts, church committee. At the age of thirty-four he turned to writing inspirational novels, most of them for and about young males, on the subject of success and how to get it. Some writers produce one good book; Alger managed more than a hundred bad ones, but they brought him fame. As a child, Nat had torn through stacks of them before moving on to Dostoyevsky and Tolstoy. The male Cinderella stories had simple heroes, threats of foreclosed mortgages, adventures in depraved cities like New York, and often a therapeutic journey to the American West. Poor, dumb boys always win by means of hard work and down-home determination — good old luck and pluck — especially with the patronage of a protective older man. In Alger's literary terrain, there are no unhappy endings. Repackaging Alger's best-selling recipe, Nat added a few flourishes of his own: sex and violence, sick jokes, and disgusting subplots. And because happy ends made him gag, he designed a gruesome fate for his hero.

Rigging up a work space in the piggery, he began feverish, five-hour daily sessions. With previous books it took a week of laborious meandering to complete one page, but no more. He wrote in pencil as fast as he could in hopes of getting through a first draft by early November. Without his hotel salary, he could not afford to dawdle and a new book had to be sold quickly. He had an option clause with Harcourt, agreeing to submit his next work for consideration before it was offered to other publishers.

The new book surpassed *Miss Lonelyhearts*, he assured Max Lieber; he was starting a second draft right away and expected to submit a completed manuscript to Harcourt by December 1. When this deadline proved impossible, Cap Pearce agreed to settle for the first half plus a synopsis of the remainder, and promised a quick decision. Scrambling to knock out the second portion before the holidays, Nat confidently told his friends that the novel was scheduled for Harcourt's spring list.

A Cool Million is the story of a teenage boy living with his mother in the Vermont village of Ottsville, a naive youth who will set off for the metropolis to make a fortune and save the family homestead from foreclosure. In the course of his adventures, Lemuel Pitkin encounters Nathan "Shagpoke" Whipple, the corrupt ex-president of the United States and likely a pedophile, who becomes his mentor; the probably gay, suspiciously Jewish New York decorator Asa Goldstein; and also Betty Prail, Lem's Ottsville sweetheart, a perky Little Red Riding Hood who spends most of the book flat on her back after abduction by white slavers. Jailed, robbed, and repeatedly tricked, Lem fends off a sodomy attack, but worse is yet to come. In the closing chapter, Lem meets a startling end. "His teeth were pulled out. His eye was gouged from his head. His thumb was removed. His scalp was torn away. His leg was cut off. And, finally, he was shot through the heart." After being dismantled, he is declared a martyr by the fascist National Revolutionary Party.

Detouring from his main theme of how bad things can befall cute young boys, Nat exhibited a gallery of unwholesome characters whose likes would not be seen again until the late 1960s with the pyrotechnics of Monty Python's Flying Circus and its glorious dead parrots, silly walks, and the invincible dismembered Black Knight ("I'll bite your legs off!"). One of Nat's funniest inventions is a formidable entrepreneur named Wu Fong, a graduate of Yale University (Shanghai branch) who captures the true spirit of American enterprise. With illegal labor recruited from white slavers, Wu Fong successfully revolutionizes the sexual services business by launching a luxury brothel named "House of All Nations," featuring choice merchandise from all over the world. When profits drop off after the Crash and Wu Fong must hustle to find a new business model, he abandons the global supermarket in favor of "Buy American." He introduces fantasy sex play, pairing hedonism with patriotism to create multiple tableaux: "Log Cabin Pioneer," "Western Cattle Days," and "Victorian New York." In his "Old South" scenario, a luscious, hoopskirted Georgia peach, Alice Sweethorne—surrounded by sconces and chandeliers and exquisite pieces of old Sheraton—graciously serves her customers sow-belly grits and fine bourbon.

Wu Fong, overlooking no nook or cranny of the sex services market, satisfies his homosexual clientele with a selection of pretty boys and special rooms whose closets are fitted with peepholes for voyeurs. (In one of Lem's low points, Wu Fong sells him to an Indian maharajah who has ordered a "pithy thailer boy.")

With the Harcourt deadline closing in, pressed for time, Nat decided to salt the prose with bits of dialogue copied from Horatio Alger novels loaned to him by Josie Herbst. Probably he started out cherry-picking a few words or sentences here and there from *Andy Grant's Pluck*, but before long he went on to root around in other Alger books. It didn't matter which one he picked up because they were all much alike. Nobody would be likely to notice. Using Alger's gooey speeches made it possible to take shortcuts and add a dash of authentic flavor. As Nat knew from writing *Miss Lonelyhearts*, colloquialisms spice up a narrative. In both novels, his plagiarism was hardly accidental, and definitely not unconscious, the lame excuses that plagiarists typically offer to explain how they happened to steal another writer's words. Neither was it a case of creatively using historical source materials in fiction, as some boldly insist is a novelist's right. Nat understood all too well what he was doing. Some years later, preparing a screen treatment of *A Cool Million*, his protagonist shrugs off cheating by declaring that "no one cared how you got your million as long as you had it . . . When a chance came along he . . . knew how to grab it," which was Nat's philosophy in a nutshell. Certainly he had nothing against poaching from Horatio Alger, any more than he thought twice about appropriating Nathan Weinstein's grades at Tufts. From where he sat, it was more important to make Harcourt's spring list than to worry about Alger's piteous prose, vomited into the national psyche for the last seventy-five years.

While plagiarism is actionable in civil law, common law does not treat unauthorized use as a criminal offense; still, this is nothing that a writer would want known. In Nat's case, the uncredited passages went undetected by agents and editors, reviewers and readers. It would be thirty years before a pair of professors at State University College of New York at Fredonia, accidentally catching similarities between *A Cool Million* and *Andy Grant's Pluck*, succeeded in identifying a fair number of plagiarized passages.

From *Andy Grant's Pluck*:	From *A Cool Million*:
"Come in, Grant, and have some whiskey," he said.	"Come on in," he said, "and have a whiskey."
"Thank you, but I don't care for whiskey."	"Thank you," said our hero, "but I don't care for whiskey."
"Perhaps you would prefer beer?"	"Perhaps you prefer beer?"
"I don't care to drink anything, thank you."	"I don't care to drink anything, thank you."
"You don't mean to say you're a temperance crank."	"You don't mean to say you're a temperance crank."
"Yes, I think I am."	"Yes, I think I am."

Further investigation revealed plagiarism from *Joe's Luck*:

From *Joe's Luck*:	From *A Cool Million*:
"Sho! How many teachers did you shoot when you was a boy?"	"My," said Mr. Whipple with a smile. "How many teachers did you shoot when you were a boy?"
"Only one. The rest heard of it and never dared touch me."	"Only one. The rest heard of it and never dared touch me."

All told, roughly 20 percent of *A Cool Million* was written by Alger. Sometimes Nat reworked his prose, some passages he transported word for word, and still other text was in all likelihood pinched from works not yet identified, perhaps by Bret Harte. Most of the plagiarized material seems to appear in the final chapters, the very section in which the writing is noticeably flat. On the other hand, if 20 percent is Alger, 80 percent is Nat at his most uninhibited, reeling off the wonderful gallows humor that he liked to call his "particular kind of joking." Certainly the novel would have benefited from more West, less Alger.

The movie version of *Miss Lonelyhearts* came out on December 13, opening in New York at the Rivoli Theater, accompanied by a Disney cartoon, *Santa's Workshop*. For a writer it was always exhilarating to collect movie money, even though there were no guarantees the repackaged property would ever reach the screen. Getting a book actually filmed by a major studio ranked as massive good luck, but even more prestigious was to see your picture open during the holidays at one of New York's grand movie palaces. Regardless, had Nat not been distracted by a tight deadline, he might have reasonably felt like killing himself. The film was a disaster bearing almost no resemblance to his novel.

Partly to blame for the catastrophe was a piece of bad luck. In August the novel had come to the attention of *Harrison's Reports*, a movie industry newsletter that advised theaters of forthcoming releases. A conservative watchdog, the newsletter did not hesitate to describe *Miss Lonelyhearts* as a tasteless, twisted book unsuitable for a film adaptation. It stank of "degeneracy" and should never have been published in the first place. "It cannot be defended on the grounds of art; it has none; it is just low and vulgar, put out undoubtedly to appeal to moronic natures."

In general Nat had nothing against appealing to morons and degenerates, but fearing the newsletter might hurt business, he demanded that Harcourt sue *Harrison's*. Cap Pearce told him there had been too few sales for the report to cause damage, but he would use it to generate publicity. The publisher obligingly put out a press release quoting critics who had praised the book, but this did little to stimulate sales. Josie sadly noted it had sunk "almost as soundlessly as a stone into water," a fate shared by her latest novel.

There was good reason to be apprehensive. In his next report, editor E. G. Harrison turned up the heat. He scalded *Miss Lonelyhearts* as beyond the bounds of decency, "the lowest, vilest, filthiest book that I have ever read." Exhibitors were urged to boycott the movie unless the offensive book was "discarded in its entirety and a brand new story written around the title." And this is exactly what happened. Thoroughly bullied, Twentieth Century further diluted a story that had already been hacked to death, the characters renamed, the plot practically unrecognizable except for the fact that it took place in a newspaper office. Studio boss Darryl Zanuck took special care to explain that he had bought Nat's book only for rights to the title, but even that found its way to the cutting room floor.

The leading role in *Advice to the Lovelorn* was acted by Lee Tracy, a popular comedian who had played the crack reporter Hildy Johnson in *The Front Page* and since then been typecast in movies as a stereotypical fast-talking newsman. Revamped, the film was half light comedy, half melodrama about an ace Los Angeles reporter demoted to the agony column who subsequently gets mixed up with a bunch of evil drug manufacturers and inadvertently kills his mother, but marries happily in the end. The screenwriter, an acquaintance of Sid's, was a veteran British-born writer, Leonard Praskins, whom Sid mocked as "a shell who spits out scenarios." Faced with the tricky task of transferring *Miss Lonelyhearts* to the screen, Praskins took the path of least resistance and simply cut and pasted the Hildy Johnson character onto *Miss Lonelyhearts*'s title character.

Adaptations bearing little resemblance to their literary sources were not unusual. Still, Nat felt heartsick over the casual mutilation of his work. The only blessing was that *Advice to the Lovelorn* swiftly disappeared from movie houses and people's memories as well. At the same time, the Paramount film Sid had worked on during the summer was showing a few blocks away. *Sitting Pretty*, made-to-order for the holiday, was a comedy starring Ginger Rogers and Jack Oakie, memorable for its hit song "Did You Ever See a Dream Walking?" Not surprisingly, it was a huge box-office success. Sid exhibited his customary indifference. Both his and Laura's attention was focused elsewhere: their first play, *All Good Americans*, had just arrived on Broadway a few days earlier. It was a nostalgic biography of their dear friend Beatrice

Mathieu and her Lost Generation circle of expatriates, drinking and acting rowdy on the Left Bank in the twenties, a period that seemed as distant as King Tut and the pyramids. It was also a museum piece that bored first-nighters, audience and critics alike (one review called it "a second-rate Barry comedy"). Notwithstanding its Broadway failure, the play would be an important steppingstone for Sid and Laura because it established them as collaborators and led to jobs as a husband-and-wife screenwriting team.

A cold snap in the first week of February sent temperatures plummeting to fifteen degrees below zero. Toasty in the farmhouse, with a log fire in his baronial stone fireplace, Nat awaited word from Cap Pearce, but the decision sent him into a tailspin. To his disbelief, Pearce said that Harcourt was passing on *A Cool Million* for financial reasons. No apology accompanied the rejection. It was cut-and-dried, business as usual. Nat believed that he understood how publishing worked. Wasn't it a company's policy to publish all of an author's work, not just books that might sell?

"I can't recall liking the book or disliking it," Pearce said later. "It wasn't an easy time to get a book accepted." In fact, it was one of the worst years publishing had known, but the real problem lay elsewhere. Compared to *Miss Lonelyhearts*, *A Cool Million* was disappointing, blackly funny but also hardly memorable. Pearce had counted West as a large talent, but his future now appeared "uncertain." Maybe *Miss Lonelyhearts* was a fluke. Pearce's judgment about fiction was normally keen; very shortly afterward he bought an impressive first novel, a work in progress by a *New Yorker* short story writer, an Irishman seen around town, usually drunk and unshaved, with the likes of Dorothy Parker and Robert Benchley. When *Appointment in Samarra* was published in August, stores could scarcely keep John O'Hara's book in stock.

Nat felt shell-shocked. For a year he had been calling himself a writer. And now? What would his mother say?

For two nerve-racking months, Nat bit his nails, until Maxim Lieber placed the manuscript with Covici-Friede. Founded by Pascal Covici, originally a Chicago bookseller and publisher, and former Liveright vice president Donald Friede, the company had been in existence less than two years when the Depression struck and sent it limping toward bankruptcy. Aside from a few serious titles (Radclyffe Hall's banned lesbian novel *The Well of Loneliness*, the plays of Clifford Odets, Jack Conroy's proletarian fiction), its most profitable book was a sex manual, *Ideal Marriage*. By 1934, the publisher was doing whatever it could to survive. At one point, to publicize *Speakeasy Girl*, a potboiler efficiently produced in six weeks, it had distributed a thousand aluminum cocktail shakers to book buyers. As houses went, Covici-Friede was marginal, but Nat, jittery and disillusioned, felt grateful for any sale at all.

It took Covici-Friede only ninety days to release the book. The jacket illustration, copied from Horatio Alger's 1900 novel *Adrift in New York*, shows a boy wearing a coonskin cap and toting a squirrel rifle, and on the back appears an author biography (presumably supplied by Nat) claiming he was born in 1904, attended a New England prep school, and spent two years in Paris. With the addition of a subtitle ("The Dismantling of Lemuel Pitkin"), a dedication (to Sid), and an epigraph made up like an old adage ("John D. Rockefeller would give a cool million to have a stomach like yours"), the first edition of three thousand copies was ready for release on June 19, 1934. That night, Covici-Friede hosted a boozy publication party, the kind that had become stylish since the repeal of Prohibition in December. In keeping with the book's ill-starred history, the author could not be present. A storm hammering Bucks County the previous night had knocked an oak tree onto his porch.

Maxim Lieber sold the film rights to Columbia, no small accomplishment with a property whose hero winds up dead and dismembered. That Nat's Horatio Alger story was obviously unsuitable was acknowledged by Columbia's story department, which summed up the theme as "honesty will buy you pain and disgrace." Credited by the *Nation* as "bitterly hilarious," and by the *New Republic* as "unkindly fun," the novel was nonetheless measured, usually poorly, against *Miss*

Lonelyhearts. Some critics recognized the Horatio Alger spoof (but not the plagiarism), while others compared Lem Pitkin to Candide.

The book failed to excite readers and wound up remaindered for twenty-five cents the following year. Nat was still feeling bitter when, five years later, he tried to get it reissued in an inexpensive paper edition. Bad timing had accounted for the book's sickly sales, he thought. At the time, however, he blamed the book's failure on Covici-Friede, which had evidently dropped the ball. From Hollywood, Sid reported rumors that they owed Gene Fowler eleven thousand dollars for a biography published three years earlier. He warned that the company was "famous for being rascals." Covici-Friede was struggling to stay afloat. Promising sales of *Speakeasy Girl* encouraged the house to assembly-line publish similar bodice rippers with provocative titles—*Bachelor's Wife, Boy Crazy, Alimony Jail*—fiction that found its audience and fared considerably better than *A Cool Million.*

As Nat fumed about being victimized, he continued to pray for royalty checks, commonly referred to by the family as "Covici gelt." In a moment of masochism, he decided to tally up his previous earnings from writing and realized he was "absolutely unable to make even the beginning of a living." At the end of three years and two books (*Balso* and *Miss Lonelyhearts*), he had eked out $780.

The summer of 1934, while Sid was on the Coast looking for work, Laura lived at the farm and waited to be sent for. She was miserable.

When he had work, Sid's weekly salary had climbed to $600, about twenty times that of an average wage earner. While he sympathized with Laura's boredom, there was no point wasting $142 on her train fare if he failed to get anything and had to come back. Practically every day he wrote long letters describing the frustrations of obtaining an assignment, along with sanitized accounts of how and with whom he passed his evenings. After five years of marriage, Sid did not mind spending weeks or even months apart from his spouse. During these separations, he was involved with a variety of women. After he and Dashiell Hammett ran into each other at the Brown Derby one night in 1931, they had adjourned to Hammett's house. Afterward, Dash wrote Lillian Hellman how he "gave him some Bourbon, and wound up by doing a little pimping for him." Sid's infidelities would not have surprised Laura, whose reaction was resignation. She was heard to talk matter-of-factly about having "lost her husband" in Hollywood.

If Sid's social life was "dull as old paint," as he assured Laura, being cooped up on the farm was worse. A Geigel Hill neighbor piloted her around the county, but she was such a tedious woman that Laura never wanted to lay eyes on her again, she told Sid. His encouragement to write him "even when you have nothing to write about" did little to alleviate her loneliness. She made no effort to seek out new friends, nor did she have anything in common with neighbors like Josie. With nothing to do, she became obsessive about her schnauzers, Gurke and Asta, took up collecting bric-a-brac (tiny china dogs and cats), and enjoyed occasional visits from her mother and her pregnant sister. Mainly she clung to her brother for solace.

Watching the Weinstein family drama fascinated Josie, and the person of most interest out of the entire clan was the somnolent Laura. Paying a social call one summer day, Josie burst into the cool, shadowy parlor to find Nat and Laura in facing chairs listening dreamily to a Mozart recording. Between them, on a glass table, were placed two untouched drinks and a plate of two carefully iced cupcakes. As it was clearly a special occasion of some kind, she quickly excused herself. But she had felt awkward, as if she had drifted into a watercolor depicting a tender moment shared by intimates. The Arcadian scene—the perfect cupcakes against Laura's dainty white dress and green snakeskin slippers, the watery light bathing the room—would stick in her memory long afterward.

In Tinicum Township, people did not know what to make of Nat. For one thing, his driving alarmed them, and when he barreled down River Road toward New Hope, motorists with squeamish stomachs hugged the shoulder until he had passed. His relationship with the Perelmans set the tongues of gossipmongers wagging. Nat and the kids were perceived by some locals as more a triangle than a family. As recently as the 1980s denizens of Tinicum Township continued to trade gossip about incest, completely undeterred by lack of evidence.

That summer a visitor caught a glimpse of Nat, playing with his new hound puppy, chatting about hunting and dog training, joking about writing a book to be titled *The Louse in the Fright*. He appeared totally relaxed, a man without a care in the world. In fact, his situation was getting dire because cash was dribbling out, but no Covici gelt flowed in. Desperate, he instructed Maxim Lieber to submit several of his short stories, including "Tibetan Night," a spoof of the best-selling Shangri-la novel *Lost Horizon*. Prior to Sid's departure for the Coast, they had begun collaborating on *Even Stephen*, a play satirizing book publishing, about a female novelist who visits a New England women's college (like Pembroke) in search of material for an exposé of flaming youth. Sid had "a lot of faith" in it, and as he was savvy in these matters, Nat assumed there would be no trouble interesting a producer.

Another idea was to grab free money, and in September he applied for a fellowship from the John Simon Guggenheim Memorial Foundation, which was giving away grants worth two thousand dollars to scholars and artists. It was like a bank heist with none of the risks. In the literature category, the grants always went to so-called serious writers. Did *Miss Lonelyhearts* qualify as a literary work? Nat hoped so, despite the humiliation of *Advice to the Lovelorn*. Encouraged by Edmund Wilson and Josie, both of whom were themselves intending to apply, he outlined in a one-page proposal a novel about "a young man of my generation" who had come of age in the boom years but faced the real world—"the discovery of economics"—during the Depression. The committee might think of it as A *Portrait of the Artist as a Young Man* meets *The Education of Henry Adams*, he suggested. For the requested references, he approached an assortment of local intellectual heavyweights—Wilson, Malcolm Cowley, and George S. Kaufman— all of whom supplied suitably thoughtful tributes, including Wilson's assurance that the only word for *Miss Lonelyhearts* was *extraordinary*.

Nat wanted someone with more star power, though, and decided to ask F. Scott Fitzgerald, whose new novel, *Tender Is the Night*, had been published that spring. Presumably, Fitzgerald admired *Miss Lonely-hearts*, because he had mentioned Nat as a writer worth watching in his introduction to a Modern Library edition of *The Great Gatsby*. With an apology for imposition, Nat humbly presented himself as a naif who knew "very few people" and practically nobody whose name would carry weight with the Guggenheim committee. If Fitzgerald would agree to write a letter of recommendation, it would make him "very happy." Fitzgerald dragged his feet for several weeks before sending the foundation a hemming-and-hawing letter that included his personal gripe about its misguided tendency to emphasize poetry. He finally complimented Nat as "a potential leader in the field of prose fiction." It was a lukewarm recommendation, but beggars can't be choosers.

One by one, his undertakings seemed to come apart: *A Cool Million* failed to find readers, his short stories found no publishers, nobody was interested in *Even Stephen*, and his Guggenheim application would prove to be a waste of time. For a few months he had fooled himself into believing he was famous, but at this juncture, his high-flying career had fallen back to earth, dismantled as completely as Lem Pitkin's poor body.

A while back, Josie's husband had hiked over to visit with Nat and accidentally barged into "a family powwow." Crazy Anna and the materialistic Weinstein uncles, reported John Herrmann, were trying to push Nat back to his previous life in the hotel business, and from what John could tell, they were succeeding.

Then he was a fool, Josie exclaimed, and started to cry. Lots of writers ran out of money. He should show some gumption. Let him pare back—sell his car, mortgage the farm. (Nat would have found any such solution unacceptable.)

Those days, his demeanor seemed unusually depressed. Around Josie he was a changed person, glum, withdrawn, and for the first time they could think of little to say to each other. However, late one night he appeared at her door looking cheerful. His family had been there

all day, he said, formally summoned by his mother for the express purpose of bringing him to his senses. Being so good in business, he would
have no problem finding another hotel to manage. Of course they were
right. His life had gone off course, but if he had to live in a salaried jail,
it would be one of his own choosing.

Josie, silent, watched him chain-smoke as he insisted that family
pressure had made him see the light. It was Sid and his example that
suggested a sensible solution: a couple of those obscene Hollywood
paychecks would whip up a respectable nest egg and make him self-
sustaining. Moving to the Coast for a few months would replenish his
bank account, and then he would be back. The studios had become
a magnet for novelists and playwrights, including the most successful, who treated movies as personal cash cows. If Sid could take the
money and run—if Lily and Dash and Dottie Parker and John O'Hara
all could make a quick buck—so could he. See, he assured Josie, he
had "crossed the Rubicon." Movie writing wasn't the end of the world.

Josie had no use for Hollywood, which she believed to be a dangerous place for writers. Saddened, she struggled to hide her disapproval,
and finally replied, "Well, if that's the way it's to be, I'm glad to see you
take it on the chin." When the chips are down, it's better to make some
decision than none at all, she guessed. Still, she thought he was selling
out. But after all his determined talk, he continued to dally at the farm.
It was Sid who came to his rescue. From Hollywood, he began sending Nat spending money, thirty-five dollars every week, to cover his expenses and also give his mother ten dollars. If this wasn't humiliating
enough, his personal life had reached a new low.

For the past year his relations with women had been limited to
those he met on his periodic visits to the city, either his usual chippies
or impersonal encounters with people he sometimes brought back to
Erwinna. "What do you think of the new one?" he would say to Josie,
who was absorbed in her own marital problems. Talking to those bone-
headed women of his was impossible, she replied. They were all alike,
good-looking but boring. That didn't bother Nat. A meaningless frolic
suited him, because it could be easily ended.

Without thinking, he made the mistake of getting involved with a neighbor, like himself a gentrified New Yorker who had moved to the country in search of cheap real estate. Ten years his senior, she was convenient—and married—which, together, somehow convinced Nat the relationship would be safe. But she turned out to be not only possessive but indiscreet, bragging about the relationship to people in the village and arousing her husband's suspicions. Soon a scandal threatened when she began talking of divorce. In desperation, Nat attempted to ditch her by beating a hasty departure to New York and lying low in a Village hotel room (a short walk from the building in which Eileen and Ruth McKenney were about to rent an apartment, so close they might have passed on Eighth Street). Reestablishing contact with old friends, he joined Jim Farrell and other writers in picketing on behalf of a labor strike against Ohrbach's department store on East Fourteenth Street. Along with scores of picketers, he wound up arrested for disorderly conduct.

Sid, in the meantime, was continuing to disburse weekly checks. Nat told his sister that he appreciated the favor but the remittances were not really sufficient. Nor were they regular. (In fact, they were regular, but he had neglected to have his mail transferred to the Brevoort Hotel from Erwinna.) Sid blew his top to Laura: "AND FOR JESUS CHRIST'S SAKES AMEN I WANT AN ANSWER FROM HIM SO IF THE CHECKS DIDN'T ARRIVE I CAN STOP PAYMENT." As for increasing the amount, Nat would just owe him more. "What is he doing?" Sid scolded. Did he have any prospects?

None whatsoever. Worse, there was no telling when he would. And just as he deluded himself into believing the danger at the farm was over, his angry neighbor appeared at the Brevoort. In an emotional scene that soon got out of hand, he stood firm and managed to break off once and for all. This frightening experience accomplished something that his family had failed to do: it blasted him out of his rut. Short of throwing up barbed wire, living at Eight Ball Farm had become impossible for the time being. It was Hollywood or nothing.

In the spring he returned to Erwinna to collect his belongings and close up the house. Before driving back to the city, he swung along Upper Tinicum Church Road to say goodbye to Josie, alone after John began seeing another woman. The sight of the buoyant, sartorially obsessed young bachelor she knew of old brought a smile to Josie's lips.

"Watch out," she teased. "You may live to be one of the best dressed men in America."

As a man who had bungled his life in two states, Nat was impatient to make his getaway. The land of Mickey Mouse was bound to be better.

15

14 GAY STREET

GAY STREET WAS a crooked, dollhouse lane tucked away between Christopher and Waverly in the West Village. The building itself was tiny, a quaint, white-washed brick row house designed for the comfort of small human beings. In the winter of 1935, the landlord was determined to rent his basement apartment to the girls from Ohio for the exorbitant sum of forty-five dollars a month. It was, he swore, "the best value for your money you'll get in New York."

By the time Eileen and Ruth reached 14 Gay Street, they had been trudging around in the cold all day. Scarcity of apartments was not the problem. In practically any neighborhood of Manhattan could be found suitable one- or two-bedroom apartments for reasonable rents, but Ruth was determined to live in the Village. For decades the picturesque neighborhood had been popular with writers and painters, just like the Left Bank in Paris.

Edmond Martin, listing reasons why they should rent the apartment, insisted the place was a bargain sure to be snapped up by the next day. Take his word for it, they would find nothing comparable. But Eileen, fresh from Silsby Road, had her doubts. The place was a dump, a pitiful underground version of the peasant shanties that the likes of her great-grandfather Patrick Flinn had left behind a century earlier. The family in Cleveland would be horrified. Besides, calling it an apartment was a whimsy. The low-ceilinged room was a cellar re-built to resemble an apartment. Its only good feature was a handsome white fireplace. Otherwise, the pair of ratty daybeds, the built-in book-cases, the table and wooden folding chairs, the broken-down stove, looked terribly dilapidated. But Martin even had the gall to praise the taste of his wife, Ramee, who, he boasted, had personally supervised the décor. A Pullman kitchen contained dime-store dishes and flat-ware. In the bathroom, so cramped that only one person could squeeze in at a time, something disturbing was growing from the ceiling. The basement's two windows, below street level, revealed a parade of legs going by. Did people ever bend over and look in? Certainly not, Mar-tin told them; no such thing ever happened.

Martin suddenly pointed them down a hallway and out a rear door. Behind the house, a rubble of tangled brown branches and rusty cans filled a small triangular yard that he called a private garden for the ex-clusive use of his tenants. In summer, blue jays and mourning doves nested in the pear and sycamore trees. They could step outside and sunbathe in the middle of Manhattan, sip cocktails on the patio, sleep under the twinkling stars. Bundled in their overcoats, they stood shiv-ering in the wind-whipped garden as Martin continued to paint an idyllic tableau. Finally, they told themselves it would be an adventure and signed a one-year lease. Not only was Gay Street enchanting, but it was also within spitting distance of the Christopher Street subway station at Sheridan Square, and even the outrageous Martin could be viewed as a colorful character. Born in Brooklyn, the son of an immi-grant French sailmaker, Edmond Martin referred to himself grandly as an artist, but he was in fact the proprietor of a real estate company that owned a dozen buildings in the West Village, and his chief talent was making shrewd property investments. Apart from renting his base-ment to the McKenney sisters, his only newsworthy act would occur twenty-five years later, when he challenged the city's fair housing law by claiming he had a constitutional right not to rent to black tenants and prominently displayed a sign to that effect in his office.

The basement apartment was burglarized the first week. A thief broke in to get his hands on a bottle of gin and four empty milk bottles the girls were meaning to return for the deposit, and scooped up their radio while he was at it. What was more, the cellar was a fishbowl for Peeping Toms, mostly men unable to resist stooping, kneeling, and slipping their noses through the iron railing as if studying polar bears at the Bronx Zoo. The last thing Eileen and Ruth saw every night were legs marching past the windows. And they would sometimes be awoken by voices outside that scared the daylights out of them: "Who lives here?" Knowing better than to answer, they lay quietly in bed. They soon began keeping the curtains drawn in the daytime. A couple on the second floor fought viciously—Ruth said it would be unwise to call the police—and a neighborly ex-football player, clad in shorts and sneakers summer and winter, shared another apartment with his girl-friend, who went to work all day while he stayed home to look after the cooking and ironing, tippling gin as he did the chores. He once offered to do the sisters' ironing, at no charge, but drew the line at laundry. That was women's work, he said.

To spruce up their "walk-down," they replaced Ramee Martin's decorations and bought a set of good china and a new radio. The floor had not been painted in a long time, they pointed out to Martin, to no avail.

"Paint your own floor," he barked.

With a single furnace serving all seven of Martin's buildings, there was never an abundance of heat. Freezing on a day when the temperature inside the apartment dipped to forty degrees, they invited him down to judge for himself. As they huddled in overcoats and gloves, he promptly issued his verdict: no problem. As if to underscore the point, he crawled out of his coat and danced around in his shirtsleeves.

"My, my," he said. "I didn't know the modern woman was a weakling." Enraged, Ruth uncorked her Irish anger, which resulted in a five-dollar rent reduction, later rescinded.

Their biggest complaint, though, was the unexplained, mushroom-colored mold spilling out of the bathroom ceiling. The nasty brown slime could have been mildew or rot, some species of fungus maybe.

Without knowing its technical name, they were quite sure it was unhealthy and unsanitary. Eileen hated it. Edmond Martin didn't.

"I think it's sort of pretty," he said.

Eileen and Ruth found their footing in new surroundings and gradually learned how to be New Yorkers. In Midtown, the late-night sky was obscured by a brocade of illuminated advertising signs. The avenues were thick with phalanxes of Checker cabs. Schools of subway riders washed up on the sidewalks, bobbing in all directions without regard for traffic. If Times Square twinkled like the boardwalk at Coney Island, Greenwich Village was a Wild West town and Sheridan Square its main street, without a sheriff. At no hour was the corner of Seventh Avenue and Christopher Street completely deserted. The end of Prohibition the previous year had given rise to scores of clubs and saloons frequented by carousing customers who spewed into the narrow streets, making a nuisance of themselves until the early hours. Some of these cowboys eventually found their way to 14 Gay Street, where they squealed "Hi-ya, babes!" and begged to be let in.

Every once in a while Eileen wondered why she had left Cleveland, and there were moments when she felt homesick for the sight of her father sitting contentedly on the porch with his *Saturday Evening Post*. But she never seriously thought of going back, not for a million dollars. In New York she studied Picassos at the Museum of Modern Art, gorged on gooey pecan rolls at the Jumble Shop on Eighth Street, dug into big, free platters of whatever was most expensive on dates at the Brevoort Hotel (on Fifth Avenue, where, at that very moment, Nathanael West was packing in preparation for his departure to Hollywood). The April sun warmed the sky above Gay Street, and the wisteria around back blazed with mauve blossoms. By summer, the patch of garden looked picture-perfect, blooming just as magically as Martin had promised, probably the only honest thing he had ever said to them. Occasionally she and Ruth threw parties, although before the guests arrived Eileen had to trim the bathroom fungus with her manicure scissors.

By this time Ruth's friend from the *Akron Beacon Journal* was also living in the city and working for the *Post*. Earl Wilson, after many un-answered letters to Walter Lister, finally received a coolly worded wire advising him to "go back to the farm and be happy," to which Earl replied that he didn't want to be happy. He'd rather work for Lister. Eileen, by then a Manhattan insider, welcomed Earl and helped him find lodgings in a rooming house on Washington Square South. There he quickly fell in love with another boarder, a dark-headed secretary who had bolted East St. Louis, Illinois. Rosemary Lyons had a beau back home, but, says their son Earl Jr., "they were perfect for each other, both escapees from the farm world." It was the kind of real-life New York romance in which he could say to her, "If I don't make it by the time I'm thirty-five I'll kill myself," and she could answer, "You'll make it." Earl and Rosemary were married one day in January, dur-ing her lunch break, she wearing her office clothes, but had to skip a honeymoon because he rushed off to cover an execution at Sing Sing.

Even O. Henry couldn't make that up.

With the windows always kept open, the air in the *Post* city room hummed with the buzzing of flies and the whirring of ceiling fans. Whenever a breeze gusted off the river, the unmistakable smell of fish wafted through the office. On the third consecutive day of a heat wave, Ruth was assigned to the Brooklyn waterfront, where a Brazilian train-ing ship had anchored on a goodwill tour. Getting to Brooklyn by cab (a non-reimbursable expense), Ruth was greeted by an explosion of sailors throwing their hats in the air and crying out in Portuguese. The Brazilians mistook her for a welcoming city dignitary, no doubt an em-issary of Mayor Fiorello La Guardia's.

Eventually escaping back to the newsroom, she was sipping a choc-olate soda when five sailors in white uniforms came strutting down the aisle toward her desk, bowing and waving their hats. Rarely had such a commotion been seen at 75 West Street. Reporters stood on their desks laughing and whistling, and then the business and movie departments began to crowd in. Unfortunately, the Brazilians refused to go. Ruth fi-nally was obliged to leave the office, ducking into the sooty bowels of the subway with the sailors scampering at her heels. At home, Eileen had just stumbled through the door and collapsed on her bed. She was stretched out, eyes closed, with her hat on the pillow beside her and thinking of a cold shower. Hearing Ruth come in, she opened her eyes. Five pairs of eyes were watching her.

"They're Brazilians," Ruth hissed. Squeezed on the opposite bed, the sailors sat in a row smiling happily while Ruth complained about her day. Wasn't it a scorcher?

Forget about the heat, Eileen said. "Get rid of the Navy." It was just like Chubb to drag home a bunch of randy sailor boys looking for an orgy. Unable to recognize the slightest bit of humor in the incident, Eileen afterward referred to the intruders with disgust. *L'affaire Brazil*, she would say snidely.

Gotham swarmed with attractive men, solemn thirtyish types sporting Rogers Peet suits and expensive haircuts, endlessly chain-smoking. At business receptions, to which Eileen found herself invited for no special reason (except being female), they strolled around drinking complimentary cocktails and trying to pick up women. As New York was the country's publishing capital, quite a few of them turned out to be writers or aspiring writers. Having no great interest in writers, who generally impressed her as self-involved and infantile, Eileen was bored by their conversations about books she had not read and magazines so effete they were not sold on newsstands. While waiting to meet a really good guy, preferably a nonwriter earning a lot of money, she attended another of these business gatherings and met somebody she liked very much. Luckily, he was no highbrow intellectual either.

Morris Jacobs was a good-looking man of twenty-four who worked in the advertising department of a local radio station. Eileen liked his easygoing manner and boyish looks, the brown hair, his narrow, five-foot-nine frame. In his sporty V-neck sweaters, he had the air of a gentlemanly college student. He kept her amused with his zingy sense of humor, and was fond of having a good time. They got dressed up and went to nightclubs and cozy Village restaurants, nice places that

showed his eagerness to please her. In the only snapshot of them together, they are sitting on blankets, facing each other, on a grassy hillside. Eileen's knees are tucked under a schoolgirlish pleated skirt and
she is wearing a dark blouse and ankle socks. Morris is facing away
from the camera, but Eileen's expression shows a woman in love.

Morris was an Ohioan, born in Cincinnati to Jewish immigrants
from Romania, the third of eleven children. Joseph Jacobson was a
cabinetmaker, a specialist in office furniture, who scrambled to put
food on the table for his growing brood. Growing up on Ridgeway Avenue, Morris attended public and Hebrew school, although he refused
to be bar mitzvahed. He was a high-strung, restless kid, a bit wild, easily
dissatisfied, and frequently at odds with his father. After sixth grade he
left school for the same financial reasons that caused his older brothers
to cut short their educations. At twenty, a clerk in a retail paint store,
he decided to accompany his brother Harry, older by two years and
an illustrator, to New York in the hope of a more rewarding life. The
brothers landed jobs in an advertising agency, where their names got
shortened to Jacobs after a bookkeeper accidentally misspelled Jacobson on their checks.

Morris had much in common with Midwestern transplants like
the McKenney sisters and Earl and Rosemary Wilson. "He had always wanted to work in show business," one member of his family said.
"Getting to New York and being on his own was the first step." In his
adopted city, self-assured and outgoing, he gave the impression of being an open, happy-go-lucky type, ambitious but never taking himself
too seriously. But Morris was actually quite guarded. He was "a secretive guy," his brother Julius Jacobson says, "a good guy but he didn't
open up about himself, or what he did." In letters home, he emphasized how highly he was regarded by the radio station. For a grade
school dropout and a former paint salesman, he was doing pretty well.
In all probability, he avoided revealing much of his Ohio life to Eileen,
the Cleveland Heights princess whom he wished to impress. He would
have informed her that his family were plain, working-class folks, but
maybe not bragged about a hardscrabble childhood in which his fa-

ther struggled to make ends meet. Having lived in New York for several years, and achieved a veneer of sophistication and a love of big-city excitement, he preferred the role of bon vivant.

Ruth did not like Morris. To be sure, he was crazy about Eileen but he also was uneducated, provincial, shallow, especially clueless about economics and politics. And he was often soused, which suggested to Ruth, a virtual teetotaler, that he might be a bad influence on her sister. In no respect was he good enough for Eileen, who had always placed a high value on her worth. She was throwing herself away on Morris. Ruth's concern for the masses—lettuce pickers, rubber workers, newspaper reporters—did not necessarily extend to radio station admen eager to jump into bed with her sister.

Regardless of Ruth's disapproval, Morris stayed in the picture. In fact, her attempts to break up the relationship only succeeded in making Eileen defensive. What made Ruth imagine that some blue-blooded banker was waiting to carry her away? Admittedly Morris earned a modest salary but he was making a go of it in the entertainment world, and she felt proud of him. She convinced herself that Ruth had it all wrong—possibly she was jealous—therefore, her romantic advice was worthless. In any case, Chubb knew nothing about men. Meanwhile, as the courtship progressed, Eileen still had not found a job. In those awesome skyscraper offices, the competition for secretarial positions turned out to be more intense than at home. Ruth suggested she was pretty enough to model or go on the stage, but attractive women were abundant in New York, and they didn't stutter either.

Months after their arrival in the city, Ruth remained the family breadwinner, paying the rent and doling out pocket money to her sister. The two of them just barely got by on her salary. Eileen, she would complain, was "always needing something and no matter how much I made" it was never enough.

Eileen married Morris at the Manhattan Municipal Building on August 31, 1935, a cool Saturday with a hint of fall in the air. There was little fanfare: no frilly gown and veil, no father of the bride, vows witnessed by the bride's sister and their friend Earl Wilson. It was not the way weddings were done at home, but live-and-let-live New Yorkers seemed to place less store on tradition. What role Morris's Jewishness played—how warmly Syd McKenney embraced a Jewish son-in-law, or Joseph Jacobson a Gentile daughter-in-law—is not clear. "We never met Morris," says Eileen's brother Jack. "She kept him away from Cleveland Heights."

In September, the newlyweds moved into an apartment at 40 Monroe Street on the Lower East Side. After eight months in the Village, Eileen gladly left Edmond Martin and his catacomb to her sister, who couldn't face living there alone and moved to Bank Street. Eileen's new home was Knickerbocker Village, the city's first major public housing project to offer affordable homes for middle-income tenants. Sandwiched between the Manhattan and Brooklyn bridges, the community stood on three acres of land once notorious as one of the island's worst slums. It was now a towering blockbuster of 1,600 apartments in two twelve-story buildings, featuring modern amenities such as automatic elevators, incinerators, parquet floors, luxury bathrooms, enclosed radiators, and stylish, high-end kitchens with metal cabinets. Every apartment overlooked either the street or a central courtyard with gardens and playgrounds. Rentals averaged $12.50 a room.

The opening of the massive complex the previous fall had made news when disappointed tenants launched a rent strike after not receiving all the amenities promised. Some had moved in to discover cement floors and bathrooms lacking toilet seats. By this time, however, the kinks had been worked out, and the Jacobses took possession of a comfortable four-room apartment, as bright and airy as Gay Street had been dank. The Knickerbocker rent was about the same Eileen and Ruth had been paying Edmond Martin.

All through September Eileen settled in to married life. Her job was to launder, vacuum, serve attractive meals, get her husband off to work in the morning, greet him at the end of the day, and entertain his friends. They had frequent parties. The guests one night included a surprise: one of Morris's brothers showed up unexpectedly at their door. Seventeen-year-old Julius and his cousin had hitchhiked from Cincinnati "without a dime between us," recalls Julius Jacobson. There was no cordial welcome, and in fact, Morris refused to let them stay. "He handed me ten dollars and told me to go home," Jacobson says. He remembers meeting Morris's wife for the first and only time and deciding she was a "nice-looking girl."

Before long, a few clouds appeared on the horizon: money and alcohol. All too often Morris drank to excess, Eileen discovered. Baby brother Julius could have told her that Morris was known at home as "a serious drinker." Otherwise, the big problem must have been in bed.

From the beginning, strong physical attraction had been complicated by Eileen's fears. Most likely she found sex disappointing, maybe even actively disliked the physical side of marriage, but nonetheless she was determined to be a successful wife. Morris had a roving eye, and she worried he might be unfaithful; his behavior around women was a bit too cozy for comfort. Six months after the wedding, Eileen chose the standard formula for securing a marriage. She became pregnant in March 1936.

"We kissed McKenney goodbye yesterday," Walter Lister reported to one of Ruth's *Post* colleagues. She was going to Ohio "to write a book about how union labor has brought Christ to Akron."

At twenty-five, Ruth didn't love the paper anymore. She began to wonder if it was worth trying to claw her way up in a field that seemed to offer a dead end for women. Many times she had wanted to quit, but "I was always in too far on the expense accounts." She quit anyway, in order to research a serious work of history documenting the first big CIO (Congress of Industrial Organizations) strike—fourteen thousand rank-and-file workers versus the giant rubber companies, Firestone, Goodyear, and Goodrich. *Industrial Valley* would be a heroic David-and-Goliath fable, always Ruth's cup of tea.

Lister was glad Ruth left for something she wanted to do. She was obviously "going places, somehow." With her passion, and her big mouth, she reminded him of "a female John Reed." She wasn't profound, "not even logical," he thought, but she had plenty of brass and "come the revolution, she'll be good for the troops."

As secretary of the Newspaper Guild's local chapter in 1935, she had established herself as a tough organizer willing to ruffle the feathers of management. By that point a member of the Communist Party, she attributed her embrace of Communism to rage ("I just wanted to smash up things"), but in fact she shared a set of beliefs with many others of her Depression generation, grappling with fear that the country had taken a wrong turn and was heading down a path of disaster.

Lister, impatient with her leftist views, compared her to the outspoken labor organizer "Mother" Mary Harris Jones and jokingly dubbed her Mother McKenney. In the winter the paper had sent her on an unusually grueling assignment, a two-week trip on a Greyhound bus riding across the country from New York to Los Angeles. The journey was a circulation stunt, but Ruth had done an exceptional job. Now she was gone, and he did not believe she would return to the business. "She could have been one of the best in New York but she not only would not learn, she never considered the possibility of improvement in herself."

To Eileen, giving up a steady job to write a book about Akron sounded stupid. Maybe those rubber workers were excellent folks, but fooling with Reds never put food on the table. How did Ruth plan to live without a salary? Whenever Ruth mounted her soapbox to lecture about saving the world, Eileen tuned her out. She didn't care about wildcat strikes and the *Daily Worker*, refused to hear another word about Generalissimo Franco and the Lincoln Brigade volunteers, even when Ruth called her backward, lacking in class consciousness. Unless people got serious and began uniting, there was going to be another world war, and it was shirkers like Eileen who would be responsible.

"Hire a hall," Eileen replied.

Before departing for Akron, Ruth treated herself to a vacation in Litchfield County, Connecticut. The area around New Milford, a small community some eighty miles north of New York City, had become a miniature mecca for certain celebrity literati, mainly writers and editors who, when young and poor in the twenties, had hung out in Paris but ended up working for *The New Yorker* and the *New Republic*. Among those former exiles who had put down roots in Gaylordsville and Sherman were Matthew Josephson, Robert Coates, and Malcolm Cowley. With publishing the main topic of conversation at social gatherings, Ruth felt encouraged to bat out a couple of light pieces and submit them to *The New Yorker*. Even though it was a humor magazine and Ruth was by no means a humorous writer, she decided to give it a try because she badly needed the money. (An informant identifying himself as "a former high functionary in the CP" told the FBI in 1951 that the party directed Ruth to "penetrate" the magazine.)

From New Milford on October 12 she addressed a query to "Dear Sirs." For a series of articles, the *New York Post* had sent her to California and back on a bus last winter, but not all of her research had been used. She offered two sketches, "Angel Child" and "The Class-Conscious Gambler." By return mail she received a reply from the fiction editor, Katharine White. Rejecting one of the stories (but suggesting revisions), Mrs. White went on to say that she would accept the second piece—about a bus-riding gambler who spends his time and money helping unions win their strikes—if it were "considerably" cut and edited. They would pay seven cents a word.

Ruth, overjoyed at her success, followed instructions about cutting, but while awaiting payment, she suddenly found herself in the hot seat. The piece rang a bell for the executive editor, Ik Shuman, who became vigilante angry to learn the material had already appeared in the *Post*. But this particular angle was unused, Ruth argued. Mrs. White promptly jumped in and ordered an investigation to verify if "the girl gets paid, whether she is honest." A single misstep could get a writer banned for all eternity, and Mrs. White had to be alert. She thrived on the role of office pit bull.

In the end, after it was determined that the two pieces were sufficiently unlike, "The Class-Conscious Gambler" was published on December 12, 1936. Ruth, feeling obliged to make a show of servility, penned a groveling letter wondering if the magazine would ever trust her again.

The New Yorker had been established eleven years earlier by the inimitable Harold Ross and his then-wife, Jane Grant (whose role would be purged from the magazine's history after their divorce in 1929). Ross needed a tough female to keep the editorial side operating, and Katharine White could be scary. An awesome taskmaster, Mrs. White, as she preferred to be addressed, had the drawing room manners of a Wharton character and the demanding temperament of a Captain Bligh. Like most of the magazine's editors, she was not exactly comical. She had a Calvinist streak that seemed at cross purposes with a humor magazine, but she did bring noteworthy assets to the operation. She happened to be an extremely good editor, a connoisseur of English prose, equipped to nurture the likes of John O'Hara and Vladimir Nabokov. It was her Yankee efficiency at squeezing the proverbial lemonade out of lemons that single-handedly elevated Ross's often slipshod operation into a magazine known for the excellence of its writing.

Katharine Sergeant was born in Brookline, Massachusetts, and educated at Bryn Mawr. After wedding a Cleveland attorney, Ernest Angell, she lived in his hometown for several years before relocating to New York. Their marriage, a miserable one (Angell was openly unfaithful), limped along for almost fifteen years, until Katharine divorced him and married a man seven years her junior, a writer with whom she worked at *The New Yorker.* Forty-four years of age, she twisted her hair into a stern bun at the back of her head, which made her look like a dour, switch-wielding schoolmarm. Along with two children from her first marriage, and a son from her second, she had to tend a husband with peculiar emotional peccadilloes, E. B. (Andy) White, and scores of contributors with other eccentricities.

It was not easy being Katharine Sergeant Angell White, and over the years Ross's fiction deity left some people trembling with rage, secretly of course, in light of her status as the house goddess. When their iconic humorist Sid Perelman pounded her, years later, in a blistering private letter, as "a stupid, tyrannical, and tactless old bitch" who was "throttling the life out of the magazine," and swore never to work for *The New Yorker* again (he withdrew his threat), his fury spoke volumes about the unexpressed feelings of both contributors and staff. Insider Brendan Gill likewise shafted her publicly, in his memoir *Here at The New Yorker*, when he likened her extreme dogmatism to "some weighty glacier working its way down a narrow Alpine pass."

Ruth, oblivious to Katharine White's personal situation, treated her like someone with only one concern in life: the writing of Ruth McKenney. In her letters (typically without regard for commas or margins), she expected a motherly interest to be shown for her ideas, her plans to lose weight, her decision to read *Gone with the Wind*, which she was finding surprisingly sexy. Between November 1936 and May 1937, while living in Akron with her Aunt Margery and researching the rubber industry, she bombarded the editor with stories of her experiences, involving bass viol players, lunatic uncles, Georgian princes, and Cuban vaudeville. Many of the ideas tended to be either half baked or completely unpublishable. Diplomatic, sometimes even benevolent, White would regularly deflate her efforts with outright rejections or requests for revisions. Ruth, she repeated for maybe the hundredth time, needed to think out her stories, to edit them before submission. She was too florid, too facile.

In the meantime Ruth tried to ingratiate herself with a second editor at the magazine. St. Clair McKelway, an accomplished writer who had joined the staff in 1933, was managing editor for fact articles, in effect the twin of White, whose responsibility was fiction and poetry. Gifted writers were commonplace to Harold Ross. What he needed at the helm were extracompetent editors, saviors who knew how to get things done—"jesuses," as some called them—and so he snatched up McKelway. Ruth, still tempted to recycle ideas from her junk heap, trotted out a provocative essay about Akron and the rubber industry. Normally, McKelway replied, they never accepted reports from other cities, "but yours is so well written." Ruth led off by giving readers a private tour of a city that "smells like a rubber band smoldering in an ash tray." Akron was "dirty and ugly and, at the moment, full of suspense." McKelway published "Uneasy City" the week following the gambler piece. That the citizens of Akron were howling in outrage delighted Ruth.

• • •

In the apartment on Monroe Street, there was never enough to do. Isolated in the boredom of pregnancy, Eileen read Ruth's letters complaining about her life in Akron. When Ruth was not gathering information on the rubber workers or showering Mrs. White with stories, she visited with their grandmother Celia. There were regular reports on her diet, because she was going to be "thin if it kills me." One week, starving herself, she proudly reported the loss of seven pounds. Homesick for New York, she was counting on Eileen and Morris to put her up when she came back for a visit in her newly acquired 1928 Ford.

Ruth's patronizing attitude toward her brother-in-law had not changed. After knowing Morris for a year and a half, she still considered him a bad lot. He drank too much and probably cheated on her sister. Certain that the marriage was a failure, she tried to introduce Eileen to another man. Her letters to St. Clair McKelway contained frequent references to her sister, whom she described as living in Knickerbocker Village and expecting to give birth any minute. (There was no mention of Morris, almost as if he didn't exist.) Suggesting that McKelway look up Eileen, she helpfully provided the mailing address, but if he preferred to telephone, "she's in the phone book." As a married man with plenty of women on the side, McKelway declined to take the bait. Still, Ruth kept after him, recalling the time Eileen worked for the credit bureau and burned up the surveillance film. Her sister was blessed with a special wit, she told McKelway. Very likely she could write some amusing personal-experience pieces for the magazine.

Ruth joined Eileen at the end of January. It had snowed that week, but it was a rainy wet snow that chilled the bones, the ugly kind that smears to rivulets of gray slime. Eileen went into labor the very next day. Out on the slushy street, Ruth and Morris bundled her into a taxi and raced uptown to Wickersham Hospital on East Fifty-ninth Street. Later that day, January 29, 1937, Eileen gave birth to a son. Morris, relegated to a walk-on role, was not permitted to name the boy. Mother and aunt decided to honor the most important male in their lives — Grandpa Flynn — and so the dark-haired, blue-eyed boy was named Thomas W. Jacobs. His most noticeable feature was large protruding ears.

At home, the baby cried practically nonstop for the first ten days and nobody could figure out the reason. Ruth recalled that "we just stood around and wrung our hands and hoped it wasn't dying, which it wasn't." She had no interest in babies, which impressed her as "pretty much a lump of flesh and not worth looking at." Ensconced in his bassinet, Tommy received visitors who signed their names in Eileen's baby book, an elaborate album adorned with cherubic watercolors of yellow-haired, blue-eyed infants. All of the signatures—Rosemary and Earl Wilson, a former editor of the *Beacon Journal*, a magazine music critic—belonged to friends of Ruth's. Shortly afterward she rushed back to Akron and left Eileen on her own.

Almost immediately, friction began to develop. Neither Eileen nor Morris had the slightest idea of how to care for a baby, but it was Eileen who bore the responsibility, because Morris tended to make himself scarce. Although she loved Tommy, the diapers, feedings, and wails of a newborn seemed overwhelming. At twenty-three, she very much wanted to be in control of her life. She had done the right thing, taking pains to prove she was a grown-up woman, comfortable with the traditional roles of wife and mother. But for what? A snarly husband and an infant needing his bottom wiped six times a day.

In her spanking-new apartment with the parquet floors and the nice kitchen cabinets, it could get unbearably lonely.

16

CHEAPSVILLE

I N THE SPRING of 1935, Nat was back in Hollywood. His agent at William Morris assured him that on the basis of his three novels he could be peddled as a rising literary star, a New York Dostoyevsky known for quality, innovative fiction. In spite of Jim Geller's certainty, Nat was not so confident.

Hollywood was just as he remembered, the same California sun pouring down on the Tudor cottages and Mediterranean villas, the same weird carnival of switchboard operators masquerading in bandannas, slacks, and tennis sneakers. First thing was to line up a place, he decided, followed by a decent deli and then a new pair of sunglasses.

He took a room at the Parva-Sed-Apta apartments, a three-story, brown-beamed Tudor Revival building with a roof garden at 1817 North Ivar Street, not far from the luxurious Knickerbocker, where he had lived two years earlier. Newspapers were rife with ads for extended-stay residences—furnished apartment hotels, garden bungalows, scruffy trailer courts—but this one stood out for its pretentious Latin name. Although *parva sed apta* means "small but suitable," the hotel's ad translated the phrase as "Little, but Nice." All Nat could afford was a one-room unit, costing forty dollars a month. The décor was Early Holiday Inn, with a few nondescript easy chairs, a tiny kitchen, and a Murphy bed. That it wasn't the Sutton Club Hotel did not matter because his stay would be temporary, and the only hours he planned to be there would be spent asleep. As soon as he had a regular paycheck, he could move to more suitable accommodations.

Halfway through June, still at the Parva-Sed-Apta and still unemployed, he was getting discouraged. For all Jim Geller's efforts to place him at a major studio—and a number of promises of work—nothing had materialized. Sid had warned that arriving in Hollywood without an assignment was notoriously risky, but Nat did not really pay attention. Of course there was no comparison between a novice like himself, who would not turn down a meat-and-potatoes salary, and a seasoned writer in Sid's elevated pay category. But despite his modest expectations, nothing was happening and his faith in Geller's judgment had begun to wear thin. After burning his bridges in New York and Bucks County, though, he was forced to stick it out in Hollywood. He missed Danny, his pointer, left behind at the farm.

In the previous decade, Hollywood had undergone a seismic shift. "Wait a minute, wait a minute"—Al Jolson cried in *The Jazz Singer*, sometimes considered to be the cosmic blast of motion-picture history—"you ain't heard nothin' yet." While the best silent-film writers easily migrated to talkies, the introduction of sound in 1927 transformed the screenwriting profession to embrace different types of writers. With the emphasis on good spoken dialogue, there was a rush to recruit notable journalists, critics, novelists, and Pulitzer Prize–winning playwrights whose names stood for class.

Suddenly studios found themselves in the unpleasant position of having to put up with prima donnas from the East, and they didn't like it a bit. These uppity A-list writers, including denizens of the Algonquin Round Table, took themselves very seriously as creative people, even though they behaved like money-grubbing shopkeepers. Movie writing was slumming, they said dismissively, and Los Angeles was a distant galaxy where you couldn't get a good bagel, "seven suburbs in search of a city," as Alexander Woollcott described it. To entice them to the Coast, in addition to outrageous wages, movie companies were obliged to pay their way, first class on the Twentieth Century Limited and the Santa Fe Super Chief. Then they turned out to be foul-mouthed workers who strutted in late (sometimes hung over), made personal phone calls, and forgot to turn off the lights at night.

Unaccustomed to being pushed around, the mighty studio lords tried deflating the writers by means of contempt, calling them the highest-paid secretaries in the world, or in the words of Jack Warner, "schmucks with Underwoods." The Underwood schmucks had the last laugh by making the studios pay a high price for their secretarial services. It was Herman Mankiewicz who famously wired Ben Hecht, a playwright whose credentials included successful plays like *The Front Page:* "Millions are to be grabbed out here and your only competition is idiots. Don't let this get around." Word did get around, and soon the exodus to El Dorado was under way. It became a familiar routine for the New York carpetbaggers: an invitation to visit Hollywood with expenses paid on the Twentieth Century; a few weeks or months of work; then scattering back home at one's own expense when options were dropped. It was a different story when options were renewed. Then they would travel back and forth or stay on permanently, becoming enamored with luxury goods and sunshine, adept at fawning in a company town where sycophancy was mandatory.

By the time Nat arrived, in 1935, as many as 130 writers were working under contract at MGM (called Metro), 120 on the Warners lot, 100 at Paramount, and additional scores at RKO, Universal, and Columbia. On the studio payrolls at various times were F. Scott Fitzgerald, William Faulkner, Lillian Hellman, Philip Barry, John O'Hara, William Saroyan, Aldous Huxley, George S. Kaufman, and Clifford Odets. One of the few important writers to resist the lure of Hollywood was Ernest Hemingway.

According to payment hierarchies created by the studios, the top was a hefty $2,000 ($30,000 today) a week, and $1,500 was considered very good, while a few screenwriters, like Ben Hecht, one of the highest paid, pulled in even more. F. Scott Fitzgerald got $1,250 from Metro, William Faulkner earned $1,000 at Twentieth Century Fox. Only a small percentage commanded those salaries; around half earned less than $4,000 a year. Still, even the lunch-pail writers who had flocked to Hollywood for as little as $50 a week, pocket change for the Hechts, could aspire to move up the studio food chain.

In the Depression, the average per capita income was less than $800 a year, income taxes were minimal, and a loaf of bread cost 9 cents. While most people were counting their pennies, the Underwood schmucks were buying whatever they liked. When Dorothy Parker and her actor-writer husband, Alan Campbell, came panning for gold in 1934, Paramount offered them a combined salary of $1,250 a week ($1,000 for her, $250 for him). Four years later they would be in the $2,000-a-week category (and at their peak $5,000). As a houseguest of the Campbells, John O'Hara reported to Scott Fitzgerald that they were living in "a large white house, Southern style," enjoying "a brand new Picasso, a Packard convertible phaeton, a couple of Negroes, and dinner at the very best Beverly Hills homes." With money to splurge, the couple bought a farm in Bucks County just a few miles from Geigel Hill Road.

But as an incessantly downbeat Sid liked to point out, everything is relative, and wealth by ordinary criteria meant little by Hollywood standards, because movie stars and studio executives were preposterously rich. Nobody outside the industry recognized writers' names, which were "writ in water" and would be soon superseded by others. Screenwriting might be "no worse than playing piano in a house of call," he supposed. On the other hand, prostitutes did not have to perform their services in wretched Triangle Shirtwaist sweatshops turning out "movie feces" for disgusting "yahoos."

Dorothy Parker, the poet laureate of the Underwood schmucks, hated Hollywood as much as Sid. Excoriating one movie mogul, she said that "he hasn't got enough sense to bore assholes in wooden hobbyhorses." But what could be expected from a business full of "poops," where a director thought nothing of sticking his finger in Scott Fitzgerald's face and saying, "Pay *you*. Why, you ought to pay us." Still, she had to admit that she loved the weather and her house on North Canon Drive in Beverly Hills with a nice yard for her dog. And the money, of course.

During Nat's first months in the movie colony, lacking friends of his own, he inherited Sid and Laura's social crowd: Dorothy Parker and Alan Campbell, Frances Goodrich and Albert Hackett (writers of the *Thin Man* film), and Arthur Kober. Ordinarily, such people might have scorned association with a nobody like Nat, but a brother-in-law of Sid's was sure to be welcomed. One of the most successful screenwriters was Dashiell Hammett. Six times between 1934 and 1936, his fiction had been converted into profitable movies, which enabled him to swan around in chauffeured limousines, occupy a six-room penthouse suite at the Beverly-Wilshire Hotel, then move to exclusive Bel Air Road in West Los Angeles, where he lived like a maharajah with his black valet, Jones, and Jones's lover. It was a lot of luxury for an ex-Pinkerton detective.

Nat liked Dash, which was why, at the risk of his job, he had allowed him to live rent free at the Sutton Club for almost eight months while he completed *The Thin Man*. They had spent an uncounted number of hours in each other's company. After release of the *Thin Man* movie in June 1934, a box-office success starring Myrna Loy and William Powell, Dash had persuaded Metro-Goldwyn-Mayer to buy the rights to a highly regarded labor novel, *The Foundry* by Albert Halper, and Metro hired him to write the screenplay at his usual weekly rate of $1,750. Hearing that Nat was looking for an assignment, he promised to get him shoehorned into the film project. Confident that he would soon be writing for Metro, the Waldorf-Astoria of Hollywood studios, Nat relaxed and waited for the call from producer Hunt Stromberg.

To his disappointment, none came. Dash had forgotten all about their conversation. At a party at his house one evening, when Nat referred to the project, his benefactor pretended not to understand. Then the pitch of Dash's voice rose so that everyone could hear.

"I haven't any money to lend you now," he said condescendingly, "but call me next week and I'll lend you some."

Nat felt mortified. Never had he asked for a loan, even though he was strapped for money and Dash knew it. They had only discussed his search for employment. Baffled and humiliated, he reported the incident to Sid and said that Dash "made me eat plenty of dirt." Did Ham-

mett's freeloading at the Sutton slip his mind? This was the thanks Nat
got for being a Good Samaritan.

Dash continued to kick Nat when he was down. Another evening,
one of Dash's guests declared herself thrilled to meet the author of
Miss Lonelyhearts, and Dash abruptly warned the woman to "leave
him alone. He hasn't got a pot to piss in." Shaken by Dash's determination to rub his nose publicly in his difficulties, Nat made no comment and slipped away. "I sneaked out early and spit all the way home
to get the taste of arse out of my mouth," he told Sid, who might have
explained that a "taste of arse" was the first law of Hollywood. Dash, sober, was exceptional company, generous with his money, very much
like his charming fictional character Nick Charles. Boozing, however,
he was not only unpleasant but cruel, known to turn sharply and attack. In the end, there was no opening for either of them with Hunt
Stromberg. When Metro dropped its option on *The Foundry*, Dash was
frozen out of a job too. In Hollywood, every writer was dispensable.

Meanwhile, Sid and Laura had followed Nat to the Coast, this
time to offer themselves as a writing team. At MGM the kids went on
the payroll of an Irving Thalberg picture (the never-produced *Greenwich Village*), at a joint salary of $1,000 a week, $400 above Sid's previous solo pay. Even with the raise, Sid remained sour on the business, which was run by "beetle-brained wind-suckers." Laura, equally
contemptuous, was soon describing dinners she had attended in behemoth Tudor palazzi with first editions in the library and mezuzahs on
the doorposts, where wives spoke Yiddish and their snarling husbands
smashed chairs if a spouse used the wrong fork.

Over the Fourth of July holiday, Hammett gave a party on Bel Air
Road. For entertainment, he hired a prostitute from Lee Francis, the
madam who operated Hollywood's swankiest sporting house, where he
was a regular customer. Lee Francis stood for quality, meaning medically inspected personnel decked out in style and trained to engage in
intelligent conversation. Her brothel was frequented by the cream of
Hollywood, both men and women (she offered "lezz" services). In an
upstairs bathroom at Dash's, one of her employees disrobed and set

up shop; her first customer was Sid Perelman. After noticing her husband's lengthy absence, Laura grew worried and started to hunt for him. Finally, opening the bathroom door, she caught him in flagrante delicto.

Before Sid could find his trousers, Laura made a beeline for the front door. Running away had become her typical response whenever driven over the edge, and sometimes she stayed out all night. This time was different, because she failed to show up the next morning. "There was hell to pay," said Albert Hackett, another guest at the party. As a rule, the person most distressed by her disappearances was Nat, who, in Manhattan, was known to walk the streets until daylight in search of her. This time, it was a hysterical Sid phoning everybody he could think of, short of the police. Nobody had seen her, Dash was absent too, and it became apparent they were together. Declaring a state of emergency, he finally notified Lillian Hellman in New York that it looked as if Dash had run off with Laura.

Although Lily subsequently would inflate her relationship with Dash, pretending it was a great passion, the physical aspect had lasted only a short time. By 1935, his sex life was mostly with whores, romanticized by Lily as "casual ladies." Sid's call infuriated her. What made him imagine she would want to know Dash was sleeping with Laura? How thoughtless could he be? It would be many months before she forgave him. As for Hammett, she would never get over his Independence Day fling with Laura. Four decades later, and even after his death in 1961, she wished he were alive "so I could kill him."

In San Francisco, the runaways were not having a good time. Although Laura's infidelity was only a twenty-four-year-old's payback for six years of Sid's philandering, there is no question that she found Dash alluring. But Dash fell ill, and in place of a lover she found herself with an invalid who wanted to talk about his love for Lillian. After several days, Laura returned to Hollywood, worn out, still extremely upset, and by no means happy to see her husband. Waving off a reconciliation, she proclaimed her intention of staying with Dash, who, she said, needed her. Nat, always obsessive in his efforts to protect her, knew that going off with Dash was a crazy idea. Whatever it took, her marriage had to be pasted back together.

"After twelve hours of being talked to," Laura recalled, she resigned herself to going back to Bucks County with Sid. So great was her reluctance that Nat was forced to escort them across the country. When the plane touched down at Newark Airport, Laura was still angry, still unsure she wanted to stay with her husband. "If Pep hadn't been along," she wrote Dash, "I would have probably turned back and you would have found me on the couch at Bel-Air." In a dramatic letter to Lillian she reported that Dash was "well and sober," and advised her to call him "if you love him as much as he does you." Or if Lily preferred "to phone Pep the number is Gladstone 1236." Lily did not phone either one.

The Perelmans retreated from Hollywood like an army that had wandered too deeply into enemy terrain. Shunning the film colony did not by any means prevent all further domestic friction, but they did manage to stick it out until the bitter end, or almost, living in the farmhouse on Geigel Hill Road, sometimes in a New York apartment, with short stays in Los Angeles, because entirely turning their backs on movie money was not possible. Laura became pregnant after six years of marriage and gave birth to their son, Adam, in October 1936. A daughter, Abby, was born in 1938.

Nat returned to Hollywood to find himself in the same situation as before. In his absence, Jim Geller had doggedly continued to put up his name for assignments. Everyone said they were very keen for him and it was only a matter of the right assignment. Jobs that looked like cinches slid out from under him. His agent always sounded upbeat, but Nat realized that it meant nothing. When he reported that something might be frying at Warners, Nat refused to get his hopes up. Warners had showed interest in him before. Bracing himself for another rejection, he reminded Geller that he wasn't fussy. He would work for fifty dollars a week, even take a reader's job. In story departments, the job of reader was an essential but noncreative position that entailed evaluating manuscripts and preparing reports. For a scriptwriter the pay was peanuts, the professional equivalent of rattling a cup on the corner of Hollywood and Vine. But for a person who didn't know how he was going to feed himself without family handouts, peanuts were better than nothing.

For months he had been killing time in California, and now it was suddenly September. Whenever he talked about going home, people urged him to be patient. Since there was nothing awaiting him in New York, or anywhere else, he hung on, holing up at the Parva-Sed-Apta and cutting himself off from the Perelmans' rarefied circle.

Some of Nat's difficulties finding work can be traced to William Morris, a powerhouse talent agency that kept proposing him to the top studios, where competition was heaviest. Geller had told him that his six weeks as a junior writer at Columbia qualified him for a first-class job. In fact, he was a newcomer whose marginal connection with movies counted for little. As Nat would learn, those high-salaried Underwood schmucks at Metro and Paramount constituted a tiny minority of the profession. These were not the people for whom the Screen Writers Guild had been organized in 1933. William Morris continued to shop him while Nat relied on the kids for weekly stipends. Before leaving New York, he and Sid were in Sardi's one night when Sid made an offhand remark about never expecting to see his money again. Nat had taken it as an insult but no longer blamed him. As his debt kept mounting, he began to fear it could never be repaid.

In Nat's fiction, the Parva-Sed-Apta would reincarnate itself as both the Chateau Mirabella, a scruffy hotel whose halls reeked of disinfectant, and the slightly more attractive San Bernardino Arms. North Ivar Street would be nicknamed Lysol Alley for its large population of hookers and their pimps. In reality, the 1800 block of North Ivar was a quiet street of unremarkable bungalow courts, red-tile-roofed Spanish colonial houses, and gardens hazy with the smell of magnolias. His building, a short walk up the hill from Hollywood Boulevard, was within the downtown business district but not at the heart of it. Only five years earlier, Hollywood had been a small town with few decent restaurants and nothing to do at night, but now Hollywood and Vine was beginning to resemble Times Square West, a clutter of beauty parlors, dime stores, and soda fountains jammed among flashy hotels and cocktail lounges. On nearby Hollywood Boulevard, he poked around Stanley Rose's bookshop, a writers' hangout, and next door was the Musso & Frank Grill (Musso Frank's), a popular chophouse known for beef goulash and chicken potpie.

Adrift without the company of the kids, missing his dog more than ever, Nat would pass the time browsing the Hollywood sex market and its variety of services, gay, straight, and Gillette blades (local slang for bisexuals). Bookstores retailed extensive selections of pornography, with some offering free delivery, toting orders in suitcases with false bottoms. Entrepreneurs like Lee Francis used standard marketing practices, booking appointments in advance and opening charge accounts. She and a panoply of competitors, conveniently located in the best neighborhoods, served caviar sandwiches and Champagne. It was heaven for a hooker consumer like Nat, or would have been if he had money. (The alternatives to clean girls were the street girls or the crib houses, unappetizing joints with scratchy sheets.) Hollywood was equally broad-minded about homosexual activities. "Nances" and "Sapphic ladies" were routine sights along Sunset Boulevard, while the big stars (Greta Garbo, Katharine Hepburn) and directors (George Cukor) lived discreetly gay lives and it was assumed that Cary Grant, a matinee idol, would marry to conceal his relationship with partner Randolph Scott. The city's homosexual subculture fascinated Nat.

Aside from the lively sex scene, the town was swarming with a vast population of immigrants, lured to Southern California by visions of new-model Pontiacs and modest homes without mortgages, a parallel universe to the cliché Hollywood of swimming pools and private screening rooms. Multitudes of hat-check girls and carhops dreamed of hitting the jackpot as movie stars, but most would seek to become one of the fifteen thousand technical workers—grips, cutters, seamstresses, electricians—to whom the studios provided steady incomes.

For others, success meant employment as bit players or nonspeaking extras, who could earn as much as $16 a day, or $50 to $75 a day for babies. As Nat rambled along the streets and studied the people around him, he realized that Hollywood was a factory town. What struck him as unnerving were not the hardworking laborers—the insurance salesmen in Tyrolean hats—but a different group altogether, an invasion of outcasts who loitered on street corners and stared at the passing crowds. Their expressions radiated boredom, resentment, and unmistakable hatred. He could almost imagine them to be another race, a plague of prairie people in ill-fitting Sears, Roebuck suits who had streamed across the country to find the place where it never snowed, their idyllic travelogue of sunshine and oranges. These infestations of "locusts," unbeknownst to themselves, came to California "to die." They had been cheated and betrayed, not just by the false promises of Hollywood but by life as well.

If the kids had not gone home, had he found employment, he might have overlooked subterranean Hollywood, the underbelly crawling with what he called its screwballs and screwboxes. He would have traded the Parva-Sed-Apta for a comfortable house in the Hollywood Hills. He might have celebrated his thirty-second birthday with new friends. There would have been invitations to cocktail parties and Sunday barbecues, all the tribal rites of Beverly Hills. As it was, at loose ends, he made a halfhearted attempt to start writing again. In a discouraged letter to Josie Herbst, he reported reading Sinclair Lewis's latest novel, *It Can't Happen Here*, and making plans to return home after the first of the year. "I've written a book," he confided, "but I'm fed up on books and it's going to be the last." But there was no book at all, only vague ideas that came to nothing. Sailing away to a tropical island in the South Seas remained one of his favorite fantasies. Repeatedly he suggested to Josie the idea of a six-month voyage to "the Indies," just the Herrmanns and himself. He thought they could charter a boat for a thousand dollars. "Is such a trip possible?" he asked. It wasn't.

Several years earlier he had clipped a newspaper article about a California soldier-of-fortune type who had been implicated in a local murder, because Nat thought the man might make an interesting character. One of his book ideas involved such a man's scheme to operate private cruises to a Pacific island. The story, part comedy, part drama, incorporated his old voyage-of-freaks idea: a child actor and his mother, a family of Eskimos, a movie cowpoke, a wiseguy dwarf, a vaudeville actor and his movie-struck daughter, and a screenwriter who keeps a rubber horse at the bottom of his swimming pool. The most picturesque passenger was a seven-foot lesbian who shaves every day.

The ship-of-fools motif, a theme in art and literature for centuries, had been used successfully in Vicki Baum's *Grand Hotel* (1929) and would surface later in Katherine Anne Porter's *Ship of Fools* (1962). But Nat's vessel refused to sail, and when he transferred some of the boat people from the high seas to a theatrical boardinghouse, this too proved a false start. He had strung together a group of peculiar characters, but there was no story. It would be many months before he teased out the connections between these creations. Instead, he began a short story about a cowboy.

All day long Earle Haines waits outside a saddle shop on Vine Street. Nat's cowboy wears a ten-gallon hat and high-heeled boots, and every thirty minutes he thumbs his pockets for tobacco and papers to roll a smoke. A professional extra in full costume, Earle wears dungarees with wide, turned-up cuffs. That he is dumber than dirt doesn't matter; he can ride, and he is handsome in a tumbleweed, hipless sort of way.

Earle rouses himself when his girlfriend pulls up in a Ford touring car. She is jailbait, with long legs and tiny breasts like "the twin halves of a lemon." Her bleached platinum hair is pulled back with a baby-blue ribbon. At seventeen, Faye's goals could not be more traditional. She is determined to become a movie star.

"Hello, cowboy," she says.

Earl removes his hat. "Lo, Honey."

The cowboy actor Tom Mix, a megastar of silent movies, made more than three hundred pictures. During the Depression, as Hollywood fed the undiminished American appetite for cowboy heroes and horses, men came in from the ranches seeking jobs in the low-budget Westerns, which paid considerably better than raising cattle and breaking horses. They gathered in full cowboy attire—Stetsons, boots, big belt buckles—to wait for work on the corner of Sunset and Gower, until the intersection came to be nicknamed Gower Gulch. Outside the CBS studios on Sunset was a saddle shop with a hitching rack. The sight of cowpunchers sitting there by the hour, familiar to passersby, smelled like literary material to Nat.

Unlike Sid, who complained that Hollywood stifled his literary creativity, Nat had no trouble shifting his focus to fiction. "Bird and Bottle," his story starring a cowboy and a thrill-seeking adolescent in a tight sweater, would be published in *Pacific Weekly*, a left-wing journal founded by the muckraker journalist Lincoln Steffens. But the mouthwatering Faye and her buckaroo would be back.

It was fire season, the hot, dry Santa Ana winds rolling over the San Gabriel Mountains, the wildfires bursting out of control in the dusty hills north of the city. In his room at the Parva-Sed-Apta, the whiff of charred sumac in his lungs, Nat had no trouble imagining fire streaming through the canyons and turning the city to ash. As a juvenile firebug he had pictured the New York Public Library a mass of red flames, and the idea of fiery biblical cataclysm remained sweet. In "Burn the Cities," a poem written several years earlier, he had managed to torch Jerusalem, Paris, and London. ("Paris will burn easily / Paris is fat"). Omitting Los Angeles was an oversight.

Around the time of the fires, Nat was unexpectedly visited by more personal afflictions when he discovered that he had contracted gonorrhea again. The infection occurred in both penis and rectum. It was no comfort to know that gonorrhea, commonplace among screenwriters, was a frequent subject of humorous gossip. Dash, soon to check into Lenox Hill Hospital in New York, had similar problems, as did John O'Hara. Noticing O'Hara's car parked outside a doctor's office, Sid once left a note on the windshield: "Dear John, it's no worse than a bad cold." Sid was no fan of O'Hara's, whom he considered a "smirky, sneaky" anti-Semite. O'Hara, extremely peeved, accused Sid of spreading vicious lies.

Nat developed complications, a congested prostate that contributed to his misery, and soon his testicles had bloated to the size of oranges. He could barely sit ten minutes in a chair before flopping on his back. Both walking and sleeping became difficult. With the Murphy bed pulled out, his room seemed smaller and hotter. On muggy nights, dripping with sweat, he dozed in half-hour snatches, and often lay awake smoking and waiting for the sun to rise. Against his doctor's orders, he would swallow two more morphine tablets, which would give him horrible headaches. His thoughts circled endlessly around how to repay Sid (a debt eventually amounting to $1,500), find a decent job, and start another book. He told himself that he had "nothing to say, and no talent for writing. I have deteriorated mentally."

His doctor was a lighthearted sort. No need to worry, he chirped. The g.c. had no bearing on his prostate, just an unfortunate coincidence, a spot of bad luck. Any man over thirty could have a congested prostate, he assured him. Probably it was caused by lack of intercourse or by masturbation during the gonorrhea treatment. Nat hoped Dr. Seagal would "rot in hell." Too weak to get out and about, he found himself a prisoner of the Parva-Sed-Apta, forced to rely on others to chauffeur him to the appointments. Even had he been offered a job by L. B. Mayer himself, he thought, he couldn't take it.

After the gonorrhea healed, he was shocked by his appearance. Losing twenty-five pounds made him look older than thirty-two. None of his clothes fit, and the outfits he had brought from New York needed to be replaced. The seat of his striped flannel pajamas rotted away, his underwear in pitiful tatters, he turned to his sister. Send a couple of cheap Brooks button-down-collar sport shirts, he said. He had two left, but no white ones, and the collars were falling apart. Regardless, he continued to make jokes in his letters to Sid. "Here's the twisteroo," he wrote. A man knocked on his door to ask if he had any shoes needing repair. Without thinking, he handed over a pair for new heels. The footwear failed to return, however, and several days later he read in the paper about a ring of shoe thieves operating in the neighborhood.

On January 17, 1936, Nat reported for work at 4024 North Radford Avenue in Studio City. Entering the main gate of Republic Productions, Inc., wearing a belted, box-pleated Norfolk jacket, he was assigned an office at the rear of the writers' building. Out the windows was a pastoral view of trees and twittering birds, which immediately upset him, because he spotted birds that looked like shrikes, the predators he had always found revolting. The next day, to the alarm of the writer sharing the office, he came in carrying an air rifle. "I hate shrikes," he announced, and spent half the day trying to kill them. After ten months marooned in Parva-Sed-Apta limbo, some two and a half rocky years after walking out of the Sutton Club, Nat felt enormously grateful to be back in the workforce and refused to allow shrikes to mar his happiness. His weekly salary was two hundred dollars, with employment on a week-to-week basis but no provision for increases, not surprising for an outfit like Republic.

During the Depression a collection of mom-and-pop production companies had opened around Sunset and Gower and began turning out Westerns, serials, and detective mysteries. Before long, the corner became known as Poverty Row. Four of these dinky operations—Liberty, Monogram, Majestic, and Mascot—had been receiving credit from Consolidated Film Industries. Then Consolidated's owner, Herbert J. Yates, decided in 1935 to take over and merge them into one organization that might compete with the major studios. It was to the cigar-chewing, hard-nosed, fifty-five-year-old dealmaker and his fledgling operation that Nat owed his serious entrée into the film business.

Compared with front-runners like MGM, Yates's conglomerate was a midget. Its biggest advantage was a modern plant in the San Fernando Valley, encompassing ten buildings, six soundstages, and extensive back-lot sets for action shooting. In the writers' building, uncomfortable offices offered the regulation desk, swivel chair, and filing cabinet. Some of the more fastidious writers objected to the horsey smells permeating the building from the many Westerns being shot. Nat disliked the institutional linoleum floor, and when he discovered an office down the hall with a rug, he began stretching out on the floor in the late afternoons, perhaps thinking about what a character would say next, but just as likely napping.

Republic Productions has since been called "Repulsive Productions," the studio that never made a decent picture. Thirties Hollywood produced many good movies, but also many stinkers. Probably Republic's fell at the high end of the stinker list. A more accurate description of the company would be Cheapsville: its factory assembly line spewed out a constant stream of quickie action pictures using the most economical methods. Writers were given three weeks, or less, to do a script. Hurry-up shooting schedules operated from dawn to dusk. Flubbed lines seldom resulted in reshoots. Footage was reused, sometimes in the very same film. Theater owners often booked Republic releases when they couldn't afford better pictures. In order to be profitable, the studio had to keep its rental fees low, and that meant shooting on the cheap.

In Cheapsville, writers and performers tended to be second-string. Nevertheless, Republic's lineup of writers was not devoid of talent. It had Horace McCoy, author of hard-boiled Los Angeles fiction (*They Shoot Horses, Don't They?*), and a future director, Samuel Fuller, whose first screenwriting assignment at age twenty-five was a collaboration with Nat on *Gangs of New York*. In the acting category, Republic could boast of more stars with four legs than any other studio in town; its superstars were the squeaky-clean singing cowboys Gene Autry, with his horse Champion, and Roy Rogers riding Trigger. Other human stars on the lot were Bela Lugosi, Jackie Cooper, Wendy Barrie for dramatic roles, and comedienne Judy Canova for hillbilly comedies. In addition, two Hollywood legends were working there during Nat's time: John Wayne and Rita Cansino, before being renamed Rita Hayworth (*Hit the Saddle*, 1937).

Nat's first feature film, *Ticket to Paradise*, was an amnesia comedy about an executive (Roger Pryor) at a white-shoe company who loses

his memory after an auto accident, regains it thanks to a fetching heroine (Wendy Barrie), and—the twisteroo—promptly forgets the fetching heroine. When the film was released in June, *Variety* thought the
dialogue was amusing and the *New York Daily News* called the caper
"cute," but other dailies used words like "stupid" and "juvenile," and
one paper recommended the film to "students of amnesia." *Ticket to
Paradise* can hardly be called an auspicious debut. Nat's performance
demonstrated, though, that he could get together a viable script and
handle the work with competence and speed. In May, Republic raised
his weekly pay to $250 and offered a standard six-month contract promising further increases every six months until his salary reached $1,000.
Those clauses were laughable, because $400 was the highest wage any
Republic writer received, and some of the staff took home $25 a week.
It was said, jokingly, that Republic was so cheap it fired all its writers
the day before Thanksgiving and reinstated them on Friday.

Nevertheless, Nat was delighted by the new contract because he
could begin repaying Sid. He left the Parva-Sed-Apta for a house on
Alta Loma Terrace, one of the winding streets in the hills above Sunset Strip. With a place of his own, he was able to send for Danny and to
mate him. The pup he kept was a gloriously mischievous, liver-colored
bitch, "full of all kinds of little evil tricks—a thief and a liar, but lots of
fun and full of laffs." Despite complaints about how Julie and Danny
took over his bed, he never kicked them off. As long as he had his dogs,
he was happy.

Although Republic was Horseworld, Nat never worked on a Western. All his projects were "problem" stories featuring characters who
were established at the outset as good or bad, with no shades of gray.
The simple, predictable plots were suitable for the second half of double bills at neighborhood theaters, where they opened and disappeared
nearly overnight. Following *Ticket to Paradise*, Nat worked on *Follow
Your Heart*, a cornball operetta designed as the screen debut of Metropolitan Opera star Marion Talley. As this type of musical production
was offbeat for Republic, they went overboard, with showy coloratura
arias and expensive dance sequences, but it failed to measure up to the

light-opera pictures made popular by Nelson Eddy and Jeanette Mac-Donald. Marion Talley had a beautiful voice but no gift for acting.

On *Follow Your Heart,* Nat was partnered with senior colleagues Samuel Ornitz and Lester Cole, the latter a friend of Sid's. Born Lester Cohn to a Polish immigrant cutter in a neckwear factory, Cole dropped out of school at sixteen to become an actor. During his four years in Hollywood, he had managed to assemble a string of writing credits at studios like Fox Films and Columbia, but lately his career had stalled—blackballed due to his union activities, he believed—making it necessary to take cuts in pay and prestige. (Nat suspected the real reason was "his truculent, quarrelsome personality.") Lester and Sid were fond of spending afternoons at the Santa Anita racetrack, followed by nights of partying at the Clover Club on Sunset, where Lester droned on about redecorating his house on the cheap, how he got a woman friend to pick out curtains and his Filipino servant to paint the walls. It seemed odd to Nat that Lester should be leading such a cushy life in Beverly Hills; he was a cocky, evangelizing Communist supposedly driven by concern for the working class and had thrown himself into organizing the Screen Writers Guild. He was always trying to elevate Nat's political consciousness with invitations to join Marxist study classes, but Nat resisted.

Unlike most of the other writers—from Robert Benchley, with his Harvard degree, to Lester Cole, the high school dropout—Nat had earned an MBA from the Kenmore Hall and Sutton Club hotels, where he had gained a firsthand understanding of how to operate a business. Five years a manager, now an employee, he believed in giving respect and good value to an employer. Without much thought, he was inclined to treat screenwriting as a business, the pictures a commodity from which to turn a profit, or loss. He constructed a career in movies as meticulously as Max Weinstein had put up an apartment building. The Underwood schmucks could scoff at "movie feces," but Nat took his work seriously.

During the whole decade of the thirties, Sid received screen credit for eight feature films. Several more were uncredited or unproduced, and none was successful except two Marx Brothers movies. By contrast, Nat in only two years would have a hand in ten movies, most of them actually filmed, by showing up day in and day out and getting the job done. He aggressively approached every project: a loopy Inspector Clouseau–type detective chasing missing emeralds (*Jim Hanvey, Detective*); a police officer doubling as a New York racketeer (*Gangs of New York*); a punk college kid stealing exam questions (*Stormy Weather*); blue-collar buddies saving a dam from collapsing (*Born to Be Wild*); a songwriting hoax in Tin Pan Alley (*Rhythm in the Clouds*); diabolical Main Street fascists threatening illegal immigrants with deportation (*It Could Happen to You*); a boy and his trusty dog against the world (*Orphans of the Street*). Sprinkled throughout are lovable animals, fishing trips, and a sweet elderly father named Max.

To be sure, these B pictures were not likely to win Academy Awards. He insisted that he wrote "grade-C scripts only—dog stories and such things for low pay. If the director's wife finds them sloppy enough, then they are accepted."

The picture usually singled out as one of his best—definitely his best at Republic—is no dog story. *The President's Mystery*, adapted by Nat and Lester Cole, attracted attention for its social conscience, documenting the struggles of the cooperative movement in America. It is a solemn film based on an idea of President Franklin Roosevelt (a bedtime reader of whodunits). Jim Black is a corrupt Washington lobbyist who disappears after his wife is murdered. Starting over in a small town, he takes up the cause of local farmers and cannery workers in organizing a cooperative. In the end, the little guys triumph against big business with the support of Jim, in love with the cannery owner's daughter, and everybody lives happily. Advance word on *The President's Mystery* was excellent, and the *New York Times* reported that preview screenings "set the industry buzzing." But a first viewing by the head of Republic practically blew the roof off the projection building. "Who's responsible for this propaganda, this Roosevelt communist crap?" roared Herbert Yates. "Put that communist shit on the shelf." But once President Roosevelt won a second term by a landslide two months later, the Communist crap was released after all. It was the kind of moralizing, boring picture that won respectful reviews along with audience yawns. "The heavy hand of propaganda" prevented its making the grade as entertainment, chided the *Washington Post*.

Nat was unconcerned. By the end of his second year at Republic, then represented by Feldman-Blum, a top talent agency, he was pulling in a steady income of $350 a week, small potatoes compared to the $1,000 to $2,000 being drawn by the Underwood schmucks but gratifying nonetheless. Repulsive Pictures enabled him to live more affluently than he could by managing a hotel or doing almost any other job in those years. Others might sneer at Hollywood hackwork, but he never underestimated his good fortune.

In the parking lot behind Musso Frank's one night, Nat sensed somebody following him. A familiar voice said, "It's a long way to Viele Pond."

Without missing a beat, he said, "Scotty."

John Sanford had recently arrived in Hollywood. Publication earlier that year of his second novel, *The Old Man's Place*, brought an offer from Paramount of a six-month, $350-a-week contract. He was working on another book and attending meetings of the Anti-Nazi League and the Communist Party.

They walked around to the entrance of the restaurant, chatting about nothing, and gave each other a half salute before going their separate ways. Scotty recognized Nat by his ungainly gait, like "a man embarrassed by his feet." Their last contact had been the ugly exchange at the Sutton Club.

While living on the farm, Nat had received a letter from Scotty tentatively proposing a reunion for old times' sake. It was unfortunate, he replied, "but your note came just as I was preparing to leave here to go away for several weeks." He would get in touch at a later date. Scotty, feeling snubbed, made no further attempt to rekindle their relationship. In Hollywood, they ended up having regular—but accidental—social contact, bumping into each other at Musso's bar or next door at

Stanley Rose's bookstore, where John bought Communist literature. Sometimes Nat would be standing on the sidewalk chewing a tooth-pick. The occasions they joined each other for dinner, usually im-promptu, Nat held forth on "duck-shooting, guns, and bird-dogs." He still couldn't light a cigarette without using both hands, Scotty noticed. They were no longer friends but rather adopted the roles of male ac-quaintances, classic bachelors at loose ends and appreciating the sight of a familiar face.

Nat had developed a close friendship with the bookstore owner Stanley Rose, who was to play an important part in the genesis of Nat's next book. Rose was born at the turn of the century into a farm family on the southern fringe of the Texas Panhandle. After his father's early death, his mother remarried a horse rancher twenty years her senior, and Stanley and his younger siblings grew up among cattlemen and cowboys. He never went beyond the fourth grade, but neither did a lot of people in Motley County. Rose's slow migration from rural be-ginnings in Texas to Hollywood bookseller and authors' agent suggests that neither profession requires any special love of literature. His close friend of twenty years, Bill Saroyan, once asked if he ever read any of the books he sold.

"Well," he replied in his extra-slow Texas drawl, "not all the way through maybe, but I know what every book in the shop *is*." In his early days in Hollywood, sometimes living on the edge of the law as a boot-legger and pornography distributor, he once spent three months in jail after publishing a copyrighted book by comedian Charles ("Chic") Sale without permission. "He was a sonofabitch," said a woman who worked for him, "but he loved his mother."

While living on North Ivar Street, Nat wandered into the store one day and immediately felt at home. There were books and art on the street floor, an erotica section on the balcony, and at the rear of the store a separate room that was almost like a private club. Admission was by invitation. The regulars represented a Who's Who of literary names—William Faulkner, Scott Fitzgerald, Gene Fowler, Erskine Caldwell, Dashiell Hammett, Carey McWilliams—as well as half a dozen less well-known novelist-screenwriters like John Fante and Horace McCoy. Stanley's was not the only popular bookstore in Hollywood, but it was the only one that doubled as a literary salon where writers could relax with a glass of homemade orange wine and gossip about the movie and book business.

Rose may not have been much of a reader, but he loved the company of writers, especially writers like Nat. He made affectionate fun of his Ivy League dress code, calling him Tweedy Boy, and Nat, in turn, referred to Stanley as Jeeter, after Erskine Caldwell's ignorant tenant farmer in *Tobacco Road*. With Stanley as a guide, Nat was able to tour some of the disreputable places never publicized by the Hollywood Chamber of Commerce, its lowlife population of cockfighters, drug peddlers, smugglers, and unrepentant pimps. Without Stanley, Nat would have written another novel of course. But not the same novel.

17

SISTER EILEEN AND MRS. WHITE

OUTSIDE THE TOWN of New Milford, Connecticut, the mountaintop house overlooked dense woodlands and speckled wildflowers, poetic as a Hudson River School oil painting. The crumbling, seventeen-room clapboard residence had been built at the turn of the century, when big families employed plenty of servants, but years of neglect had turned it into a cobwebbed wreck without electricity or running water. No doubt the long-unoccupied house was a bargain at fifteen dollars a month, if one was willing to put up with certain drawbacks—mosquitoes, dozens of windows without screens, a woodstove, the outhouse, a bumper crop of poison ivy. Still, there was the pleasure of swimming in nearby Candlewood Lake.

After six months in Akron, Ruth had returned to New York, at the end of May 1937, in an exceptionally good mood. Not only was her old Ford sagging with the books and research folders needed for her account of the United Rubber Workers strike, but months of dieting had paid off: she weighed 135 pounds. Her plan was to spend the summer in Connecticut working on the book, and during her week's stopover in the city, she arranged to rent a house in the town where she had vacationed the previous fall. On the day of her departure she was not alone. Eileen and the baby came with her.

Eileen had to admit that her sister was right: Morris was a very bad choice. During pregnancy she had counted on their baby to change him, but the drinking moods, his robust attacks of bile, the cutting sarcasm continued. Sober or hung over, he managed to argue her under the table: All right, he drank, but so did lots of people. Didn't he bring home a paycheck every week? Unwinding with a couple of drinks was a man's right. In the end, attempts to coax him off the bottle proved fruitless because they merely sent him retreating to the alcoholic's classic fallback position: he was the victim, his wife the wet blanket. After twenty-one months of marriage, their lives a war zone with alcohol the winner, she decided to file for divorce.

Shortly after taking up residence on the mountain, Eileen and Ruth were befriended by Matthew and Hannah Josephson, a couple living in nearby Sherman. Matty, one of the country's most popular biographers, coined the phrase "robber barons" for the title of his book on how the Rockefellers and other Gilded Age capitalists got their money. Ruth made it her business to cultivate the couple, though in later years she sniped sarcastically about Matty's "mighty brain," calling him "a slightly pinker than ordinary liberal." For the time being, laughter and good times prevailed, and the Josephsons' young son, Carl, always looked forward to a baseball game with Ruth as "great fun."

Another local resident to befriend them was St. Clair McKelway, the *New Yorker* editor who had purchased Ruth's piece about Akron. Mac, as everyone called him, lived a stone's throw away in Gaylordsville, and after getting a firsthand look at Eileen the sparks ignited. "I fell for her immediately," he said, recalling her bewitching aquamarine eyes, the lilting laugh, the endearing stutter. He also enjoyed her directness, which struck him as unusual for a woman. That she seemed willing to make fun of herself—to readily admit personal defects—unsettled him at first, but he grew accustomed to her straight-talking manner. She never asked for sympathy and did not expect it, he noted.

He immediately set out to improve her, however. What especially impressed him were her self-deprecating anecdotes about the situations she got into, confessional humor rich in deadpan wit. With her ear for comedy, she ought to write, he said.

Of course, competing with her sister would be unthinkable. Rarely did she wade through a book, let alone contemplate writing anything more strenuous than a nicely written letter. So she rebuffed McKelway's encouragement by saying that she had no interest whatsoever in writing, and furthermore, she had nothing to say. Writing ability came born in you, like double-jointedness. Ruth had it; she didn't.

Nonsense, he argued, because "she could do better than Ruth."

She didn't have any ability, she said stubbornly.

But a flair for writing seemed to run in her family, he insisted; she should try.

Eventually she mustered the courage to attempt a story, just to please him, but gave up after deciding it was awful.

One reason for Mac's earlier indifference toward Eileen, her pregnancy notwithstanding, apparently had to do with Ruth, who had impressed him as gauche. When he did meet Eileen he was greatly surprised to find she was nothing like her brassy sister. She had style, refinement, poise, and natural good taste. Never did he feel uncomfortable squiring her anywhere, whereas he would have been mortified to be seen in public with Ruth. He fell into the habit of driving over from Gaylordsville, showing up unannounced because there was no telephone on the mountain, until, one summer evening, he and Eileen became lovers. The fact that he was married seemed incidental; he and his wife kept in touch and shared an apartment in town, but generally led separate lives.

"Blond, bland St. Clair McKelway," purred *Time* magazine. He was the most agreeable of men, a tall, mustached blond with an aristocratic name and a patrician manner as smooth as a jigger of Southern Comfort. Not only did he enjoy women, he also fancied the idea of being a husband, so much so that he had tried it three times and would do so twice again (but never successfully). Friends, dubbing him "Marry the Girl Mac," teased that he would wed almost any good-looking woman who asked.

Born in Charlotte, North Carolina, the eldest son of a Presbyterian minister, he was deaf to the holy call of the church. It was love of the newspaper business that coursed more powerfully through three generations of his family, beginning with his prominent, namesake great-uncle, the longtime editor in chief of the *Brooklyn Eagle*, and including his younger brother Benjamin, who would become editor of the *Washington Evening Star*, and finally his own career, spanning some sixty years as writer and editor.

When Eileen met him in the summer of 1937, he was thirty-two years old, a model of cool self-possession. Other than a habit of quietly mumbling his words, there were no rough edges to mar his bland blondness. From the age of fourteen, as an office boy at the *Washington Times-Herald*, McKelway distinguished himself on a number of well-known papers, yet remained an adventurer at heart. For three years he lived in Siam, where he edited an English-language newspaper, the *Bangkok Daily Mail*. After his return to the United States in 1933, he worked for the *New York Herald Tribune* before being hired by *The New Yorker* as a staff writer. When Ross appointed him managing editor for fact articles, he agreed, on three conditions: a rigid separation of duties that restricted Mrs. White to fiction; the high annual compensation of fifteen thousand dollars; and the right to step down after three years. Why three? Ross wanted to know.

Because of some mysterious affinity for the number, he replied— three years in Washington, three in Bangkok. Ross held up his hand to interrupt: "I don't want to hear it." All around, the arrangement worked out satisfactorily, even when McKelway hired a recent Yale graduate, Brendan Gill, at an overly generous salary. "Don't play God, McKelway!" Ross barked, but otherwise did not interfere with his judgment.

True to his agreement, McKelway would step down in 1939 and leave the post to one of his assistants, William Shawn (who, after succeeding Harold Ross in 1952, would edit the magazine for thirty-five years). Returning to full-time writing for the magazine, Mac won a place in the *New Yorker* family as a favored son, alongside Andy White and Wolcott Gibbs, drawing praise from colleagues for both his work and his charisma. "Mr. Congeniality" to his colleague Gardner Botsford, he epitomized cosmopolitan fashion for Brendan Gill, who admired his "broad shoulders, a graceful walk, and well-cut clothes." He twice made waves by marrying within the magazine's family. At the moment, his wife was Ann Honeycutt, a wiry, chain-smoking, heavy-drinking, ex–oil wildcatter from Louisiana who worked in the music department at CBS. Around *The New Yorker*, Honey had been known as James Thurber's girlfriend, although she also dated White and Gibbs. At one point she was spending so much time in the office that Ross assumed she must work there. For eight years, the besotted Thurber pursued Honeycutt, ceasing only when she decided to marry McKelway.

In New Milford, Eileen's summer romance with her big blond began happily. Mac was the nicest, kindest man she had ever known, an opinion she shared with Ann Honeycutt, who saw her courtly husband as "ever a gentleman. No tantrums. Good looking. Self-possessed," adding that "he could hold his liquor." More than anything, Eileen longed to be adored by someone classy, and no question, Mac fit the description. Sexually experienced, he soon figured out that she was frigid, but he apparently made her feel at ease, because they got on well in and out of bed. Many a man would have regarded a squirmy six-month-old as an encumbrance, but the presence of Tommy did not seem to faze Mac, himself the father of a five-year-old son, with whom he had little contact. For Eileen it was a relief to sink into a desperately needed safety zone, even if it proved a temporary fling. Enveloped in mountaintop greenery, autumn seemed a long time off.

"Katharine White discovered Ruth McKenney," St. Clair McKelway was to declare emphatically years later. Despite having bought one of Ruth's first pieces for *The New Yorker*, he took no credit for bringing her into the fold. At the magazine's water coolers, gossip maligned the new contributor as a militant rabble-rouser and an inept writer whose submissions were generally rejected, rewritten (sometimes several times), then resubmitted and sometimes accepted, after which they required massive editing. It was entirely due to the patience of Mrs. White that her work appeared in the magazine at all, or so some believed.

The New Yorker had been slowly straying from its earlier humor content to higher literary ground but still liked to think of itself as primarily entertaining, and its core readership continued to buy it for yuks. Mrs. White, a major-league prune despite her racy office romance with Andy White, was responsible for bringing in bread-and-butter comic pieces from their stable of humorists and also developing new funny writers. Ross had a soft spot for personal humor—nostalgic episodes from family life—and in this department she had done extremely well. Among her pets were two longtime contributors: Clarence Day, whose stories about his parents had been running since 1933, and Sally Benson, the St. Louis–born writer whose "Junior Miss" and later "Kensington Avenue" ("Meet Me in St. Louis") stories would become popular films. The most notable example of all was James Thurber, whose beloved stories about his youth in Columbus, Ohio, had been published as a book, *My Life and Hard Times*, four years earlier. To Mrs. White, it was clear that Ruth was no female Thurber—her writing was impressively undisciplined, a paean to excess—and yet nothing was impossible. She might be whipped into satisfactory shape after all. Mrs. White had developed a trouble-free, affectionate relationship with Clarence Day, and she had no problems with Benson, a prolific staff writer said to like her cocktails. But dealing with Ruth McKenney was to take biblical patience.

While Mrs. White never sugarcoated her opinion of Ruth's writing, which she considered wordy, careless, incoherent, and loose, she once did acknowledge her as "a swell writer" who got fewer rejections than most of their contributors. (It would be interesting to know who got more.) During the decade in which the magazine would publish Ruth's work, Mrs. White attempted to instruct her in the craft of fiction. "Full of irrelevancies" was a typical criticism. But getting Ruth to stick to a point was like asking a camper to give up marshmallows. In hair-tearing exasperation, Mrs. White once made a telling observation about stories featuring Grandpa Flynn, calling the character "really *too* preposterous and too freakish." Once Mrs. White had moved to Maine (to accommodate Andy) and her duties were assumed by

Gustave Lobrano, he continued to reject Ruth's pieces. "Make an effort to under-write rather than over-write," he urged. When two of her submissions happened to fall into the hands of William Shawn, by then McKelway's replacement as nonfiction editor, he shuddered. The pieces were, Shawn told Gus Lobrano, "both unbelievably bad, carelessly slung together, full of generalities."

Mrs. White's blunt comments seemed to slide off Ruth's back. Ruth seemed more intent on cultivating the editor with dinner invitations (Mrs. White did not socialize with novice contributors) or jollying her along with tidbits from her personal life. Mrs. White was not a jovial woman. Indeed, she was practically humorless, at least where it concerned contributions to *The New Yorker*. But not only was Ruth a person who hated to take no for an answer, she also was desperately hard up for money. Rummages through her childhood yielded gooey stories that could be dramatized into salable sketches. Her earliest ideas focused on homespun Ohio. They featured a homely, Huck Finnish tomboy and her cutie-pie kid sister, two jaunty tykes in an old-fashioned, prewar, extended Irish family with an overbearing father and a shadowy mother. That the stories exuded a whiff of mothballs, and sometimes the unmistakable flavor of corn, did not offend Mrs. White, who knew her readers' appetites.

Of all Ruth's vignettes the most frequently rejected were those about Tom Flynn; the ones most interesting to Mrs. White were stories featuring Eileen. She particularly enjoyed reading about the fortunes of the grown-up sisters once they left Ohio and struggled to make their way in the city. Ruth began fine-tuning her sketches by expanding the sister's role and at the same time retaining her role as stage manager–narrator, with events and impressions filtered through her sunny memories. What began to evolve was a distinct picture of Eileen, albeit a faded, inaccurate snapshot dated circa 1915. Whether six or sixteen, the Eileen character in the pages of *The New Yorker* is a lovely girl with a tilted-tip nose and bubbly personality but not a lot upstairs. The other sister is pudgy, homely, capable Ruth, the exceptionally smart character who accomplishes things despite her liabilities.

At some point during the summer of 1937, Eileen found herself being nudged onto the path of fame. Accustomed to being unheeded by
the world, she was not in the habit of seeking attention, certainly not
when she had done nothing to deserve notice. It is doubtful that she
and Mrs. White ever met, at least not in 1937, but it was White who
would be responsible for changing her life. As McKelway pointed out,
Katharine White discovered Ruth. But she also discovered Eileen.

During those languorous days of June, Eileen was crazed as only a
woman desperate to discard a man can be. She wrote letters to her attorney, yelling at him instead of Morris. The only grounds for divorce
in New York State was adultery, with evidence from a third party; however, it was possible to fulfill a six-week residence in Nevada, which
granted decrees on the grounds of extreme cruelty. What if a woman
had no money of her own? In that case, the lawyer informed her, the
husband paid. But what if the husband had not agreed to a divorce, because he was expecting the wife to return? Eileen was trapped.

Meanwhile, money was again an unpleasant issue between her
and Ruth. Their agreement was to divide the household labor, with
Ruth writing her book and pitching in with the cooking (typically
ham hocks and string beans, corned beef on Saturday) while Eileen
earned her keep like Little Orphan Annie, washing dishes and sweeping the floors. A local girl came up to help out with Tommy, who, at
six months, still passed much of his day asleep in a wooden box on the
porch. The hired girl cooled his bottles in the well, boiled undershirts
on the woodstove, and draped them on bushes to dry, because the purchase of a clothesline never occurred to Eileen.

Over Independence Day the country was transfixed by the disap-
pearance of Amelia Earhart, who had strayed off course in the Pacific
on a world flight. As the search continued, people stayed glued to their
radios for the latest news. Without electricity, Eileen and Ruth had to
drive down to the village to find out if the wayward aviator was dead or
alive. But such excitement seldom ruffled their pastoral existence during the week. Weekends were different; almost every Sunday Ruth's
Communist friends trooped up from the city. Some of the comrades

expressed indignation to Eileen that her sister should be forced to work for a frivolous magazine like *The New Yorker*. The only publications to meet their approval were the party newspaper, the *Daily Worker*, and the *New Masses*, a prestigious Marxist journal publishing writers like Theodore Dreiser and Ernest Hemingway. Eileen could not help resenting some of these visitors—obviously they came for a free meal, knowing full well the sisters were pinched for money. It was unfortunate that their sole source of income was the *New Yorker* checks, not only modest but also unreliable, since so many stories wound up rejected.

From time to time, Eileen proposed material that turned out to be witty and salable, including the story of their favorite tramp, Chickie, and another about 14 Gay Street, with its bathroom fungus. Ruth changed Edmond Martin's name to Spitzer, but the portrait fit the rattlesnake landlord to T. A third story, "Beware the Brazilian Navy," recalled the detestable Brazilians who had followed Ruth home from Brooklyn. Mrs. White thought it was too long and awash in "loose writing," but it was so amusing that, pending revisions, she penciled it in for a summer issue. She also sent a thirty-dollar bonus and raised Ruth's word rate to eight cents from seven. After that, Eileen didn't hesitate to suggest ideas, urging Ruth to get a story in the mail quickly so they would receive another check.

One morning in late July, Ruth came back from the post office with a letter from some joker who said he was collaborating on a book about labor leaders. Claiming to be associated with the *New Masses*, this John Stuart began dropping names: Granville Hicks the Communist literary critic, Bruce Minton the labor editor and historian, with whom he was coauthoring *Men Who Lead Labor*, a collection of biographical profiles of men like John L. Lewis and Harry Bridges. After a smart-alecky buildup, Stuart requested information on the history of the United Rubber Workers of America. He wanted it by return mail because he and Minton had passed their publisher's deadline. For her convenience he was enclosing a self-addressed envelope. All this made Ruth bristle.

Eileen thought Stuart sounded like a jackass. "What gall!" she said.

After Chubb had spent months mucking around in Akron, after filling six cartons of research material, she should not be bullied by Marxists doing an armchair analysis.

Ruth regarded the rubber workers as "mine, all mine." Even so, she felt ambivalent. Should she be insulted or flattered? These *New Masses* bullies were the very best Communists. Not only were they aware of her project, no doubt having read "Uneasy City" in *The New Yorker*, but also must have thought it sufficiently important to steal. Dispatching a terse reply to John Stuart, she said that her research had been conducted solely for her own book and therefore obliging him was out of the question. If he cared to visit her some Sunday in Connecticut, she might be willing to discuss the subject with him. Finally, she was not acquainted with this Bruce Minton, whoever he might be.

Eileen warned her not to mail the letter. Stuart would be up there in a minute.

Not likely, Ruth thought. It was a two-hour drive from the city, and those types of fat cats had better ways to spend their weekends.

A telegram arrived the next afternoon. Stuart and his associate would be arriving Sunday, August 1, on the 9 A.M. train.

Ruth picked them up at the station in dirty overalls and a straw hat. In a foul mood, she felt under no obligation to look attractive or behave graciously. Stepping off the train came a rotund twenty-five-year-old who introduced himself as John Stuart and immediately took charge of the conversation, smiling and chattering nonstop. His companion, a scrawny fellow, hung back and said very little. Stuart announced that his friend found Ruth's letter insulting and had not wanted to come. But he refused to leave him in the city on a boiling-hot Sunday, brooding all by himself.

"His wife's in Reno divorcing him," Stuart reported, with ill-considered relish.

At that point, Bruce Minton, who had remained aloof from the conversation, interrupted. There was nothing to brood about, he snapped. He and his wife had been separated for years. As they drove up the mountain, the two kept screaming at each other to shut up.

At the house, Eileen was waiting on the porch. She decided that the self-important Stuart must be the distinguished Marxist historian and the skinny, nervous guy his lickspittle Minton.

Welcome, Minton, she mistakenly greeted Stuart. "I understand you *write*." She was about to follow up with a volley of cutting remarks when the situation unexpectedly turned complicated. At that very moment, a taxi, one of the few in Danbury on a Sunday morning, rattled up the steep hill and Morris hopped out. The sight of two men standing on his wife's porch made him jump to conclusions. Without prelude, he ignored Stuart and turned on the string bean. "Who are you?" he yelled at Minton. Word of her fling had got back to him, and he believed he stood face to face with the man making love to his wife.

But this was not McKelway, she protested, who, incidentally, was nothing more than a platonic friend.

Morris continued to rant. Traveling all the way from the city to visit his son, he had found her entertaining a bunch of guys. And the condition of the house was shocking. There was no running water, not even laundry facilities for washing the baby's diapers. The sight of Tommy, suffering from a bad case of heat rash, sent him off on another tirade about substandard conditions. He threatened to report Eileen to family court for endangering the welfare of an infant.

After a flurry of name-calling, Morris gathered up the baby and went off to play. Shirt stripped off, he parked on the sun-dappled back veranda with a view of the Housatonic River valley and cradled Tommy in his lap. Having come prepared with a camera, he enlisted the help of the babysitter to snap pictures of himself with Tommy. A few hours later, he had run out of things to say to a six-month-old, and as the rest of the household continued to ignore him, there seemed no point in hanging around. He slogged down the hill on foot and headed for the station.

In the meantime, another drama was unfolding inside the house. Bruce Minton announced that his name was not really Bruce Minton —a nom de plume, he called it—but Richard Bransten. The reason for the alias was his family, who disapproved of his radical activities. John Stuart, it turned out, was not John Stuart either. His real name was Harry Winegar. To Eileen, rolling her eyes in disbelief, these men seemed a silly pair playing a cloak-and-dagger game of spies and secret decoder rings.

For the rest of the morning, the visitors huddled with Ruth to talk about the United Rubber Workers, but as noon approached they began making hints about lunch. Eileen and Ruth, scurrying around the kitchen, assembled a humble meal of corned beef on white bread with dill pickles, and served the remains of a jar of peanut butter for dessert. Minton hated corned beef but had the good grace to eat his sandwich without complaint. In the afternoon Eileen became the recipient of Stuart's braying denunciation for her lack of political consciousness. When it became clear the men were in no hurry to depart, Ruth suggested driving down to Candlewood Lake for a swim, to a special rock, where the startlingly clear water was thirty feet deep. Near the shore Ruth and Richard floated as they continued to talk, while Stuart, who could not swim, squatted on a rock reading the *Daily Worker*. Eileen, tired of feigning interest in Harry Bridges and his tedious longshoremen, absented herself by swimming to an island in the middle of the lake.

That evening the men treated them to hamburgers at a drive-in and caught the 9:30 to Grand Central.

Back at the house, Eileen and Ruth sat in the dark and slapped away the mosquitoes. After leaving Bransten and Stuart at the train, Eileen was eager to swing by Gaylordsville and tell Mac all about the silly *New Masses* Marxists. To her surprise, Ruth insisted on driving straight home. On the porch, unusually subdued, she said that Richard had promised to write.

Ridiculous, Eileen replied. And the way she had been making a fool of herself—those goo-goo eyes, practically wagging her tail at the lake—was "revolting." Mark her words, he would never be heard from again.

So she was an expert on men, Ruth said angrily. Look how long it took her to wise up to Morris. When she rose from her rocker to take a swing at her sister, Eileen ducked the punch.

Suspicious of people who used aliases, Eileen thought that the entire name business sounded fishy. But what did it matter? A year from then Ruth wouldn't even remember this Minton-Bransten.

Ruth was sure she would.

"He won't write," Eileen said.

But she was wrong. Just eleven days later, Ruth and Minton-Bransten were married by a justice of the peace in Bridgewater, Connecticut.

Richard Bransten, Harvard class of 1927, grew up in a family of San Francisco merchants. The patriarch, Richard's German-Jewish grandfather, Joseph Brandenstein, made his fortune in the late 1800s selling tobacco, and later coffee and tea. By the turn of the century, M. J. Brandenstein and Co. — or MJB — had become a leading coffee brand along with Folgers and Hills Bros. In reaction to anti-German sentiment during World War I, the family anglicized its name.

Richard, born in 1906, was an overprotected, bookish youngster who suffered from tuberculosis. Subsequently cured but medically traumatized, he carried himself even as a grown man with an air of uncertainty that reflected deep insecurity. When Ruth met him he was thirty-one, pasty-cheeked, and painfully underweight at five feet eleven and 131 pounds. A man who knew him around that time said he was "spectacularly thin," but his typically tense expression was "gloriously dissolved when he laughed." "I was always attracted to living skeletons," says the main character in Christina Stead's *I'm Dying Laughing*, a novel whose real-life subjects were Ruth and Richard. (Stead was an Australian writer whose friendship with the Branstens began in the late thirties.)

Two years after graduating from Harvard with a degree in literature, Bransten married Louise Alice Rosenberg, a twenty-year-old Vassar-educated heiress to a dried-fruit fortune. This alliance between the Branstens and the Rosenbergs had all the earmarks of a royal grocery-store coupling, two Bay Area youngsters united by Ivy League educations and a world of privilege, but with the souls of rebels. In the aftermath of the stock-market crash, convinced of the necessity to burn down their fathers' houses, those evil empires built by caffeine and fruit, they fervently embraced the idea that they could help destroy capitalism. As a matter of principle, they joined the Communist Party. In *I'm Dying Laughing*, the character based on Richard tells his incredulous mother, "In a better world I might have been born a good son to you. But it's a worse world." In the worse world, he took the pen name Bruce Minton and wrote a book that went unreviewed (and likely unread) about the fascist menace in America; the couple made a six-week tour of Russia and habitually supported good causes—a longshoremen's strike, for example. But after eight years of marriage, Louise was in Nevada with their seven-year-old son, Thomas, for a divorce. Returning to New York that October, she must have been startled to learn that her ex-husband was now married to a woman he had known only a few days.

The marriage was even more astonishing to Ruth's Ohio relatives. That Ruth—bullheaded, mentally disturbed, and fat—had managed to land the scion of a coffee fortune with meteoric speed was beyond belief.

In *I'm Dying Laughing*, Stephen Howard (Richard) jokes about falling in love with his wife Emily on first sight: "You had just scored a bull's eye in the entertainment field and I figured I could live off you for the rest of my days." In reality, Ruth's home run would not occur for another year. She was an impecunious freelancer living on ham hocks and green beans when Richard met her in New Milford. The key to their pairing appears in one of Ruth's letters to him shortly after their marriage: not only did they share the profession of writing but they were both Communists, which meant there was "a common tie of working our whole lives for a good and beautiful thing."

Eileen did not begrudge Ruth her happiness. It appeared to be a perfect match, a fairy tale come true for a sister who had known so many hardships, and so she set about getting to know her brother-in-law. It soon became apparent, though, that Richard disliked her—and the feeling was mutual.

St. Clair McKelway surrounded by *New Yorker* and Algonquin Round Table friends. Seated: Fritz Foord (McKelway's therapist), Wolcott Gibbs, Algonquin Hotel manager Frank Case, and Dorothy Parker. Standing: Alan Campbell, McKelway, Russell Maloney, and James Thurber. Eileen decided not to marry McKelway.

Katharine White (center) and her husband, E. B. White (left), sailing in Maine with Franklin Pierce Adams. Katharine was the *New Yorker* editor who discovered Ruth McKenney.

The Parva-Sed-Apta apartments, 1817 North Ivar Street in Hollywood, inspired Nat's settings for *The Day of the Locust*.

Joseph Schrank collaborated with Nat on a Broadway play, *Good Hunting,* about the insanity of war. It closed after two performances.

Nat and Sid Perelman at the West house in the Hollywood Hills. Unlike Sid, who hated both Hollywood and screenwriting, Nat established a successful life for himself in California.

The best novel ever written about Hollywood was finally filmed in 1975, with Karen Black and William Atherton as Faye Greener and Tod Hackett in *The Day of the Locust.*

Eileen and her son getting a fresh start in Hollywood after her marriage to Nat in 1940.

Budd Schulberg and his wife went to nightclubs with Nat and Eileen in Hollywood. Nat "seemed like a different person" around Eileen, Schulberg said.

After giving up on New York, Eileen found a job with the Disney Studio in Hollywood.

A glamorous Eileen in slacks and a sun hat was the perfect wife for a Hollywood screenwriter.

Fishing was one of Nat's loves, but bird hunting became an obsession. Eileen turned out to be the better shot.

The last known photograph of Eileen, posing alongside the Wests' new Ford station wagon with Danny and Julie in the fall of 1940.

EILEEN McKENNEY WEST, pictured at the shoulder of her author-sister Ruth McKenney, who immortalised her in "My Sister Eileen" and "The McKenney Carry On," was killed yesterday in an automobile collision in California. Her husband, Nathaniel West, novelist and scenarist, also was fatally injured. A play based on "My Sister Eileen" is scheduled to open here Thursday.

'My Sister Eileen' Is Killed
Dies With Husband in Auto Crash

"My Sister Eileen," the rollicking heroine of Ruth McKenney's madcap magazine articles, two of her books and a play scheduled to open Thursday on Broadway—was killed yesterday in an automobile accident near El Centro, Cal.

Eileen's husband, Nathaniel West, novelist and movie scenarist, also was fatally injured when a station wagon in which the couple were returning from a trip to Mexico collided, driven by Joe

and is scheduled to open Thursday at the Biltmore Theatre — unless the tragedy results in a postponement.

Mrs. West, who was 26, married twice. Her first husband was Morris Jacobs, a New York radio production man. They were wed in 1935 and divorced in 1936, dividing the custody of a child, now three years old. At the time of Mrs. West's death, the child was in her care, according to friends here.

West Was 'Promising'

Signed: Green Snakes

Among the pupils at Public School 221, Empire Blvd. and Troy Av., Brooklyn, Detective Bernard Carney believes, there is a villainous 9-year-old who writes kidnap threats and says he is "The Three Green Snakes," drawing three snakes in green crayon to prove it.

Detective Carney, a little surfeited with Mother Goose, the River Boys and the other juvenile literature he has had to

On Lea To Britai

Overwhelming supp President Roosevelt's for losing or mortgagi equipment to the Britis voiced today by leading icans in a survey made Post.

Outstanding represen of industry, labor, relig cation, politics and organ interested in the role of in the second World W almost unanimous in th the President's plan.

The proposal, which t dent expects to presen new Congress Jan. 5, that the U. S. might future British orders fo ments in this countr lease or mortgage th ducts to Britain on the tion. After the w plan provides, the return the supplies if in good condition, o them.

Of all the telegra to The Post's que out the nation nar wholeheart the plan. One not go far eno that Congress which, or cons dent's fa

An outright port for the W William Green, pr American Federatio who telegraphed:

"My opinion Presid to extend aid to Ga by lending war ma sound and necessary support it."

George M. Harriso dent of the Brothe Railroad Clerks, we farther:

"I favor lending o right implements Great Britain as cratic nations def selves against ag such nations are un the situation throug efforts. . . . If demo be preserved we Great Britain. . . .
Britain can hold off the dictators it will giv our country of meetin ture attack from this

Warning that the the war is here, Char mour, president of Y versity, telegraphed:

"I heartily approve F Roosevelt's plan . . . and that it will develop give a decided impetus port of the British broadest basis. the Europeans w and if it is to by the

The car crash that killed Eileen and Nat in December 1940 shocked the public more than it did friends, who knew him to be a reckless driver.

My Sister Eileen opened to acclaim four days after Eileen died. The play became one of the biggest hits in Broadway history. Jo Ann Sayers and Shirley Booth played the sisters, Morris Carnovsky their nutty Gay Street landlord.

Nat and Eileen's grave in Mount Zion Cemetery, Queens, New York. Eileen's ashes were placed in the coffin.

18

DESTINED TO BE A HEROINE

SUMMER GONE, EVERYONE drove down from Connecticut to the city, but nobody stayed long. Immediately, Richard went to Spain for the *New Masses*, Ruth to join him in Paris for a belated honeymoon, St. Clair McKelway to a drying-out sanitarium in the Catskills. Only Eileen was left, returning to Knickerbocker Village and Morris because she had no other place to go. It was only for the time being, she warned him, for Tommy's sake, and yes, she still was going to Reno as soon as the cash could be found.

When Mac came back from Dr. Fritz Foord's sanitarium at Kerhonkson, a four-star retreat favored by *New Yorker* staffers, he left the apartment he officially shared with Anne Honeycutt. He rented Eileen an apartment on West Fourth Street in the Village and kept separate quarters at the Mansfield, a hotel near the *New Yorker*'s offices on West Forty-third Street. This helped but did not begin to solve her financial problems as a single mother. She applied for stenographic openings in what would turn out to be a succession of dead-end jobs, with most of her wages going to child care. Tommy stayed with babysitters during the day and many evenings too, because she went out with Mac. On weekends when Tommy was not with Morris, he sometimes wound up without his mother anyway because Mac liked slipping away to Skytop Lodge in the Pocono Mountains with Eileen. In a snapshot of

Tommy at eleven months, outside Eileen's brownstone, he is glowing with pleasure. But another photograph taken four months later shows a forlorn little boy with "sticking-out ears," unmistakably the face of a sadder child who has learned a thing or two about the world.

That fall, and throughout the winter of 1938, Eileen's life with Mac centered around eating, drinking, and parties where the martinis never ran out, frequently in the company of his coworkers. Mac's sober return from Foord's sanitarium did not mean abstinence, but rather scaling back. Teetotalism would have been difficult in an office where alcohol abuse was the norm. The morning routine of one staffer was to get out of bed, throw up, shower, and shave. (Did he throw up *every* morning? asked young Brendan Gill, who did not drink. "Of course," E. J. Kahn, Jr., said. "Doesn't everyone?") After work Mac routinely headed for the Algonquin Hotel or saloons handy to the office, like the Cortile. When Eileen joined him later, the two of them would go out for a night on the town at the "21" Club or El Morocco. The clubs, the house seats at Broadway openings, the thousand and one cocktail parties, where she learned to pass up all hors d'oeuvres except caviar—because crumbs made a woman look sloppy—made for an exciting but grueling daily schedule, one that required costly outfits impossible on a stenographer's wages.

On an excursion to Saks Fifth Avenue, she made the mistake of charging a show-stopping white satin gown to her brother-in-law's account and signed herself as Mrs. Richard Bransten. The bill provoked outrage from Richard, who considered it insane to spend $129.50 (around $2,000 today) for an evening dress. Ruth couldn't have agreed more, but loyally defended the purchase by saying that Eileen must have needed it.

Before long, intimacy began to expose some of her beloved's shortcomings. Superficiality, for one. In addition to editorial duties at *The New Yorker*, he wrote first-rate profiles—of the African-American religious preacher Father Divine, and another in progress on gossip columnist Walter Winchell—and he wrote and rewrote short pieces for the "Talk of the Town" department at the front of the magazine. While that was all well and good, Eileen couldn't understand why a person of his abilities took so little interest in subjects of a more serious nature. Did he ever consider the underdog? What about injustice, fascism, or the situation in China? He was really rather a frivolous person, she teased. To such badinage, no matter how playfully phrased, he reacted with increasing irritation; possibly the taunts hit a sore spot.

Sooner or later, she must have noticed distressing similarities between Mac and her husband. Each tended to be shallow, and each probably cheated on her (she chose to look the other way). The most obvious resemblance was that both were alcoholics who got to their offices in the morning nursing hangovers. There were marked differences in their drinking, of course. Morris, tangled in denial, was an unattractive drunk. Mac, however, a considerate alcoholic versed in the fine points of mixing a martini, readily acknowledged his problem and periodically withdrew to Foord's sanitarium in order to dry himself out and get back on course, a process accompanied by endless sessions with his psychiatrist. As some of his friends and coworkers knew, he suffered from a manic-depressive condition that resulted in periodic mood swings and delusional episodes. Had Eileen looked at the fine print, she could have noticed evidence pointing to an impairment not much different from her sister's. But this was something she did not wish to see.

The Spanish Civil War, in its second year, was providing American Communists a focal point for their fight against fascism. All sorts of people, Communist and non-Communist alike, were volunteering to fight, drive ambulances, deliver medical care, and do firsthand news reporting. Prominent writers such as Ernest Hemingway, Dorothy Parker, and Josie Herbst went to Spain, as did Richard Bransten, for the *New Masses*. As a home-front soldier in the war on capitalism, Ruth had to content herself with party recruitment, education, and other housekeeping matters, about which she sent frequent progress reports to her husband overseas. Some of her letters would come to light six years later, when the FBI's New Haven field division, spying on the

Branstens, photographed quantities of their private correspondence, which had been stored in a local warehouse. Apparently one of Ruth's priorities was drawing her sister into the fold. Her goal, she wrote Richard, was connecting Eileen with a blue-collar unit in Brooklyn or the Bronx, where she could hand out leaflets on street corners and engage in "some good old-fashioned educational work."

Whether or not she distributed leaflets, Eileen did agree to attend Marxist study classes and found herself increasingly involved in party activities. Her commitment remained ambivalent, however; party pieties put her to sleep. She could see that the world was going to hell, fascism was evil, capitalism's days were numbered. It upset her no end that people were dying in Spain, and she felt sorry for farmers who lost everything in the Dust Bowl. But she was a person who had a hard time distinguishing between the AFL and the CIO. As St. Clair McKelway would recall, she was a "mild" Communist, the sort never seriously interested in party theory but "deeply sympathetic to the poor." He believed that she joined the party out of loyalty to Ruth, and others who knew her also assumed this. In fact, there is no evidence that Eileen ever became a member. (A Freedom of Information Act request filed in 2005 failed to turn up FBI records that would indicate any official involvement.)

With Mac in tow, Eileen once showed up at a Communist Party outing on the New Jersey Palisades overlooking the Hudson River in a chauffeured Carey Cadillac. They emerged from the limousine toting a hamper full of fancy picnic food catered from the "21" Club.

Eileen would remain a picnic-basket Marxist, who professed strong enough belief in the party's goals to pay lip service but not enough to become a member. She was too much of a skeptic—far too unsentimental—to embrace the idea of a life on the barricades.

In the autumn of 1937, Eileen and Ruth seemed to have stabilized their lives. Eileen had an emotionally (and financially) committed boyfriend, Ruth a husband whose mother controlled his money and doled it out with strings attached. Neither was a perfect situation, but both were more appealing than corned-beef sandwiches. When Ruth returned from her honeymoon, she and Richard took a floor-through apartment on West Eleventh Street and she resumed writing for *The New Yorker*. Not long afterward she crashed, corkscrewing into a condition she called crippling arthritis. As she almost always referred to severe depression as crippling arthritis, or another physical ailment, this seems likely to have been bipolar disease. In manic-depressive psychosis, there can be long periods when symptoms temporarily disappear. Although Ruth's mood swings seemed mild in recent years, her impulsive marriage to a man she barely knew strongly suggests a manic high, just as the stress of the new relationship and setting up a household were the prelude to depression.

Unable to work, she kept to her bed. At one point, she almost went to Arizona, she wrote Matty and Hannah Josephson. "Eileen had the train schedules all looked up and about ½ my clothes packed when I decided I couldn't." One reason she couldn't was her Aunt Lyda and Uncle Otto Thomas, who had made a trip to New York and expected to be guided around the sights. Ruth had to make an effort to pull herself together. "Dear god, what suffering," she moaned afterward. She still felt fond of Lyda but couldn't stand squares like Otto, who believed the infamous Haymarket anarchists were guilty as convicted. When the Thomases left she went back to bed and stayed there, gaining weight and reading Matty's ten-year-old biography of Émile Zola. Ever eager to impress Josephson, she offered effusive praise and announced she was ordering a separate copy for her sister, though it was exactly the kind of book Eileen would never read.

In Christina Stead's *I'm Dying Laughing*, the Richard Bransten character calls his sister-in-law a dullard who "spreads boredom around her fifteen inches thick and anything the man says is right."

Oh, but she is really "a soft hearted girl," his wife argues.

Not at all, he says. She is "a third-rate whore."

From the outset there was no love lost between Richard and Eileen, a situation that escalated once he realized somebody had moved the goalposts and he had married two women, one of them a practitioner of financial anarchy. Making up for years of privations, Ruth bought wildly. From the time they set up housekeeping in the Village, and Ruth spent four dollars apiece on blue-ribbon figs at Balducci's gourmet market, they lived above their means. Whenever she had a few dollars in her pocket, she turned into a runaway spendthrift, but Richard was not much better. Spoiled as a child, married to an heiress, he was a trust-fund person never required to support himself. Faced with a marital bank account in perpetual ruin, he nagged Ruth about the need to curtail expenses, particularly those involving Eileen. At first, he agreed to give Eileen and Tommy a weekly allowance of twenty dollars. When he also was persuaded to underwrite Eileen's Reno divorce in 1938, entailing a six-week stay at a dude ranch for her and the child, he felt badly used.

After Eileen discovered the curious elasticity of Richard's nest egg, she decided that twenty dollars represented a small sum for him. It was unfortunate she had to accept his money, but even with his allowance, Mac's payment of her rent, and Morris's paltry contributions, she was barely scraping by.

What caused the most trouble was Eileen's use of Ruth's charge accounts.

Why must she always dress to the nines? Ruth said, exasperated.

For practical reasons, Eileen said. She needed clothes for work — and for the clubs where Mac was accustomed to spending his evenings.

Ruth seemed sympathetic; Richard remained unmoved.

The Branstens, meanwhile, were at each other's throats. Ruth furnished their apartment with top-of-the-line furniture from Macy's, then employed a cook because, she argued, his first wife fed him cold cuts and she wanted to be a better wife than Louise.

Fractious as the relationship was, Ruth loved her husband very much. He was "a splendid Communist, thoughtful and devoted," who knew so much more than she did, "but you can teach me."

"I never meant to write about you," Ruth told Eileen later. She just wanted to sell a few stories to *The New Yorker* because she needed money. Neither had she given much thought to the book, which was "an accident." She hoped Eileen didn't mind, to which Eileen laughed and replied, "Why should I mind?" because what else could she say? The book was in the stores.

In fact, there was nothing accidental about the book. In early 1938, having sold The New Yorker more than a dozen sketches, most of them autobiographical, she had begun pursuing the idea of collecting them. The idea was hastily snapped up for Harcourt, Brace by Charles Pearce, Nathanael West's erstwhile editor, who had dismissed him so casually, an act he would never forgive. Cap Pearce judged Ruth's girl-power stories irresistible, a delicious meringue of good times and hope that melded the country's heartland, the crucible of corn, with New York, the crucible of coolness. Not only did he work with Ruth to link four-teen of the stories into a unified fable, but it was very likely the shrewd Pearce who originated the title My Sister Eileen, perhaps suggested by Clarence Day's enormously popular Life with Father.

Cap Pearce's instincts proved correct: My Sister Eileen became an immediate success. Chosen as a Book-of-the-Month Club selection prior to its release in July, it soared to number 2 on the New York Times bestseller list (outperforming nonfiction works by Thomas Mann and Dale Carnegie), and by the end of the year it had gone through eight printings. Katharine White, to whom the book was dedicated, pro-nounced it "grand" and herself "thrilled" by its success. Ruth ought to follow up with a sequel, she said: "getting yourself and Eileen mar-ried, Eileen's baby, your appendix, your pure white apartment and your black cook, your job and your husband." But now that she could do whatever she liked, Ruth told her, she intended to focus on serious subjects, like Industrial Valley, her history of the United Rubber Work-ers strike, scheduled for publication in February. After that she was go-ing to write a novel about a union organizer. But she was already think-ing about how she might dramatize the stories for a Broadway comedy. Harold Ross, who kept track of his contributors, sent a memo to Gus Lobrano: "Understand she's using the Eileen motif for her play."

At the Chatham Hotel, Harcourt, Brace threw a flashy publication party, at which Eileen became the center of attention in a simple black taffeta suit with frilly white organdy collar and cuffs, white gloves, and a delicate spray of mauve orchids. The suit was on loan from a friend in her office, a dollar an hour plus the cost of dry cleaning. Ruth, tipping the scales at 183, was stuffed inside a navy print dress, despite Eileen's warnings that fat girls should never wear patterns. In her nervousness, Ruth lost her handbag and forgot to introduce her husband, who, to his great annoyance, was being addressed by the guests as Mister McKenney.

Still, it was a splendid event, as was the party Ruth gave later that evening to celebrate Cap Pearce's thirty-second birthday. Regardless of her resemblance to a rumpled Gertrude Stein, she had become an overnight literary celebrity, practically another James Thurber or S. J. Perelman, suddenly in demand on the author-luncheon tour. And, to Eileen's surprise, everybody wanted to get a look at the cute little sister. In publicity appearances together, they were billed as the Fabulous McKenney Sisters or the Incomparable McKenney Sisters, like vaudeville headliners on the Orpheum circuit.

In a flurry of interviews Eileen presented herself as an "honest to goodness heroine." According to her standard script, she was employed as a private secretary to the president of a large advertising agency located in Rockefeller Center. Although she and her dates frequented El Morocco and the Stork Club, she was nevertheless a serious, contemplative person who, after work, traded her silk hose for lisle-cotton stockings and spent the evenings in Village cafeterias, talking with friends about "battles of the working man." She was a "strong sympathizer of China." Asked about her boyfriends, she blinked her lovely blue-green eyes and made vague allusions to her stable of beaux, too numerous to count. Women at parties, she said, hurried to "pull in their husbands when they realize they are coming face to face with a heroine, who is supposed to be a man-killer." That made her laugh, because she really believed "I'm no glamour girl." Readers did not need to know about her marriage, divorce, and child. Or about Mac. In these matters she took her lead from Ruth, who skipped lightly over her life as wife and Communist.

In every interview Eileen could count on being asked the same question—why didn't she write a book of her own?—to which she had prepared an automatic response. She was "destined to be a heroine," not an author.

Book reviewers complimented Ruth for old-fashioned storytelling that seemed "as richly American as a three-decker sandwich." The *New York Times* rhapsodized, "There is something Thurberian about the McKenneys' tales of a tumultuous childhood in Ohio; there is something of the Clarence Day manner in the harrowing episodes of Manhattan days and nights." But not everybody agreed. In his *New York Post* column, Franklin Pierce Adams admitted he couldn't stomach Ruth's stew of "hoydenish nostalgia," which seemed to be asking "Weren't we the fascinating little devils!" No matter, because, heartwarming or hokey, those Manhattan days and nights were extremely appealing, especially for female readers enthralled by the experiences of sisters who had traded Ohio for a storybook life in New York City.

In Cleveland, meanwhile, reactions of family and friends ranged from sheer ecstasy to dismay to sour grapes. There was plenty of excitement among the Flynns, who had the pleasure of recalling the events on which the stories were based. They argued over the identities of various lightly disguised crazy people and marveled how cleverly Ruth had altered certain details, referring, for example, to Apex Electrical as the Gladsome Washing Machine Co. For her cousin Dick Selvey, the stories "always contained a string of truth" even when events appeared exaggerated, but the portrait of Eileen failed to ring true. Her high school friend Ruth Beebe Hill agrees: "It definitely wasn't the Eileen I knew."

The conservative McKenneys struggled to smile. Syd, for the past year, had watched his life smeared in public, thankfully in a small magazine (circulation 134,000), not in his beloved *Saturday Evening Post* (circulation in the millions). Finding himself a character in a book selling briskly in his own backyard, at Halle's Book Shop, was quite a different matter. He rose to the occasion by explaining to the *Cleveland Press* that his daughter, even as a child, was always making up stories, and so while the experiences in her book might appear factual, the details were considerably embellished. Nevertheless, he gave her credit for spinning good yarns. "My Dad was very very proud of Ruth," says Jack McKenney. Ethel, though, wanted no part of the stagy sisters.

If the stories struck Ruth's family as embroidered, they left outsiders wondering if they were fiction or nonfiction. In fact, the stories were neither, though listed as both; they were typical *New Yorker* "casuals," light sketches existing in a literary no-man's land. "I had to doctor things up a bit," Ruth once confessed. "Not much—just here and there, a slight touch." All she did was add "just the least little bit of fiction to what is undeniably fact," a compulsion that had driven Walter Lister crazy at the *Post*. And so, while Ruth's humorous anecdotes could be called true, they were not necessarily accurate. Readers didn't care, and neither did Mrs. White—her position after all was *fiction* editor, and she did not subject Ruth's material to the same fact checking that the magazine gave to nonfiction. Her rejections were made on the basis of weak narrative, not inaccuracy.

My Sister Eileen was a Depression lollipop from a picture-postcard city of skyscrapers and bright lights. Just as the country flocked to see escapist pictures starring frisky comediennes like Carole Lombard and Katharine Hepburn, it was quick to embrace the Ohio sisters, Cinderellas with sass.

Although the book's success made Eileen a household name, she would discover that fame did not count for much—it offered no financial security. Eileen, famous for being famous, was unable to capitalize on her image, especially one that was entwined with her sister's. Complicating the situation further was a disturbing question: Was she still the same old Eileen McKenney, or was she Ruth's make-believe Sister Eileen?

Within the space of a year, her life had twisted 180 degrees from Ruth's. Her sister was the wife of a millionaire's son with a cook and the best false teeth money could buy; Eileen had broken four of her front teeth diving into a half-empty swimming pool and was trying to pay off the five-hundred-dollar bill for their replacement. When she felt disheartened, Mac would caution against yielding to despair. A devout believer in psychoanalysis, he visited his therapist five times a week and routinely dispensed advice to Eileen. Counseling had performed wonders for him. Prior to treatment with Dr. Foord, he had been a nervous wreck, but now that he was a new man, the doctor enjoyed meeting him for cocktails at the Algonquin.

Her trouble, in Mac's view, was a sense of inferiority that accounted for marrying Morris and making so little of her abilities. The situation was exacerbated by writings that presented her as a dippy literary character glamorized from a very pretty girl in life into a ravishing beauty. She naturally had become a mass of resentments, and the person at fault was her sister.

His negative view was to be expected, because Mac scorned Ruth as a vulgarian. Her conversation was peppered with coarse *whooplas*, *phooeys*, and *whees*, often backed up by a chorus of *poohs* and *eh-heeeehs*—expressions that no well-bred human being would dream of uttering. Her writing, emotional and inclined to fantasy, was highly overrated. Recently he had resisted her attempt to sell him a fact piece about a Communist rally. But, Ruth joked, her idea contained no "wicked old propaganda." And no point of view either, he snapped back.

Psychiatric treatment was by no means common at the time, but Eileen eventually worked up the courage to try it. When she asked Ruth for financial assistance, her sister turned to her husband. He failed to understand why it was necessary for Eileen to air her dirty laundry to a doctor for fifteen dollars an hour.

Because, Ruth replied, she wanted to be normal.

Normal, he repeated with a laugh. None of her relatives were normal.

Eileen's treatment got off to a predictable start. Detouring around the sorrow of her mother's death, the scheming stepmother's rock-hard heart, the golf-obsessed father's impatient belittling, she blazed with resentment toward Ruth. The very first sessions triggered considerable rage, not only over publication of the sketches but events stored deep down in her unconscious for much of her life. At one point the doctor expressed surprise that she didn't dream of strangling her sister. The person she wanted to strangle was the therapist, for saying "mean things" about her sister. Having herself denounced Ruth did not mean she would tolerate his criticism, not even in order to address her conflicts.

Around Ruth and Richard, she used Freudian terms like *transference* and *fixation* and tried to give the impression that the doctor (called "Dr. Memburg" in one of Ruth's books) was a jerk. He had bad breath and buckteeth, she declared, and of course he had a crush on her. Before long she was developing unflattering comic routines about Memburg, a married man not averse to a bit of adultery on the side, and how he kept chasing her around the couch or inviting her to Voisin for duck à l'orange. But in his office, three times a week, there was no tomfoolery. Talking about her sexual difficulties, including blocked memories of the almost-rape, made the sessions especially upsetting. Once these painful emotions were unstoppered they were hard to turn off, and she went home and confided the incident of sexual violence to Mac. That trauma, he said, would account for her need to make men suffer. Wasn't she always ready to believe the worst? (Not without reason, because he did cruise to Bermuda with his former wife while Eileen was in Reno.)

Her treatment continued for several months, until Richard refused to cover Dr. Memburg's bills. In the winter of 1939 she had reached another turning point in her life, possibly hastened by the therapy. After almost two years with St. Clair McKelway, months of perfectly stirred dry martinis, an accidental pregnancy, and an un-Chickie-like abortion, she sensibly decided to part company with the big blond. He seemed impervious to the reasons the relationship fell apart. Long accustomed to medicating himself with alcohol, he had no problem doing an excellent job as Ross's indispensable Jesus. Eileen, acutely sensitive to drinking husbands, even a high-functioning editor who exuded alcoholic niceness, did not wish to repeat her experience. A reminder must have occurred when Morris lost his job and moved into her apartment. He acted like a "dawg," Ruth informed Matty and Hannah Josephson, so that Eileen couldn't eat and looked like a "ghost." She was obliged to kick him out.

The men who next entered her life were interesting but equally flawed. One was Robert Josephy, a prominent book designer and a nephew of Alfred Knopf's. Thirty-six, also a big handsome blond man, he had a wife and a five-year-old daughter, but the marriage was unhappy and would soon end in divorce. After Josephy, she tumbled into a romance with the foreign affairs editor of *Newsweek*, a highly successful journalist married to a writer at the *Washington Post*.

By the spring of 1939, Eileen had racked up several more reasons for believing the worst about men. She had learned that psychoanalysis was not the answer, that all problems could not be conquered, that blessings conferred by *The New Yorker* and its staff are not necessarily godsends, and that New York was not the right place for her after all. In four years, she had lived in a basement, fallen in love and married, become a mother, divorced, fallen in love with and spurned an admirable man, moved on to other men of considerable intelligence. Short on formal education beyond Heights High, she had learned how to comport herself in the company of educated older men and how much to tip the ladies' room attendant at the "21" Club.

With more knowledge but fewer illusions than when she had left Ohio, she decided to fold up her tent and move to the West Coast, where they had sunshine and oranges at least.

19

AN ARSONIST'S GUIDE
TO LOS ANGELES

A DIRECTOR AT Republic told Nat that a script of his wasn't worth five cents, because it did not contain a single new idea. Think of the audience. "It isn't funny enough to make them piss in their seats—it isn't sad enough to make them snuffle," and there's no lesson for people to take away. Get a message, Burt Kelly said. Advice like this would become Nat's Rosetta stone, and it was at the Piss and Snuffle School of Film Writing that he gradually began to master the fundamentals of his craft.

At the same time, he was beginning to understand how Hollywood worked. He learned to befriend directors and keep track of people's careers, who's on top, who has muscle, whose star is dipping. After fifteen months Republic offered him the opportunity to become a story supervisor, but he turned it down. Marathon conferences all day long were "not for me! I had much rather write any time," he told Sid. Besides, he had his eye on sweeter things. A producer anticipated a move to Metro and promised to take Nat with him. "I wouldn't mind leaving this place," he said, but he first hoped to get his weekly salary increased from $250 to $350, an overdue raise. "I have screen credit on practically every good picture that has been made here," he declared with satisfaction.

Granted, a "good picture" at Republic was pretty much an oxy-moron, and there was little resemblance between Cheapsville writers and the celebrity screenwriters living at the Garden of Allah on Sun-set Boulevard. The swank hotel had become a way station for transient New Yorkers waiting to rent a baronial Bel Air mansion. At sundown they gathered around the pool, before retreating to private bungalows, where they swigged epic pitchers of very dry martinis and traded witti-cisms. Meals were at eleven, if they remembered to eat at all. By con-trast, a nuts-and-bolts writer like Nat was sitting in his furnished house cracking open a cold bottle of Schlitz and worrying about contract renewals.

In the winter of 1938, Nat was finally getting his life together. In ad-dition to repaying his debt to Sid, he had saved several thousand dol-lars and was planning his first vacation in two years, a summer trip back to Erwinna. In a letter to Sid he reported that his main anxiety—don't tell Mother, he warned—was the health of his dog Danny, who despite pounds of raw liver was in the hospital, "just a skin and bones tragic looking guy, almost the size of a puppy." He had Julie but, he said, "Dan is more important to me."

He mentioned nothing about his new novel: yahoos bored with their lives in the hinterlands flock to California in search of nice weather and citrus fruit, discover that heaven on earth is a fake, get ticked off, and behave badly. He was calling it *The Cheated*.

"Stage Nine—you bastards—Stage Nine!" It's late in the afternoon and the fake infantry and cavalry that have been fighting the fake battle of Waterloo straggle in the direction of a fake Mississippi riverboat. On the first page of Nat's novel, Tod Hackett leaves his office at Na-tional Movies and rides the streetcar to Vine Street, where he mingles with switchboard operators dressed up like tennis players, insurance salesmen camouflaged as mountain climbers, pretend Rhine castles, plaster-and-paper Samoan huts, exotic Japanese temples. What a howl, Tod thinks: how absurd, tasteless, and completely pitiable. But he is not laughing, for "few things are sadder than the truly monstrous." In three pages of cinematic images, Nat renders the DNA of the film capital, planet Hollywood as it might be viewed from space, a Hogarthian landscape peopled by a host of tanned perverts and demented raw-food faddists. If Tod Hackett couldn't manage a laugh, his creator could.

At the San Bernardino Arms, an apartment building similar to the Parva-Sed-Apta, Tod rents a room after noticing a moonfaced platinum blond in the hall. Right away he wonders what will happen should he leap on her. "It would be like throwing yourself from the parapet of a skyscraper," he decides. His heart would pop out of his chest, his back crushed, his teeth pounded into his skull "like nails into a pine board." He can't wait to die.

Tod is a Yale graduate, newly surfaced in the movie capital to learn set and costume design but determined to work on a painting of his own that he calls *The Burning of Los Angeles*. He finds himself sucked into the lives of his neighbors at the "San Berdoo": Abe Kusich, the overwrought, foulmouthed dwarf who can get you a horse, a cockfight, an apartment, or a woman ("What a quiff!"); and the blond bit player Faye Greener and her rubber-faced, vaudevillian father, who peddles homemade silver polish door-to-door. It is through the Greeners that Tod meets the self-effacing Homer Simpson, a masturbating, middle-aged hotel bookkeeper who has left Iowa for a rest cure in paradise but whose orderly life is about to be destroyed by Faye. Completing the collection of screwballs and screwboxes are the Gingo family of Eskimos, a horny Mexican adept at cockfighting, a ten-gallon-hat buckaroo named Earl, the life-size rubber horse at the bottom of a screenwriter's pool, the cornball evangelicals, a hateful child actor named Adore Loomis and his raw-food-eating mom, a Gertrude Stein–loving madam who screens stag movies, and a giant butch tennis champion. And behind these pour throngs of atmosphere players, the so-called extras, Midwesterners enticed to California by visions of sunshine and oranges. "All their lives they had slaved at some kind of dull, heavy labor," Nat wrote. The promised land turns out to be a disappointment. True, there is plenty of sunshine and a surfeit of oranges and avocados, but so what? These poor, lonely transplants "slaved and saved for nothing."

In the book's ambiguous final section, a tinselly premiere is taking place on Hollywood Boulevard, with klieg lights and cameras. On hand are hundreds of police to keep in check the worshipful fans pressing forward to catch a glimpse of their favorite stars. It is into this tinder pile that Tod and Homer Simpson accidentally stumble. Falling apart under the weight of Faye's indifference, Homer turns into a wild man and attempts to stomp Adore Loomis to death. Engulfed by a mob now ready to kill anybody, he is last seen being ripped to pieces. Tod, his leg crushed in the mayhem, is rescued by police and driven away screaming.

Nat declined to offer a satisfying conclusion. There is no possibility of escape for his crazed hotel bookkeeper, delivered to vigilante justice, but is Tod's breakdown permanent, or is he just having a bad day?

Some critics found Nat's characters a frightening crew of misfits and retards. West's books, W. H. Auden complained, are peopled by "cripples." Nat would have given the "fingeroo" to somebody like Auden. There was nothing he loved more than creating stories about real people, cripples or not.

None of Nat's characters can be called autobiographical—he is no more Tod Hackett than he is Balso Snell or Miss Lonelyhearts—but each of the imagined pivotal characters—Tod, Homer, and Faye, all dreamers seeking a land of promise—closely reflects some facet of the author's emotional history. Tod and Homer emerge from Nat's dual professional life, the fusion of the artist and the hotelman, the detached intellectual and the slow, clumsy cold noodle who struggles with twitching hands and sleeplessness just like his creator's. Tod falls somewhere between a detached observer standing on the sidelines, in the vein of Fitzgerald's sensitive Nick Carraway, and a hero-participant who catalogs his own downfall, as would Holden Caulfield in *The Catcher in the Rye.* He speaks for himself while studying those he meets, but he is so vulnerable that he soon gets mangled in the Hollywood dream dump ("for there was not a dream afloat somewhere which would not sooner or later turn up on it"). But Nat's most intriguing disguise as a literary character is the actress Faye Greener, the dream dump incarnate, a template for the legions of hungry movie blonds whose careers would stretch over the duration of the century: the seemingly untalented Norma Jean Bakers unapologetically posing nude for calendars, the Lana Turners discovered at Hollywood soda fountains. Nat's Faye is a seventeen-year-old virgin, "shiny as a new spoon," an actress who has one line in a picture and manages to speak it badly. Skill is unnecessary because her physical presence, even her affected mannerisms, exercise a dramatic effect on the opposite sex. Faye has stockpiled a card file of daydreams in her mind. Lying on her bed, she can pass the entire day shuffling them until she picks one she likes and then melts into make-believe. Like her creator, she believes that "any dream is better than no dream," even when you're going nowhere.

In Nat's hands a tight, uncomplicated story—"cablegrams to a distant country," Malcolm Cowley called his economical writing, "with the words so expensive that he couldn't waste them"—has the power to disturb. On all sides splash sickening images, visions of a nightmarish future, and flawed characters doomed to hopeless existences. From first page to last, from the soldier extras being herded to Stage Nine to the mob that burns the city, the novel is steeped in violence. To Nat, the story illustrated one of his principal beliefs: since the universe is essentially rigged against us, efforts to improve this lousy world are futile and the only intelligent response is laughter. Reproached for making "private and unfunny jokes," he got defensive, once telling Scott Fitzgerald that "I do it my way." He may not have been a Robert Benchley or a Frank Sullivan (or, god forbid, an S. J. Perelman), but "I do consider myself a comic writer." He distinguished between comic writing on serious subjects, a tradition going back to Aristophanes and the Greeks, and modern-day humorous writing like Sid's. "I am not a humorous writer I must admit and have no desire to be one." Whatever he was, he certainly took pleasure in the role of provocateur.

Tod's ambitious painting, *The Burning of Los Angeles*, provides a chart to Nat's intentions. Across the top, Tod has drawn the burning city, the flames licking at the cardboard houses. Down a long hill in the center of the canvas sweeps the torch-waving mob with baseball bats and joyous faces, the people yowling for blood after the city has snatched away their hopes. In the lower foreground are individuals fleeing the avengers, Faye and Harry, Homer, Claude Estee. Tod has stooped to pick up a small stone. In an upper corner appears Nat's signature, one of his private jokes—a Corinthian column holding up the palm-leaf roof of a nut-burger stand, presumably offering the cheated and betrayed a nutritious meat substitute. In Nat's eyes, *The Cheated* was not just comical but also a musical of sorts, because it included four tunes—five, actually, counting "The Star-Spangled Banner." What more did people want?

Nat needed to buy time for the novel. When his contract came up for renewal in January 1938, he asked Republic to release him, and, except for a week's assignment at Columbia on a gangster picture, he did not take another film-writing job until June. In those months, his writing flowed fast and smooth. He bulldozed ahead on a typewriter instead of writing longhand. He could see that *The Cheated* was going to be more than twice as long as *Miss Lonelyhearts*. After completing another draft, he decided that it might be in shape for submission. With his previous publishers out of business or the object of his unfading rage, he was ready to move on. It was important to get a first-class house that would appreciate him, or at least not do him dirt. As it happened, Sid had published a collection of essays, *Strictly from Hunger*, with Random House the previous summer. Despite disappointing sales, he remained enthusiastic about Bennett Cerf, the editor in chief, with whom he had become quite chummy. Nat, who had once met Cerf at Stanley Rose's store in the fall of 1935, saw him again in Los Angeles on Valentine's Day and promised him a first look at the manuscript.

When *The Cheated* arrived at Random House in May, reaction for "this lunatic scheherazade" was rapturous. Saxe Commins, Cerf's veteran senior editor, was electrified, advising him that "we must by all means publish this delirious book." It was "a fantastic riot with a deep bite in it and written with such a sure hand and such lavishness of episode and crazy invention that it's pretty hard to choose favorite sections or even favorite characters." What was more, it was "a far, far better book than LONELYHEARTS."

On May 17, Cerf sent Nat the kind of thrilling telegram that authors dream of: "Definitely accept The Cheated for Random House. Hope you will make few minor changes about which I am writing you today. It is a swell book." Nat had not yet learned that a publisher's fervor was no guarantee of success.

Bennett Cerf and Nat had grown up in the same tight-knit corner of Harlem, both sons of affluent Jewish families. Although Bennett went to P.S. 10 instead of the Model School, and to Townsend Harris instead of Clinton, they belonged to the same crowd of uptown boys. In his younger days, Bennett Cerf had been a dashingly handsome six footer, briefly married to a movie actress, Sylvia Sidney, and in his middle age would be known to television viewers as the chirpy, balding, bow-tied panelist on the game show What's My Line? But when he accepted The Cheated in 1938 he was forty and impressive, the kind of enterprising hustler brimming with charisma and energy who would seem like an ideal son to a Harlem mama like Anna Weinstein.

Nat's feeling of comfort around Cerf may have owed something to nostalgic boyhood memories, but more likely it had to do with his being Sid's publisher. Despite Sid's disappointment over sales of his recent book, he liked Bennett and intended to publish his next book (Look Who's Talking) with Random House. He took pleasure in sending him extra-affectionate letters: "Please plant a passionate kiss on the foreheads of Don[ald Klopfer] and Saxe Commins, and do write your little school-fellow."

A few years later, the affection would end when Sid assigned Cerf a permanent position on the S. J. Perelman blacklist. Privately lambasting him as a "pinchpenny," he suggested to James Thurber that they sneak into Random House and crown "America's Sweetheart" with a toilet, making certain the commode was crunched "snugly down over his ears." Eventually Sid's animosity could no longer be satisfied by personal correspondence. He wrote a mocking New Yorker piece ("No Dearth of Mirth—Fill Out the Coupon") in which he transformed the effervescent Cerf into a screaming flibbertigibbet and christened him Barnaby Chirp.

Random House offered an advance of five hundred dollars against royalties and an option on Nat's next two books, a more than decent deal. (Sid received a three-hundred-dollar advance for his first two collections, in 1937 and 1940.) Even if Bennett Cerf was giving Nat a bear hug, that did not mean he considered *The Cheated* perfect. Revisions were needed.

Cerf's objections concerned unpalatable content and authorial voice. For instance, "Joan Schwartzen," the bearded, seven-foot lesbian, a segment that he delicately referred to as "the little Lesbian interlude," made him recoil. A "pretty horrible" passage about a black hen detracted from the "magnificent" cockfight scene later on, and the introduction of Abe Kusich the dwarf and the drooling nude cellist seemed overdone. The story had enough "incredible and grotesque characters" without "this monstrosity." He also questioned the awkward first-person narration of Claude Estee, the artist-turned-screenwriter serving as Nat's alter ego. A character with no purpose should be eliminated, Cerf suggested.

Behind Nat's back, Cerf mentioned to Sid that his brother-in-law wasn't as good at descriptions as with characters and dialogue, comments that got back to Nat immediately. When confronted about them Bennett said his remarks weren't really significant. Nonetheless, Nat might think about cutting back some of his descriptive passages.

At this point, he was agreeable to practically anything Random House asked, ditching the "lesbian stuff," prettying up the dwarf's first scene, sanding down Homer's disgust over a scabby black chicken. He didn't want to "shock just for shocking's sake," he wrote Bennett Cerf (whose name he misspelled as "Bennet" for the next two years), an assurance that does not ring true. But most important, the revised version has Tod Hackett telling the story. Into this character Nat conflated leftover traits of the screenwriter Claude Estee, whose role was reduced to two brief appearances as a friend of Tod's. Nat handed in a revised manuscript that was smooth and controlled, showing "a great deal of improvement," he wrote Cerf in July. He sure hoped Random House could publish in October—"1939 is so far away." The only thing that continued to trouble him was the title—how about *Grass Eaters?*— and by the way, where was his advance?

Having grown fond of the Hollywood Hills, Nat moved from Alta Loma to a handsome, red-tile-roofed Spanish-style house on nearby Canyon Terrace, and not long after that to another fine place at 6614 Cahuenga Terrace. Houses were a necessity when rooming with dogs. But more and more, his second Hollywood home was Stanley Rose's bookstore, especially its pleasant back room. There was rarely a woman to be found, just a bunch of guys trading studio scuttlebutt, whining over how they had sold their souls for a pittance of five hundred dollars a week. Usually, Stanley mocked their good clothes, their nubile young women, their steaks at Musso's. "So cry a little bit and go back there tomorrow and fart around for an hour or two for another hundred bucks." Because, where he came from, "any man who earns a hundred dollars *a month* is a big success." Of the coterie of backroom writers, it was Nat who most interested Yetive Moss, one of Rose's young women clerks. Even though he appeared to be a respectable gentleman, Yetive decided that "it was a big act." His cheerful manner made her suspicious too. Who knew what lay behind the mask?

Into the tank of big-fish writers one day paddled an exotic minnow, a baby-faced twenty-two-year-old fresh from Dartmouth College who wrote for Selznick International and attended a Marxist study group by night. In contrast to the published writers, Budd Schulberg was Hollywood royalty. The eldest son of B. P. Schulberg, head of Paramount Pictures, and Adeline Schulberg, a powerful talent agent, he had spent most of his life in the throne rooms of the film kingdom. In an insider memoir about his early years as a member of the royal Schulbergs, he subtitled the book "Memories of a Hollywood Prince." This prince was a brainy kid who had the misfortune to stutter.

Silent as wallpaper, Budd came to sit at people's feet and pick up secrets, listening to conversations not as a management spy but as a reverent apprentice. More than anything he wanted to make his mark as a novelist and, to him, Nathanael West was a celebrity. As a rule Nat was guarded and secretive, but he treated young Schulberg with gentle affection. The boy, a dozen years younger, had been born in Harlem in a Fifth Avenue apartment house facing Mount Morris Park, only three blocks from the Weinsteins on Mount Morris Park West. At the bookstore, Budd tried to eavesdrop on conversations between Nat and Bill Faulkner, hoping to "glean some philosophical pearls," but felt disappointed to hear them gabbing about hunting wild boar on Santa Cruz Island, a three-hour trip off the coast. Even more, Nat enjoyed shooting waterfowl with Stanley Rose. It was obvious to young Budd that Rose and Nat had "a special relationship because they went off together on long trips." In a tone of admiration, Rose one time confided to Budd that "Pep would rather hunt than write, hunt than eat, hunt than hump." Yetive Moss could vouch for that, because "I don't ever recall him showing any romantic interest in women." Certainly the women with whom he kept company were not the kind you took on dates or introduced to women like Yetive.

Increasingly, his weekends were devoted to shooting ducks and doves, one of the only activities that made him truly happy. Nat's secretary, Jo Conway, knew that on Mondays and Tuesdays in season "I would get a rundown on the weekend's hunt, then we might work Wednesday and Thursday, but on Friday preparation for the hunt began."

Sometimes these expeditions took him far from home: to Brawley in the Imperial Valley and to Arizona for doves, San Joaquin Valley for ducks, and Baja California, Mexico, where he shot quail, geese, and ducks on the ranches of Mexicali and Ensenada. He never missed an opening day. His decoys and equipment were kept in excellent condition, although, usually in a hurry to get away, he would neglect to bring blankets and dry clothes. "If he was wet or cold, he simply endured it," said one of his regular buddies, the MGM writer Wells Root. The two of them had devised a system that squeezed the maximum amount of shooting into less than two days. On Friday nights they would pile their dogs into Root's truck, which was fitted with comfortable cots and compartments for their stash of legal and illegal game. Before setting out they swallowed sleeping pills and gave the chauffeur Benzedrine. Reaching their destination, having had a good night's rest, the medication schedule would be reversed, and the driver popped a sedative. In the false dawn they began sneaking through the shallow rushes to bait the pond with rubber decoys. Then, muddy and soaked, they cocked their custom-made Sauer and Parker Brothers shotguns and waited for the migrating birds, on their way to Mexico and South America for the winter, to home in on the seductive decoys resting calmly on the water.

The details of this routine, which impressed Sid as "crazy and wonderful," struck others as crazy and pathological. It would have surprised Nat to know that his choice of sport was regarded disapprovingly by some of his friends. Malcolm Cowley informed Josie Herbst that Pep's hobby was nothing but a twisted, machismo obsession. Josie did not disagree—a love of guns suggested sexual inadequacy—but she speculated that what impelled him to kill were feelings of cruelty and the "need for attack on something." Spotting him with his gun and dog in the Erwinna woods, she had been surprised by "his happy face." In her novella about him, *Hunter of Doves*, she recalls his poor marksmanship in hunting animals—he was pathetically unsuccessful even with dumb raccoons—but he had better luck killing helpless birds. Once he discovered doves, he gladly "fled as often as he could to the enchanted woods."

Nat's passion for stalking and hunting was probably a carryover from childhood and his love of *Field & Stream*. In Central Park, he and his cousins had taken pleasure in tracking the sexually occupied couples, concealing themselves in the bushes, silently observing, then hollering their heads off like a pack of angry Indians. As an adult, the sport satisfied basic emotional needs. It was a womanless activity that provided a legitimate excuse for red-blooded regular guys to be in intimate company with other red-blooded regular guys. The manly bonding in a duck blind provided a cozy, tactile intimacy that would have been suspect in any other surroundings.

On occasion Nat dated women, whom he described as "dull as hell and still more selfish," but his social life was mostly with individuals like himself (or like Stanley Rose), unmarried, presumably heterosexual men living alone. In mock lamentation, he began comparing himself to Arthur Kober, Lillian Hellman's ex-husband, who was famous for falling asleep at half past nine.

Living directly across the road from the Perelmans at Eight Ball Farm was a playwright and film writer named Joseph Schrank. When he mentioned leaving for the Coast to work at Warners, Sid said, "Oh, you should meet my brother-in-law, Pep."

Joe regarded his neighbor as "a nasty little fellow," but in Los Angeles he discovered that the brother-in-law was "an awfully likeable chap." The only mystery was how a man in as advanced a stage of grumpiness as Sid Perelman could have such a nice guy for a relative.

Schrank, a genial man of puckish humor, grew up in the Bronx, the son of a street fiddler whose death caused him to drop out of Stuyvesant High School. He had to his credit two successful Broadway shows, one a comedy he had written that ran ten months and the other a hit musical revue about union workers, *Pins and Needles*, to which he had contributed sketches. Nat, who had always wanted to write a play, was impressed. For years, he had envied Sid and Laura for their comedy *All Good Americans*. Recently he had been pushing Sid about *Even Stephen*, the play they had written together in 1933. Probably it was a dead noodle, but "how about turning it over to an agent," he suggested. "Try at least." Sid didn't feel like trying. Joe, however, proved to be more receptive to Nat's frustrated stage ambitions.

Joe Schrank found Pep—who still carried the childhood nickname —entertaining, in particular his stories of various wild sex escapades. The really hot prostitutes, Nat said, were Japanese, Chinese, Mexican, and Filipino. He liked to sample different nationalities, he explained. With a straight face, he rattled off a tall tale about his plan "to lay an American Indian," no simple matter, because Indian prostitutes were rare. Nevertheless, he had located a brothel in Arizona near a reservation.

Afterward, Joe was eager to hear the details. "How was it?"

"Okay," he said solemnly. "But she smelled of bear grease." When faced with a receptive audience, Nat never let truth stand in his way. The sex weekend was most likely one of his dove-hunting trips, the "girls" whitewings.

At dinner one evening Nat described a book he had been reading, an analysis of military strategy and the tactical mistakes made by the Allies in the Great War. "You wouldn't believe how stupid these generals are," he told Joe. The twenties had produced tomes of antiwar literature, notably the poetic novel *All Quiet on the Western Front* by Erich Maria Remarque and Laurence Stallings and Maxwell Anderson's play *What Price Glory*. These were serious efforts, but Nat wondered if the subject might lend itself to satire. The central character could be a stereotypical British gentleman who commands his regiment by telephone, according to the rules of war in an old school textbook. Field officers would get dispatches wrong. Even the Krauts would be boobies. Joe agreed it was a swell idea.

During 1937, when Joe was working at Warners and Nat at Republic while writing *The Cheated*, they completed three drafts. In *Gentlemen, the War!* scatterbrained British officers, using a church in France as their field headquarters, map out their preparations while sounding exactly as if they are planning a Sunday shooting expedition. Their daily routine includes breakfast at eleven, tea in the garden, and an afternoon nap. None of the generals has an ounce of sense, and the appearance of generic German officers reveals them to be equally insipid. The play owed much to Gilbert and Sullivan's *HMS Pinafore*, in which nincompoop Sir Joseph Porter rose to First Lord of the Admiralty without ever going to sea. The collaboration proceeded so smoothly that Nat and Joe were able to give the finished play to an agent in November 1937; an option followed shortly thereafter. The producer was Jerome Mayer, an eager fellow in his twenties who had already produced several Broadway shows, all of them flops. Any producer was better than no producer.

Like it or not, Nat needed two careers to survive. Being a full-time novelist was hardly possible when his books went practically from the printer to the drugstores, as he once joked. Writing fiction while working a steady job was not easy, but not impossible either. He wrote *Miss Lonelyhearts* while managing two hotels, *The Cheated* at Republic's sweatshop. So it was maddening when friends back east dismissed the necessity for "hack work." "You are an artist," Edmund Wilson once chided, with no business in "a ghastly place" like Hollywood. Running out of apologies, tired of explaining his financial situation, Nat simply stopped talking about his pictures, even the ones that were good. Neither did he brag when, in 1938, he leaped from Poverty Row studios to the big leagues.

The first major studio to hire him, RKO, was known for A pictures like *King Kong* and the Astaire-Rogers musicals, but also operated a B-picture unit that turned out profitable low-budget films. RKO Pictures was a big step up, even though his established weekly pay remained $350. He was assigned to *Five Came Back*, a B picture about a plane full of Americans that crashes in an Amazon jungle famous for its headhunters. Racing against time, the crew patches together the damaged aircraft and builds a makeshift runway, but owing to the temporary repair and low fuel, the plane can carry only five of the passengers to safety. Who lives, who dies, who decides?

That summer, while working on the plane-crash script, Nat was also teaming with two of his close friends, Wells Root and Gordon Kahn, on an independent project that drew on one of his favorite pastimes, duck hunting. It was an original story about a Justice Department agent looking for the killers of a North Carolina game warden who uncovers a gang of illegal hunters. The part of Special Agent Kane was written with the most bankable star in Hollywood, Clark Gable, in mind. MGM paid $7,500 for the fifty-one-page treatment, titled *Flight South*, but never produced the picture.

In six weeks, Nat completed a draft of *Five Came Back*, for which he anticipated a solo credit and the chance to break out of his $350 pay bracket. It was deflating to learn that his credit would be shared with Dalton Trumbo and another writer, who had done a polishing job. (Trumbo, an ardent Communist, converted the anarchist villain into a hero.) Chester Morris, John Carradine, and Lucille Ball starred under the direction of John Farrow (Mia Farrow's father). Setting the standard for plane crash survival movies, *Five Came Back* was remade in 1956 under the title *Back from Eternity*, with Rod Steiger playing the lead. For probably the first time, Nat began to take real pride in his screen work. And though he never admitted it to friends, he reveled in the money. Waiting in line to collect his check, he was overheard saying with glee, "I like working out here. It makes me rich beyond the dreams of avarice."

Among the writers at RKO, he attracted attention for often spending his lunch hours strolling around the lot instead of joining them in the commissary. Garson Kanin was a twenty-six-year-old directing his first film. An admirer of *Miss Lonelyhearts*, he made a point of introducing himself. What was the new novel about?

"Hollywood," Nat replied.

"Pro? Con?"

Nat hurried to correct himself. "I shouldn't have said Hollywood," he told Kanin. "It's about people—people *in* Hollywood."

In fact, *The Cheated* was not the only Hollywood novel; plenty of good writers had been seduced by the same raw materials. The hero of Scott Fitzgerald's new book was rumored to be modeled after Irving Thalberg, MGM's boy wonder, who had died in 1936. Other notable novelists busy moonlighting as screenwriters included John Fante, whose *Wait Until Spring, Bandini* would be followed in 1939 by the peerless *Ask the Dust*; and Horace McCoy, Nat's coworker at Republic, whose last novel, *I Should Have Stayed Home* (1937), a bitter story of movie extras, seemed to use ideas alarmingly close to those in *The Cheated*. A few months earlier, John O'Hara had published a Hollywood book that surprised and infuriated Nat because it was a stinkola, a humdinger, a lollapalooza, and a twisteroo, but most of all an insulting fingeroo.

In recent years, O'Hara had written two best-selling novels, *Appointment in Samarra* and *Butterfield 8*, and he also put in time working in Hollywood for Paramount and MGM. Among the East Coast expatriate writers he was a familiar, but not particularly beloved, figure. He was a tennis player, an uncouth braggart, a heavy drinker who often acted crudely, and an unrepentant "Pal Joey" type of heel with women. At Stanley Rose's, he would mix with Budd Schulberg and William Saroyan in the back room or try to pick up the female clerks who worked up front. To Nat, he was nothing more than a casual acquaintance who had once been Quentin Reynolds's roommate.

In O'Hara's novella, a Hollywood screenwriter is pursuing a bookstore clerk who is a Communist sympathizer and Anti-Nazi League activist, but Peggy Henderson refuses to sleep with Jim Malloy, because she doesn't like him. Another man whom Peggy dates is Herbert Stern, a sophisticated Jew who is writing a novel about Los Angeles. Not about movie people, Herbert insists. "These Iowa people that come here," wear crazy clothes, and do what they couldn't do at home in their one-horse towns. O'Hara describes Stern as a terrible driver (Peggy is "frightened to death" to ride with him), a man who hangs out at a bookstore, writes arcane books, and suffers from a chronic disease (TB). There was no mistaking the person O'Hara meant.

Hope of Heaven was published by Harcourt, Brace and edited by Charles Pearce. Nat must have wondered why Cap did not encourage his author to modify or disguise Nat's identity. Not only was this disagreeable portrait in thunderously bad form, but it reeked of anti-Semitism. Its publication earned O'Hara a frosty reception at Stanley Rose's store.

Luckily for Nat, *Hope of Heaven* did poorly.

Joe Schrank had turned out to be an ideal collaborator. *Gentlemen, the War!* (retitled *Blow, Bugle, Blow*) had been completed in little over a year and was set for a Broadway opening that fall. In early August, Nat took the Santa Fe Super Chief to New York, a four-day journey across the prairies in cars that "rattled like hell, making it almost impossible to sleep." Dorothy Parker and Sid and Laura preferred to shuttle back and forth by air. Not Nat. Flying, he suspected, was basically unsafe, and having recently completed *Five Came Back* added to his jitters. Unwilling to admit his fear of flying, he compromised by deciding to travel east on the train and return by plane. If he had to die, there was no point doing it before his Broadway debut. At Grand Central he was met by Joe, who had invited him to stay with him and his wife, Bertha, in Erwinna. It was convenient because the Perelmans were away and the farmhouse was closed up.

Scheduled to open in September, the show kept getting postponed: the third act needed an overhaul, actors left town, backers bowed out, theaters suddenly became unavailable. When the producer encountered financial problems, Nat shelled out a thousand dollars in the hope of fixing the problems. His collaborator, a seasoned professional, refused to do likewise. (Joe "never put money in anything," says his daughter Sarah Gold.) More troubles ensued when the opening had to be postponed again and the out-of-town tryout canceled. If the delays continued, Nat warned Jerome Mayer, he would have to leave, but this was an empty threat.

By late September, Nat wrote his secretary Jo Conway that he felt rotten for having "just fooled away the last six weeks in barrooms, waiting." In reality, no time was wasted in bars, not with the grinding pressure of rewrites and production meetings—plus a final revision of *The Cheated*. Exhausted at the end of the day, he either returned to Erwinna for a few hours or stayed in town at the Hotel Lincoln on Eighth Avenue.

He did manage to get in some visiting. In the nearby town of Pipersville, he and Joe dropped in on Dorothy Parker ("a kindhearted little Jewish woman," Joe joked) and her husband, Alan Campbell ("delicate, but I wasn't his type"). Nat spent another evening trying to get a rise out of Josie Herbst, by telling, "with both revulsion and pleasure," she recalled, perverted tales of Hollywood sex, drugs, and scandal. Did she hear the one about the studio bosses who did not deign to wipe themselves or flush their own toilets, but kept servants for those tasks? He also made the rounds of his immediate family, dropped in on Bennett Cerf, and looked up old friends like Jim Farrell, who was unimpressed by a spicy story about the Hollywood scene and the practice of hiring two prostitutes at a time. Curiously, his native city roused little interest for him. His thoughts kept returning to the Coast, where duck season was starting and piggybacking writers were fussing with his *Five Came Back* script; he found himself missing the lush weather.

Did his Metro check for *Flight South* come through yet? he wrote to Jo Conway. He was expecting to see her by November 10. And this time, he vowed, "I won't leave Hollywood for several years and will do my damndest to make a career out here and get more money."

Rehearsals got under way on November 6, the opening was slated for November 21 at the Hudson Theater, and the title changed for a second time, to *Good Hunting*. By this point Nat's mental state was so shot that he appeared almost anesthetized. On the way to the theater with Joe one day, he drove out of the Lincoln Tunnel into Midtown Manhattan and proceeded to ignore eleven consecutive red lights. Swerving around a streetcar, he barreled through an intersection and sideswiped a taxi. The damage turned out to be minor, and Nat offered the cabbie cash on the spot. Joe was speechless—but not paralyzed. He hopped out of the car and set off for the theater on foot. On another occasion, winding along a side road in Tinicum Township, Nat suddenly pulled into the traffic on River Road. "Sonofabitch, you're going to kill us!" Joe screamed. From then on, he refused to drive with Nat.

In appreciation of the Schranks' hospitality, and possibly to make amends for Joe's near-death experience, Nat presented the couple with a handsome piece of furniture—an antique pine hutch.

What cheered him most during this difficult period was Random House. "Everything," he reported to Jo Conway, "is O.K. on the novel thank God." Publication was scheduled for January 10, and "the publishers think it will do fine." Certain sections, especially the opening chapters, he thought were "bad," but he was "sick of it" and could do no more. At the same time, he felt it was his best work. An indication of his confidence is that he showed the manuscript to Josie, the one person sure to give him a straight opinion. Irrespective of her high regard for his writing, she did not care for the book's ending, which shows Tod caught in the maelstrom of a riot. But her main objection centered on the way Nat depicted sex and violence, especially a disgusting cockfight. It was overdone, she thought. What was his point? Privately, she was repelled by his characters, the whole bunch of repulsive misfits, but especially the females. She didn't like his "quite hideous women" one bit.

If Nat felt no desire to tone down the mayhem, he did make a significant revision by deleting the final three pages, in which Tod predicted class warfare and the triumph of the proletariat in America—it was certainly too Marxist for his personal taste. In the new ending, Tod is laughing maniacally, which closely mirrored Nat's personal attitudes.

Still up in the air was the book's title, which failed to reflect the content, and in any case Saxe Commins said Nat was "inventive enough to offer something suggestive and quite mad." Deciding that *The Cheated* sounded "a little too pretentious," Nat changed it to *The Grass Eaters*, which Bennett thought sounded like a book about some African tribe. The biblical title Nat would have liked, *Days to Come*, had already been grabbed by Lillian Hellman for her labor play. Turning again to Scripture, he came up with verses suitably apocalyptic from Exodus and Revelation about plagues of locusts, which seemed pertinent to both the final riot scene and to the torchbearers in Tod's painting. *The Day of the Locust* had a nice doomsday ring to it.

The long-awaited night of the opening, November 21, 1938, was the Monday before Thanksgiving. Before the performance, the partying got under way with an alcoholic dinner at an Eighth Avenue saloon, in a crowd of friends, including George Milburn, the Oklahoma short story writer who had driven cross-country with his wife just for the occasion. Then everybody sloshed over to the Hudson Theater on Forty-fourth Street, where the curtain rose on an impressive set, the interior of a fifteenth-century church. The audience behaved as decorously as worshipers at a midnight Mass, not a good sign. Throughout the first act, when nobody laughed, Nat began to audibly grind his teeth, and at intermission fled down the street to a bar, where he spent most of the second act trying to quiet his nerves. Forcing himself to return for the third act, he found the actors gamely plugging away onstage as the audience awaited deliverance with expressions of polite suffering. Obviously something had gone wrong.

The production brought facetious remarks from newspaper reviewers. The *Wall Street Journal* managed to slip in the old chestnut "laid an egg." The *Times* critic described *Good Hunting* as "nitwit theatre" notable for "faint and tedious jokes" and "disastrous direction." Still, Brooks Atkinson advised his readers, "if you hurry, you may find some reputable actors defying doom in a damp whizbang." The play closed after two performances, which was better than opening and closing the same night. It had found no favor at all beyond the authors' immediate families and friends.

On Thanksgiving Day, in Erwinna with Joe and Bertha and the Milburns, Nat "hunkered down under a tree like a stunned ox," Joe recalled. "He simply didn't know what hit him." What hit him, Nat admitted later, was "a rain of stones." During the day a blizzard bore down and wrapped the farm in whiteness, as softly pretty as a picture postcard. As soon as it was possible to dig out, the Milburns prepared to drive back to the Coast. "Pep decided to go along with them," said Joe. Without a word, "he just stepped quietly into the car and off he went, away from it all."

Two explanations may account for the harsh pummeling received by *Good Hunting*:

A. *War.* The "peace in our time" Munich agreement of September 29 divided Czechoslovakia among Nazi Germany, Poland, and Hungary, thus appeasing Hitler and broadening the conflict that had been heretofore confined to Spain. Most Americans, fearing another bloody European war, were not in the mood to laugh. They were praying for the nightmare to go away.

B. *Poultry.* The play was a turkey.

B seems most likely.

Nat returned to California feeling as if he'd been "batted over the head with a stick with a nail in the end of it," he told Edmund Wilson. The failure of *Good Hunting* was a humiliating blow. It did teach him a lesson, though: he had no talent for writing plays.

20

STINKOLAS, HUMDINGERS, LOLLAPALOOZAS, TWISTEROOS

N AT WAS GETTING IMPATIENT. It was January and still no book. Random House bumped the publication date to its spring list, and obtaining even the most basic information meant prodding Bennett Cerf to be "a good fellow" and give him the production schedule and questioning Saxe Commins on "what's the jacket going to look like?" He made suggestions for appropriate designs—he liked the tasteful, black-and-white jackets on Aldous Huxley novels—but Cerf steamrolled over his ideas. The jacket was in the hands of a "really high-priced artist," he said, publishing code for mind your own business. The next thing to alarm Nat was the catalog copy, which presented his characters as a grab bag of freaks. Explaining his dissatisfaction to Commins, he emphasized that, despite a comic style, the novel was "serious in implication." Before long, his apprehension had escalated into a full-blown case of prepublication jitters.

It culminated in Stanley Rose's store on the Monday in April after Nat got his first look at the dust jacket and discovered it was red. To his eyes it looked garishly, clownishly bordello red. Budd Schulberg remembers Nat charging around the store like an angry bull.

"I'm going to kill that Bennett Cerf," he cried. The son of a bitch had spoiled the whole thing by giving him "a cheap, lousy-looking jacket!" Both Schulberg and Rose tried to quiet him down. So the jacket was red. What was wrong with that?

"I'm ashamed for people to see it," he declared.

In a fit of rage, he began to yank books from the shelves, mainly Random House authors like Eugene O'Neill. To Nat it seemed abundantly clear that Cerf stayed in business by catering to his glamorous authors and shortchanging the ones he expected to fail. After misrepresenting the novel's content and then misjudging its audience, the incompetents at Random further trivialized the book with a sleazy jacket.

In fairness to Cerf, there was nothing particularly unusual about the jacket. The front cover, a bold cherry red, is illustrated with a butter-yellow, three-legged movie camera and a black strip of celluloid that unspools blurbs from Dashiell Hammett ("the Hollywood that needs telling about") and Dorothy Parker ("brilliant, savage and arresting—a truly good novel"). It was a fairly typical commercial-fiction jacket.

But Nat always fussed over the smallest details of outward appearance. Even after Stanley Rose constructed a pyramid of *Locusts* in the bookshop window, Nat refused to shut up about it, lashing out at Cerf for betraying him. In a telegram to Cerf, he demanded the recall of books already shipped for the May 16 publication date. He offered to pay for jacket alterations to remove the yellow movie camera, because three colors—red, white, and black—were quite enough, and the red binding looked, he said, like "bait for vampire bats." Whom did Bennett expect to buy this book? "Drunken Mexicans?" Bennett didn't respond.

Complaining lifted his spirits. By firing a warning shot at the company, he meant to serve notice that he was no greenhorn schmuck but a person with taste who did not take such a hideous jacket lightly. In private, he called Random House "just as stupid" as Liveright or Covici-Friede.

To Nat's irritation, a title issued several weeks before his was turning out to be the fiction sensation of the year. It was John Steinbeck's tenth novel, *The Grapes of Wrath*, which blasted onto the bestseller list. Selling 2,500 copies a day in its first month, it rolled on to win a Pulitzer Prize, and Twentieth Century Fox turned it into a successful film directed by John Ford and starring Henry Fonda. Allowing for Nat's respect for Steinbeck, the droves of readers rushing to embrace his California-bound "Okie" sharecroppers—Viking Press was shipping 83,000 copies a month—was galling. Nat felt obliged to praise the work that was grabbing the glory he wanted so badly for his own. As he confided to Malcolm Cowley with barely concealed disdain, *Grapes* was "swell"—he wished Steinbeck the best—but he could not believe in Ma Joad, the pivotal mother character, nor in the daughter-in-law. (No starving stranger would ever be breast-fed in West's fiction.) To him it seemed a wordy, proletarian melodrama. All the tearjerking pamphleteering about good triumphing over evil and hope for a better world left him wanting to "laugh or at least smile." Nat was one of those people who can't help subverting and offending. In his attempts to depict Big Themes, he came off looking like the Marx Brothers. When he tried to describe a meeting of the Hollywood Anti-Nazi League in *Locust,* an all-American organization with the most exalted objectives, toward which, by the way, he felt totally sympathetic, he had upended his good intentions by writing a brothel scene featuring a pornographic movie.

As he pointed out to another friend, "there is nothing to root for in my work, and what is even worse, no rooters."

Few fantasies bring a writer greater pleasure than the prospect of large sales and unqualified praise. As notices began trickling in, it became clear that Nat was going to get neither. The *New York Times Book Review* thought it "an effective grotesque," but it was the assassins who tended to stand out; Clifton Fadiman, who had spurned sample chapters of *Miss Lonelyhearts,* told readers of *The New Yorker* to expect "a nice bit of phosphorescent decay," original but "unpleasant"; the cannibals at *Time* dispatched the novel as "screwball grotesque"; the reviewer from *Books* called it "emotionally inert" and "two dimensional." Distinguishing the good reviews from the bad could sometimes be tricky; the *Los Angeles Times* described it as a "dirty" novel that was "riotous and sidesplitting."

In reviews by Nat's friends, seemingly generous references to his admirable qualities barely concealed a show of fangs for the novel at hand. In the *Saturday Review*, George Milburn, friendly enough in Stanley Rose's back room, drubbed Nat for "hasty, disjointed writing." Edmund Wilson, after complimenting Nat as "brilliant" and the novel as "remarkable," padded his *New Republic* review with sour details that undercut some of the praise. In West's universe, wrote the critic, the people were not just bizarre but "sordid and senseless," the plot failed to provide even a marshmallow of a center, and—a surprisingly unfriendly dig—the novel displayed "less concentration than *Miss Lonelyhearts*." Wilson was not the only one to compare *Locust* unfavorably with the previous novel.

John Sanford bought a copy at Stanley Rose's but could not bring himself to read it. "Nothing could make me read The Locust," Scotty wrote to friends back east who knew Nat. "It's the God's honest truth that he's the only human being on the face of the earth that I really detest." It wasn't true, as some imagined, that Nat didn't understand those poor goofballs and their hurts. "He understands them well," Scotty insisted. Nat handpicked his freaks as carefully as Hitler selects "the inconsequential Jew as a suitable German goat." No person he had ever known "has less pity for the insulted and the injured."

From Scott Fitzgerald, appreciative of the grueling effort that went into a novel—and usually kind to other writers—came a note of congratulations. Nat gamely replied with a baseball analogy. "So far the box score stands: Good reviews—fifteen percent, bad reviews—twenty five percent, brutal personal attacks, sixty percent." As for sales, "practically none." (His subscription to the Argus Press Clipping Bureau proved to be a waste of money, as the book was not widely reviewed.)

Nat had hoped for some nice notices, some nice sales, maybe even a movie option. The likelihood of any studio wanting film rights seemed small, but wackier things had happened in Hollywood. *Nobody* wanting to buy the book was the real surprise. The humiliation made him confrontational with Random House.

For a few weeks he tried to get them to advertise, offering to share the cost of a campaign, but like any other publisher, Random House was not going to pony up for a losing title. Perhaps *Life* or *Look* might be persuaded to run a photo story about bit players and extras whose lives were often more compelling than the mythology that passed for star biographies. Nat would be happy to collaborate of course. Nothing came of this proposal either.

After earlier rejecting Cerf's suggestion that visiting stores sold books, he decided to sacrifice his dignity and make an appearance at the Broadway-Hollywood, a department store that offered a Thursday afternoon book series. Numerous best-selling authors (including Edna Ferber) had participated in the programs. Facing an auditorium of around sixty shoppers, most of them older women, Nat chain-smoked throughout a speech on the conflict between daydreams and reality, certainly pertinent to *Locust* but not of great concern to those in attendance. Afterward, he reported to his mother that the old ladies gave him a polite round of applause, then left scratching their heads and wondering if he was a nut. It was doubtful if many, or any, of them purchased the novel.

Like every author with a new book, he fell into the role of agitator, trying to goad his publisher into action. Surely there was something he could do to fire up sales. But Cerf had nothing to suggest beyond the customary excuses that only word of mouth sold books. The major book audience, Cerf supposed, was women. And by the way, he hoped Nat's next book would treat the opposite sex a bit kinder, because some female friends of his had expressed disgust for *Locust* in "very emphatic terms."

No magic strategy? Nat persisted.

None that Bennett knew of.

Very well, said Nat, sounding cheerful. He would have to assassinate Adolf Hitler.

Cerf excused *Locust*'s miserable showing by insisting that Hollywood novels didn't sell. "By God," he declared to Nat, if he ever published another one it would be "My 39 ways of making love," by Hedy Lamarr. What he really meant was that Hollywood novels like *Locust* didn't sell. At that very time, he was planning to publish a first novel by Budd Schulberg, a behind-the-scenes account of the movie business. Budd's Sammy Glick, a merciless rat, is a repulsive character who claws his way to the top. Nevertheless, Cerf's ear for what would sell turned out to be pitch-perfect in this instance. *What Makes Sammy Run?* became an instant bestseller when released in 1941. It was, he thought, "probably the best book about Hollywood ever written."

But it is *The Day of the Locust* that continues to be rated as the most penetrating novel ever written about Hollywood. Seventy years after publication, it remains the gold standard in its genre, followed by F. Scott Fitzgerald's unfinished *The Last Tycoon* and Budd Schulberg's *What Makes Sammy Run?* The novel has inspired a deluge of theses, dissertations, and essays by those West called "the literature boys whom I detest." He has been appointed a poet of the profane, a disciple of the Marquis de Sade, the originator of sick humor, and—how he would have loathed this one—"the most indisputably Jewish writer yet to appear in America."

Other Westologists have contended that his motifs anticipated the rise of Hitler, World War II, and the Holocaust. He was hardly alone, though, in his premonitions that the world was heading for trouble; similar ideas were floating in the air throughout the thirties. Those who extolled his books as apocalyptic visions would especially annoy Josephine Herbst, who believed that he was "the last person interested in the prophetic." In years to come, she would remind these eager academics ("bright boy," she impolitely called one of them), "Don't put the fool's cap of prediction on Pep West's dead head." The man she knew was lovable and sweet-tempered, a stylish, dignified gentleman, very different from the scofflaw writer launching "a savage unloving assault" against anything in his path.

Taken together, West's four novels can be viewed as the history of both his and his father's lives in roughly 420 pages. *Balso Snell* was a rebellious adolescent's parlor trick designed to shock and offend the grown-ups and show off the number of books he had read. In *Miss Lonelyhearts*, he had developed the maturity to meditate on the meaning of life (none) and the possibility of alleviating human suffering (hopeless). *A Cool Million*, produced the year after his father's death, attempted to document how easily a lifetime of raw labor could amount to nothing—or, as he called it, shirtsleeves to shirtsleeves in one generation. Similarly, the ghost of Max Weinstein hovers over the torchbearers in *Locust* expecting to claim their earthly rewards in Southern California. But one aspect of West's fiction had no acknowledged part in his own or his father's life.

At a time when gay fictional characters were practically nonexistent, every one of West's novels contains unmistakable homosexual motifs and homosexual characters, closeted, outed, and in-between. Balso Snell couldn't pass by an anus, even when it belonged to a horse. Peter Doyle rips open Miss Lonelyhearts's fly ("What a sweet pair of fairies you guys are," his wife teases). The clean old man brutalized in the Madison Square Park toilet has "homosexualistic tendencies." Similar tendencies can be seen in Shrike, who can hardly suppress his acute erotic interest in Miss Lonelyhearts, who in turn dies in the arms of a man who has discharged a bullet into him. That unsentimental capitalist innovator Wu Fong handpicks poor Lem Pitkin for the pleasure of a gay maharajah. In openly gay Hollywood, a tennis star is a strapping, seven-foot Amazon of a lesbian, the stylish female impersonator at the Cinderella Bar wears French garters under her red dress, and Faye Greener taunts Homer: "Do you know what a fairy is?" In his child's prudishness, he does not. "I hate fairies," Faye announces vehemently.

Tod shoots back that "all women do."

"They're dirty," she replies.

In the 1930s, the reality was that no American novelists—not even Josephine Herbst—dared identify themselves as gay or bisexual. Revealing one's homosexuality was unthinkable, the equivalent of career suicide. West's obsessive attraction to the forbidden subject could pop out and march around center stage in his work, but could never be overtly examined.

• • •

By the beginning of July 1939, Nat's hopes for *The Day of the Locust* had crumbled. He was shocked to learn of sales figures, an incomprehensible 22 copies between June 1 and 13, and Cerf's projection that he would be lucky to sell 1,400 copies total (half the printing). Deducting the copies purchased by the Wallensteins and Weinsteins, by his hunting pals and Stanley Rose's friends, the total was truly negligible. *Locust* was "a definite flop," he reported to Edmund Wilson. He was always being told by people like Wilson that he should give up Hollywood hackwork and behave like a real writer, but "no market whatsoever" existed for his work. The public was not just apathetic, but some reviewers actually went out of their way to excoriate his defenders. Nat tried not to show Wilson that he was deeply hurt. Already he had begun blocking out his next novel, he said. "I haven't given up."

In truth, he was overflowing with bile. In an angry letter to Sid, he complained that book publishing was not about books at all, but rapacious companies out to screw their authors. Why did so many people want to write books when it was actually a trap, the gateway to ruin? Please, he urged Sid, stick to writing for *The New Yorker*. He confessed to feeling "quite depressed today," although depressed described his mood most days. Unable to plan a new novel, he conjured up a "spec" script, a rehash of *Five Came Back* that he described to Sid as "pure, unadulterated bubameiser"—he meant an old wives' tale—into which he threw everything but the kitchen sink. It was "a real guzma"—exaggeration—"about aviators, lost cities, jungles, and such guzmarie." When the *bubba meiseh* script found no takers, he went back to RKO in November.

Bennett Cerf now disgusted Nat. He seemed less despicable than Cap Pearce, who would always head Nat's list of publishing phonies, but never again would he place any faith in Bennett's loyalty. Unfortunately, Nat needed him. With a contract that gave Random an option on his next two books, he realized there was nothing to be gained by waging war.

It was some time before he felt able to suggest another idea. Learning that Saxe Commins was visiting Los Angeles, he set up a meeting in order to pitch a story "clearly in my mind and [I] know just what I intend to do with it." Before this presentation he had mentioned to Cerf an idea that would "make us both rich," something he vaguely referred to as "a Joseph Conrad–like story of adventure," but he also jokingly promised him an uplifting novel—"simple, warm, and kindly"—of the sort he was incapable of producing. The idea he presented to Commins, nothing like the earlier subjects, dusts off the setting for *Miss Lonelyhearts* and takes place in a newspaper office. The editor's reaction was courteous but tight-lipped. All he could promise was to relay the idea to Bennett along with Nat's request for an advance.

Nothing prepared Nat for Cerf's swift reaction. "You ask for a $1000.00 advance on a new book for which not a line has been written as yet," he scolded. *Locust* had sold exactly 1,464 copies. That meant Random would sustain a gross loss of more than six hundred dollars, "entirely exclusive of any overhead charges." His editorial team, likewise his promotion and sales crew, deserved credit for untold man-hours on the project. In fact, he personally had given Pep "a great deal of time." But despite Random House's efforts to champion the book, "most people definitely didn't like it," and so the company had written it off as "a failure." In his opinion, Pep's new project was "interesting" but stale; it had already been done unsuccessfully by a dozen other writers. Besides, it was no concern of Cerf's if an author was "a starving coal miner or a pampered scenario writer who gets $5000 a week turning out bilge for MGM and RKO." On the basis of Pep's track record, "you shouldn't ask for any advance at all," but he was willing to offer an advance of $250 as a gesture of confidence in his ability. In closing, he claimed to be speaking as a friend, for his own benefit, and he hoped Pep wouldn't be angry with him.

Nat was so infuriated that he could not reply. He knew for certain that he had been too trusting of a man plainly not his friend. Possibly his request for a thousand dollars was a bit cheeky, but in order to push ahead on the book he expected to take time off from his movie work. Surely he could depend on Random House for eating money. A year earlier, Bennett had promised with fatherly affection that he would be a Random House author "for the rest of your natural life," which Nat took literally. Now the paterfamilias gave him a biblical poke in the eye with a sharp stick.

If Cerf's brass-knuckles attack on screen work as bilge was especially outrageous, more offensive were his disparaging comments about rich movie writers seeking escape in "a little white farmhouse in New England" and novels expressing their "true soul." His $250 offer, less than the $350 Nat was earning each week as a screenwriter, would buy hardly more than a Hooverville shanty.

After a month's delay, he managed a response to Bennett's "hard letter" that suppressed his urge to bite back. From then on, his correspondence with Cerf would sound like Oliver Twist in the workhouse begging, "Please, sir, I want some more." As a tactical opening, Nat made himself apologize for having requested an advance. Of course Bennett was right. He didn't deserve one, but surely Bennett could tell he was frightened. It was "psychological." He felt vulnerable and feared for his sanity.

He reminded Cerf that he was not one of those soul-searching fellows making $5,000 a week. He was an average guy, and all he wanted was a little butter for his bread. Whenever one of his studio contracts expired, he was instantly unemployed again. During the dry spells he had "a tremendous sinking feeling in his stomach." This was not actually the case. If four years in the business had not made him rich, he was nevertheless able to afford a very comfortable lifestyle. During the first nine months of 1939, he had taken home $12,600 (around $200,000 in 2009 currency). It was more money than he had ever imagined, far more than he could have earned in the hotel business. His latest picture, and his second-best after *Five Came Back*, was the successful *I Stole a Million*, about a crook planning to go straight after pulling one last job. If Cerf had seen the film, with big stars George Raft and Claire Trevor, he did not acknowledge it. By all accounts he never complimented Nat on any of his movies.

After Nat's tin-cup routines proved ineffective, he caved in and accepted the $250 advance.

• • •

Meanwhile, still badly upset by the failure of *Locust,* Nat wondered if he should forget about fiction for a while. Whenever he stepped "one foot on the ladder of success somebody moved the ladder," he told Sid. Instead, he began talking about a book of vignettes modeled on Ivan Turgenev's 1852 classic, *A Sportsman's Sketches.* The Russian novelist had recorded his observations hunting hares and birds. Nat's account, set in modern Hollywood, would chronicle his hunting adventures with ducks and doves, sleeping pills and Benzedrine. But the idea was quickly shelved. Probably Nat sensed that it would never appeal to Bennett, whose sports were tennis and swimming.

In October he was laid low by another shockeroo, the return of his venereal disease, which forced his departure from Universal, where he had been working for ten months. In Merced County, California, with Wells Root for the opening of duck season, he walked to a duck blind toting his heavy gear. Several hours later, he climbed out again and abruptly lay down in the brush. It was only an upset stomach, he said. Back in Hollywood, he collapsed from inflammation of the urethra. At first the urethritis promised to be more easily treatable than the combined gonorrhea–congested prostate that had wiped him out in 1935. But when pre-antibiotic sulfa drugs brought no relief, he wound up in Cedars of Lebanon Hospital. The condition resisted treatment, and he developed a fever and a rash. He was discharged two weeks later, but had to undergo a series of extremely painful outpatient treatments before the condition cleared up.

Not long after leaving Cedars of Lebanon, he met Eileen Mc-Kenney.

21

EILEEN IN DISNEYLAND

EILEEN RENTED ROOMS for herself and Tommy in the home of a family living on Fuller Avenue in West Hollywood. The house was "a disgusting little concrete bungalow, painted vomit-pink," but she didn't mind because the landlady agreed to care for Tommy while she looked for work. A few weeks later she was hired for a secretarial job in the promotion department at Disney Studio.

In June of 1939, when Eileen arrived in Hollywood, the country was still trying to scramble out of hard times, but the picture business continued to bask in its glory years, its apogee represented that year by two smash movies, *The Wizard of Oz* and *Gone with the Wind*. Every day, Hollywood was overrun with openmouthed tourists hoping to see movie stars like Tyrone Power. On street corners vendors hawked maps directing visitors to the private residences of the people they had read about in *Modern Screen*. Those newcomers planning to become permanent residents in Hollywood found no such helpful maps to establishing an ordinary life, which could be both expensive and complicated. Eileen found the weather disappointing. Expecting swimming pools and bougainvillea, she had not bargained for the oppressive heat or the fog that seemed to lift only "between two and four."

Her employment at Disney was a lucky break. Since they opened their first cartoon studio in a garage in 1923, Walt and Roy Disney had become rich and successful by making stars out of a bunch of mice, ducks, and dogs, named Mickey Mouse, Donald Duck, and Pluto. There seemed to be no end to their technological innovation. In 1937 the studio released its first full-length feature, the eighty-three-minute *Snow White and the Seven Dwarfs*, an immense success at the box office. By the time Eileen arrived, Disney had become a factory employing hundreds of highly skilled technicians—writers, directors, animators, in-betweeners, background artists, inkers—and preparations were under way for expansion to a still-larger plant in Burbank. In various stages of development were the fairy tale *Pinocchio* and a delightful mixture of classical music and animation titled *Fantasia*. Eileen, initially hired in a secretarial position, soon reassigned to the story-research department, could see opportunities for something better. She was hoping to get special training and join the artisans who hand painted scenes on transparent sheets of celluloid acetate in the days before computer animation.

Again she struggled with the logistics of being a single mother. Early in the mornings she boarded a streetcar to the Disney studio on Hyperion Avenue in the Silver Lake district, and when she returned home Tommy clung to her. Yanked from the sidewalks of West Fourth Street, plopped down in the midst of palm trees and strangers wearing sunglasses, the two-year-old passed hot, boring days growing more fearful than ever, always frantic for his mother. Dealing with Tommy's tears was left to the landlady, who must have resorted to the age-old custom of comforting an unhappy child with sweets. As an adult he would self-medicate with candy, then drugs and alcohol. (In his last years, he practically lived on Hershey bars and peanut butter.)

Around the opposite sex Eileen could be abrasive, a weary, combat-hardened veteran back from the front. But though the demands of her job and her son left little time for socializing, she was eager for companionship and went on a date with a Metro writer who took her to a South Sea Islands restaurant. Over a plate of sweet-and-sour ribs in the pitch-dark bamboo hut, she told herself she should have ordered a Seeing Eye dog. The food and the tropical surroundings made her feel as if she had fallen into a Somerset Maugham story. Her date, the owner of a block-long Mercedes, was wearing a two-day beard and a sappy, hand-painted yellow necktie with a green shirt, and his conversation consisted of a monologue, about himself of course. It stood to reason that the men who could afford tropical restaurants were generally writers.

That summer Eileen kept in touch with Ruth by mail, and sometimes by phone despite Richard's howls about the bills, but they were drifting apart, and geographical distance was only one reason. There seemed to be no place for her in Ruth's life anymore. The long, gossipy letters that Ruth wrote to friends frequently mentioned her husband, rarely Eileen. By then the Branstens had assumed a public identity as professional Communists. Much of their time was devoted to making speeches, signing petitions, teaching classes, entertaining comrades. Separately, Ruth was swamped by her writing commitments, which included regular contributions to the *Daily Worker* and the *New Masses*. In April, when the *New Masses* teetered on the edge of extinction, Ruth had appealed for contributions—"any amount you can"—to save the magazine. She continued to write for *The New Yorker*, notwithstanding her animosity for Mrs. White, Harold Ross, and the whole bunch of snobs on West Forty-third Street, and she also worked tirelessly to develop additional *Sister Eileen* projects, including a Broadway play script and a sequel to be titled *The McKenneys Carry On*. At the same time, she complained that the first book had been embarrassing, sometimes dismissing it as her "sister Eileen funny book." (Earnings from the funny book provided a reliable annuity that supported her for the rest of her life.)

To friends, she denied being a humorist: she had "a sort of oblique way of digesting experience, that's all." All she cared about was that *My Sister Eileen* made money for the "busted Branstens." She talked of doing more books like *Industrial Valley*, which had been published to favorable reviews earlier that year.

By then Ruth and Richard had outgrown their one-bedroom apartment in the Village, and Ruth felt eager to bring down the curtain on New York. In typically dramatic fashion, she was now referring to the city as "death." Soon after Eileen moved to the Coast, the Branstens purchased a two-acre property in Westport, Connecticut, complete with a blue-shuttered, white-shingled house and a silvery brook. Ruth threw herself into home improvements and, even though children had always left her "totally cold," began toying with the idea of adopting a baby. (Nothing came of it.) As always, she enjoyed hosting social events, and invitations to her Westport parties and picnics became prized by Communist Party bigwigs and fellow travelers. Comrade Ruth seemed to have the best of both worlds.

Eileen, meanwhile, was managing to squeeze a few social benefits from the party. The close-knit community of Hollywood Communism welcomed fresh faces, especially celebrities. She began showing up occasionally at meetings, where she was fawned over by people like Lester Cole, a prominent figure in the local party. One of the best places to meet people in the film colony was at party functions, she had discovered. She sometimes wondered if she should move back to New York and marry Mac. This confidence led to Ruth's suggesting to Bennett Cerf that he look up Eileen on his next trip to the Coast. Her beautiful sister was slaving away at Disney, "a morgue," and could do with "a little extracurricular livening up."

Eileen's former husband now worked in Los Angeles as a radio writer, and even though she welcomed Morris's presence for Tommy's sake, she had absolutely no intention of allowing him to reenter her life.

After five months in Hollywood, she met Nat. One night in late October, she was invited to a get-well dinner for a friend of Lester and Jonnie Cole's, who lived with their two baby sons in a bungalow on Ranchito Street in Burbank. Lester briefed her beforehand about his old friend Pep, the screenwriter and novelist with whom he had worked at Republic and Universal, most recently on *I Stole a Million*, and who'd recently been in the hospital. To Eileen this information didn't mean much. When she entered the Coles' house he was wearing a Brooks Brothers suit and clamping a cigarette between his fingers. If he looked familiar it was because half the men in the movie business were prematurely balding middle-aged Jews with a hint of a potbelly. He was not as cute as Morris or as sexy as Mac, despite the sweet, Clark Gable mustache. When he spotted her walking into the Coles' house she seemed to ooze sass and strong opinions, a fearless, jaw-jutting, be-low-Fourteenth-Street party babe, the Red Square–Sheridan Square connection. She was a big person, tall and athletic and a bit loud, one of those girls who has all the answers. There was no question about her fondness for martinis (a couple of Mexican beers satisfied him). From watching her cheerful manner in relating woebegone stories about herself, funnier than one would expect, Nat may have concluded that the poor girl could use some help in managing her life.

To Lester and Jonnie, it was poor Pep who needed help. He was the lonely single man, whose highest priority seemed to be killing birds, an obsession that made Lester wonder how much Nat really wanted to be a writer. Having only recently met Eileen, the Coles were favorably impressed by her personality and reputation as the fairy-tale heroine of a bestseller, but knew nothing about her otherwise. That she might not want to cast her lot with a field-and-stream boyfriend, off someplace with a shotgun two days a week, must never have occurred to them.

The mood that evening was somber. The Nazi-Soviet nonaggres-sion pact had been signed in the last days of August (and supported by American Communists). After the invasion of Poland, and the British-French declaration of war on September 3, all of Europe was going to explode. At dinner the war was the main subject of conversation. After-ward, Nat politely offered Eileen a lift home. By the time they reached Fuller Avenue, he had decided to invite her out the following evening, even if she was a hothead Red who might easily become annoying if she began pontificating on social justice. Still, she seemed intelligent and her company might be enjoyable for a few hours. Besides, it was an amusing situation: when a writer invites another writer's quasific-tional character to go on a date, should the person be treated as real or imagined? Nat was familiar with *My Sister Eileen*, but there is no indi-cation he had read the book. It was typical *New Yorker* ham and grits, nothing that would interest him.

The next morning, Eileen decided to buy one of Nat's novels, so that she might study up for an intelligent discussion of the plot. In the course of the day she managed to locate a copy of *Miss Lonelyhearts* and began skimming it as "homework." When he showed up at Fuller Avenue she had not yet finished.

Almost apologetically, she proposed dining at her place instead of a restaurant, hoping he wouldn't find "the homely touch" too phony. Ruth later maintained that her sister deliberately offered a home-cooked meal because Hollywood restaurants were expensive and she had the impression that Pep might be hard up, but there was no reason to suppose such a thing. Most likely the reason for the cheap evening was Tommy, who came out to be introduced clutching his mother's skirt, clearly reluctant to let her out of his sight. She must have wanted to see if Pep hated kids. Getting cozy with a man annoyed by her child's clingy behavior would be more trouble than it was worth. Nat, who had always enjoyed the company of his nephew Adam Perelman, three months older than Tommy, was touched by the boy, who was bright and inquisitive, with big ears, like Nat's own.

In his autobiographical *Hollywood Red*, Lester Cole took credit for introducing Eileen and Nat, an old-fashioned case of love at first sight, in his living room; Ruth's version in her memoir *Love Story* sounded similar. She remembered that Eileen wrote to her that same evening. "Don't laugh, dearest Chubb, but after all these years, I *think* I'm in love." Over the next few weeks Eileen and Nat continued to see each other. On Sunset Strip one evening they did the nightspots with Budd Schulberg and his wife, Virginia. "Eileen tried to teach Pep to jitterbug," Schulberg recalls. "He didn't want to dance but she made him, and then he kind of liked it." They were obviously happy together. "She was naturally congenial, the opposite of Pep, and she really pulled him out of himself. He seemed like a different person."

At the heart of the unplanned relationship were the feelings of two lonely people starved for fun, emotions that would creep into a screenplay Nat was writing that fall. "It's funny what makes you like people," a character muses; sometimes it can be as subtle as a tiny gesture. And, he adds, some people spend years seeking success only to discover it is too late to have fun. "Nonsense," replies the heroine. "It's simply that you've worked so long you've forgotten how to play—Or perhaps you just have no one to play with."

Initially, their relationship was more companionable than sexual. Despite Eileen's sessions with Dr. Memburg, she had never managed to develop any great enthusiasm for physical intimacy, and Nat was still in treatment for urethritis. A normal physical relationship was temporarily out of the question.

Otherwise, Eileen's first impression of Nat—perhaps similar to Josie Herbst's—must have been of the courtly, soft-spoken Ivy League intellectual, his Clark Kent, hotel-executive personality. Had she known his work beforehand—if she'd thoroughly read his most recent novel—she would have been forewarned, to some degree. Appearing on the second page of *The Day of the Locust* was a biography of his alter ego, Tod Hackett, as "a nest of Chinese boxes" containing numerous sets of personalities. To those like Josie who had come to know him, or to a sharp observer of the opposite sex like Dorothy Parker, some of those shiny boxes were complete fakes. There was, Parker thought, nobody like Pep, but she never thought him a good catch as a husband. If—a big if—Eileen had read all of his four novels, she would have detected his fear of women, the contemptuous portraits ranging from the castrating Fay(e)s to the bovine Betty Prail, raped, sold, and degraded without protest. In none of the books is there a healthy relationship between a man and woman.

Nat's attraction to Eileen seems predictable. A fastidious man who fussed over the cut of his conservative suits, he tended to be picky about the women with whom he associated. Run-of-the-mill women held no interest whatsoever. In his twenties, he had ended the relationships with brainy Beatrice Mathieu and glamorous Alice Shepard when they threatened to become serious, possibly before consummation. At this stage, now that he was financially if not emotionally ready, Eileen must have impressed him as an appealing trophy. That she was better known than he did not faze him a bit; indeed, it added to her allure. And he was equally pleased by the rest of her—a pretty woman, outgoing, and good fun. It makes sense that he would seek emotional support given the setbacks he had suffered in recent months. But there was one troubling note, and it was not her dislike of reading or her lack of a college education or that she was a secretary, none of which he evidently considered significant.

What he found especially unattractive was her political righteousness. The previous year, when Matthew Josephson met Nat during a visit to Hollywood, Matty was a bit surprised to hear him talking so disdainfully about friends of his, smart people, who were hewing to the party line with religious fervor. He specifically mocked Burt Kelly, his former boss at Republic, as a do-gooder who needed "an ointment"— Communism. To Josephson he made it clear that he had no patience with misty leftist mumbo-jumbo. (His advice for a no-win world, he confided to Malcolm Cowley, could be summed up in a single word: "beware.")

When it came to politics, Nat constituted a party of one. While the hoopla over alleviating the world's miseries might sound noble, he lacked faith in a solution, an awkward position given that so many of his friends had become fellow travelers or card-carrying comrades, including Budd Schulberg, Dash Hammett, Dorothy Parker, Lester Cole, Burt Kelly, Samuel Ornitz, and Gordon Kahn. Scotty too had recently joined the party, attending the so-called housewives' meetings reserved for party spouses not on a studio payroll. In Bucks County, even Laura and Sid allowed themselves to be carted off to party meetings by their best friends, the playwrights Ruth and Augustus Goetz. People frequently lectured Nat, but he sneaked out the back door when nobody was looking. It was a free country; there was "a place for the fellow who yells fire and indicates where some of the smoke is coming from without actually dragging the hose to the spot."

Surrounded by people dragging hoses, buckets, and ladders, he finally embraced an attitude of deference and tried to blend in. He went out of his way to express concern for the heroic Spanish war dead and offered respectful murmurs about the terrible plight of the world, and in fact he was truly sorry. Nevertheless, he was wary of Marxist tenets, which he considered fairy tales. "Nihilistic pessimism," Josie Herbst labeled his bone-deep cynicism, while another friend, Bob Coates, rated him "about the most pessimistic person I have ever known." For all the years John Sanford knew him, he'd shown "no interest in reforming the system he lived under," and "any reference to politics, particularly to socialism, had evoked almost always derision or disdain."

This disdain of all that Eileen thought was good—or at least important in 1939—provided her with a clear mandate to do political missionary work. To reeducate him, she talked—reasoned, persuaded, no doubt lectured—and forever tried to push him into a Marxist study class; he did not welcome her efforts. It was just as well that he did not have an opportunity to meet Ruth and Richard, whom he might have ridiculed as wacky cartoon revolutionaries. A few years hence, Ruth would characterize her sacred commitment to party doctrine as the misguided faith of a Don Quixote: She knew it was "only a windmill but we had to tilt for our souls' sake," she claimed. To the world's overwrought Quixotes, Nat preferred the part of Sancho Panza, the realistic, unemotional sidekick. Communism wasn't ideology, he thought; it was a product found on the medicine-cabinet shelf. It was Vaseline jelly.

If Nat's stubborn ridicule of her political beliefs dismayed Eileen, there were other things about him that gave her the willies: for one, he drove like a maniac. When a cop pulled him over one day, he was quick to protest his innocence. Despite an amiable conversation, Nat's explanations failed to sway the officer, who proceeded to write the ticket. "Nice guy, bad driver," he was heard to remark as he prepared to ride off.

Eileen could not resist turning the incident into an anecdote. The punch line—"Nice guy, bad driver"—usually got a laugh. The trouble was, Nat would not admit to being a bad driver. On the contrary, he prided himself, after some twenty-five years behind the steering wheel, on never having been in a significant accident, lost his license, or driven drunk. And he glossed over a habit of taking his eyes off the road to talk with people in the backseat or to absent-mindedly light another cigarette.

On one occasion he narrowly avoided a fatal accident when his car almost hurtled off a bridge into an irrigation ditch. If these kinds of near misses did not happen every day, safety violations were all too routine. During rush hour, he would impulsively torpedo a U-turn across six lanes of traffic on Ventura Boulevard. More than once he was guilty of swerving over the center line, driving on the wrong side of the road, and passing on hairpin curves. Whenever one of his passengers started yelling at him, he would respond soothingly, promising in the manner of a priest administering last rites that there was nothing to worry about.

His denials centered on the kinds of rationalizations—the distorted thinking that leads to disasters—that social psychologists would one day call cognitive dissonance. Seemingly indifferent to personal safety, he cracked nobody-lives-forever jokes and maintained that caution did not necessarily forestall misfortune. What he did not seem to realize was that his actions might cause damage to others.

When Eileen warned him to stop driving or, at least, to avoid carrying passengers—a drastic solution in the motor capital of the world—he felt hurt. He reluctantly acquiesced to her doing the driving, but clearly his masculine pride was bruised, because he would make her stop a block short of their destination and switch places with him. The subject of his driving would become increasingly touchy.

On a sticky day right after Thanksgiving, when the temperature hit ninety-eight degrees, the Perelmans descended on Hollywood, vowing that "this is *really* our last trip here, forever." This time the tribe included two children, a schnauzer, and a nursemaid. Once Abby and Adam were deposited at Nat's house and Gurke in a kennel, Sid and Laura checked themselves into the air-cooled Hollywood-Knickerbocker Hotel. After an eight-day drive from Pennsylvania, they were frazzled. Nat "doesn't mind the noise," Sid insisted. Actually, it was the children's grandmother Anna, also a houseguest, who didn't mind. Just past sixty, she looked spry but had become deaf.

Unable to earn such an extravagant living elsewhere, the couple intended to work for eight months before shutting the door on screen-writing. If they had only one life to live, "it isn't going to be led here," Sid grumbled characteristically. The town, which "smelled like a laundry," was crawling with losers wearing "the fierce deranged stare of paretics." The diatribe was vintage Perelman. He and Laura sought comfort and corned beef in "the only Hebe delicatessen in town."

After several weeks the Perelmans repaired to a house in the fashionable section of Beverly Hills and eased back into the writers' lifestyle. Although it took them two months to find employment at United Artists, on a picture never to be produced, their time was not wasted; they began writing a stage play, *The Night Before Christmas*, in which bumbling ex-cons attempt a Yuletide heist by tunneling from a luggage shop to a bank vault next door. Nat's mother's attention was diverted to her grandchildren, and to her daughter, with whom she engaged in a running battle over the supposedly defective hearing aids Laura had provided her. Nat, uninvolved in the chaos, was relieved to escape to his RKO office.

After the debacle of *Locust*, Nat could at least console himself with his success at RKO. On the basis of *Five Came Back*, the studio assigned him to develop a treatment for *Before the Fact: A Murder Story for Ladies*, by the English crime writer Francis Iles. The 1932 novel, in which a dead woman relates how she consented to being murdered by her husband with a poisoned glass of milk, had been kicking around for years because nobody could figure out how to film it. Nat was teamed with a Russian writer-director named Boris Ingster, to whom RKO had offered an opportunity to direct the picture if a script could be coaxed out of the novel. Seven weeks later, they had an approved script and Laurence Olivier's tentative acceptance to play the murderous husband. Then everything fell apart.

Working on the RKO lot was Alfred Hitchcock, who became interested in the Iles novel while seeking a story for Cary Grant. Grabbing the rights, Hitchcock decided to throw out the Ingster-West script and use his own staff to craft a different version. In both novel and film, the key scene is the glass of milk. Does Lina drink the poison? Yes, according to Francis Iles; no, she shoots her husband, imagined Nat and Boris. Hitchcock came up with a third possibility, that the milk isn't poisoned at all and Lina is a suspicious neurotic and the picture ends happily with the wife (Joan Fontaine) discovering her husband is innocent after all. *Before the Fact*, released in 1941 under the title *Suspicion*, would become RKO's biggest box-office hit that year and win a Best Actress Oscar for Fontaine.

Nat shrugged off the loss of *Before the Fact*. Not only was regret a useless emotion for a screenwriter, but he had no time for self-pity. Immediately, he was assigned to a picture about a reformed-alcoholic pilot who loses his life testing experimental aircraft. In two months he cooked up a 127-page script for *Men Against the Sky*; without a single day off, he found himself working on a Bob Crosby musical, *Let's Make Music*, that required emergency repairs. He heard nothing more about the aviation movie, but one day he caught the producer in the hall. What happened to *Men Against the Sky*? Didn't he know? the producer replied. It had started shooting Monday. What's more, he was to receive a solo credit and his compensation was being raised to four hundred dollars a week.

With all the commotion over the Perelmans' arrival, Nat had managed to avoid bringing up the subject of Eileen McKenney to his mother. He himself was unsure of his feelings. As he did every year, Nat planned to go off and shoot birds with his good buddy Wells Root on New Year's. This news prompted a tongue-lashing from Eileen: she damn well didn't care what he and his cronies used to do. Now he had her, and she was not asking for much, only a date on New Year's. Her hollering led him to make a swift exit out of town, confiding to Wells that Eileen's behavior had really upset him. She was "sore as hell" at him for leaving her on the holiday. In Root's recollection, Pep complained that his weekends were becoming "a problem," that Eileen was trying to "louse up his hunting life."

That an unmarried male of his age would be set in his ways was hardly surprising. Nat provided good reasons for Eileen to think twice about a permanent relationship. For one thing, he was in baby-talking love with his dogs, even slept with them. She was not going to put up with dogs in her bed, but it had become apparent that the dog problem was not the worst of it. Despite her best efforts, he continued to drive like a lunatic. And his notion of free time was sitting in a freezing duck blind trying to kill birds, his concept of fine art a collection of hand-carved wildfowl decoys ordered from Charles "Shang" Wheeler, a prizewinning Connecticut artist.

Somehow their shaky relationship survived the New Year's crisis, but the future remained up in the air. It was his poor physical health — this time a large kidney stone lodged in his urinary tract — that elicited her sympathy. In January he began undergoing procedures that Sid humorously described to Gus Goetz as Pep lying "flat on his pratt" with "a battery of doctors peering up his pecker." Dissolving the stone ("of the Triassic period") was not quite so amusing as Sid made out; Nat confided to Wells that he passed out from the painful treatments. A houseful of mayhem added to the strain. Anna fretted hysterically over his medical problems, the children brawled, and Laura spread sore throat and cold germs. It was, Sid said, a regular Donnybrook Fair.

As a little boy in Harlem, Nat stood alone and watched other children playing marbles. Nat at thirty-six was still secretive and solitary, his life packaged into airtight compartments. After dating Eileen for several months, he bought her a ring, a diamond flanked by a ruby and a sapphire, but no engagement announcement accompanied the ring; on the contrary, few who saw them together assumed it was a genuine courtship. Probably he would continue to see the new girlfriend for a number of weeks, even months, but when the bloom wore off he would backpedal to the safety of paid sex at Lee Francis's brothel. In the winter, Nat's mother returned to New York knowing little — possibly nothing — about Eileen, certainly unaware that her son was seeing a divorced Christian and the mother of a small child.

Since Eileen and Nat made such an odd couple, there was predictable gossip: what had induced an intellectual like Pep West to go slumming? The flip side of that question—what interested a celebrity like Eileen in an obscure novelist like Pep West?—evidently did not arise. Nobody believed that the spendthrift princess in Ruth's stories could be Nat's equal, and some speculated that a shallow woman would prevent his writing serious literature. These smears incensed Ruth, who had initially greeted the romance with elation. Instantly on the defensive, she sputtered that it would not be Eileen's fault if he never wrote another word. For years he had been working in Hollywood and living in self-indulgent comfort. Her sister was a responsible, levelheaded woman. West was the neurotic one, who squandered his money on all manner of knickknackery to support an expensive hunting habit. Ruth would still be fuming about the backbiters twenty-five years later.

One day Nat and Eileen dropped in on Scott Fitzgerald, who was renting a guesthouse on the Edward Everett Horton estate in suburban Encino and working on his Hollywood novel. Few visitors came there, and Scott and his girlfriend, Sheilah Graham, a syndicated gossip columnist for the North American Newspaper Alliance, rarely ventured out socially. The person Eileen met was a frail, pasty-white, middle-aged man overwhelmed by the weight of professional and personal troubles. A recovering alcoholic, he suffered from a heart condition and tired easily. "He had stopped drinking," says his then-secretary, Frances Kroll Ring, "but he smoked and ate all the wrong things." Most days he stayed in bed, where he wrote longhand, and gave Frances the manuscript pages to type.

Although vaguely familiar with Scott's work, Eileen had not read anything from his halcyon days. At forty-three, six years after publication of *Tender Is the Night*, which sold poorly, he was increasingly regarded as a relic. By this time, his works were not even regularly stocked in the major Los Angeles bookstores, and although *Esquire* had recently published his story about an alcoholic hack screenwriter (the first in the Pat Hobby series), he was sometimes assumed to be dead. Unaware of this, Eileen chided him for writing fiction that glorified rich people in love with their money. What about the little guys?

Where was his political consciousness? She took it upon herself to en-
lighten him on world events. When fascism was sweeping Europe, failure to get involved in the terrible political battles of their time was
more than a personal shortcoming—it was unthinkable.

Scott did not take kindly to criticism. Any holier-than-thou lectures
tended to ruffle his feathers, and here was a mouthy youngster regurgitating half-baked ideas whose meaning she obviously lacked the brains
to figure out for herself. Nat, embarrassed, began chattering nervously,
which made Scott wonder if "he's long-winded as a defense mecha-
nism," as a way of keeping people at a distance and saying "don't like
me." Scott had an unusually close relationship with Sid, whose suave
manners he always said reminded him of his wealthy expatriate friend
Gerald Murphy. After Abby Perelman's birth Scott had recommended
a baby nurse, and he recently purchased Sid's 1937 Ford. The two of
them, Scott said, were so simpatico that "we had no need to talk." Little
of this affection rubbed off on Nat, whose "heaviness" made Scott uncomfortable. Usually he referred to him distantly as Sid's brother-in-
law or Laura's brother. "He was fond of Sid and Laura but he didn't
like Pep that well," recalls Frances Ring. He admired Nat's writing, but
the stories thoroughly depressed him. And if his fiction was "morbid as
hell, doomed to the underworld of literature," his taste in women was
miserable too.

Once the callers had gone, Scott made a disparaging entry in his
notebook referring to Nat's "foolish passion for that tough and stupid
child Mc_____." In any case, he added, "Sid knows what I know so well
that it would be blasphemy to put it into conversation." He had no desire to embarrass Sid by discussing Eileen or the visit. "He thought
Eileen was a silly girl," says Frances Ring.

Nat's hunting companions disliked Eileen too, especially when he
invited her to join them. Although the presence of any woman would
have interfered with their camaraderie, the athletic Eileen proved to
be a good marksman—in fact better than Nat. Wells Root thought she
was a showoff, "outspoken and talkative in any group and on any subject." Specifically, she was "not much bothered with facts, figures, and

historical perspective." Her habit of pouring forth "flip generalities and pat opinions" made Root cringe. If her behavior had the power to annoy him, he hated to think how it must embarrass Nat, a thoughtful man, well read and highly educated. Of course, those opinions of Eileen's reflected her politics, shared by plenty of people in the movie business, ideologies for which Root evidently felt no sympathy. In the end, he became resigned to her. The relationship might possibly work, he told himself, but only because Pep was "incredibly good natured and tolerant." Thirty-five years later, Wells Root objected to a *Los Angeles Times* article portraying Eileen as lonely and insecure. She was no such thing, he declared. On the contrary, she was a large, raucous woman with a wild sense of humor who loved her martinis.

News of the romance startled some of Nat's longtime friends. Josie Herbst, living quietly in Erwinna after the breakup with John Herrmann and completing a new novel (*Rope of Gold*), had seen Nat briefly the previous fall. She privately wondered if he might be secretly bisexual or homosexual, a natural suspicion, because he had shown considerable interest in same-sex relationships in his fiction. As for opposite-sex relationships, he told her that he subscribed to a double standard: his wife would have to be a virgin or "the next best thing," and extramarital affairs are "all right for husbands but not for wives." In both situations, "his attitude was rigid." Josie could not imagine him marrying any woman, virgin or not. The idea of him suddenly gravitating toward someone of Eileen McKenney's background—"hardly a one-man woman"—left Josie scratching her head. There must be some essential fact of which she was unaware. Perhaps Eileen, whom she had never met but presumed cosmopolitan, was secretly childlike "and Pep fell hard for her child." Eventually, after she gave up trying to understand, she would conclude that "it was a genuine love match and I never expected Pep to make one."

Probably the one person who found the love affair completely understandable was St. Clair McKelway. Obviously Eileen would adore an egghead like Nathanael West, "a serious guy" with a fun-loving side, "not a heavy handed or heavy thinking leftist." That he was a highbrow

intellectual, a self-involved, donnish type wracked by doubts and hesi-
tations, must have been irresistible, he thought. No doubt the cerebral
West was enthralled by "her animated, suffering humor."

Bennett Cerf, on a trip to Los Angeles, made no attempt to analyze the relationship but offered flattering congratulations on Eileen's
charm and good looks. "I don't think I have ever met a more attractive
girl in my entire life," he declared. Budd Schulberg says that Eileen
failed to fit the local stereotype concerning beauty but was "strikingly
attractive by eastern standards." He liked her for being "hearty, funny,
warm, outgoing, constitutionally cheerful, and loving."

At a dinner party hosted by screenwriter Guy Endore during the winter
of 1940, Nat bumped into Scotty, who had married a Metro contract
writer, Marguerite Roberts. It was the first time they'd seen each other
in a while, but some things never changed. When Scotty started quoting the opinion of a CBS commentator who broadcasted news from
London—"Major George Fielding Eliot says . . ."—Nat interrupted.
Captain Eliot, he murmured.

Pugilistic as ever, Scotty fired back. "God damn it, it's Major!"

Nat retorted, "Oh, was he promoted?" (Major was correct.)

Scotty's anger toward Nat had cooled since the publication of *Locust,* but he continued to view him as a writer whose work was propelled
by feelings of vengeance, arising from his anger that he had not been
born a Hardy or a Dostoyevsky. He remembered how Nat, in an un-
guarded moment, had referred to himself as "only a third-rate Huxley."
Nevertheless, Scotty managed to rein himself in and the rest of the evening passed amicably. Nat asked Scotty and Marguerite for a lift home
because his car was in the shop. As they were passing C. C. Brown's ice
cream parlor on Hollywood Boulevard, Nat insisted on stopping for hot
fudge sundaes, and so everybody was in a good mood by the time they
said good night. At his door he turned with a grin of apology and said,
"You know, Scotty, I think you're right. He is a major."

At no time during the evening did Nat mention a girlfriend, much
less plans to get married. Habitually secretive, he also found himself at

a fork in the road, unable to move north or south. A few weeks later, he told Bob Brown, his trusted friend from *Contempo* days, who had sent him a couple of cookbooks, that "I gave three of them to the girl that I might marry, and the fourth to my sister." To his friends he appeared happier than anybody could remember, but even so, Budd Schulberg says, "Pep's decision to marry Eileen amazed everyone."

Eileen knew that Nat was in no hurry to get married, despite the diamond ring and his assurances of really wanting to be with her. All of her efforts to set a wedding date met with excuses: script deadlines, weekend hunting dates, lack of time for a honeymoon. He was a master of dragging his feet, but she finally got him to settle on a date, April 19, two weeks after her twenty-seventh birthday. Immediately she ordered a simple gold wedding band, inscribed "For NW from EMK 4 1940," and engraved wedding announcements:

MR. JOHN SYDNEY McKENNEY
announces the marriage of his daughter
EILEEN
to
MR. NATHANAEL WEST
on Friday, the nineteenth of April
One thousand nine hundred and forty
Beverly Hills, California

Eileen had not seen her father in several years. There was no dramatic falling-out, but she had come to feel as unwelcome in his house as Ruth did and distanced herself accordingly. If the father of the bride would not be there to give her away, neither would other Cleveland relatives make the long, expensive trek to the Coast. Nor did Ruth attend. She was booked to address a peace rally at City College, where she planned to lambaste the press for pushing the country toward war, but she sent a flurry of congratulatory telegrams.

On April 19, following the seventh consecutive day of pouring rain, the sun came out. Charles J. Griffin, a judge known for performing movie-star marriages, officiated at the ceremony, and there was a din-

ner afterward at Chasen's, an overrated chili parlor on Beverly Boulevard. Until the very last moment, Sid and Laura failed to take the
marriage seriously. (The last person to know about it was Anna Weinstein, now back in New York.) When it did happen, Sid announced
the news to his Bucks County friend Gus Goetz as an afterthought to
talk of the rainy weather and his recent ordeal of having to return a
three-month-old bloodhound puppy. He was more interested in Nat's
musings about maybe buying another farm in Pennsylvania. Did Gus
know of anything for sale?

Monday morning after the wedding, the newlyweds returned to
their respective jobs, Eileen to Disney and Nat to RKO. A honeymoon
was postponed until the summer, when they could spend two leisurely
months in Oregon. Meanwhile, Eileen mailed out the traditional "at
home" cards:

> At home after the first of May.
> Sixty-six fourteen Cahuenga Terrace
> Hollywood, California

One of these cards was slipped into a note thanking Bennett Cerf for
a gift of classic literary works, which she planned to take with them to
Oregon. "Providing I'm not too busy cooking trout, I'm going to pursue a little culture in the Greeks—while Pep is busy writing your next
best seller!" Cozying up to Cerf was meant to reinforce her husband's
promises that he would return in the fall with "a gem of purest ray serene in my satchel" for Random House.

In June, accompanied by Tommy, they rented a cabin in Oregon's
McKenzie River valley, an angler's paradise for salmon and trout.
Everybody relaxed. In the late afternoons they pulled on their fishing
boots and headed for the supposedly good places in the vicinity. Only,
Eileen wrote to her new mother-in-law, "so far we haven't found many
fish waiting for us." But they were having fun and getting "plenty of exercise tramping around and wading in the river." Their leisurely routine involved sleeping until nine or even later and eating a big breakfast. Eileen did the washing up before setting out on a four-mile jaunt

for groceries, and then, she informed Anna, "Pep starts to work." Just as her letter omits any mention of Tommy, the description of what Nat did all day is misleading. Most of the time he played with Julie and Danny, dug holes to bury the garbage, and carried on about a balky, overheating stove. Sometimes he entertained friends like Wells Root and Lester Cole, when they drove up to fish.

Although Nat did some writing, it wasn't fiction. He produced pages of notes, mainly two outlines that clarified the ideas he had presented earlier to Random House. The shorter of the two, about eight hundred words, begins: "This is a story about a racket." This particular racket is little known because, unlike mob extortion, its profits are minor, but it's a crime just the same. Nat's "racket" is newspaper personals. The second, longer outline ("Foreword on Racket") presents thumbnail descriptions of the major characters and plot points. The action is built around Earl James, star reporter for the *New York Times Dispatch*, who is combing the lovelorn column and the classifieds for human-interest stories. Among the ads for acne creams and spiritual mediums is a matchmaking/dating service, the Golden Friendship Club, which promises to bring together singles seeking love and marriage. "Are you lonely? Do you wish you had a beau to squire you to delightful little parties?"

"That's it!" Earl James shouts. "There's probably a whole series in it."

Nat next introduces Alice Ronsard, a student enrolled at Bennett Cerf's own alma mater, the Columbia School of Journalism. A humorless South Dakota yokel, Alice is "no shrinking violet," Nat wrote. Dressed like an "Aberdeen heifer" in a mannish tweed suit, low-heeled shoes, and woolen stockings (and carrying a purse made from the hide of a calico pony), she initially comes across as a younger version of Miss Farkis, the bookish lesbian of *Miss Lonelyhearts*. But obviously there is another side to Alice: she later strides into the "21" Club in a "soigné" Elizabeth Hawes outfit. As the story proceeds, Earl meets the Burgess family—wife, husband, and grown son—operating its Golden Friendship Club from a Brooklyn brownstone. Convinced that he is on the track of a criminal operation, Earl deploys Alice to Brooklyn with instructions to join the social club. While performing legwork on his behalf, she can practice her reporting skills. Next thing, Alice disappears without a trace—and there the notes end.

The summer of 1940 flickered by in a haze of sunshine. Nat failed to write a single word of Random House's next bestseller, and neither did Eileen get around to Cerf's Greek classics. He frittered away the days fishing and playing with his dogs; she made believe he was writing "the gem of purest ray serene." The new book, she wrote Ruth, was going to be "the most important American novel since Dreiser, Hemingway, et cetera." But then followed a burst of joy—"Isn't it NICE to be married? Aren't we lucky?"—that was probably no exaggeration.

22

TOGETHER

For fifty-seven nights that autumn, the German Luftwaffe pounded London. The raids were being called a "lightning war," a blitzkrieg, and people took to carrying gas masks by day and sleeping underground in the tube stations.

From their house in the Hollywood Hills, Nat and Eileen followed the Blitz, reading the newspapers aloud to each other or listening on their radio to Edward R. Murrow or Quentin Reynolds reporting from London. Eileen one evening began a letter to "Mother West," whom she had yet to meet. Worry over the war, she wrote, brought her and Nat closer together and made them feel lucky they had "each other and you to love." Reassurances followed: "Believe me, we'll keep it that way."

With Anna at a safe distance on the East Coast and the war half a world away, the newlyweds nestled together on Cahuenga Terrace, but had begun planning ahead for the day they could move. Ready to enjoy the comforts of family life, they went looking for properties in the open countryside of the San Fernando Valley, long a haven for ranch-owning stars like Clark Gable. It had been two years since Nat last saw Eight Ball Farm, and he longed for space. They began shopping for a house with several acres of land, something suitable for a couple with a two-and-a-half-year-old child. What they had in mind was a simple home with five bathrooms and indirect lighting, Eileen wrote in a giggly letter to Ruth. Could anything be found for twenty-five dollars a month? "Please send all details on how to get a second mortgage."

No mortgage tips were forthcoming because Ruth was busy with the September publication of her sequel to *My Sister Eileen*. The new book, *The McKenneys Carry On*, was dedicated to "Eileen and Tommy with love." Again released by Harcourt, and edited by Charles Pearce, it offered reprints of fourteen stories that had appeared in *The New Yorker*, *Woman's Day*, and *Publishers Weekly*, a total of 219 pages that continued to depict confectionary lives untarnished by reality. In one of the pieces, the fictional Eileen is mourning the demise of their dog Bones. In "The Ides of February" she is the bratty sister who gets all the valentines at Prospect elementary school. ("My sister Eileen was made for Valentine's Day, and vice versa.") In stories about the adult sisters, the grown-up Eileen soldiers on as an unmarried New York secretary but has no romances worth mentioning. Practically none of the material was aimed at young female readers seeking escapist tales about the fun of being single in the city. The collection is padded with detailed descriptions of Ruth's marriage to Richard and their domestic arrangements in verdant Westport, in their house with "rose bushes winding over its old well." The most conspicuous omission was the Branstens' active affiliation with the Communist Party.

By 1940 *My Sister Eileen* was in its eleventh printing. Having established a franchise, Ruth was turning Eileen into a lucrative cottage industry. Against all odds, *The New Yorker* continued regular publication of the stories. Officially, Katharine White was no longer fiction editor—she had accompanied her spouse to Maine—but she pulled puppet strings on her replacement, Gus Lobrano. Periodically the magazine lowered its editorial standards to include cutesy pieces from its pantheon of homespun writers, which included Ruth as well as Sally Benson (with her "Junior Miss" stories of adolescence). Fortunately for Ruth, its readership continued to cherish these cheerful potboilers.

Money was, as usual, a cause of tension between the Branstens. While prepared to offer undying allegiance to the proletariat, they were also party nobility who lived on a grand scale. To support their lifestyle they required a steady revenue stream, but despite Ruth's manic output and Richard's trust fund, they were always broke. Ruth's profit-making ventures involving Eileen were not limited to *The McKenneys Carry On*; a Broadway show was in the works as well. When Eileen heard about the sale of dramatic rights, she made a joke of it by asking who was going to play her. Ethel Barrymore?

Such decisions were not under her sister's control. Ruth did not believe an option would necessarily lead to a production. In this case, the optioning playwrights had such an unimpressive track record there seemed to be no reason for optimism.

Jerome Chodorov and Joseph A. Fields were a team of B-movie writers working at Republic Pictures when Nat arrived there in 1936. Their movies were similar to his — cheap comedies and dramas — and though they managed to escape Repulsive for RKO and Columbia, they had failed to rack up any notable credits. While out of work and collecting unemployment in 1939, they made an offer for the rights to *My Sister Eileen*. Joe Fields, forty-four, came from a prominent show-business family: his father was Lew Fields of the popular Weber and Fields comedy act, his sister Dorothy an eminent lyricist, and his brother Herbert a successful librettist. Jerry Chodorov, sixteen years Fields's junior, had begun his career as a reporter on the *New York World*. His older brother, Edward Chodorov, was an established playwright. Regardless of their families, Joe and Jerry themselves had yet to taste success. Their single Broadway venture, a comedy called *Schoolhouse on the Lot*, had closed after fifty-five performances.

Ever since the publication of *My Sister Eileen*, Ruth had been struggling unsuccessfully to transform the tales into a stage play, or to sell the book directly to the movies (a $2,500 deal with Columbia fell through). But even after her agreement with Chodorov and Fields, she did not give up hope of doing the play herself. Options frequently lapsed for lack of production financing.

After acquiring the rights in October 1939, Jerry and Joe and their wives rented a beach house in Malibu. Combining unemployment checks, they soaked up the sun while devising a comfortable work routine, which consisted of sitting on the sand and leaning against backrests. During those weeks, Jerry remembered, they savored "barbecued steaks and chops almost every night on the patio, fresh corn on the cob and frozen daiquiris." The chief difficulty with *My Sister Eileen* was that it had no plot, only a jumble of sketches, two main characters appearing as children and adults, and a forest of deadwood. But finding a workable story line, which had eluded Ruth, was sandbox play to Jerry and Joe, graduates of the Republic writing department. "Plots were my specialty," Jerry recalled thinking to himself. By Christmas they had a first draft.

Upon his and Eileen's return from Oregon, Nat planned to start his novel. Using the notes he had prepared over the summer, he intended to continue the outline about Earl James and the friendship racket, then draw up a schedule and begin writing. Suddenly he began making excuses. It would be nice to have uninterrupted time instead of working in fits and starts. Wasn't the friendship club story too similar to *Miss Lonelyhearts*? For that matter, he could think of lots more interesting characters than the reporter and the Columbia journalism student. At one point he decided that the hero, perhaps not necessarily Earl James after all, would be climbing a mountain trail when he falls into a ten-foot snowdrift. Nat was losing interest in the plot, but that did not entirely account for his dawdling: he got sidetracked.

The previous fall, RKO had paired him with Boris Ingster, a Russian who, in spite of his country's rich cinematic heritage, was drawn to the flash and dash of American movies. They got along well, and in May, when Boris finally had made his directorial debut with the psychological thriller *Stranger on the Third Floor*, starring Peter Lorre, Nat contributed an uncredited polish job. Thanks to his rapport with Boris, Nat now found himself swamped with movie projects that left no time for writing novels. His hot streak began in September, when the two of them raked in a bundle overnight, followed by two additional meaty deals. Faced with a decision—money or dubious glory—he chose the cash. Bennett Cerf would just have to wait.

Boris's appearance—thinning pale hair, watery blue eyes, and a dough-colored face—suggested a six-foot white rabbit. Five years Nat's senior, he had studied cinematography at the Moscow Institute of Cinema with Sergei Eisenstein, whose *Battleship Potemkin* was recognized as a silent-film masterpiece. When Paramount invited Eisenstein to Hollywood in 1930, Boris came along as part of his entourage. The plan for an American film fell through and Eisenstein returned to his native land, but Boris, bewitched by Southern California, decided "this was the place for him," says his nephew Henry Bruch. Although he knew five languages and learned to speak excellent English, his writing skills remained poor. When Nat met him in 1939, his two most recent jobs were on a pair of Sonja Henie pictures.

A prodigious reader who could down two or three books in a day, the Russian was not only highly literate and a master of plot and structure, but also a smart businessman who understood where the money was. As Nat told his sister, Boris had "enough energy to drive a steam shovel," and knew "a hell of a lot about the business." It did not escape Nat's notice that he had clout with people like Darryl Zanuck at Fox, or owned a costly house off Benedict Canyon Road in Beverly Hills and drove a magnificent Packard.

No doubt the steam shovel and the garden spade seemed an odd couple, but as writing partners Boris and Nat were a perfect match. An admirer of Nat's novels and his ability to create unique characters, Boris was quick to see comic possibilities in *A Cool Million*. In only a few days, they strung together a treatment that transformed Lemuel Pitkin into an asexual, sugary-sweet Horatio Alger hero. Following in the footsteps of so many other Alger boys, Joe Williams leaves Vermont with his paper suitcase, heads for a career in the city, and instantly messes up. Sanitizing Nat's story meant sex and violence had to go. The twisted Wu Fong and his voluptuous brothel sweeties could hardly pass the Production Code, and neither could brave Betty Prail's serial rapes. The hero's eye could not be gouged out and his scalp ripped off, nor could he be shot in the heart. Instead, a few innocent missteps in bookkeeping get Joe accused of embezzling a million dollars from the bank where he works, which leads to jail, notoriety, and surprising respect as a master thief. In a Frank Capra, *Mr. Deeds Goes to Town* bit of hokum, Joe's legal travails are made to end happily after all. The kid gets to keep all of his body parts, before walking into the sunset with his girlfriend Laura, a tough Manhattan cookie "who had two answers for everything."

Although the overhauled version bore slight resemblance to the novel, Nat and Boris decided to label the treatment an adaptation. Premade material always commanded bigger prices than original stories.

Five studios bid on *A Cool Million*. On September 24, Columbia bought the treatment for the princely sum of $10,000, meaning each of the authors took in a cool $5,000 ($75,000 in today's currency). This sale was especially remarkable because Columbia already owned the rights. Obviously the story department had forgotten about buying the book six years earlier, and Nat felt no obligation to remind them. The mix-up delighted him, as the opportunity to screw the establishment didn't come along every day.

A disciplined man, Boris not only drove himself but also expected other people to produce, and Nat had to scramble to keep up with him. For the next several days, the two men worked around the clock to develop a treatment for a suspense thriller whose story they had ripped from recent headlines. Jim Osborne, a stockbroker who wins a Thanksgiving turkey in an office raffle, realizes it is no ordinary bird when people start killing to get it. The raffle turkey turns out to be "Sam," the military mascot of March Field Air Base in Riverside, California, on whose back are tattooed technical plans for a top-secret bombsight. With German bombs continuing to hammer London, any idea involving weapons and high-level government espionage got attention. Only two weeks after selling *A Cool Million*, their twenty-six-page treatment for *Bird in Hand* was snapped up by RKO for $25,000, the equivalent of $380,000 in today's figures.

Nat was getting giddy. The turkey idea had worked out to $1,000 a page. What they ought to do, he told Boris, is open an office on Hollywood and Vine and advertise their wares like custom tailors. NEED A TREATMENT? CALL US. They scored another coup when RKO green-lighted them to write the screenplay besides.

The winning streak continued. On the basis of their *Cool Million* sale, Columbia had offered them the chance to do a treatment and screenplay for one of its own properties, a gambling caper called *Amateur Angel*. The story was inspired by the popular vaudeville ditty "The Man Who Broke the Bank at Monte Carlo" as well as the 1935 Ronald Colman picture of the same title. Columbia's version moved the action from the Riviera to a cruise ship in the United States, and the man who breaks the casino is a geography professor who deliberately calculates the effect of river waves on the roulette wheel. So that Nat and Boris might honor this commitment to Columbia, RKO gave them permission to begin the bombsight screenplay after completing *Amateur Angel*, at which point they would be guaranteed three or four months' work with a weekly salary of six hundred dollars for each of them. For the first time in his adult life, Nat was looking at more money than he knew what to do with.

Meanwhile, his Random House novel was sitting on the back burner, getting cold. People who scoffed at the power of money "will someday have their fingers burnt or their snooks cocked," he believed. Nat was determined to not get his snook cocked.

Chodorov and Fields were finished after eight months of alterations and revisions. Ruth was alone in Westport the morning of July 23, 1940, when the script arrived by air express, registered mail. It took her a few minutes to crack. Then she ran around the house shrieking hysterically. "I was never so outraged in my entire life," she said later.

In order to transpose *My Sister Eileen* to the stage, Jerry and Joe discarded twelve of the fourteen pieces in the collection and told the story of the adult sisters living in New York. By focusing exclusively on "Mr. Spitzer and the Fungus" and "Beware the Brazilian Navy," they managed to push Ohio into the background and conflate the Flynn and McKenney clans into a third-act walk-on by Syd McKenney. The compressed action takes place entirely in a one-room basement apartment in Greenwich Village.

In the Chodorov-Fields version, one sister is the leader and the other the follower, but both sisters come off subtly changed. Although Ruth remains the feisty, two-fisted writer, she is described as "well-built" but not fat and definitely not unattractive; Eileen is the saucy "beauty in the family" who has "a swell figure" and ambitions to be an actress. Other characters from the original stories were too good to lose—for example, the awful landlord and the ex–football player upstairs—and no sane playwrights would have dropped the Brazilian sailors. Chodorov and Fields also added a subplot and new characters, mostly men in pursuit of Eileen. The most important is Robert Baker, a sophisticated editor (not unlike St. Clair McKelway) who works for a literary magazine (not unlike *The New Yorker*) and takes an interest in the sisters. Tacking on a love story certainly made sense, but Fields and Chodorov gave it an inspired twist. Against all expectations, it is plain old Ruth and not her beautiful sister who gets the man at the final curtain.

BAKER: It looks as if you're stuck with me, Ruth—. (*He crosses to her and takes her hand.*) Like it or not.

The real Ruth was so angry that she tried to get the rights back. The Fields-Chodorov story was unpardonably offensive, she thought. How dare those Hollywood fools turn her experiences into a bubble bath and pair her romantically with a *New Yorker* editor? How could this nonsense possibly be explained to Katharine White or to St. Clair McKelway, much less to her comrades in the party? She refused to accept the legal realities, imagining that it was not too late to get a reversion of the rights. After all, this was her sister, her stories.

Neither Nat nor Eileen, still vacationing in Oregon, took part in Ruth's crisis. Eileen seemed to be resigned, if not exactly thrilled—"I wonder if it's dignified. Oh, well." And the whole thing rolled off Nat's back. At Republic and RKO he had been friendly with Jerry and Joe, sometimes lunching together, and could fully sympathize. He understood what went into the task of getting a workable script and had grown philosophical about such matters.

After legal maneuvers proved fruitless, Ruth tried to deal with the *Sister Eileen* situation on a personal basis. In a telephone call to Jerry Chodorov in Los Angeles, she unnerved him by saying that he and Fields could go ahead with the play, but "I just don't want it to be about my sister and myself."

"*What?*" he yelled. She wanted him to cut the sisters?

Not exactly, she replied. Just change the names.

But Ruth had no leverage at all. Richard and her agent eventually persuaded the playwrights to change the name McKenney to Sherwood, and also Cleveland to Columbus, but everything else would be left the same. Ruth was still unhappy. Her last hope was that they would find no backers.

Unbeknownst to Ruth, the playwrights holed up for six weeks that fall at the St. Moritz Hotel in New York, lopping deadwood and punching up exit lines, and soon after the play went into production. With the encouragement of Moss Hart, they succeeded in interesting a first-rate producer, Max Gordon, and persuading people like Hart and Alexander Woollcott to invest. Their luckiest break, though, was enlisting the theater's top-ranked comedy director, the prestigious George S. Kaufman. When readings for the role of Eileen got under way in November, word-of-mouth interest was evident. "They were looking for a blond," remembers Jo Ann Sayers. "I got a call to come to the theater, and there was a mob, just hordes of girls." Jo Ann, a Seattle movie actress, didn't know Ruth's book—in fact, had only a vague idea of Eileen's being a living person. She found a telegram stuffed under her door at the Barbizon-Plaza: REPORT FOR REHEARSAL 10 AM MONDAY.

As Jo Ann Sayers began rehearsing at the Lyceum Theater in New York, the real sister Eileen was preparing to settle into a new house in the San Fernando Valley. Nat, rolling in money, was treating himself to a deluxe Ford station wagon costing $950. By 1940, station wagons were status symbols, and Nat's was a beauty: streamlined wood-paneled body, sealed-beam headlights, hydraulic brakes, steering-column shift, leather seats and dashboard.

In November, the Wests took possession of 12706 Magnolia Boulevard, a brick farmhouse set on two acres in North Hollywood. It was a house that conjured memories of Bucks County, but instead of the woods and pastures on Geigel Hill Road, it was surrounded by a tangle of flower gardens and groves of pear and walnut trees. Built four years earlier by an Australian comedian, Clyde Cook, the structure had brick walls, dark wood paneling, wide-planked hardwood floors, exposed ceiling beams, and an old-fashioned fireplace. It was a man's retreat, but Eileen swiftly made it her own. Scouring local department stores, she bought a trestle table and a Welsh cupboard for the dining room, a pair of wooden rockers and a Sheraton desk for the living room. There was also a sofa and matching easy chairs covered in blue, lavender, and pale green floral chintz. She installed shelves to hold Nat's collection of Shang Wheeler wildfowl decoys and the books—some three hundred volumes ranging from Wordsworth to *The Geography of Witchcraft*—he had accumulated over the years, and she covered the walls with Mexican serapes and prints of Audubon watercolors.

Some of Nat's friends secretly made fun of the backwoodsy furnishings, which they thought conspicuously tasteless and smacking of installment-plan Sears, Roebuck. Wells Root called the house "slightly unkempt."

With money not a consideration, Eileen embarked on a shopping spree. Following the furniture came luxurious paraphernalia she had never been able to afford during her marriage to Morris. At the best stores she selected cookware and cocktail shakers, towels and bed linens, and the latest appliances. She stockpiled highball glasses and imported china, including a spectacular set of blue-and-white Spode. At Brooks Brothers she splurged on a leather-trimmed wicker picnic basket that contained service for two with crystal glasses and a wine-bottle holder. Her only nod to economy was the purchase of a secondhand typewriter. Before long, the house was cluttered with so many crates and delivery cartons that it would be weeks before all of them could be unpacked. Money, Nat mused, was truly "a wonderful thing" that could never be overpraised. "Good old money. Good young money, too."

Eileen was not sorry to give up her job at Disney, because now she had a chance to be a full-time mother for the first time. It was tremendously satisfying to provide Tommy with a normal childhood, in a house with a big yard and dogs. She employed a regular babysitter, Rose Fisher, to look after him when she had to be away from home.

Feeling free to do much as she liked, free not to worry about money, Eileen made an effort to take more of an interest in books, although she would never be a reader. Applying for a borrower's card at the Los Angeles Public Library had less to do with a newfound love of literature than her desire to please Nat and appear well read around his friends. Her main concern was taking care of her husband's needs. She assumed responsibility for overseeing every aspect of their lives— the house, the shopping, the driving, but especially the psychological stroking and patting that Nat had been starving for his whole life. In the eyes of his wife he became a top novelist who wrote literature but could also handle a big career in films. She made efforts to support important professional relationships that might bolster his growing reputation as a screenwriter, at the same time carefully ungluing him from some of his less savory bachelor buddies, like Stanley Rose. Even before all the china was unpacked, the Wests began having people to dinner. They invited writers and their wives, couples such as Ring and Silvia Lardner, Ian and Alice Hunter, Boris and Wilma Ingster, Gordon and Barbara Kahn, as well as directors like Burt Kelly and Nat's hunting friend Wells Root. There were good wines and after-supper dancing. Eileen, never much of a cook, had no idea how to prepare party food and didn't even attempt it. Her parties relied on cooks and serving maids. On Thanksgiving, Ian Hunter remembered sitting down to a handsome turkey plump with chestnut stuffing. Nat, staring haplessly at the bird, made a big production of sharpening a knife. When he finally plunged the blade into the turkey and began carving, the boned and stuffed bird collapsed into elegant, presliced portions.

Eileen regaled guests with sidesplitting jokes about Nat's dogs, which she had banished from their owners' bed. Her Rin Tin Tin routines about the wonder dogs Danny and Julie, Wells Root said, could "hold a dinner party spellbound with the hilarious tale of her nightly rivalries with them."

Success in playing the Hollywood social game did not mean Eileen ignored her own interests. She continued to attend Communist Party meetings and tried to get Nat involved too. To please her, he agreed to enroll in a study group that met on Wednesday nights. The news got around quickly. When Joe Schrank was informed that "your friend Pep is taking indoctrination," he laughed. Impossible, he said. Joe had no patience with Red screenwriters, who, he believed, lacked a sense of history and were plainly "stark raving nuts" to boot. "Of course Pep didn't tell me," he was to say. "He'd be too embarrassed."

23

EL CENTRO

I T WAS A FEW DAYS before Christmas when Ruth and Richard drove their Hudson down from Westport to attend a dress rehearsal of *My Sister Eileen*. Catching her first glimpse of the set, Ruth could not get over its resemblance to "the vile, dank hole I called home" on Gay Street. Her astonishment deepened at seeing Eileen as a sprightly blond and herself looking "very, very pretty" (after having "gone to pot on the grand scale," she was now seventy pounds overweight). The whole show was incredibly "eerie," she thought.

The script that had made Ruth so furious had somehow metamorphosed into a real play, capitalized at fifteen thousand dollars and scheduled to open on Broadway the day after Christmas. Neither of the leading actresses was well known, although both impressed Ruth as really fine. Jo Ann Sayers was a B-movie actress who had done a Boris Karloff picture, while the role of the older sister had gone to Shirley Booth, a talented forty-two-year-old character actress whose fifteen appearances on Broadway had yet to make her a star. In the late afternoon, riding home on the Merritt Parkway, Ruth decided the production was not so bad as she feared. "Do you think it will pay off the second mortgage?" she mused to Richard, perhaps mindful that she had a 40 percent financial stake in the play.

Eileen and Nat decided against attending the opening. A cross-country trip would be inconvenient for Nat, who was pushing himself hard on the *Amateur Angel* script and felt unable to take time off. He had even resigned himself to forgoing his usual New Year's hunting trip. Neither did a New York trip appeal to Eileen, who was preoccupied with plans for her first Christmas in the new house and giving Tommy a traditional holiday, with stockings and all the trimmings. Eileen warned her mother-in-law not to expect them but promised a big reunion in the spring.

One of the events on her social calendar, her most ambitious party to date, was a dinner for some of Nat's literary friends. Among the expected guests were Dorothy Parker and her husband, Alan Campbell; Scott Fitzgerald and his girlfriend, Sheilah Graham; and Elliot Paul, who had written an excellent memoir about the Spanish Civil War (*The Life and Death of a Spanish Town*) and was now celebrating the publication of a new mystery novel. She also invited Hilaire Hiler, Nat's Parisian painter-pianist friend living in San Francisco, where he had created murals for the city's marine museum. It was an interesting, if somewhat reckless, combination of people who were in some cases more than casually acquainted. Scott and Dottie once enjoyed a brief fling, but that was six years ago. Even so, Sheilah considered Dottie a bitch who smiled at her face while smearing her as a gold-digging floozy behind her back. In public they conversed sweetly with each other, but that fooled nobody. As for Scott, he still found Eileen hopelessly grating, but managed to conceal his feelings on social occasions.

The party was scheduled for Friday the 13th, but Eileen's major concern was not the bad-luck date but rather coaxing some of the guests out of their homes. Several were in bad shape. While shopping in Schwab's drugstore two weeks earlier, Scott had suffered a heart attack, and his doctor ordered bed rest. Feeling stronger by this time, he wrote to his editor at Scribner's that he hoped to complete a first draft of his novel by January 15, and that evening he managed to drag himself from Sheila's ground-floor apartment on North Hayworth Avenue to Magnolia Boulevard to break bread with the Wests. Dorothy Parker had yet to recover from a hysterectomy, an operation for fibroid tumors that ended her attempts to bear a child. Her husband Alan had reached the limit of his patience after weeks of playing nursemaid, finally sending to Bucks County for Dottie's favorite dog in the hope of cheering her up.

But the night of the dinner they took their seats at the trestle table, eight men and women laying aside their woes for a few hours. Fittingly, the conversation turned to their younger days, to Paris in the twenties, which for several of them was not just a gentler time but perhaps were the best years of their lives. Sentimental and drunk, except Scott, who sipped soda, they conjured up the old familiar sights and faces—the Jockey Club and the Dingo Bar, Zelda, the Murphys, Hadley and Ernest and Bumby. In ragged voices they began singing, "The last time I saw Paris, her heart was warm and gay," a nostalgic tune about the fall of Paris in June, which moved Elliot so greatly that he would eventually write an idealized memoir titled *The Last Time I Saw Paris*. The Friday the 13th party ended in a blur of tears and happiness.

Eileen finished her shopping the week before Christmas, and then she did Nat's as well, because he claimed that shopping bored him. Customarily organized, she wrapped the presents and stored them in a closet before turning to preparations for other holiday festivities, including a Christmas Eve party for Tommy. Suddenly Nat began talking about a quick weekend trip across the border to Mexicali in the splashy new station wagon. Not only did he need a few days to unwind after an exhausting schedule, but he was dying to use some beautiful new guns before the end of quail and duck season. At an auction recently he had picked up a matched pair of custom-made Purdey shotguns—James Purdey & Sons was the Rolls-Royce of English gun makers—that retailed for $2,000, but he had been lucky to get them secondhand for $750.

Under other circumstances, Eileen might have been interested, because she had grown to accept and even enjoy their trips. Reconciled to Nat's hunting as a fact of her life, she had equipped herself with a rugged field jacket, calf-length capri trousers, tinted glasses, and a canvas game bag. But there was too much to do Christmas week, she told Nat. His male friends showed no interest either. Wells was heading east to visit his family, and Boris pleaded last-minute shopping. On Friday morning Nat telephoned Jimmy Alvarez, manager of the Leon d'Oro tavern in Mexicali, who had made travel plans for him on previous trips. A local character, Alvarez was a pal of Hollywood celebrities like Hedy Lamarr. The hunting was splendid, Alvarez assured him, and he could set him up with Jesus the Yaqui Indian guide; he must come down. Their conversation left Nat unconvinced because, he told his secretary, the Mexican's first priority was coaxing rich gringo tourists down to spend money.

When he reached home, he made another attempt to sway Eileen. It would be fun, he said, a fast four-hour drive to the border and a night at an expensive hotel. If they set out at once they would have all day Saturday plus Sunday morning for shooting. He figured they could get back on the road early Sunday afternoon and be home by dark, which would leave two days for decorating a tree and last-minute shopping. Eileen could consider the weekend his Christmas present, a few days of relaxation before he had to get his nose back to the grindstone. Under the circumstances, she could hardly refuse.

And so they went after all. Hastily loading the Ford station wagon, they left Tommy at Rose Fisher's house and dropped off Danny at Jimmy Lindsay's kennel on Tujunga Avenue. By eight in the evening, with Nat at the wheel and Julie in the backseat, they were on their way.

The international border crossing at Calexico, some 230 miles southeast of Los Angeles, was a picturesque outpost consisting of a few hundred residents and clusters of low structures. Beyond the border in the Mexican state of Baja California lay Mexicali, one of the biggest cities in the country, a tourist attraction of gambling clubs, sidewalk markets, and a lively red-light scene. Late that Friday night, Eileen and Nat pulled up to Calexico's Hotel De Anza, a whitewashed inn catering to American sportsmen and film celebrities happy to pay for the privilege of being treated like royalty. Its overdecorated lobby matched the meals offered in the dining room, where sated guests struggled to cram in a slice of carrot cake, the house specialty. Each year, before dove season began in September, the De Anza would run ads in the *Los Angeles Times* reminding hunters to book early because rooms were going fast.

Just as Nat promised, the excursion passed quickly. Before dawn on Saturday the Wests met the Yaqui guide and crossed the border for a day of shooting, followed by a merry evening at Jimmy Alvarez's tavern, where Nat greeted people he had not seen since his marriage. In a relaxed mood, he cracked jokes while swigging his favorite Mexicali beer. On Sunday they squeezed in a few more hours with the guide before wending their way back to the Leon d'Oro for a farewell drink, and by half past two they were ready to depart. The station wagon was parked under the Hotel De Anza portico while Nat ducked into the lobby to pay the bill. After a splendid two days, the cargo bay was stuffed with limp dead birds and bottles of beer. Nat slid behind the wheel, Eileen climbed into the front passenger seat, and Julie jumped on the backseat. On the outskirts of town, he pulled up to a gas station, and then they headed north through the Imperial Valley, only ten minutes until Route 111 met U.S. Highway 80, four miles east of El Centro, where they would turn off toward Los Angeles. Probably they were going to be home by seven, enough time to fetch Tommy from Rose Fisher's before his bedtime, even to swing by the kennel and get Danny.

It was typical late-December weather in the Imperial Valley, pleasant temperatures in the mid-sixties with cloudless, milky white skies and visibility rippling for more than a mile. On Sunday afternoons the two-lane ribbon of highway between Calexico and El Centro was usually deserted. The road sliced a solitary path through fields of crisp head lettuce.

The 1937 Pontiac sedan was traveling west toward El Centro, chugging along below the speed limit at forty miles an hour. Its occupants were a husband and wife and their two-year-old daughter in the backseat.

They were on Route 80, approaching the four-way boulevard stop with its red reflective sign at the intersection of Route 111, and the view out the windshield that afternoon was clear as crystal. There was hardly any traffic, but in the distance Joseph Dowless spotted a car hurtling up the Calexico-Brawley road. "It was moving pretty fast. However, I didn't pay much attention to that because I knew there is a boulevard stop." But the next time he looked out, the car was suddenly on top of them.

"He didn't stop," Christine Dowless cried. Before her husband could answer, the car smashed into them.

When state highway patrolman Tillman Daley and his sergeant pulled up to the intersection twenty minutes later, they heard a screaming baby and a dog that kept barking. In the ditch a Pontiac two-door sedan, license no. 9Z2672, was facing west with its front end squished and its driver trying to rescue his family. On the highway pointing north stood an empty Ford station wagon, license no. 6Y5287, the hood thrown up, tailgate sagging, and doors gaping open. Its radiator had burst. Evidently the impact had whipped the wagon around and tossed its occupants into the air, because Daley found two people lying unconscious on the ground. Behind the station wagon was a woman with her head shattered in the ditch, where she appeared to have alighted after being knocked aloft between the two spinning vehicles. Up ahead of the station wagon Daley discovered a man sprawled on the highway. A bleeding dog, limping and howling crazily, was trying to jump back into the Ford.

Daley first stanched blood spurting from a severed artery in the arm of the Pontiac driver, then noted the couple from the Ford were knocked out, dead for all he could tell. Leaning over the man, he could smell liquor, always an important concern, but turning back to the woman, he could detect no odor. He made further note of an open bottle of liquor a few feet away, and the presence of splinters in the dog's bloody paws from the glass that showered the highway.

Three miles away, near Heber, an ambulance was parked outside

Imperial County Hospital—and it remained there even after the emergency summons had been received. Imperial was a clinic set up to provide first-aid care to farmworkers. There was limited staff and no blood bank, and its single ambulance was not permitted to leave without assurance of absolute need. Upon clearance of the red tape, the ambulance drove away but carried no equipment or rescue personnel.

Had the accident occurred on Sunset Boulevard, an ambulance from Hollywood Presbyterian would have swooped in and picked up the Wests. As it was, thirty minutes ticked by on Route 111. Tillman Daley began measuring the skid marks—some eighteen feet or so—made when the station wagon tried to brake. A few rubberneckers slowed down, and one car stopped. The driver, who said he was a doctor, went over to look at the bodies. Evidently he believed nothing could be done, because he walked back to the patrolmen and stood chatting until the ambulance arrived.

On duty at Imperial Hospital was Burton Brock, a twenty-eight-year-old son of an El Centro farmer who had passed the state medical board examination three months earlier. As soon as the ambulance drove in and the victims were unloaded, Dr. Brock pronounced one of them dead and began examining the other. The protocol was to administer oxygen and intravenous fluids if a patient lived longer than fifteen minutes after arrival, but just at that cutoff point the heart of the dying man stopped and no attempt was made to revive him. All that Dr. Brock could do was smell the deceased's breath "to see if there was alcohol on it. I wasn't able to." Death certificates fixed the time of death for Eileen as "abt. 3:30" and the place as "en route to the Imperial County Hospital"; Nat was pronounced dead "abt. 4P." For both of them the official cause of death was listed as "skull fracture," although an autopsy might have revealed internal injuries as well.

A few hours later the local paper sent a photographer to shoot the wreckage. Although the Ford station wagon appears only slightly damaged, the Pontiac, at the extreme right of the photo, shows a front end twisted into a nest of crumpled metal. The *Imperial Valley Press* called the fatalities residents of Hollywood. Nat was described as a thirty-six-year-old screenwriter, but Eileen was incorrectly identified as Ruth McKenney West, age thirty. That night the bodies were taken to Lemons Mortuary in El Centro. It was noted at the funeral home that the personal effects of the dead man included practically no money, and later it would be deduced that someone, perhaps a hospital worker, had rifled through his pockets. All that remained of a $25 check cashed on Saturday was a pile of loose change amounting to $1.46. Nat would have been amused to know of the twisteroo.

In Erwinna it was going to be a Yuletide of balmy temperatures and not a trace of snow expected. On Geigel Hill Road, the Perelman household was preparing to celebrate the season with a lighted tree in the parlor and the arrival of Santa for Adam and Abby, ages four and two. Old friends living in Doylestown, Joseph and Katharine Bryan, invited Laura and Sid for dinner. In a mood of exceptional gaiety, Sid swore they would be perfect guests. Laura would bring a mop and pail to scrub their upstairs bedrooms, and he was prepared to varnish the foyer floor. One minute they were decking the halls with the Bryans, the next Sid was booking a flight to Los Angeles.

Once news of the deaths went out overnight on the Associated Press wire, stories began appearing all over the country. The news peg was Eileen. Headlines announced the death of a young woman, only twenty-seven years old, familiar to the public as the bubbly heroine of two best-selling books and a Broadway play scheduled to open on Thursday. Her husband was identified as a novelist and screenwriter, whose given name was misspelled as "Nathaniel" and age listed as thirty-four instead of thirty-seven. Nat's name was largely unknown to most readers. Judging from the coverage, the couple appeared to have a typical celebrity marriage, a female notable with a supportive husband content to wait in the wings. There were references to Ruth, but no mention was made of Eileen's son.

In Los Angeles a cold drizzle began falling on Monday morning. John Sanford arrived at MGM in Culver City with his wife, Maggie, whose habit was to begin the day by scanning the papers and calling out interesting news. The front-page headlines carried news of a celebrity death, Scott Fitzgerald, who had died Saturday, of his third heart attack in recent weeks. He was only forty-four, and there was another story about a car crash, near El Centro, in which the real-life "My Sister Eileen" had been killed. Suddenly she stopped reading. "But John! This is about Pep! Pep West is dead!"

Scotty walked down the hall, took the stairs to the ground floor, turned around, and hiked up again. Back in his office, he felt sick. The day had fallen to pieces like "a bowl broken," he thought, "like something gone to smash." Driving home in the dark with his wife that evening, his eyes welled with tears. She was sorry for having "broke the news wrong," Maggie said. Scotty knew that Nat would detest his loss of control. According to Nat, people of good breeding did not raise their voices; a proper gentleman always dressed in Brooks Brothers, observed correct table manners ("only Jews speak to the next table," he counseled Scotty), and certainly never cried.

At the Biltmore Theater, the cast of *My Sister Eileen* was in the middle of a run-through on Monday afternoon, with only three days remaining before opening night. Summoned to the box office to take an urgent call, Jerry Chodorov listened as Richard Bransten informed him that Eileen and her husband had been killed.

"You're kidding," Jerry would remember replying. He was so stunned that "I didn't know what I was saying."

Richard's response sounded icy. "I don't kid about things like this." He thought that Jerry should know "in case you want to postpone the opening."

Returning to the rehearsal, Chodorov broke the news to George Kaufman, who had to decide whether or not to delay the opening. Eileen's death was sure to cast a pall over the show, and audiences might be reluctant to laugh. After consideration, Kaufman elected to open as scheduled, grimly observing that they couldn't help Eileen "by sinking our own ship." This decision, however unfeeling, proved to be the appropriate call. "The opening night audience loved it," Jo Ann Sayers remembers. "They had no idea Eileen had died." The reviews appearing on December 27 were unanimous raves. "The first completely gay comedy on the dramatic stage of New York this season," wrote the *New York Times*'s Brooks Atkinson, who was the only critic to mention Eileen's sudden death. Every other paper in town poured on the superlatives: "The laugh hit of the season" (*New York Mirror*); "Hilarious. Among the year's hits" (*New York Herald Tribune*); "Side-splitting, brilliantly integrated comedy" (*New York Post*). "Nobody was more staggered than I," Ruth would say. "My husband and I paid off the mortgage on our house and built ourselves a swell dam across our creek."

My Sister Eileen would turn out to be box-office magic, breaking theatrical records with 864 performances and becoming one of the longest-running shows in Broadway history. For decades to come there would be countless revivals, road companies, summer-stock companies, and school productions. In March 1941, Columbia Pictures acquired the property for $225,000. The screen version, starring Rosalind Russell and Janet Blair, eliminated about a quarter of the play while expanding the love story between Ruth and Robert Baker. Because of protests from the Brazilian government, the six "future admirals" became Portuguese merchant-marine cadets. A second motion picture, featuring Janet Leigh as Eileen, would be released in 1955, and a television series aired in 1960. But in its most successful incarnation, the comedy served as the basis, in 1953, for *Wonderful Town*, the Leonard Bernstein musical with lyrics by Betty Comden and Adolph Green. Ruth's stories continued to delight audiences as recently as 2003, when a revival of *Wonderful Town* opened on Broadway to golden reviews, ran 497 performances, and received a Tony nomination for Best Musical Revival.

He was not to blame, Joseph Dowless said. "We had been living over in Yuma for a few days while working there. We were coming to El Centro to spend the night." By time he realized the station wagon was running the stop sign, it was ten feet away, making it impossible for him to do anything. This was, he added, the first accident in his life.

On Tuesday, the day before Christmas, the coroner's jury convened at Lemons Mortuary to determine the cause of the collision that had led to the deaths of Nathanael West, writer, and Eileen McKenney West, housewife. More than two dozen highway fatalities had taken place in the Imperial Valley that year, several of them at the same intersection, and so the inquest was expected to be routine. The Imperial County deputy coroner conducted the hearing, which was attended by a representative from the district attorney's office and a stenographer recording the testimony. For the seven jurors it was an unpleasant civic duty to perform on Christmas Eve. There were few witnesses: the state trooper, the doctor from Imperial Hospital, and a Los Angeles attorney who had come down to identify the bodies. The driver of the Pontiac explained what led to the collision and how he had tried to keep his car from overturning, how his wife had sustained a broken leg and pelvis. He knew nothing about the parties in the other vehicle.

Joseph Dowless, twenty-seven, and his twenty-one-year-old wife, Christine, and their daughter, Ann, made their home with Christine's family in El Centro. A migrant farmworker, he was employed by one of the big produce companies that harvested and packed the winter head lettuce, the broccoli, and the cabbage, followed in the spring by crops of Sweet Imperial onions and the mountains of cantaloupes grown in the "World's Greatest Melon Center." The handpicking, carrying, and crating, for a piece rate of pennies, was a backbreaking job. Christine's family, at one time farmers in Manchester, Ohio, had emigrated to Southern California in 1930, hoping they could do better on the broad, even plains of the fertile Imperial Valley, where the sun shines all year. They had done worse, sad to say, dragged down by the hard days of the Depression.

People like Christine and Joe had never seen a Broadway play or heard of *The New Yorker*. Impoverished, uneducated, owning few possessions except a car, sometimes sleeping in campground trailers, they might have been characters in a Nathanael West novel. In *The Day of the Locust*, they would have been the disappointed transplants who had come to California with expectations, the very ones waving the torches in Tod Hackett's painting.

At Lemons, a central issue was whether the judgment of either driver had been impaired by alcohol. The smell at the scene, it was determined, did not come from either of the deceased parties but from the smashed Mexicali beer bottles. A half bottle of Bacardi rum was also found in the ditch near the station wagon.

A juror questioned Joe Dowless, "Had you had any drinks at all?"

"No, sir, I hadn't."

An hour and it was over. The seven jurors quickly rendered their verdict:

> We, the undersigned, find that Nathaniel [*sic*] W. West and Mrs.
> Eileen McKenney West died as a result of negligent driving on the
> part of Mr. Nathaniel W. West. In our judgment, Mr. Joe Dowless
> was in no way to blame for the accident.

As reports of the deaths began circulating around Hollywood, those who knew Nat weren't surprised; he had been such a careless driver. One time, in a rare concession to reality on the subject, he told Joe Schrank's wife, Bertha, that probably he would die in a crash. But even though the worst had come to pass, his friends still hoped the inquest might uncover a plausible excuse—mechanical failure, alcohol, heart failure, fatigue. No such factors emerged. In the end, seven practical men reported that Nathanael West, driver of a 1940 Ford station wagon, plowed through an intersection and slammed headlong into Joe Dowless's 1937 Pontiac. They were at a loss to explain why he had done so.

Following the inquest, the remains were taken to Los Angeles. Upon arrival at Pierce Brothers Mortuary (on Santa Monica Boulevard, not the one on West Washington Boulevard, where Scott Fitzgerald lay), several complicated decisions had to be made. Sid, just landed after ten sleepless hours on a plane, had the responsibility of representing both families. With the preferences of the deceased unknown, and the McKenneys too distraught to make specific requests, Sid was left to do his best with the arrangements. The main difficulties were how to handle Nat and Eileen's burial—and where. When a husband and wife perish together, a joint interment seems appropriate. This would not be possible were Nat to be placed, as his mother wished, in the Weinstein plot at Mount Zion, owing to the prohibitions against Gentiles being buried in Jewish cemeteries. To circumvent these rules, a decision was made to cremate Eileen's body and place her ashes in Nat's casket. The person responsible for taking this unusual—and deceptive—action is unclear, but presumably it was Sid, the only family member on the scene, who carried out the wishes of the Weinstein family.

The night after Christmas, the casket left Los Angeles on the 8 P.M. Santa Fe Super Chief, accompanied on its transcontinental journey by Sid, who had exhausted himself with both the funeral arrangements and futile attempts to locate the West dog. Julie, her feet cut by broken beer bottles, had limped away before the ambulance arrived. As it turned out, she was rescued by a farmer who, after taking her to a vet, refused to return her until Sid brought legal action.

On December 30, the Weinstein family gathered with Syd McKenney and Ruth and Richard Bransten at the Riverside Memorial Chapel, the same Upper West Side mortuary where Max Weinstein's service had taken place. Later that day at Mount Zion, the casket containing Nat's remains and Eileen's ashes was lowered into the ground near Nat's father on Path 27R, Lot 25. The cemetery remained unaware of the family's private solution. "We would have had no way of knowing if there were another's ashes in the casket," says April Franzino, the present general manager of Mount Zion. "Certainly we would not have permitted it because she was not of the Jewish faith. In addition, we bury one person per box per grave. So on two counts it would not have been allowed."

When the headstone was erected six months later, its wording made a further attempt to disguise the true situation.

NATHANAEL W. WEST
HUSBAND OF EILEEN
Oct. 17, 1903
Dec. 22, 1940

The inscription offers no information about the anonymous wife—no surname, no vital statistics, no indication that this is her grave as well. A large, single word—SON—is carved on the top of the square marble slab.

John Sanford, flooded with memories, couldn't turn off his sorrow about Nat's death. He offered condolences to Laura and suggested in a separate note to Sid that somebody—preferably Sid himself—should write a tribute, perhaps a memorial essay for the *Clipper*, a leftist West Coast literary periodical. In no mood to eulogize Nat, Sid numbly refused. Such a tribute sounded like a good idea, he agreed, but unfortunately he had no perspective, nothing but "a dull sense of shock and unreality," which he suspected would never disappear. Almost anybody could do an essay on Pep, he said, an invitation that left open the door for Scotty himself.

Phantom images of the doomed station wagon—"a debacle of metal, wood, and glass"—continued to haunt Scotty. Nat had never been good at operating machinery. Even the mechanics of marbles had befuddled him. Reminders of his clumsiness made him wonder if Nat had been attempting to brake and mistakenly hit the gas.

Several weeks after Nat's death, Scotty and his father were walking along Taft Avenue, talking about the unpredictability of life and how deeply the accident had shocked everyone. Scotty recalled Nat standing outside the De Peyster naming the cars that would prove his undoing, the sleepy-eyed kid who didn't know how to "run, skate, kick a football, shoot a marble. He just stood around and watched." The two of them had never grown close again after their falling out in 1932, he told his father. Nat had not invited him to his wedding, or to visit his new home. There was no introduction to his wife, not even a hint that he was getting married. But he would not have become a writer without him. In a strange way, he had always written for one person, Nat Weinstein.

As they stopped at the corner of Hollywood Boulevard, a red streetcar rolled toward them. Philip Shapiro said, "Is that the only reason you miss him, Julian?"

"No. Not the only."

Dead before reaching middle age, Nat left behind no children, no literary reputation of importance, no fine *New York Times* obituary ensuring immortality, no celebrity eulogies, just four short novels, two of them unforgettable. When a writer lives only thirty-seven years and ends up with very little reward, it might seem a waste, until you look at what he did. For Nathanael West, what he did seems enough.

POSTSCRIPT

SHIRLEY BOOTH (1898–1992) followed up her work in the theater with a distinguished late-life movie career, receiving an Academy Award in 1953 for *Come Back, Little Sheba.* In the 1960s, she twice won Emmys as the television sitcom maid in *Hazel.*

LOUISE ROSENBERG BRANSTEN BERMAN (1908–1977) became one of the American Communist Party's most important financial angels. Subpoenaed by the House Committee on Un-American Activities, she came under scrutiny as a Soviet spy (code-named Map) passing atomic secrets to Russia. To dispel that image, she told the committee that, as the mother of a teenage son, she "shared with all mothers the deep desire for peace," before invoking her Fifth Amendment right against self-incrimination. In the post–Cold War era, she was a respectable philanthropist devoting herself to good works. Her family's Rosenberg Foundation currently funds programs in the fields of children's education and health care.

BENNETT CERF (1898–1971) embellished his career as Random House publisher with a variety of sidelines: compiler of joke and riddle books, cofounder of the Famous Writers School correspondence courses, panelist on the *What's My Line?* TV show for sixteen years, and host of the Miss America pageant. Cerf's request for the return of the dead

West's last book advance, a sum of $250, pushed Sidney Perelman to the boiling point. In retaliation, he created snide caricatures of Cerf as characters named Barnaby Chirp and Emmett Stag, and as Harry Hubris in his 1962 Broadway comedy *The Beauty Part*.

JEROME CHODOROV (1911–2004) and JOSEPH FIELDS (1895–1966) went on to score many more successes on Broadway: *Junior Miss* (1941), *Wonderful Town* (1953), *The Girl in Pink Tights* (1954), *Anniversary Waltz* (1954), and *The Ponder Heart* (1956). Chodorov was blacklisted in the 1950s as a member of the Communist Party, wrecking his career as a screenwriter, nor did he have much luck with his solo Broadway efforts in the 1960s. Fields cowrote with Anita Loos the book for *Gentleman Prefer Blondes* and collaborated with Oscar Hammerstein II on the book for *Flower Drum Song*.

LESTER COLE (1904–1985) turned out to be one of the "Hollywood Ten," a group who defied the House Committee on Un-American Activities investigating Communism in the movie business. Convicted of contempt of Congress, he served ten months in prison, was blacklisted, and thereafter wrote scripts (the best known is *Born Free*) under pseudonyms. In later life he taught screenwriting at the University of California, Berkeley.

JOSEPHINE HERBST (1892–1969) and JOHN HERRMANN (1900–1959) separated in 1935. Herbst's major fiction achievement was a trilogy (*Pity Is Not Enough*, *The Executioner Waits*, and *Rope of Gold*) depicting an American family from the Civil War through the Depression. As a journalist her reports appeared in *Partisan Review* and the *New Masses*, and she later recounted her experiences during the Spanish Civil War in a much-praised memoir, *The Starched Blue Sky of Spain*. Her 1954 novella, *Hunter of Doves*, stitches together an uncannily observant portrait of Nathanael West. Herrmann wrote three novels (*What Happens*, *Summer Is Ended*, and *The Salesman*) before turning to full-time work for the Communist Party. A courier who traveled the country collecting dues, he later became associated with the covert "Ware group" (party operatives within the U.S. government) and is said to have first introduced Alger Hiss to Whittaker Chambers in 1934, at a Chinese restaurant in Washington.

BORIS INGSTER (1903–1978), an early director of film noir pictures, is best remembered as the producer of *The Man from U.N.C.L.E.*, one of the most popular television series of the 1960s.

MORRIS JACOBS (1910–1971) removed his son Tommy from the West household immediately after Eileen's death, with the intention of raising him. He refused his brother Philip's offer to adopt the boy, but did not reckon with Ruth McKenney, who convinced the courts that she could offer a more stable home. Jacobs spent twenty-six years in the U.S. Air Force, a career that began with his wartime enlistment in 1942 and ended with retirement, as a master sergeant, in 1968. Over the years he had little or no connection to his son, a break initially caused by the upheavals of war and then compounded by the Branstens' decision to live abroad. With his second wife, Stella Mae, he adopted two daughters, but the couple eventually parted over his drinking.

THOMAS JACOBS (1937–1986) was adopted in 1941 by Ruth McKenney and Richard Bransten and renamed Patrick. His uprooted childhood was spent in New York, Hollywood, Westport, Washington, Tucson, Brussels, and London. As an adult, he lived in England, where he worked at menial jobs, including gas station attendant and motor vehicle deliveryman. Married three times and the father of four, he struggled against obesity and abuse of prescription drugs and alcohol, reports his daughter Hillary Hillson.

BEATRICE MATHIEU (1896–1976) married a Freudian analyst, Dr. Allan Roos, in the 1950s. The couple became known for their extensive collection of modern art, including the works of Picasso, Rouault, Magritte, and Kahlo. A freelance beauty-and-fashion writer and consultant, she contributed occasional pieces to *The New Yorker* over the years.

ST. CLAIR MCKELWAY (1905–1980) stepped down from his post as *New Yorker* fact editor in 1939 but continued to work as a staff writer until 1972. His manic-depressive disorder worsened with age. During World War II, while serving in the Pacific as an Air Force information officer, he became convinced that the Supreme Commander, Admiral Chester Nimitz, was committing high treason and so notified the War Department. Quietly shipped back to the States for the duration, after a period of psychosis he briefly surfaced in 1948 in Hollywood, where he wrote two screenplays and married for the fourth time, to the ex-wife of actor Victor Mature. Once his mind slipped permanently into dementia, he had to be confined to a nursing home.

RUTH MCKENNEY (1911–1972) and RICHARD BRANSTEN (1906–1955), expelled from the Communist Party in 1946, abandoned the United States to live as expatriates in Brussels and London, where they turned to writing travel books. Their family included Thomas, Bransten's son with Louise Rosenberg, Eileen's son Tommy/Patrick, and a daughter, Eileen, born in 1942. Among Ruth's later writings were *All About Eileen* (a second sequel to *My Sister Eileen*), *Love Story* (a memoir of her marriage), and three novels, *Jake Home*, *The Loud Red Patrick*, and *Mirage*. Ruth's later years were laden with heartache. Bransten committed suicide on November 18, 1955, her forty-fourth birthday. Returning to New York, her writing career over, she spent the rest of her life in poor mental and physical health. Her final *New Yorker* piece had appeared in 1946. Eileen Bransten, in a 2003 interview with the *New York Times*, said that her mother "never quite recovered from her sister's death." She certainly never rallied from her husband's.

CHARLES A. PEARCE (1906–1970) left Harcourt, Brace in 1939 to co-found Duell, Sloan & Pearce, a small, quality house that published such best-selling authors as John O'Hara, Erskine Caldwell, and Louis Fischer.

SIDNEY J. PERELMAN (1904–1979) has been called the funniest writer in America, if not the world—an exaggeration, but there is no question of his unique talent. His comic stories continued in *The New Yorker* until 1979, an association lasting a half century. In books, plays (*One Touch of Venus* and *The Beauty Part*), and the movie *Around the World in Eighty Days*, he continued to enchant audiences. With advancing age, he suffered from depression and a troubled personal life. While he still ranked tops with admiring readers, he developed increasingly bad-tempered relations with publishers, Bucks County neighbors and shopkeepers, children, and his wife, whom he considered divorcing in the year she died. In his posthumous memoir, *The Last Laugh*, he tidied up the messiness of Nathanael West's life by primly describing him as "an amiable and well-spoken young man" who had expertise in running hotels but loved books best of all.

LAURA PERELMAN (1911–1970) teamed with her husband on six Hollywood screenplays and two Broadway plays (*All Good Americans* and *The Night Before Christmas*). When their professional collaboration ended in 1942, she spent the rest of her life mostly residing in Erwinna and raising her children. After her death from cancer at the age of fifty-eight, her husband sold the farm.

QUENTIN REYNOLDS (1902–1965) was one of the most prominent correspondents during the Second World War, not to mention the author of twenty-five books. In a 1955 landmark libel case, *Reynolds v. Pegler,* he successfully sued Hearst columnist Westbrook Pegler and won a judgment of $175,001, at the time the largest such award in U.S. history.

STANLEY ROSE's (1899–1954) bookstore closed around 1940. Always a heavy drinker, his last years were spent in and out of the Veterans Hospital in Los Angeles undergoing treatment for chronic alcoholism. He died in Colton, California, where he was living with his wife and son.

JOHN SANFORD (1904–2003) wrote twenty-four books, including fiction, history, memoirs, and a magisterial five-volume autobiography, *Scenes from the Life of an American Jew,* which contains numerous memories of Nathanael West. He and his wife of fifty years, the screen-writer Marguerite Roberts, were blacklisted during the McCarthy pe-riod. For a complete account of his writings, see Jack Mearns's *John Sanford: An Annotated Bibliography*, Oak Knoll Press, 2008.

JO ANN SAYERS (1918–) appeared in fourteen films and is familiar to cult fans as Boris Karloff's costar in *The Man with Nine Lives*. She left *My Sister Eileen*, her only Broadway role, in 1942 to marry and raise a family. Widowed, the actress lives in Princeton, New Jersey.

JOSEPH SCHRANK (1901–1984) enjoyed a successful forty-year career in stage, screen, and television. He wrote pictures for such leading ladies as Judy Garland, Betty Grable, and Esther Williams, but his most im-portant screenplay was *Cabin in the Sky*, with Louis Armstrong and Lena Horne. In 1965 he adapted Rodgers and Hammerstein's *Cinder-ella* for television. Not the least of his efforts was a series of humorous essays about life in Bucks County, published in the *Tinicum Bulletin* in the early 1980s.

BUDD SCHULBERG (1914–2009) wrote novels, screenplays, and articles for almost seventy years. His most notable works are two novels, *What Makes Sammy Run?* and *The Harder They Fall*, and the film classic *On the Waterfront*, which won eight Oscars, including Best Picture of 1954. He broke with the Communist Party over its attempt to influence the content of his first novel. Political controversy, however, dogged his life after he appeared as a friendly witness before the House Commit-tee on Un-American Activities.

ALICE SHEPARD (1908–1972) married Bernard Dougall, a lyricist and mystery writer, who was the great-grandson of Brigham Young as well as the stepson of librettist Otto Harbach. A resident of New Rochelle, New York, she became the mother of two daughters.

LYDA FLYNN THOMAS (1881–1983) became known for her volunteer work delivering home-baked cakes and cookies to patients at Cleveland State Hospital (where her sister Mildred had lived most of her life). On her ninetieth birthday, in 1971, she received a congratulatory greeting from President Nixon for her inspirational good works.

ANNA WALLENSTEIN WEINSTEIN (1878–1945) changed her name to Anna West after her son was killed. She died almost five years to the day after his accident and lies next to him in Mount Zion Cemetery.

KATHARINE SERGEANT ANGELL WHITE (1892–1977) continued working as a part-time *New Yorker* fiction editor until her retirement in 1961, with most of the years after 1938 spent in Brooklin, Maine, her home with E. B. White. Her popular gardening articles were collected posthumously as *Onward and Upward in the Garden*. She once summed up Ruth McKenney as "a very intense, emotional Irish girl with natural Irish humor. I liked her."

EARL WILSON (1907–1987) retired in 1983 after forty-eight years with the *New York Post*. The crew-cutted Ohioan, whose gossipy show-business column was syndicated throughout the country, was known to readers as Broadway's Boswell. His affectionate memories of Eileen McKenney were reflected in a 1958 column, when he wrote, "She might have become one of the great personalities of her time."

THE WORKS OF NATHANAEL WEST

I. FICTION

The Dream Life of Balso Snell. Paris and New York: Contact Editions,
    1931.
Miss Lonelyhearts. New York: Harcourt, Brace, 1933. First published in
    1933 by Boni & Liveright.
A Cool Million: The Dismantling of Lemuel Pitkin. New York: Covici-
    Friede, 1934.
The Day of the Locust. New York: Random House, 1939.

II. COLLECTIONS

The Complete Works of Nathanael West. New York: Farrar, Straus &
    Cudahy, 1957.
Nathanael West: Novels and Other Writings. Edited by Sacvan Bercovitch.
    Library of America, 1997. Includes 12 unpublished writings and
    fragments and 29 letters.

III. ESSAYS

"Euripides—A Playwright." *Casements*, Brown University, July 1923.
"Through the Hole in the Mundane Millstone" (leaflet). New York:
    Contact Editions, 1931.
"Some Notes on Violence." *Contact*, October 1932.
"Some Notes on Miss L." *Contempo*, May 15, 1933.

"Business Deal." *Americana*, October 1933.
"Soft Soap for the Barber." *New Republic*, November 14, 1934.

IV. FILMS

The Return to the Soil. Columbia Studios, 1933. Never produced.
Beauty Parlor (released as *Blind Date*). Columbia Studios, 1934.
    Uncredited.
Follow Your Heart (with Lester Cole and Samuel Ornitz). Republic
    Pictures, 1936.
The President's Mystery (with Lester Cole). Republic Pictures, 1936.
Ticket to Paradise (with Jack Natteford). Republic Pictures, 1936.
Bachelor Girl (with others). Republic Pictures, 1937. Never produced.
It Could Happen to You (with Samuel Ornitz). Republic Pictures, 1937.
Jim Hanvey, Detective. Republic Pictures, 1937. Uncredited.
Osceola (original story). Never sold or produced.
Rhythm in the Clouds (with Olive Cooper). Republic Pictures, 1937.
Stormy Weather. Republic Pictures, 1937. Never produced.
Born to Be Wild. Republic Pictures, 1938.
Broadway Bible (treatment). 1938. Never sold or produced.
Flight South, aka *Heritage of the Wild* (with Gordon Kahn and Wells
    Root). Metro-Goldwyn-Mayer, 1938. Never produced.
Gangs of New York. Republic Pictures, 1938. Uncredited.
Ladies in Distress (treatment). Republic Pictures, 1938. Uncredited.
Orphans of the Street. Republic Pictures, 1938. Uncredited.
Before the Fact (with Boris Ingster). RKO Pictures, 1939. Never produced.
    Alfred Hitchcock's version was released as *Suspicion* in 1941.
Five Came Back (with Jerome Cady and Dalton Trumbo). RKO Pictures,
    1939.
I Stole a Million. Universal Corporation, 1939.
The Spirit of Culver (with Whitney Bolton). Universal Corporation, 1939.
Amateur Angel (with Boris Ingster). Columbia Studios, 1940. Never
    produced.
Bird in Hand (with Boris Ingster). RKO Pictures, 1940. Never produced.
A Cool Million (with Boris Ingster). Columbia Studios, 1940. Never
    produced.
Men Against the Sky. RKO Pictures, 1940.

Stranger on the Third Floor. RKO Pictures, 1940. Uncredited.

The Victoria Docks at Eight. Universal Corporation, 1940. Never produced.

Let's Make Music. RKO Pictures, 1941.

V. FILMS AND TELEVISION SHOWS ADAPTED FROM WEST'S WORKS

Advice to the Lovelorn (Leonard Praskins). Twentieth Century Pictures, 1933.

I'll Tell the World (Henry Blankfort). Universal Pictures, 1945. Based on *Miss Lonelyhearts.*

Lonelyhearts (Dore Schary). United Artists, 1958.

The Day of the Locust (Waldo Salt). Paramount Pictures, 1975.

"Miss Lonelyhearts" (Robert E. Bailey and Michael Dinner). American Film Institute/PBS, 1983. TV adaptation.

VI. PLAYS

Even Stephen (with S. J. Perelman). 1934. Never produced.

Good Hunting: A Play in Three Acts (with Joseph Schrank). 1938. Published in the Library of America collection.

VII. OTHER ADAPTATIONS

Miss Lonelyhearts (play), Howard Teichmann, 1957.

Miss Lonelyhearts (opera), Lowell Liebermann, libretto by J. D. McClatchy, 2006.

NOTES

All dialogue is drawn from primary sources: interviews, letters, journals, diaries, depositions, and autobiographies. In these firsthand accounts, quoted speeches are the memoirist's approximate reconstruction of conversations taking place earlier, sometimes decades earlier, and while they are presumed to be reasonably accurate should not be taken as exact.

The following abbreviations are used for frequently cited sources:

NW	Nathanael West
SJP	Sidney J. Perelman
LP	Laura Perelman
RM	Ruth McKenney
EM	Eileen McKenney
JS	John Sanford
JH	Josephine Herbst
BM	Beatrice Mathieu
BC	Bennett Cerf
EW	Edmund Wilson

LOA	*Nathanael West: Novels and Other Writings* (Library of America, 1997)
MSE	*My Sister Eileen* (Harcourt, Brace, 1938)
New Yorker Records	Rare Books and Manuscripts Division, New York Public Library
DOL	*The Day of the Locust*
FOIPA	Freedom of Information and Privacy Act archives
Beinecke	Beinecke Rare Book and Manuscript Library, Yale University

Mugar   Mugar Library, Boston University
Huntington   The Huntington Library, San Marino, California
HRHRC   Harry Ransom Humanities Research Center, University of Texas at Austin

•

page 1. IN THE HOTEL

1   "Nothing happens": NW to BM, Mar. 16, 1930, HRHRC. An echo of the memorable quote from *Grand Hotel*: ". . . always the same. People come, people go. Nothing ever happens."

2   "Listen to everything": Frank Case, *Do Not Disturb* (New York: J. B. Lippincott, 1940), 229.

Brooklyn Daily Times advice columns dealt with all sorts of problems: "Dear Miss Chester, I have a fully broken Beagle hound which I will be glad to give to anyone living on Long Island who has room for it, and who will give it a great home. MRS. RUTH B." (Jan. 27, 1929). Presumptuous requests annoyed Susan Chester. To a regular named BROWN EYES, she replied, "Dear Girl, you ought to know by this time that the column is *not* an advertising medium. If you have a room to rent, the place to write to is the classified advertising columns of some paper. SUSAN." (Jan. 2, 1929).

3   "comic superficialities": SJP, *The Last Laugh* (New York: Simon & Schuster, 1981), 163.

Perelman-Reynolds collaboration: The novel was published as *Parlor, Bedlam and Bath* (Horace Liveright, 1930).

4   "people and things": NW to BM, Apr. 12, 1930, HRHRC [LOA, 769].

5   "You are a swell girl": NW to BM, Mar. 16, 1930, HRHRC.

2. DUSTY ESKY IN HARLEM

6   "Dion-Bouton": JS, "Nathanael West," *The Screen Writer*, Dec. 1946. Also see *Intruders in Paradise* (Urbana/Chicago: University of Illinois Press, 1997), 147–148.

"The red car's": Ibid.

7   Harlem contemporaries of West's: Richard Rodgers, Howard Dietz, Milton Berle, John Sanford, Bennett Cerf, and Henry Roth.

8   "'sedate'": JS, *The View from Mt. Morris: A Harlem Boyhood* (New York: Barricade Books, 1994), 1.

9   Sleepy nickname: Author interview with Joyce Green.

"Merriwell": JS, *The View from Mt. Morris*, 81.

"It's Natchie": Ibid.

10   "two books alternately": Hinda Rhodes to Jay Martin, Sept. 30, 1966, Huntington.

10 "no good Americans": James F. Light, *Nathanael West: An Interpretive Study* (Evanston: Northwestern University Press, 1961), 8.

"one badly-made boy": JS, *The View from Mt. Morris*, 80.

"as if his sleeves": Ibid., 137.

"Dasty Evsko": JS, *Screen Writer*.

11 Weinstein family immigration: Author interview with Joyce Green, daughter of Leon Weinstein West and granddaughter of Jacob Weinstein; U.S. Census (Max Weinstein's year of immigration is listed variously as 1885, 1888, and 1889). Author interviews with Nancy Silbert and James Ross; "The Jarcho/Wallenstein Family History"; U.S. Census (family surname listed as Walstin in 1900 Census).

16 "gentle to the limit": JS, *Screen Writer*.

Business careers of the Weinstein-Wallensteins: Office of Metropolitan History, "Manhattan NB Database 1900–1986," www.metrohistory.com.

Weinstein-Wallenstein prosperous lifestyles: The creation of successful businesses in the world's financial capital allowed the brothers to enjoy lives of abundance. Pauline and Charles Weinstein's townhouse on West 120th Street boasted a music room for the family's baby grand together with another special room to house their collection of ivory and Chinese sculptures. Their daughter Susanne (whose engagement gown is preserved at the Metropolitan Museum of Art's Costume Institute) was wed at Delmonico's. Anna and Max Weinstein, observant Jews active in their congregation, were instrumental in importing a rabbi from England so that no foreign accent would be heard in the synagogue.

"a timid shy boy": Hinda Rhodes to Jay Martin, Sept. 30, 1966, Huntington.

17 "plainly wild": JS, *Screen Writer*.

"preposterous": NW, *The Dream Life of Balso Snell*, LOA, 15.

"the shakes": JS, *The Waters of Darkness* (Santa Barbara: Black Sparrow Press, 1986), 104.

"ideas of American history": NW, "Proposal to the Guggenheim Foundation," LOA, 464.

"gaunt caps": JS, *View from This Wilderness* (Santa Barbara: Capra Press, 1977), 171.

18 "The Son": LP notebook, c. 1930.

3. MISHAWAKA

19 John Sydney McKenney education: After three years in the engineering program at Ohio State, he dropped out to become a mechanical draftsman, his job at the time that he met Marguerite. His technical background and ambitious mentality quickly led to more senior positions.

Flynn family history: Patrick Flinn, Eileen's great grandfather, came from Killarney, in County Kerry. Driven out of Ireland by the Potato Famine in the late 1840s, he settled in the southwest region of New York State, married fifteen-year-old Catherine Hubbard, and fathered four sons and two daughters. During the Civil War, Patrick, forty, enlisted as a private in the New York Voluntary Infantry Regiment, signing up for three years to qualify for a $1,500 bonus. In May 1863, his company took part in the siege of the Confederate garrison at Port Hudson, Louisiana; the Union victory signaled a turning point in the war. Patrick, wounded shortly after the assault began, died four months later from a combination of his injuries and inflammation of the lungs (*American Civil War Soldiers* database).

The struggling Flinn family split up, and the four boys went to live with neighbors and relatives. Patrick's youngest son, Thomas Henry, Eileen's grandfather, was three years old when his father died. He would not remember him or feel close to his siblings.

In the late 1860s, Tom's oldest brother, James, was partially blinded in a steam-blast accident while working for the railroad. Settling in Cleveland, he first found employment in a furniture store, then in the closely related businesses of coffin making and undertaking. In 1869, he and two partners established Flynn-Abel & Froelk Funeral Directors, which would become one of Cleveland's premier funeral homes. Their advertisements in Cleveland streetcars were so familiar that people joked about a Flynn's funeral being the only foolproof way to reach heaven. Today the company name is DeJohn Flynn-Mylott Funeral Homes.

Tom Flynn, however, rejected the undertaking profession and became a teamster. Later he worked for a factory that made iron fences, mailboxes, and prison equipment, working his way up to foreman. His marriage to Mary Pierce, an English girl from Somerset put out to service as a kitchen maid at the age of eleven, resulted in nine children, three of whom died in infancy.

20 McKenney family history: William McKenney, descended from Scottish-English Presbyterians, was a Canadian who migrated to Kansas around 1880 and married a girl from Michigan named Celia Smith. His eldest son was John Sydney, born in 1885, followed by a daughter, Margery, and a second son, William. In the tiny community of Paola, an exceedingly rich town after natural gas was discovered in 1882, William was employed by a flour mill. By 1892 the McKenneys were in Medina, Ohio, thirty miles south of Cleveland, a farm area known for its bees and honey. There, William made a successful switch to the fertilizer business, in which he fared so well that his youngest son would follow in his footsteps. His daughter married a doctor.

"no McKenney": RM, *The Loud Red Patrick* (New York: Harcourt, Brace, 1947), 13.

21 "a wide circle": *Mishawaka Enterprise*, Feb. 13, 1920.

"I was homely": RM, *All About Eileen* (New York: Harcourt, Brace, 1952), 111.

22 "wigwam trading post": Ibid., 31.
"gross, primeval": Ibid.
25 "pale, unimportant people": RM to Herman Shumlin, Feb. 14, 1947, Harcourt, Inc., Records Center.
"nervous": RM, *All About Eileen*, 32.

4. SAN JUAN HILL, NEW YORK

29 "bright and clean": NW, "The Adventurer," LOA, 449.
"a storehouse": Ibid., 448.
31 "We would wait": NW, "The Adventurer," LOA, 454.
"Poor Alice": JS, *View from This Wilderness*, 197.
32 "harmful influences": Camp Paradox brochure, 1918.
33 "a quiet chap": Ira S. Robbins to James F. Light, Oct. 23, 1957, quoted in James F. Light, *Nathanael West*, 7.
"felt like going home": NW, "Western Union Boy," LOA, 427.
34 "If anyone": NW, "The Adventurer," LOA, 449.
35 "twitching crowd": Ibid., 448.
"a closet": Ibid., 449.
Arson fantasies: NW, "Burn the Cities," LOA, 458. The unpublished poem was found among West's effects, but an earlier version, "Christmass Poem," appeared in *Contempo*, Feb. 21, 1933.

5. THE STENOGRAPHER FROM CANTON

38 "a broken heart": RM to Herman Shumlin, Feb. 14, 1947, Harcourt Inc., Records Center.
39 "a normal family": RM to Katharine White, Dec. 1936, *New Yorker* Records.
"She was a rebel": Author interview with Robert McKenney.
40 "She was unprepared": Author interview with Richard Selvey.
"in one word": Author interview with Robert McKenney. Ethel and Syd would have three children together: Jack, born in 1922, Robert, 1942, and Sara Jane, 1951.
"a hell of a time": Author interview with Jack McKenney.
"I always heard": Author interview with Robert McKenney.
41 "terrible": RM to Katharine White, Jan. 16, 1946, *New Yorker* Records.
"she did it": *Cleveland Press*, Sept. 9, 1940.
"read each other's": RM, *All About Eileen*, 90.
42 "mush": RM, *The McKenneys Carry On* (New York: Harcourt, Brace, 1940), 79.
"lick her chops": Ibid., 77.
"I used to spend": Ibid., 39.

"as dumb": RM, *My Sister Eileen* (New York: Harcourt, Brace, 1938), 53.

"it put a mark": Ibid., 53.

43 Ruth suicide attempt: RM, *All About Eileen*, 88–90.

"You make me sick": Ibid., 91.

44 "a problem child": Quoted in wire service story, *Ironwood* (Michigan) *Daily Globe*, Sept. 20, 1938, and other papers.

Bipolar disorder: The cause of this long-term illness is believed to be a combination of genetic and other factors. Stressful life events, such as a death in the family, may trigger the condition, which can develop a life of its own and so the cycles continue. Symptoms typically begin in adolescence or early adulthood.

"the homeliest girl": RM, *All About Eileen*, 72.

"a serious": Interview in *Ironwood* (Michigan) *Daily Globe*, Sept. 20, 1938.

"Tiring of suicide": RM, *Love Story* (New York: Harcourt, Brace, 1950), 28.

45 "infinitely despicable": RM to Doris Schneider, Harcourt, Brace editor, and other unidentified individuals, May 10, 1944, Harcourt Inc., Records Center.

"primeval beasts": Ibid.

"not at all sad": Author interview with Robert McKenney.

"bitter": RM to Matthew and Hannah Josephson, Feb. 1939, Beinecke.

6. CRIMES AND MISDEMEANORS

46 "Hair permanently waved": Hinda Weinstein diary.

Tufts admission: Amy Miller, Tufts University Alumni Office; Tuft archivists Susanne Belovari, Michelle Romero, and Melissa Griffin; Walter J. Degnan, DeWitt Clinton High School principal, to James F. Light, Nov. 6, 1957; James R. Strawbridge, Tufts registrar, to James F. Light, Nov. 15, 1960. Tufts archives, especially pre-1960, are sketchy. Information about West's acceptance based on a DeWitt Clinton transcript, cited by Light, *Nathanael West*, no longer exists; neither does Light's correspondence with school officials in 1960. However, a 1921–1922 freshman roll lists Nathaniel Weinstein as a B.S. candidate from New York and a resident at the Phi Epsilon Pi House.

47 "became a sixth finger": JS, *View from This Wilderness*, 171; JS to Tom Dardis, Apr. 1975, quoted in Dardis, *Some Time in the Sun*, 143.

Ivy League restrictive enrollment: Irving Howe, *World of Our Fathers* (New York: Harcourt Brace Jovanovich, 1976), 411–412.

49 Tufts University student records: Tufts Freshman Class Roll, 1921–22, 251.

"poor kid": Hinda Weinstein diary.

50 "all smashed up": Ibid.

The other Nathan Weinstein: Grade sheets supplied by Tufts Digital Collections and Archives confirm that an N. Weinstein who in 1920–22 had maintained a grade C average in his premed courses, departed in June 1921 for Tufts Medical School, where he subsequently graduated, in 1925, while a second N. Weinstein dropped out in Nov. 1921. The two Weinsteins can easily be distinguished by grade sheets detailing courses and dates of enrollment.

51 West's unexplained admissions to Tufts and Brown: No documentation exists, but West's family is clearly responsible for both deceptions. West, a minor, lacked the financial means to carry out the scams.

52 "Coming from the bathroom": NW, *The Dream Life of Balso Snell*, LOA, 45.

53 "a bloody wreck": Quentin Reynolds, "When Pep Was a Ghost," *Brown Alumni Monthly*, Dec. 1957.
"I've challenged": Ibid.
"couldn't fight": Ibid.

54 "to find him": Frank Hough to James F. Light, Mar. 4, 1958, quoted in Light, *Nathanael West*, 17.
"very young": Jeremiah Mahoney to James F. Light, Feb. 20, 1958, quoted in Light, *Nathanael West*, 32.
"Tell me something": Philip Lukin to James F. Light, Feb. 20, 1958, quoted in Light, *Nathanael West*, 22. Another classmate reported that West became violently ill after smoking opium (Frank O. Hough to Light, Apr. 13, 1958, quoted in Light, 24).

55 "warm and fanciful": SJP interview, in Jay Martin, *Nathanael West: The Art of His Life* (New York: Farrar, Straus and Giroux, 1970), 68.
"a most depressing book": SJP to Abby Perelman, Apr. 15, 1954, in SJP, *Don't Tread on Me: The Selected Letters of S. J. Perelman*, Prudence Crowther, ed. (New York: Viking, 1987), 163.
"warm, sympathetic": Quentin Reynolds to Cyril Schneider, July 30, 1952, UCLA Special Collections.

56 "you want a degree": Quentin Reynolds, *By Quentin Reynolds* (New York: McGraw-Hill, 1963), 47.
Euripides: NW, "Euripides—A Playwright," *Casements*, July 1923, LOA, 393.
"self-torture": Philip Lukin to James F. Light, Nov. 12, 1959, quoted in Light, *Nathanael West*, 29.

57 "became a writer": Quentin Reynolds, "When Pep Was a Ghost."
Sources of West's writing: Israel J. Kapstein (Brown class of 1926), editor, novelist, and longtime Brown English professor, knew S. J. Perelman from their days together in high school, and knew West from college. Kapstein considered West a revenge writer who used fiction to "discharge all the resentment he could not discharge in fact." A chip on his shoulder drove him to get even with people who had rejected him. I. J. Kapstein to Daniel Walden, Mar. 9, 1970, quoted in Daniel Walden, "Nathanael West: A Jewish Satirist in Spite of Himself," in Ben Siegel, *Critical Essays on Nathanael West* (New York: G. K. Hall, 1994), 216.

"Pep was on college": Philip Lukin to James F. Light, Feb. 20, 1958, quoted in Light, *Nathanael West*, 22.

58 "To predict his future": *Liber Brunensis* (Providence, 1924), 142.

West's reputation at Brown: Author interview with Laurence B. Chase ("The Plastic Agents," unpublished paper, 1962, 89).

7. BECOMING "NATHANAEL WEST"

60 "lit-rachoor": NW and Julian L. Shapiro to the *New York World Telegram*, Oct. 20, 1931, LOA, 770.

61 "to the point": Robert M. Coates, Introduction to *Miss Lonelyhearts* (New York: New Directions, 1946), xi.

62 "Ma's hysteria": Hinda Weinstein diary.

"Oh, gosh": Ibid.

"We are a strange": LP diary, quoted in Dorothy Herrmann, *S. J. Perelman: A Life* (New York: Putnam's, 1986), 87.

"my partner": Hinda Weinstein diary.

63 "He came": Hinda Rhodes letter to Jay Martin, Sept. 30, 1966, Huntington.

"an attempt to love": NW, "Proposal to the Guggenheim Foundation," LOA, 465.

64 "Aren't you Nat": JS, *View*, 235.

65 West-Sanford meeting at Asbury Park: Ibid., 235–236.

"Ah, the names": JS, *Intruders in Paradise*, 149.

66 "Here's a story": JS, *Waters*, 27–28.

67 "a Sunday writer": NW to Milton Abernethy, Apr. 26, 1932, LOA, 772.

"acts as a laxative": NW, *The Dream Life of Balso Snell*, LOA, 15.

69 "set an example": JS, *A Very Good Land to Fall With* (Santa Barbara: Black Sparrow Press, 1987), 192.

"That day was my birthday": JS, *Waters*, 131.

70 "I was very busy": NW, "The Imposter," LOA, 416.

71 "slow and painful": Author interview with Nancy Silbert, Mortimer Weinstein's niece.

West change of name: He continued to sign business correspondence N. W. Weinstein.

72 "Did Pep hurt Max?": JS, *Waters*, 263.

"Go west": Source of the misattributed quotation ("Go west, young man, and grow up with the country") is John L. Soule, *Terre Haute Express*, 1851.

8. BALSO SNELL'S BOOK OF DIRTY LITTLE SECRETS

73 Liberia Hotel: Samuel Beckett lived there in 1938. Today the fifty-nine-room hotel at 9, rue de la Grande Chaumière is the Best Western à la Villa des Artistes.

74 "hard collars": NW, "The Imposter," LOA, 412.

74   "1000 parties": F. Scott Fitzgerald, *F. Scott Fitzgerald's Ledger: A Facsimile*, Matthew Bruccoli, ed. (Washington, D.C.: NCR/Microcard Editions, A Bruccoli Clark Book, 1972), 179.
"lit-rachoor": NW and Julian L. Shapiro to the *New York World Telegram*, Oct. 20, 1931, LOA, 770.

75   Anti-Semitism facing Jewish novelists: Edna Ferber's Pulitzer Prize for fiction in 1924 sparked disdain from certain well-known writers. Scott Fitzgerald refused to read *So Big*. He called Ferber a Yiddish descendant of O. Henry who cranked out stories about "flip Jewish saleswomen" and "earthy" carrot growers, despite the fact that her fictional farmers in *So Big* were not specifically Jewish. In scorning her work as "inferior," Fitzgerald was perhaps no more prejudiced than most Americans in the twenties. For his disparaging remarks, see *Dear Scott/Dear Max* (New York: Scribner's, 1971), 25, 76, 89; also, *A Life in Letters* (New York: Scribner's, 1994), 118–119, 154.

76   "never finished anything": NW, "The Imposter," LOA, 413.

77   "first time ever": Hinda Weinstein diary.
"God, what you can buy": JS, *Waters*, 24.

78   "typical *Yiddische hausfrau*": JS to James F. Light, Aug. 8, 1958, quoted in Light, *Nathanael West*, 33.
"a quiet, sunken-eyed": JS, *Waters*, 23.
"quit the nonsense": Ibid., 130.
West and the prostitute: JS, *Waters*, 24–25.

79   "And it still": JS, *Waters*, 24.
"the broad sweep": NW to F. Scott Fitzgerald, Apr. 5, 1939, LOA, 792.
"While walking": NW, *The Dream Life of Balso Snell*, LOA, 5.

80   "you call this dump": Ibid., 7.
"stinker": Ibid.
"I'm a Jew": Ibid., 8.
"the man who wrote": Ibid., 31.

82   "If you haven't": SJP to Lorraine Weinstein, spring 1928.

9. CLEVELAND HEIGHTS PRINCESS

83   "He worked": Author interview with Robert McKenney.

84   "Eileen was no shrinking violet": Author interview with Ruth Beebe Hill. Ms. Hill is the author of *Hanta Yo* (1979), a novel about Native Americans.

85   "quite a gal": Robert Rippner e-mail to the author, May 15, 2007.
"They looked paralyzed": RM, *All About Eileen*, 92.
"ugly tusks": RM, "Smile," *New Yorker*, Aug. 24, 1946.

86   "a pariah": RM, *All About Eileen*, 110.
Norman Douglas: Noted English writer (1868–1962) known for his controversial personal life and his 1917 novel, *South Wind*, set on Capri.
"a gruesome novel": RM to Frank Morley and Doris Schneider, Sept. 19, 1944, Harcourt, Inc., Records Center.

88 "How in the name": RM, *My Sister Eileen*, 75.

90 Probable rape: St. Clair McKelway interviewed by Jay Martin, Mar. 22, 1967.

Rape as unreported crime: Not until the women's liberation movement in the 1970s did women begin speaking out publicly about their experiences. In 1975, Susan Brownmiller wrote a landmark history of rape, *Against Our Will: Men, Women and Rape*.

10. RING OUT, WILD BALLS

91 All West letters to Beatrice Mathieu are located at HRHRC.

92 Weinstein-Wallenstein buildings: New York Department of Buildings records. The families were responsible for more than 160 commercial and residential buildings, typically Manhattan apartment houses.

93 "a two-volume edition": NW to BM, Apr. 1, 1930.
"I'll probably make": Ibid.
"these litry guys": SJP to Laura Weinstein, spring 1928.

95 "really care": NW to BM, Mar. 16, 1930.
"working pretty hard": NW to BM, Mar. 31, 1930.

96 "Life *is* worthwhile": NW, *Miss Lonelyhearts*, LOA, 59.
"the smile of an anarchist": Ibid., 75.

97 "What a kind bitch": Ibid., 72.

98 "bake my nuts": SJP to I. J. Kapstein, Oct. 9, 1930, in *Selected Letters*, 5.
"swell girl friend": Ibid.

99 "take a stick": NW to BM, May 4, 1930.

100 "His mother": Beatrice Mathieu Roos to Jay Martin, Aug. 15, 1966, Huntington.
"sort of Jewish": Ibid.
"anyone": NW to BM, Mar. 23, 1930.

101 "Violent images": NW, "Some Notes on Miss L.," LOA, 401.
"Semen and Schuster": NW to BM, Apr. 6, 1930.
"a smug bastard": NW to BM, Apr. 27, 1930.
"fat arse Fadiman": NW to BM, May 3, 1930.

102 "crazy": NW to BM, Mar. 31, 1930.
"a great writer": Ibid.
"We'll get drunk": NW to BM, May 3, 1930.
"not very nice": NW to BM, Mar. 31, 1930.

103 "No SCOLDING": NW to BM, undated telegram.
"My God": NW to BM, Apr. 3, 1930.
"pink faille shoes": BM note written on NW letter of Apr. 6, 1930.
"crying": NW to BM, May 4, 1930.
"pendulous": NW to BM, Mar. 28, 1930.
"a fat white slug": NW to BM, May 24, 1930.
"SAILING POSTPONED": NW to BM, undated telegram.

104 "an awful bastard": BM to NW, undated.
"sent letters back": NW to BM, July 20, 1930.
"phoney": Ibid.
"times are indeed hard": Ibid.

105 "find a home": NW to BM, Mar. 16, 1930.

106 "a fine feeling": William Carlos Williams, "Sordid? Good God!" in Siegel, *Critical Essays*, 60. The best-known poem of William Carlos Williams (1883–1963) is "The Red Wheelbarrow." He was posthumously awarded the Pulitzer Prize for poetry in 1963.
"Good God": Ibid.
Vanity publication: *The Dream Life of Balso Snell* was the first and last title published by Contact Editions.
"How do we go about": JS, *Waters*, 49.
"They're all *you*": Ibid., 50.

107 "Pep writes": JS to Nonie and Jesse Greenstein, Aug. 2, 1939, Mugar.
"vicious, mean": NW, "Through the Hole in the Mundane Millstone," LOA, 396.
"a good sort": "Tired Men and Dung," JS (as Julian L. Shapiro) in Siegel, *Critical Essays*, 46.
"distinguished performance": V. N. Garofolo, "A Distinguished Performance," *Contempo*, Aug. 21, 1931, in Siegel, *Critical Essays*, 45.
The most likely inspiration for *The Dream Life of Balso Snell* appears to be James Branch Cabell's *Jurgen*, the suppressed 1919 novel in which obscene humor underlies a medieval romance.
"an elaborate joke": Malcolm Cowley, "It's the Telling That Counts," *New York Times Book Review*, May 12, 1957. The first mentions of *The Dream Life of Balso Snell* to appear in major publications occurred in 1957 when Farrar, Straus & Cudahy published *The Complete Works of Nathanael West*.

108 "all it says": Martin, *Nathanael West*, 227.
"very grounded person": Author interview with Linda Seifert.
"what I can't have": JS, *Waters*, 106.

109 "tall and good looking": JS to James F. Light, Aug. 8, 1958, Mugar.
EW on Alice Shepard: EW, *The Thirties* (New York: Farrar, Straus, and Giroux, 1980), 444.
"that little flower": BM to SJP and LP, Nov. 26, 1930.
"RING OUT": Dec. 1930 cable quoted in Beatrice Mathieu Roos to Jay Martin, Aug. 15, 1966, Huntington.

11. THE BIG STEAL

110 "Son of a bitch": JS, *Waters*, 98.

111 Sutton Club Hotel: Vilifying the hotel was a favorite pastime of West's. His caustic remarks were meant to distance himself from the sort of mundane commercial employment scorned by the writers of his acquaintance. S. J.

Perelman later described the Sutton as a barracks housing Juilliard music students, impoverished copywriters, and divorcées living on minuscule alimony checks. But as a new hotel that had opened in 1930, it did not deserve such a description. During the Depression, it suffered problems similar to those of other New York hotels and slipped from its one-time elegance but certainly never become a flophouse. In World War II, it served a clientele of servicemen. Restored to its former glory after a complete renovation in the 1980s, it opened as a boutique hotel favored by political and theatrical celebrities in need of a discreet pied à terre. After a condo conversion fell through in 2007, the owners returned it to operation as a hotel for extended-stay guests. Today monthly rates range from $11,850 to $14,800.

"There's always": Ibid., 97–98.

John Sanford fiction: At Viele Pond, he completed a draft of *The Water Wheel*, published in 1933. His familiarity with the area, including a hotel stay the previous summer, would yield material for two additional novels.

"How would I shut": JS, *Waters*, 105.

"We're supposed to be": Ibid., 103.

112 "swine": JS to James F. Light, Sept. 18, 1958, Mugar.

John Sanford comments on West's driving: Ibid.; see also, *Waters*, 115–116, 123.

"You mind": JS, *Waters*, 119.

John Sanford's first novel: *The Water Wheel*, by Julian L. Shapiro (New York: Duffield & Green, 1933).

"adultery camp": Ibid.

113 "The First Church": NW, *Contact*, Feb. 1932, 80–85; see also William White, *Nathanael West: A Comprehensive Bibliography* (Kent, Ohio: Kent State University Press, 1975), 133.

114 "Miss Lonelyhearts in the Country": In addition to the summer spent in the Adirondacks, West incorporated short motor trips made to Connecticut with George Brounoff during 1931–32.

"anyone can have": JS, *Waters*, 136.

115 "a very curious type": Quoted in Paul Mariani, *William Carlos Williams: A New World Naked* (New York: McGraw-Hill, 1981), 320.

"non-political prose": NW to William Carlos Williams, late 1931, Beinecke [LOA, 770].

"I suppose": Ibid.

116 "really lousy": NW to William Carlos Williams, early 1932, Beinecke.

"business is lousy": NW to William Carlos Williams, May 13, 1932, Beinecke.

"stinkiest fake moderne": NW to William Carlos Williams, June 1932, Beinecke.

Five chapters of *Miss Lonelyhearts* appeared prior to book publication: "Miss Lonelyhearts and the Lamb," *Contact*, Feb. 1932; "Miss Lonelyhearts and the Dead Pan" and "Miss Lonelyhearts and the Clean Old Man," *Con-*

tact, May 1932; "Miss Lonelyhearts in the Dismal Swamp," *Contempo*, July 5, 1932; "Miss Lonelyhearts on a Field Trip," *Contact*, Oct. 1932. Additionally, West wrote "Miss Lonelyhearts Among the Communists," probably for use in a Communist-theme issue of *Contact*. But after the magazine folded the unpublished chapter was cut from the novel. West wrote to Josephine Herbst that he couldn't "get the communist chapter to fit, although I tried hard and wanted badly to get it in. It was too obviously artificial" (Mar. 24, 1933, Beinecke). No draft survives.

117   "so swollen": NW to William Carlos Williams, June 1932, Beinecke.
Mount Zion Cemetery: Now overshadowed by a waste-disposal plant, Mount Zion was in 1931 a pastoral eighty acres on the border of Brooklyn and Queens, historic because it contains numerous victims of the Triangle Shirtwaist Factory fire, the 1911 tragedy that claimed the lives of immigrant seamstresses. Some of the headstones are enameled with faces of the dead, an Eastern European custom. Portraits show the loved ones as they appeared in life, the young men in stiff collars and the women in picture hats, so that the cemetery looks almost like a family album. This sort of display did not appeal to the Weinsteins, whose businesslike plot on Path 27R contains somber stones.
"an awful jolt": Ibid.
"from shirt sleeves": EW, *Thirties*, 191. The adage, attributed to Andrew Carnegie, refers to first-generation immigrants who made fortunes by rolling up their sleeves and working hard. After the pampered, undisciplined second generation squanders its inheritance, the third generation must roll up its sleeves and resume hard labor.

118   "To Max": JS, *Waters*, 282.
"heartsick": NW to William Carlos Williams, June 27, 1932, Beinecke.
"straighten things": NW to Bob Brown, July 4, 1932, Morris Library, Southern Illinois University.
"No more of that snug": SJP to LP, May 1933.
"the old lady": Ibid.
"burn the books": EW, *Thirties*, 337.
chicken salad: Ibid., 356.

119   "simply and unobtrusively": Quoted in Robert K. Landers, *An Honest Writer: The Life and Times of James T. Farrell* (San Francisco: Encounter, 2004), 113.

120   "a book and author luncheon": SJP, "Ready, Aim, Flee!," *Vinegar Puss* (New York: Simon & Schuster, 1975), 96.
"the grace of someone": JH, "Nathanael West," *Kenyon Review* 23, 1961.

121   "a dandy": JH, "Hunter of Doves," *Botteghe Oscure*, spring 1954. Josephine Herbst's roman à clef, *Hunter of Doves*, is the source of scenes and conversations relating to West's relationship with Herbst and John Herrmann.
"We barely slept": JH, *Kenyon Review*.

"deathly presence": JH, *Hunter,* 322.

122 "They are swell": NW to William Carlos Williams, Nov. 1932, Beinecke.

123 "You could say": JH typed notes, Beinecke.

"Not at all": JH, *Hunter,* 318.

124 "The corpse": Ibid., 325.

"a pig-headed old kike": LP notebook, c. 1930.

125 "love pats": LP diary, quoted in Herrmann, *S. J. Perelman,* 91.

Maxim Lieber: Other clients include Langston Hughes, John Cheever, and Carson McCullers. In the 1950s, after Whittaker Chambers accused him of operating an express stop on the Communist underground railway, he left the country for Mexico and is believed to have ended up in Communist Poland.

126 "Are you bringing": Quoted in Douglas Wixson, *Worker-Writer in America: Jack Conroy and the Tradition of Midwestern Literary Radicalism, 1898–1990* (Urbana: University of Illinois Press, 1994), 199.

Child's restaurant scene: JS, *Waters,* 164–166. Years later, John Sanford was unable to account for the fight. Most likely his anger had been festering for some time though, perhaps since their summer at Viele Pond, when Nat slighted his novel, or over a dispute resulting from a story John had submitted to *Contact* magazine.

127 West's breakup with Alice Shepard: West's account to JH failed to mention Lillian Hellman. He talked about his and Alice's engagement party and how Sid and Alice slipped out of the room, which caused an anguished Laura to run away, which in turn made Nat steal a car that he wrecked against an elevated-railway pillar on Sixth Avenue. JH used his account, "with all the details, except one," in *Hunter of Doves,* and when told later that other guests at the party contradicted the story she replied, "If it was a fantasy on West's part, it would seem to me to be particularly revealing. Very often a fantasy can reveal more than a literal truth" (JH to Randall Reid, 1966, Beinecke).

128 "a devious nature": Alice Shepard Dougall to Jay Martin, May 1967, Huntington.

"the old lady": SJP to LP, May 1933.

129 "the poison": SJP, *The Last Laugh,* 168.

130 "We call the place": NW to JH, Mar. 24, 1933, Beinecke.

12. MAROONED ON SILSBY ROAD

132 "Don't they ever ask": RM, *The McKenneys Carry On* (New York: Harcourt, Brace, 1940), 104–105.

133 "just got lost": Ibid., 115.

"to keep house": Ibid., 119.

"I wrote my interview": RM, MSE, 179.

133 "unadjusted": *Ironwood* (Michigan) *Daily Globe*, Sept. 20, 1938.

Ohio State dropout: RM, "Beware Body Building," *New Yorker*, Mar. 18, 1944.

134 "an anteroom": RM, *All About Eileen*, 166.

"Mr. Wilson": Author interview with Earl Wilson, Jr.

"Governor's Daughter": RM, *Akron Beacon Journal*/International News Service, Aug. 3, 1932.

"sweated over her copy": John S. Knight, *Akron Beacon Journal*, Dec. 21, 1936.

"looked like the map": *Industrial Valley* introduction, xv.

"would run out": Author interview with Jack McKenney. Production of Cord L-29s was limited to around five thousand, but the Depression wiped out the market for such luxury cars.

135 "Robert (Bidgie)": RM, *All About Eileen*, 168.

Possible marriage: No record of a marriage or divorce between Eileen Mc-Kenney and Sterling Hubbard exists in Cuyahoga County.

136 "She expected more": Author interview with Richard Selvey.

"boil an egg": RM, *All About Eileen*, 103.

"What's wrong": Ibid., 166.

137 "intellectual gifts": Author interview with Richard Selvey.

"wretched marriages": RM to Frank Morley and Doris Schneider, May 10, 1944, Harcourt, Inc., Records Center.

"I'm just marking time": RM, *All About Eileen*, 168.

139 "Be brief": Ibid., 172.

"had to wipe": RM, *All About Eileen*, 172.

"I could look": Ibid.

"strut": Walter Lister to Joseph Cookman, Sept. 26, 1936. Courtesy of Walter Lister, Jr.

"you make me a promise": RM, *All About Eileen*, 172.

13. SCREWBALLS AND SCREWBOXES

141 "hard, brilliant": *New York Times*, Apr. 23, 1933.

West's new car: NW to Bob Brown, Mar. 9, 1933, Morris Library, Southern Illinois University.

News of Liveright bankruptcy: *New York Times*, May 5, 1933.

Miss Lonelyhearts reviews: *New Republic*, Apr. 26, 1933; *Saturday Review of Literature*, May 1, 1933; *Nation*, June 14, 1933; *New Outlook*, July 1933.

"the sheer brilliance": *New Yorker*, Apr. 15, 1933.

142 "a really swell press": NW to JH, May 10, 1933, Beinecke.

"made": JS (as Julian Shapiro) to Richard Johns, May 10, 1933, Mugar.

"wacky joint": Lillian Hellman, *An Unfinished Woman* (New York: Little, Brown, 1969), 31.

"bag of plums": Ibid., 28.

Liveright, Inc.: Following the 1933 bankruptcy, Arthur Pell reacquired the company. Liveright Publishing Corp. continued to operate until 1969, when Pell sold it to the *New Republic*. In 1974 it was acquired by W. W. Norton. The company's most valuable asset was a profitable backlist of four hundred titles by some of the biggest names in American writing.

143 "about half crazy": NW to Bob Brown, May 1933, Morris Library, Southern Illinois University. West had developed an affectionate relationship with Robert (Bob) Carleton Brown, the poet-inventor-cookbook writer.
"Pity the poor author": *Hollywood Reporter*, May 15, 1933, quoted in SJP to LP, May 15, 1933.
"A long story": NW to JH, May 1933, Beinecke.

144 Failure of *Miss Lonelyhearts*: In December 1933, Greenberg Publisher acquired the remainder of the first edition from Harcourt, Brace and sold the copies for 75 cents apiece.
"a good quick burial": JS (as Julian Shapiro) to Richard Johns, May 10, 1933, Mugar.
"If a heart": JS, *Waters*, 174.
"head in a sewer": NW to Milton Abernethy, Apr. 11, 1933, quoting *New York Evening Post*.
"dull and dirty": *Los Angeles Times*, May 28, 1933.
"a religious experience": NW, "Some Notes on Miss L.," *Contempo*, May 15, 1933, LOA, 401.
"WOMEN THREATEN": *Pawtuxet Valley Daily Times*, West Warwick, RI, May 3, 1933.

145 "Susan, don't think": Martin, *Nathanael West*, 110.
"*Dear Miss Lonelyhearts*": NW, *Miss Lonelyhearts*, LOA, 107.
"People like to see": JS, *Waters*, 105.
"Give me another *Morocco*": EW, *Thirties*, 355.

146 "Don't worry about clichés": SJP to LP, May 1933.
"god-damned sweet": SJP to LP, June 7, 1933.
"swell": NW to JH, May 10, 1933.

147 "pop": SJP to LP, May 13, 1933.
"a gigantic rat-fuck": SJP to LP, May 1933.
"a tough winter": NW to JH, May 10, 1933, Beinecke.

148 "a desert got up": NW to Milton Abernethy, July 7, 1933, LOA, 781.
"all wrong": NW to JH, July 1933, Beinecke.

149 Fate of *Beauty Parlor*: Columbia incorporated some of West's material into another property, *Blind Date*, starring Ann Sothern, released in July 1934.
"misbegotten flea-pit": SJP to Betty White Johnston, Oct. 17, 1931, in *Selected Letters*, 8.
"I am fucking sick": SJP to Deborah Rogers, 1976, in *Selected Letters*, xii.
"And the Lastfogel": EW, *Thirties*, 358.

150 "A Writer": NW to EW, July 25, 1933, LOA, 780.
"closed up as tight": NW to JH, July 1933, Beinecke.

151 "pus-pockets": NW, "Business Deal," *Americana*, Oct. 1933, LOA, 401; NW, "Three Eskimos," LOA, 456. The Eskimo family appears as the Gingos in Chapter 17 of DOL.
"screwballs and screwboxes": NW, DOL, LOA, 388.
"a horrible": JH quoted in Elinor Langer, *Josephine Herbst: The Story She Could Never Tell* (Boston: Atlantic Monthly Press, 1984), 359.
"Phooey on Cal": NW to JH, July 1933, Beinecke.

14. SHIRTSLEEVES TO SHIRTSLEEVES

152 "going to take a chance": JH, "Hunter," 326.
153 "baking, frying, and frying": SJP to LP, July 25, 1934.
154 "How's he going to eat": JH quoted in Light, *Nathanael West*, 108.
"A large White Queen": JH, "Hunter," 319.
"too much": JH notes on West, Beinecke.
"Coulda told you": Joseph Schrank, "On Geigel Hill," *Tinicum Bulletin*, Dec. 1980–Jan. 1981.
155 "the story that I intended": NW to JH, May 31, 1933, Beinecke.
"I'm doing it satirically": Ibid.
"my Horatio Alger book": NW to EW, July 25, 1933, Beinecke.
156 "the abominable": Quoted in Jonathan Ned Katz, *Gay American History: Lesbians and Gay Men in the USA* (New York: Meridian/Penguin, 1992), 33.
157 "His teeth were pulled out": NW, *A Cool Million*, LOA, 238.
158 "pithy thailer boy": Ibid., 192.
"no one cared": NW and Boris Ingster, *A Cool Million* screen treatment. LOA, 752.
159 State University College of New York professors: David Dingledy and Douglas Shepard.
"Come in, Grant": Horatio Alger, Jr., *Andy Grant's Pluck* (Philadelphia: John C. Winston Co., 1902), Ch. XXXI, www.Gutenberg.org/text, reprinted in Douglas H. Shepard, "Nathanael West Rewrites Horatio Alger, Jr.," *Satire Newsletter*, Vol. 3, fall 1965, pp. 13–28.
"Come on in": NW, *A Cool Million*, LOA, 185.
"Sho! How many teachers": Horatio Alger, Jr., *Joe's Luck, or Always Wide Awake* (New York: New York Book Co., 1913), Ch. XXVI, reprinted in Douglas Shepard, *Satire Newsletter*.
"'My,' said Mr. Whipple": NW, *A Cool Million*, LOA, 214.
160 "particular kind of joking": NW to George Milburn, Apr. 6, 1939, quoted in Richard B. Gehman's Introduction to *The Day of the Locust* (New York: Bantam, 1953), xx.
Additional instances of West's copying: Author interviews with Douglas Shepard and Gary Scharnhorst. Subsequently Gary Scharnhorst and Jack

Bales, biographers of Horatio Alger, Jr., found instances of copying from *The Erie Train Boy* (1890) and *Tom Temple's Career* (1888). Scharnhorst argues that the plagiarism could be considered an example of West "recontextualizing" Alger, that is, reconfiguring nineteenth-century prose for the twentieth, a kind of copying that a modern aesthetic would permit. The mystery to Douglas Shepard is "why would a writer of Nathanael West's caliber go to the trouble of plagiarizing from Horatio Alger? It seems very strange."

"degeneracy": *Harrison's Reports*, Aug. 26, 1933.

"almost as soundlessly": JH, "Hunter," 324.

"the lowest, vilest, filthiest": *Harrison's Reports*, Sept. 2, 1933.

161 "a shell who spits": SJP to LP, Jan. 7, 1935.

162 "a second-rate Barry": *New York Times*, Dec. 6, 1933. Closing after forty performances, *All Good Americans* was sold to MGM and released six months later as *Paris Interlude*.

"I can't recall": Charles A. Pearce to Jay Martin, Aug. 15, 1966, Huntington.

163 "honesty will buy you": Columbia Pictures files, June 12, 1934.

164 *A Cool Million* reviews: *Nation*, July 25, 1934; *New Republic*, July 18, 1934.

"famous for being rascals": SJP to LP, July 21, 1934. Covici-Friede folded four years later, despite its coup of signing John Steinbeck.

"Covici gelt": SJP letters to LP, July 1934.

"absolutely unable": NW to EW, June 30, 1939, LOA, 796. West's claim to have earned $780 in royalties did not take into account the $4,000 he received from 20th Century Pictures for film rights to *Miss Lonelyhearts*.

165 "gave him some Bourbon": Dashiell Hammett to Lillian Hellman, May 3, 1931, quoted in Diane Johnson, *Dashiell Hammett: A Life* (New York: Random House, 1983), 100.

"lost her husband": EW, *Thirties*, 329.

"dull as old paint": SJP to LP, July 1934.

166 Herbst visit to West farm: JH, *Hunter*, 339.

The Louse in the Fright: Author interview with Allen Saalburg.

"a lot of faith": SJP to LP, July 21, 1934.

"a young man": NW, "Proposal to the Guggenheim Foundation," LOA, 465.

167 "very few people": NW to F. Scott Fitzgerald, Sept. 11, 1934, LOA, 782. In 1934, FSF mentioned West's name in his introduction to a Modern Library edition of *The Great Gatsby*.

"a potential leader": F. Scott Fitzgerald to Guggenheim Foundation, Sept. 25, 1934, in Fitzgerald, *Correspondence of F. Scott Fitzgerald* (New York: Random House, 1980), 385.

"family powwow": JH, *Hunter*, 341.

168 "crossed the Rubicon": Ibid.

"Well, if that's": Ibid., 342.

"What do you think": Ibid., 340.

169 "AND FOR JESUS": SJP to LP, January 1935.
170 "Watch out": JH, *Hunter*, 344.

15. 14 GAY STREET

171 "the best value": RM, MSE, 197.
Gay Street: In 1833, the street was named for Sidney Howard Gay, a prominent historian and abolitionist. Some early residents of its row houses were
African-American servants employed by wealthy families living on Washington Square. Edmond Martin owned four row houses on Gay Street (nos. 14,
16, 17, and 18), along with three nearby buildings on Christopher Street and
a few others farther west near the corner of Grove and Bedford. The building at 17 Gay Street once housed a covert communications operation that
relayed messages between German and American Communists; twenty-
three-year-old writer Mary McCarthy lived at 18 Gay Street in 1936. In 1975,
David Ryan, an insurance company executive, moved into the basement
at 14 Gay Street, still a dump with leaks, water-warped walls, and wisteria
roots growing through the floor (which he covered with industrial carpeting). Over twenty-eight years, as Ryan's rent increased to $1,200 a month
from $340, he transformed the space into a jeweled nest. Matt Yust, a sec-
ond-floor tenant for almost twenty years, remembers that the Ryan apartment was full of candelabra and paintings, "tapestries and really nice Orien-
tal carpets. It was overdone but it had to be since it was a basement." (Matt
Yust interviewed by Rebecca DiLiberto.) In December 2003, a week after
a lengthy article about the apartment appeared in the real estate section
of the Sunday *New York Times*, Ryan perished in a deadly fire, apparently
the result of an electrical cord igniting a stack of newspapers and telephone
books. Today the apartment remains boarded up.
173 "Who lives here?": RM, MSE, 199.
"Paint your own floor": Ibid., 206.
"My, my": Ibid., 208.
174 "Hi-ya, babes": Ibid., 200.
175 "Go back to the farm": Author interview with Walter Lister, Jr.
"They were perfect": Author interview with Earl Wilson, Jr.
176 "They're Brazilians": RM, MSE, 221.
"Get rid of the Navy": Ibid.
Eileen's introduction to Morris: According to his family, they met at a social
event related to his job.
177 Jacobson family genealogy: Courtesy of Jennifer Cazier, Morris Jacobs's
granddaughter.
"He had always wanted": Author interview with Amy Jacobs Baxter, Morris's
daughter.
"a secretive guy": Author interview with Julius Jacobson, Morris's brother.

178 "always needing something": RM quoted in "Novelist Says City Has Lost Its Heart," *Cleveland Plain Dealer*, Mar. 20, 1959.

179 "We never met Morris": Author interview with Jack McKenney.

180 "without a dime": Author interview with Julius Jacobson.
"a serious drinker": Ibid.
"We kissed McKenney": Walter Lister to Joseph Cookman, Sept. 26, 1936. Courtesy of Walter Lister, Jr.
"always in too far": RM quoted in "Novelist Says City Has Lost Its Heart," *Cleveland Plain Dealer*, Mar. 20, 1959.
"going places": Walter Lister to Joseph Cookman, Sept. 26, 1936. Courtesy of Walter Lister, Jr.

181 "I just wanted to smash up things.": RM, *Love Story*, 49.
"She could have been": Walter Lister to Joseph Cookman, Sept. 26, 1936. Courtesy of Walter Lister, Jr.
"Hire a hall": RM, *Love Story*, 12.

182 "a former high functionary": FOIPA No. 1016168-000/190, FBI, New Haven field office, Apr. 31, 1951.
"Dear Sirs": RM to Katharine White, Oct. 12, 1936, *New Yorker* Records.
"considerably": Katharine White to RM, Oct. 16, 1936, *New Yorker* Records.
"the girl gets paid": Katharine White to Ik Shuman, Nov. 4, 1936, *New Yorker* Records.

183 "a stupid, tyrannical, and tactless old bitch": S. J. Perelman to Leila Hadley, June 16, 1957, Berg Collection, New York Public Library.

184 "some weighty glacier": Brendan Gill, *Here at The New Yorker* (New York: Random House, 1975), 289.
"but yours": St. Clair McKelway to RM, Nov. 1936, *New Yorker* Records.
"smells like a rubber band": RM, "Uneasy City," *New Yorker*, Dec. 19, 1936.

185 "thin if it kills me": RM to Katharine White, Nov. 1936, *New Yorker* Records.
"she's in the phone book": RM to St. Clair McKelway, Dec. 1936, *New Yorker* Records.

186 "we just stood": RM to St. Clair McKelway, Apr. 2, 1937, *New Yorker* Records.
"pretty much a lump": RM to Katharine White, Jan. 15, 1943, Bryn Mawr College Library.

16. CHEAPSVILLE

187 "Little, but Nice": *Los Angeles Times*, Mar. 11, 1932.

188 "Wait a minute": *The Jazz Singer*, 1927.
"seven suburbs": attributed to Alexander Woollcott, http://en.wikipedia.org.

189 "schmucks with Underwoods": James Silke, *Here's Looking at You, Kid: 50 Years of Fighting, Working, and Dreaming at Warner Bros.* (Boston: Little, Brown, 1976), 62.

189 "Millions are to be grabbed": Ben Hecht, *A Child of the Century* (New York: Simon & Schuster, 1954), 435.

190 "a large white house" : John O'Hara to F. Scott Fitzgerald, Apr. 1936, in John O'Hara, *Selected Letters of John O'Hara* (New York: Random House, 1978), 116–117.

"no worse than playing": National Education Television film, "On the Road to Miltown," 1966.

"movie feces": SJP, "And Did You Once See Irving Plain?" in *The Most of S. J. Perelman* (New York: Simon & Schuster, 1958), 600.

"he hasn't got": Joseph Bryan III, *Merry Gentlemen (and One Lady)* (New York: Atheneum, 1985), 112.

"poops": Dorothy Parker to Alexander Woollcott, January 1935, in *The Portable Dorothy Parker* (New York: Penguin, 2006), 605.

191 "I haven't any money": NW to SJP, spring 1935, quoted in Martin, *Nathanael West*, 266.

192 "leave him alone": Ibid., 268.

"beetle-brained wind-suckers": SJP to Betty White Johnston, Oct. 17, 1931, in *Selected Letters*, 8.

LP opinion of Hollywood: EW, *Thirties*, 313.

193 "There was hell to pay": Quoted in Diane Johnson, *Dashiell Hammett*, 123.

"casual ladies": Lillian Hellman, *Pentimento*, in *Three* (New York: Little, Brown, 1979), 472.

"so I could kill him": Albert Hackett interview with Joan Mellen, *Hellman and Hammett, The Legendary Passion of Lillian Hellman and Dashiell Hammett* (New York: HarperCollins, 1996), 95. In Hellman's 1936 play *Days to Come*, one of the characters suggests LP. Cora Rodman, like Laura, collects animal bric-a-brac and has an oddly intimate relationship with her brother, described as her best friend. The play ran for six performances.

194 "After twelve hours": LP to Dashiell Hammett, July 27, 1935. Courtesy of Peter Feibleman.

"well and sober": LP to Lillian Hellman, July 1935. Courtesy of Peter Feibleman.

197 "to die": NW, DOL, LOA 242.

"I've written a book": NW to JH, fall 1935, Beinecke.

"the Indies": NW to JH, summer 1933, in JH, *Kenyon Review*.

198 "the twin halves": NW, "Bird and Bottle," *Pacific Weekly: A Western Journal of Fact and Opinion*, Nov. 10, 1936, in Jay Martin, ed., *Nathanael West: A Collection of Critical Essays* (Englewood Cliffs, NJ: Prentice-Hall, 1971), 132. "Bird and Bottle" is one of two stories West published during his lifetime; the other is "Business Deal," *Americana*, Oct. 1933.

199 "Paris will burn": NW, "Burn the Cities," LOA, 458.

"Dear John": Quoted in Herrmann, *S. J. Perelman*, 243.

200 "smirky, sneaky": SJP to LP, Aug. 10, 1934.

"nothing to say": NW to SJP, Dec. 1936, John Hay Library, Brown.

"rot in hell": Ibid.

"Here's the twisteroo": NW to SJP, quoted in Jay Martin, *Nathanael West*, 269.

201 "I hate shrikes": Lester Cole, *Hollywood Red* (Palo Alto, CA: Ramparts Press, 1981), 148.

203 "students of amnesia": *New York World Telegram*, Aug. 11, 1936.

"full of all kinds": NW to SJP, Mar. 1937.

204 "his truculent": Ibid.

205 "grade-C scripts": Matthew Josephson interview, in Martin, *Nathanael West*, 405.

"set the industry buzzing": *New York Times*, Oct. 4, 1936.

"Who's responsible": Cole, *Hollywood Red*, 149.

206 "The heavy hand": *Washington Post*, Nov. 11, 1936.

"It's a long way": JS, *Very Good Land*, 29. The setting for Sanford's second novel, *The Old Man's Place*, was partly derived from observations collected during his summer with West in the Adirondacks.

"a man embarrassed": Ibid.

"but your note": NW to JS, 1934, Mugar.

207 "duck-shooting": JS, *Very Good Land*, 33.

bachelor dinners: Before long Scotty would meet and marry another Paramount writer, Marguerite Roberts. In 1938 they were employed by MGM, where Sanford got his first screen credit, on the Clark Gable film *Honky Tonk*.

For stories about Stanley Rose, see Gene Fowler, "A Night Among the Book Sellers," unpublished story, courtesy of Howard Prouty, www.redinkbooks. com. Rose was rumored to have gotten his start as a bookseller by swindling a wealthy Santa Barbara widow out of her husband's valuable first editions. "Madame, it's a shame. All these books are just a lotta dust catchers." Paying $218 for the library, he hired a van to cart off the thousands of books and was able to live on the profits for several years.

"'Well,' he replied": William Saroyan, *Sons Come and Go, Mothers Hang In Forever* (New York: McGraw-Hill, 1976), 71. For a brief time Stanley Rose acted as Saroyan's literary agent.

"He was a sonofabitch": Yetive Moss quoted in Ben Reuven, "From the Tables Down at Mussos," *Los Angeles Times*, Nov. 7, 1976.

208 Stanley Rose literary salon: EW called his 1941 book about six California novelists *The Boys in the Back Room: Notes on California Novelists*. The title was said to be inspired by Stanley Rose's "Algonquin Round Table West."

17. SISTER EILEEN AND MRS. WHITE

210 "robber barons": Matthew Josephson, *The Robber Barons: The Great American Capitalists, 1861–1901* (New York: Harcourt, Brace, 1934), was a staple of American history.

210   "mighty brain": RM to Richard Bransten, 1937, FOIPA.

"great fun": Author interview with Carl Josephson.

"I fell for her": St. Clair McKelway interviewed by Jay Martin.

211   "she could do better": Ibid.

Eileen's writing efforts: In January 1937, Ruth unsuccessfully prodded Eileen to write about her job at the Cleveland credit bureau. Finally Ruth herself wrote the story, "It's an Ill Wind," which appeared in the Sept. 7, 1940, issue of *The New Yorker*. In early 1938, while Eileen was involved with St. Clair McKelway, she began working on another story, subject unknown, that Ruth judged funny but aimless and in need of polishing. Katharine White, excited over the prospect of a bonus McKenney, reminded her to "send me that story by your sister" (Katharine White to RM, Jan. 26, 1938, *New Yorker* Records). But Eileen apparently put it aside, because no further references appear in the White-McKenney correspondence.

"Blond, bland": *Time*, Nov. 11, 1946.

212   "I don't want": Brendan Gill, *Here at The New Yorker*, 148.

"Don't play God": Ibid., 96.

New Yorker favorite son: Gardner Botsford, *A Life of Privilege, Mostly* (New York: St. Martin's, 2003), 225; Brendan Gill, *Here at The New Yorker*, 144.

213   McKelway marriages: A brief teenage marriage, spouse unknown, 1924; Estelle Cassidy, 1929, which produced a son, St. Clair, Jr.; Ann Honeycutt, 1935; Martha Stephenson, 1944, ex-wife of screen actor Victor Mature; Maeve Brennan, 1954, a *New Yorker* writer.

"ever a gentleman": Ann Honeycutt quoted in Harrison Kinney, *James Thurber: His Life and Times* (New York: Holt, 1995), 567.

"Katharine White discovered": Ibid.

214   "a swell writer": Katharine White to RM, Jan. 28, 1938, *New Yorker* Records.

"Full of irrelevancies": Katharine White to RM, May 6, 1937, *New Yorker* Records.

"really *too* preposterous": Katharine White to RM, Dec. 12, 1944, *New Yorker* Records.

215   "Make an effort": Gustave Lobrano to RM, Jan. 16, 1942, *New Yorker* Records.

"both unbelievably bad": William Shawn to Gustave Lobrano, Nov. 11, 1941, *New Yorker* Records.

217   "What gall": RM, *Love Story*, 13.

218   "mine, all mine": Ibid.

"His wife's in Reno": Ibid., 15.

219   "I understand you *write*": Ibid., 16.

"Who are you?": Ibid.

220   "revolting": Ibid., 20.

221   "He won't write": Ibid., 21.

M. J. Brandenstein and Co.: MJB is now owned by the Sara Lee Corporation.

"spectacularly thin": Stanley Burnshaw to Hazel Rowley, July 31, 1992, quoted in Hazel Rowley, *Christina Stead: A Biography* (New York: Henry Holt, 1993), 277.

"I was always attracted": Christina Stead, *I'm Dying Laughing: The Humourist* (New York: Holt, 1986), 301. Christina Stead met Ruth and Richard Bransten around 1938 and remained a friend throughout their lives. She and her husband, William Blake, a Communist Party member, shared the Branstens' leftist views. *I'm Dying Laughing* is an undisguised portrait of the warring Branstens, written over a period of several decades and based on personal knowledge in addition to Ruth's letters. Stead admired Ruth's strength, but felt appalled at her emotional excesses and copious greed. ("I never thought of her as anything but Gargantua.") In a 1973 radio interview, Stead said the book showed the passion of an American couple in midcentury, "who wanted to be on the side of the angels, good Communists, good people, and also to be very rich. Well, of course, they came to a bad end" (Preface to *I'm Dying Laughing*, x). The book was published three years after Stead's death to avoid possible libel suits. Her best-known novel is *The Man Who Loved Children*.

Louise Rosenberg Bransten: The Rosenberg fortune, amassed by packing and shipping California dried fruit, was the largest enterprise of its kind in the world with branches in sixty-five countries. Dubbed the Apricot Heiress by the San Francisco press, Louise was supremely photogenic, with green eyes and strawberry-blond hair. News photos of her taken years later, when she was in the headlines accused of being a Red spy, show a beautiful woman bearing a strong resemblance to Rita Hayworth. Independently wealthy after her father's death, she and her husband lived in a style typical of the aristocratic society in which they were reared. In their San Francisco apartment, with a live-in cook and maid, she had a baby and he worked at Rosenberg Fruit, although his main activity was writing short stories "full of bitterness against the hypocritical rich Jewish society in which he had been brought up," Louise recalled. (FOIPA No. 1016168-000/190. Excerpt from Louise Bransten unpublished autobiography, Oct. 21, 1945, furnished to Soviet Vice Consul Mikhail Vavilav, and subsequently turned over to the New Haven Field Division of the FBI.) Only twenty-nine at the time of her divorce, she subsequently had close associations with notables such as singer Paul Robeson, the physicist J. Robert Oppenheimer, and Bartley Crum, an attorney known for defending several of the "Hollywood Ten" writers subpoenaed by the HUAC in 1947.

222   "In a better world": Stead, *I'm Dying Laughing*, 271.

Richard Bransten's first book: Bruce Minton [pseud.], *The Fascist Menace in the U.S.A.* (San Francisco: Underhill Publishing, 1934).

"You had just scored": Stead, *I'm Dying Laughing*, 111.

"a common tie": RM to Richard Bransten, 1937, FOIPA No. 1016168-000/190.

18. DESTINED TO BE A HEROINE

224 "sticking-out ears": Author interview with Hillary Hillson, daughter of Thomas Jacobs/Patrick Bransten.

"Of course": Brendan Gill, *Here at The New Yorker*, 115.

226 FBI surveillance: Report of FBI investigation, Feb. 3, 1943, FOIPA No. 1016168-000/190.

"some good old-fashioned": RM to Richard Bransten, fall 1937, FOIPA.

"mild": St. Clair McKelway interviewed by Jay Martin.

227 Instances of Ruth McKenney breakdowns: In 1945, an FBI informant reported her hospitalization for a nervous breakdown, which Richard Bransten attributed to overuse of the over the counter amphetamine Benzedrine. A few years later, before moving to Europe, she was hospitalized in Norwalk, Conn. [FOIPA.]

"Eileen had": RM to Matthew and Hannah Josephson, Nov. 1937, Beinecke.

"spreads boredom": Stead, *I'm Dying Laughing*, 110.

"a third-rate whore": Ibid., 54.

228 "a splendid Communist": RM to Richard Bransten, fall 1937, FOIPA No. 1016168-000/190.

"I never meant": RM, *All About Eileen*, 211, 234.

229 Charles Pearce: McKenney's friendship with Matthew Josephson most likely brought her to the attention of Pearce, who was Josephson's longtime editor at Harcourt.

"grand": Katharine White to RM, Aug. 29, 1938, *New Yorker* Records.

Industrial Valley: Published by Harcourt in February 1939, the book was generally well received as "a very lively piece of reporting" (*New York Times*, Feb. 16, 1939). When Harcourt insisted she add a note explaining that some names had been changed to protect privacy, she protested the book was "a true story." But Harcourt released the book as fiction. Malcolm Cowley in the *New Republic* applauded it as a novel based on fact. In 1943 McKenney published *Jake Home*, a five-hundred-page "proletarian novel" whose central character is a Communist union worker. Reviewers were cool, sales mediocre. Once World War II began, such Depression fiction became passé.

"Understand she's using": Harold Ross to Gustave Lobrano, Jan. 1939, *New Yorker* Records.

230 "honest to goodness": *Ironwood* (Michigan) *Daily Globe* and other syndicated papers, Nov. 18, 1938.

231 "destined to be a heroine": Ibid.

"as richly American": *Forum*, Sept. 1938.

"There is something": *New York Times*, July 23, 1938.

"hoydenish nostalgia": *New York Post*, Aug. 8, 1938.

"always contained a string": Author interview with Richard Selvey.

"It definitely wasn't": Author interview with Ruth Beebe Hill.

232 "My Dad was very": Author interview with Jack McKenney.
"I had to doctor": RM, "In a Mirror Darkly," *New Yorker*, Jan. 9, 1943.

233 Ruth's pet expressions: *MSE*, vii; Ruth McKenney various correspondence; St. Clair McKelway interviewed by Jay Martin, Mar. 22, 1967.
"wicked old propaganda": RM to St. Clair McKelway, Feb. 24, 1938, *New Yorker* Records.

234 "mean things": RM, *All About Eileen*, 229.

235 "dawg": RM to Matthew and Hannah Josephson, Nov. 1937, Beinecke.

19. AN ARSONIST'S GUIDE TO LOS ANGELES

236 "It isn't funny": NW to EW, Apr. 6, 1939, LOA, 792.
"not for me": NW to SJP, Mar. 1937, John Hay Library, Brown.

237 "just a skin": Ibid.
"Stage nine": NW, DOL, LOA, 241.
"few things are sadder": Ibid., 243.

238 "like nails": Ibid., 251.
"What a quiff!": Ibid., 362.
"All their lives": Ibid., 380.
"slaved and saved": Ibid., 381.

239 "cripples": W. H. Auden, "Interlude: West's Disease," in Siegel, *Critical Essays*, 121.
"fingeroo": NW, DOL, LOA, 246. One of West's favorite words was "fingeroo."
"for there was not a dream": Ibid., 326.

240 "shiny as a new spoon": Ibid., 281.
"any dream": Ibid., 293.
"cablegrams": Malcolm Cowley, *New York Times Book Review*, May 12, 1957.
"private and unfunny jokes": NW to FSF, Apr. 5, 1939, LOA, 791.
"I do it my way": Ibid.
"I do consider myself": NW to George Milburn, Apr. 6, 1939, Huntington.
"I am not a humorous writer": Ibid.
Character names: West sometimes named characters for his friends: Albert Hackett (surname of hero Tod Hackett), Claude Binyon (first name of the Claude Estee character), Gordon Kahn (Kahn's Persian Palace Theatre, scene of the big riot). Stanley Rose was singled out for exceptional billing, perhaps West's way of publicly putting paid to an important debt. Abe Kusich's business card endorses the dwarf bookie as "'the Lloyds of Hollywood' . . . Stanley Rose." DOL, LOA, 244.

241 "this lunatic scheherazade": Saxe Commins to BC, May 17, 1938, Random House Archives, Columbia University Libraries Special Collections.

242 "Definitely accept": BC to NW, May 17, 1938, Huntington.
Bennett Cerf's publishing background: After graduating from the Colum-

bia School of Journalism, and a brief career on Wall Street, Cerf joined Boni & Liveright when it was still a classy place to work. As a vice president of the company, he realized the firm was losing money despite impressive books. Shrewdly, he and his friend Donald Klopfer purchased Liveright's distinguished imprint "Modern Library of the World's Best Books" and went into business for themselves in 1927. In the wake of Random House's first bestseller, James Joyce's banned *Ulysses*, its list began to grow with the addition of Eugene O'Neill, William Faulkner, and Sinclair Lewis. By the late thirties, Random was becoming a robust rival to Alfred Knopf and Simon & Schuster.

242   "Please plant": SJP to BC, Feb. 4, 1940, in *Selected Letters*, 22.
      "a pinchpenny": SJP to BC, Mar. 3, 1940, in *Selected Letters*, 25.
      "America's Sweetheart": SJP to James Thurber, Mar. 5, 1946, in *Selected Letters*, 67.

243   Barnaby Chirp: "No Dearth of Mirth—Fill Out the Coupon," *New Yorker*, Dec. 22, 1945.
      "the little Lesbian interlude": BC to NW, May 31, 1938, Huntington.
      Cerf's critical remarks: Ibid.
      "lesbian stuff": NW to BC, May 1938, LOA, 783.

244   "a great deal of improvement": NW to BC, July 11, 1938, LOA, 785.
      "1939 is so far": NW to BC, May 1938, LOA, 783.
      "So cry a little": William Saroyan, *Sons Come and Go, Mothers Hang In Forever* (New York: McGraw-Hill, 1976), 108.
      "it was a big act": Author interview with Yetive Moss.

245   "glean some philosophical pearls": Budd Schulberg, *Writers in America: The Four Seasons of Success* (New York: Stein & Day, 1983), 165.
      "a special relationship": Author interview with Budd Schulberg.
      "Pep would rather": Budd Schulberg, *Writers in America*, 166.
      "I don't ever recall": Author interview with Yetive Moss.
      "I would get a rundown": Jo Conway to James F. Light, Jan. 15, 1958, quoted in Light, *Nathanael West*, 147.
      "If he was wet": Wells Root, "Notes on Nathanael West," Huntington.

246   "need for attack": JH to Richard Gehman, Aug. 9, 1947, Beinecke.
      "fled as often": JH, *Hunter*, 344.
      "dull as hell": NW to SJP, Mar. 1937, John Hay Library, Brown.

247   "Oh, you should meet": Author interview with Joseph Schrank.
      "to lay an American Indian": Joseph Schrank unpublished autobiography, 293.

248   "You wouldn't believe": Ibid.

249   "You are an artist": EW to NW, 1939, quoted in Dardis, *Some Time in the Sun*, 156.

250   "I like working": Whitney F. Bolton to James F. Light, Sept. 20, 1957, quoted in Light, *Nathanael West*, 152.

"Hollywood": Garson Kanin, "West Out West," *American Film*, Mar. 1976.

251 "These Iowa people": John O'Hara, *Hope of Heaven* (New York: Harcourt, Brace, 1938), 411.

"frightened to death": Ibid., 418.

"rattled like hell": NW to Jo Conway, Aug. 16, 1938, Huntington.

252 "never put money": Author interview with Sarah Gold.

"just fooled away": NW to Jo Conway, Sept. 19, 1938, LOA, 786, Huntington.

"a kindhearted little Jewish woman": Author interview with Joseph Schrank.

"with both revulsion": JH to James F. Light, Oct. 22, 1952, quoted in Light, *Nathanael West*, 152.

"spicy story": James Farrell to Cyril Schneider, Mar. 25, 1952, quoted in Light, *Nathanael West*, 153.

253 "I won't leave": NW to Jo Conway, Oct. 21, 1938, LOA, 788.

"Sonofabitch": Author interview with Joseph Schrank.

"Everything is O.K.": NW to Jo Conway, Sept. 19, 1938, LOA, 786.

"bad": NW to EW, Apr. 6, 1939, LOA, 793.

"quite hideous women": JH to Richard Gehman, Aug. 9, 1947, Beinecke.

254 "inventive enough": Saxe Commins to BC, May 17, 1938, Random House archives, Columbia University Libraries Special Collections.

"a little too pretentious": NW to BC, June 7, 1938, LOA, 784.

biblical titles: Exodus 10:3–6, 13–15; Revelation 9:3–9.

255 *Good Hunting* reviews: *Wall Street Journal*, Nov. 23, 1938; *New York Times*, Nov. 22, 1938.

"hunkered down": Author interview with Joseph Schrank.

"a rain of stones": NW to EW, Apr. 6, 1939, LOA, 792.

"Pep decided": Author interview with Joseph Schrank.

"batted over the head": NW to EW, Apr. 6, 1939, LOA, 792.

20. STINKOLAS, HUMDINGERS, LOLLAPALOOZAS, TWISTEROOS

256 "a good fellow": NW to BC, Jan. 6, 1939, Huntington.

"what's the jacket": NW to Saxe Commins, Feb. 14, 1939, LOA, 790.

"really high-priced artist": BC to NW, 1938, in Martin, *Nathanael West*, 322.

"serious in implication": NW to Saxe Commins, Jan. 6, 1939, Huntington.

West's dislike of DOL jacket: Author interview with Budd Schulberg; Schulberg, *Writers in America*, 176.

"I'm going to kill": Ibid.

257 "bait for vampire bats": NW to BC, Apr. 1939, quoted in Martin, *Nathanael West*, 323.

"just as stupid": Ibid.

258 "swell": NW to Malcolm Cowley, May 11, 1939, LOA, 795.

"there is nothing": NW to George Milburn, 1939, quoted in Gehman, Introduction, DOL, xx.

The Day of the Locust reviews: *New York Times Book Review*, May 21, 1939; *New Yorker*, May 20, 1939; *Time*, June 19, 1939; *Books*, May 21, 1939; *Los Angeles Times*, May 28, 1939.

259 "hasty, disjointed writing," *Saturday Review of Literature*, May 20, 1939. The novel was listed in the table of contents as *The Years of the Locust*.

"sordid and senseless": *New Republic*, July 26, 1939.

"Nothing could make me": JS to Nonie and Jesse Greenstein, Aug. 2, 1939, Mugar. W. H. Auden's 1957 essay "Interlude: West's Disease" echoes some of Sanford's remarks. Auden presented West as a "self-centered" writer whose fictional cripples were a projection of self-hatred.

"So far the box score": NW to F. Scott Fitzgerald, June 30, 1939, LOA, 795.

260 "very emphatic terms": BC to NW, June 16, 1939, Huntington.

"By God": BC to NW, quoted in Gehman, Introduction, DOL, xi.

261 "probably the best book": BC, *At Random*, 119. Bennett Cerf's first wife, the actress Sylvia Sydney, had once been the mistress of Budd Schulberg's father, B. P. Schulberg.

"literature boys": NW to EW, Apr. 6, 1939, LOA, 793.

"the most indisputably Jewish": Harold Bloom's Introduction to *Nathanael West's Miss Lonelyhearts* (New York: Chelsea House, 1987), 1.

"the last person": JH notes on Nathanael West, 1947, Beinecke.

"bright boy": Ibid.

262 Forbidden themes in West's fiction: Certain areas of his life were impossible to touch upon, or even to acknowledge. One is his Jewish background and the rich source material offered by the Wallenstein and Weinstein families; for another, his use of cars as a weapon to release emotions, which resulted in an unusual kind of road rage: vehicular homicide with a ton of steel. The other unmentionable subject is homosexuality, which occurs repeatedly in his work. He was unwilling or unable to delve into his psyche and come to terms with the homoerotic undercurrents that, refusing to be contained, bubbled up from the depths and pumped throughout his writings.

"What a sweet pair of fairies": NW, *Miss Lonelyhearts*, LOA, 115.

"homosexualistic tendencies": Ibid., 77.

"Do you know": NW, DOL, LOA, 342.

263 "definite flop": NW to EW, June 30, 1939, LOA, 796.

"pure, unadulterated": NW to SJP, Oct. 1939, in Martin, *Nathanael West*, 365.

264 "clearly in my mind": NW to BC, Feb. 14, 1940, Huntington.

"make us both rich": NW to BC, Aug. 2, 1939, Huntington.

"You ask": BC to NW, Feb. 23, 1940, Huntington.

265 "for the rest of your natural life": BC to NW, May 17, 1938, Huntington.

"a little white farmhouse": BC to NW, Feb. 23, 1940, Huntington.

Random House advances: They ranged from around $250 to $1,000 or $1,500 for a multibook deal, or to sign an important author like Eugene O'Neill.

"hard letter": NW to BC, Mar. 11, 1940, LOA, 799.

"a tremendous sinking": Ibid.

266 "one foot on the ladder": NW to SJP, Oct. 1939, in Martin, *Nathanael West*, xxi.

21. EILEEN IN DISNEYLAND

267 "a disgusting little concrete": RM, *Love Story*, 174.

Eileen at Disney: Company records confirm her employment in the promotion and story research departments, but no details of her exact duties survive. Her desire to learn cel animation comes from anecdotal information supplied by West family sources.

268 Thomas Jacobs's love of sweets: Author interview with daughter Hillary Hillson.

269 "any amount": RM, New Masses Emergency Committee form letter, Apr. 15, 1939, FOIPA.

"sister Eileen funny book": RM to Matthew and Hannah Josephson, spring 1938.

"sort of oblique": RM to Matthew and Hannah Josephson, 1939, Beinecke.

"busted Branstens": RM to Matthew and Hannah Josephson, spring 1938, Beinecke.

270 "death": RM to Matthew and Hannah Josephson, 1939, Beinecke.

"totally cold": RM to Katharine White, Jan. 15, 1943, Bryn Mawr College Library.

"a morgue": Walt Edey telegram to BC, 1939, Random House archives, Columbia University Libraries Special Collections.

272 "homework": EM to RM, *Love Story*, 175.

"the homely touch": Ibid., 176.

"Don't laugh": Ibid.

"Eileen tried": Author interview with Budd Schulberg.

"It's funny": NW and Boris Ingster, *Before the Fact*, LOA, 701.

273 "Nonsense": Ibid., 700.

"a nest of Chinese boxes": NW, DOL, LOA, 242.

274 "an ointment": Matthew Josephson journals, 1938–39, Beinecke.

"beware": NW to Malcolm Cowley, May 11, 1939, LOA, 794.

"a place for the fellow": NW to Jack Conroy, June 30, 1939, quoted in Gehman, Introduction, DOL, ix.

275 "Nihilistic pessimism": JH, *Kenyon Review*.

"about the most pessimistic": Robert Coates to Cyril Schneider, June 6, 1952, quoted in Light, *Nathanael West*, 128.

275 "no interest": JS, *Very Good Land*, 168.

"only a windmill": RM to Katharine White, Oct. 21, 1946, *New Yorker* Records.

"Nice guy": Wells Root interview, in Martin, *Nathanael West*, 385.

West's driving psychology: Social psychologists use the term *cognitive dissonance* to describe the rationalization of irrational behavior.

276 "this is *really*": SJP to Ruth and Augustus Goetz, Dec. 4, 1939, in *Selected Letters*, 20.

277 "it isn't going to be led": Ibid.

Perelman's play: *The Night Before Christmas* opened to poor reviews in April 1941 and closed after twenty-two performances. The 1942 movie version, *Larceny, Inc.*, featured Edward G. Robinson and Jane Wyman; the story was recycled by Woody Allen in *Small Time Crooks* (2000).

Before the Fact: In crime fiction, Francis Iles's (Anthony Berkeley Cox) innovation was to reveal the killer at the outset.

278 "sore as hell": Wells Root, "Notes on Nathanael West," Huntington.

279 "flat on his pratt": SJP to Augustus Goetz, Jan. 27, 1940, in *Selected Letters*, 20.

280 "He had stopped": Author interview with Frances Kroll Ring.

281 "he's long-winded": F. Scott Fitzgerald, *The Notebooks of F. Scott Fitzgerald*, Matthew J. Bruccoli, ed. (New York: Harcourt Brace Jovanovich, 1978), 316–317.

"we had no need": Ibid.

"He was fond": Author interview with Frances Kroll Ring.

"morbid as hell": Fitzgerald, *Notebooks*, 316–317.

"foolish passion": Ibid.

"Sid knows": Ibid.

"He thought": Author interview with Frances Kroll Ring.

"outspoken and talkative": Wells Root, "Notes on Nathanael West," Huntington.

282 Wells Root memories of EM: *Los Angeles Times*, June 22, 1975.

"the next best thing": JH to James F. Light, Oct. 22, 1952, Beinecke.

"a serious guy": St. Clair McKelway interviewed by Jay Martin.

283 "I don't think": BC to NW, May 1, 1940, Huntington.

"strikingly attractive": Author interview with Budd Schulberg.

"hearty, warm": Schulberg, *Writers in America*, 182.

"Major George": JS, *Very Good Land*, 168–169.

"only a third-rate Huxley": JS to Nonie and Jesse Greenstein, Aug. 3, 1939, Mugar.

284 "I gave three": NW to Bob Brown, Mar. 21, 1940, Morris Library, Southern Illinois University.

"Pep's decision": Author interview with Budd Schulberg.

"Mr. John Sydney McKenney": Wedding announcement, Edmund Wilson Papers, Beinecke.

285 "Providing I'm not": EM to BC, May 18, 1940, Huntington.
"a gem of purest": NW to BC, Apr. 27, 1940, Huntington.
"so far we haven't": EM to Anna Weinstein, July 1940, in Martin, *Nathanael West*, 378.

286 "This is a story": NW, "Untitled Outline," LOA, 755.
"Are you lonely": Ibid., 757.
"no shrinking violet": Ibid., 759.

287 "The most important American": RM, *Love Story*, 176.

22. TOGETHER

288 "Mother West": EM to Anna Weinstein, Sept. 1940, in Martin, *Nathanael West*, 383.

289 "Please send": RM, *Love Story*, 176.
"My sister Eileen": RM, *The McKenneys Carry On*, 31.
"rose bushes": Ibid., 195.
My Sister Eileen profits: Apparently Eileen received no official share of the profits from *My Sister Eileen*, *The McKenneys Carry On*, or the stage version of *My Sister Eileen*. On the other hand, Ruth and Richard had generously supported her on an as-needed basis, paying for major expenses like psychotherapy and the Reno divorce.

291 "barbecued steaks": Jerome Chodorov, "Memories," unpublished manuscript, 1982, 1.
"Plots were my": Ibid.
Boris Ingster (born Boris Azarkh) came from a wealthy, cultured family. His father owned a lumber empire; his older brother Alexander Granovsky founded the Moscow State Yiddish Theater.

292 "this was the place": Author interview with Henry Bruch.
"enough energy": NW to LP, 1939, in Martin, *Nathanael West*, 366.

293 "who had two answers": NW and Boris Ingster, *A Cool Million* screen treatment, LOA, 748.
Fate of *A Cool Million* treatment: Columbia's efforts to turn the treatment into a screenplay, as a possible vehicle for Bob Hope or Eddie Cantor, or even as a comic musical, ended in failure. The property was eventually dropped.
Fate of the *Bird in Hand* treatment: A 1945 reader report stated: "This is a story about a turkey—and a more appropriate bird could not be found to symbolize this property."

294 "will someday": NW to Jerome Mayer, July 1938, quoted in Dardis, *Some Time in the Sun*, 155.
"I was never so outraged": RM, *Love Story*, 177.

295 "well-built": Joseph A. Fields and Jerome Chodorov, *My Sister Eileen: A Comedy in Three Acts* (New York: Dramatists Play Service, 1941), 7.
"It looks as if": Ibid., 84.

295 "I wonder": RM, *Love Story*, 177.

296 "I just don't": Ibid., 180.

"They were looking": Author interview with Jo Ann Sayers.

297 "slightly unkempt": Wells Root, "Notes on Nathanael West," Huntington.

298 "a wonderful thing": NW to Jerome Mayer, July 1938, quoted in Dardis, *Some Time in the Sun*, 155.

299 "hold a dinner party": Wells Root, *Los Angeles Times*, Jan. 22, 1970.

"your friend Pep": Author interview with Joe Schrank.

"stark raving nuts": Author interview with Sarah Schrank Gold.

23. EL CENTRO

300 "the vile, dank hole": RM, "In a Mirror Darkly," *New Yorker*, Jan. 9, 1943.

"eerie": RM, *Love Story*, 192.

"Do you think": Ibid., 194.

302 "The last time": "The Last Time I Saw Paris," music by Jerome Kern, lyrics by Oscar Hammerstein (1940). Although not composed for the film, the song was performed by Ann Sothern in *Lady Be Good* (1941) and won the Oscar for Best Original Song.

305 "It was moving": "Inquisition by Coroner's Jury," Imperial County, CA, Dec. 24, 1940, 8.

306 "to see if": Ibid., 10.

Death statistics: Imperial County death certificates. No autopsies were performed.

Crash-site photo: "Where Two Died, Three Met Injuries," *Imperial Valley Press*, Dec. 23, 1940.

308 "But John": JS, *Very Good Land*, 191.

"a bowl broken": Ibid., 190.

"broke the news": Ibid., 191.

"only Jews": JS, *A Walk in the Fire* (Santa Rosa, CA: Black Sparrow Press, 1989), 116.

"You're kidding": Jerome Chodorov, "Memories," 15.

"sinking our own ship": Ibid.

309 "The opening night": Author interview with Jo Ann Sayers.

My Sister Eileen reviews: New York papers, Dec. 27, 1940.

"Nobody was more": RM, "In a Mirror Darkly," *New Yorker*, Jan. 9, 1943.

My Sister Eileen stage, film, and television productions: *My Sister Eileen* (Broadway, Dec. 26, 1940–Jan. 16, 1943), directed by George S. Kaufman. Jo Ann Sayers (Eileen Sherwood), Shirley Booth (Ruth Sherwood), Morris Carnovsky. *My Sister Eileen* (Columbia Pictures, 1942), directed by Alexander Hall. Janet Blair (Eileen Sherwood), Rosalind Russell (Ruth Sherwood), Brian Aherne. *My Sister Eileen* (musical, Columbia Pictures, 1955), directed by Richard Quine. Janet Leigh (Eileen Sherwood), Betty Garrett

(Ruth Sherwood), Jack Lemmon, Bob Fosse. *My Sister Eileen* (TV series 1960–1961, CBS). Shirley Bonne (Eileen Sherwood), Elaine Stritch (Ruth Sherwood).

"We had been living": Inquest, 8.

311 "We the undersigned": Ibid., cover page.

312 "We would have had": Author interview with April Franzino.

313 West-McKenney grave: The Mount Zion website, www.mountzioncemetery .com, lists Nathaniel (*sic*) West among its notable burials, along with Lorenz Hart and the last survivor of the Triangle Shirtwaist Factory fire. According to cemetery records, the West-McKenney grave has received no care since 1993, neglect that was confirmed in 2005 when the author's assistant, Rebecca DiLiberto, cut away the brush to photograph the headstone.

West memorial essay: SJP to JS, Jan. 11, 1941, in *Selected Letters*, 37. John Sanford's essay appeared in *Screen Writer*, Dec. 1946.

"a debacle of metal": JS, *Very Good Land*, 191.

314 John Sanford's conversation with his father: Ibid., 192–193.

ACKNOWLEDGMENTS

One February afternoon in 1983, I sat at a kitchen table on New York's West End Avenue opposite an eighty-one-year-old screenwriter named Joseph Schrank. I had come to interview him about Dorothy Parker. Both he and Mrs. Parker had lived in Bucks County, Pennsylvania, in the 1930s, and I was hoping for some fresh anecdotes for my new book. To my surprise, Mr. Schrank was little concerned about Parker but instead began describing another writer, Nathanael West, who had lived there as well, with whom it turned out he had once coauthored a Broadway play. By the time I left I had learned nothing new about my subject but a great deal about Nathanael West. Without knowing it, this was my first step toward writing West's life; I later learned that Schrank was not the only one with such powerful recollections. In Bucks County lived others, now gone, eager to gossip about West's problematic driving, his spoiled dogs, his delusions of being a great hunter.

In addition to Joe Schrank, I am indebted to many, many others.

Special thanks to professional family historian Pamela Turner for her dedication in conducting my Ohio research. I was lucky to have her encyclopedic knowledge of the neighborhoods where Eileen McKenney grew up, as well as her insights and unstinting legwork.

Once again I am obliged to Patricia O'Toole and the Hertog Research Assistantship Program in the Graduate Writing Division of the School of Arts at Columbia University. A biographer could ask for no more tireless and enthusiastic an assistant than Rebecca DiLiberto.

A superb genealogist, Darcie Hind Posz, is responsible for practically everything I know about the family backgrounds of my subjects. James Ross kindly made available "The Jarcho/Wallenstein Family History."

A crowd of splendid biographers preceded me: Linda H. Davis, David Goodrich, Dorothy Herrmann, Elinor Langer, James F. Light, Jay Martin, Joan Mellen, Carl Rollyson, Mathilde Roza, Hazel Rowley, and Gary Scharnhorst. Their publications were a constant reminder of how often we stand on the shoulders of other writers.

Also indispensable to my project were numerous scholars and writers: Marlene Coburn, Peter Feibleman, Joanne Greenberg, Robert Hethmon, James Hutchisson, Tony Kahn, Daniel Nelson, Marilyn Nissenson, Lisa Paddock, Anne Pender, Joanna Rapf, David Roessel, Douglas H. Shepard, Alix Kates Shulman, David Stenn, Daniel Walden, Tom Weaver, and Ben Yagoda.

The footprints that people leave behind—their papers, letters, diaries, and memorabilia—often wind up in university or company archives, where they form precious resources for biographers. I wish to thank: Judy James of the Akron Summit County (Ohio) Public Library; Stephen Crook of the Berg Collection at the New York Public Library; Robert F. Fitzgerald, associate registrar of Brown University; Sean Noel, Laura Russo, and Maria Morelli of the Howard Gotlieb Archival Research Center, Boston University; Holly Snyder and Raymond Butti, Jr., of the John Hay Library, Brown University; Marianne Hansen of the Bryn Mawr College Library; Angie White and Trevor Levi of the Harcourt Records Center; Gayle Richardson of the Huntington Library; Max Rudin of the Library of America; Birgitta Bond of the James A. Michener Art Museum; Connie Johnston of the Mishawaka-Penn-Harris (Indiana) Public Library; Nena Couch of the Theatre Institute at Ohio State University; Tara Wenger of the Harry Ransom Center at the University of Texas at Austin; Susanne

Belovari, Michelle Romero, and Melissa Griffin of the Tufts University Digital Collections and Archives; Amy Miller of Tufts University Alumni Office; Lilace Hatayama at the Charles E. Young Research Library, UCLA; Maureen Delovio and Cecilia DiCarlo of the West Warwick (Rhode Island) Public Library; and Karen Spicher and Graham Sherriff of the Beinecke Rare Book and Manuscript Library at Yale University.

Two first-rate researchers, Carolyn Garner and Carrie Seidman, helped me to review archives at the Huntington Library and the John Hay Library at Brown University, respectively.

Among the literary executors and heirs whose generous cooperation contributed enormously to the book are Maxine Winokur, niece of Nathanael West and S. J. Perelman, who not only provided wholehearted support, wisdom, and information, but also responded patiently to my queries and requests; Jack Mearns, John Sanford's ace executor; and Linda Seifert, who spoke to me at length about her mother, Alice Shepard. For excerpts from the lively teenage diaries of Nathanael West's sister, Hinda Weinstein Rhodes, I thank Victoria West Winokur and Marissa Jaret Winokur.

Others who agreed to be interviewed about their family histories are Amy Jacobs Baxter, Jennifer Cazier, Susan Chodorov, Howard and Margaret Flynn, Rosemary Chodorov Gary, Sarah Schrank Gold, Joyce Green, Hillary Hillson, Julius Jacobson, Carl Josephson, Marge Josephson, Warren Josephy, Walter Lister, Jr., Jack McKenney, Robert McKenney, Ellen Pearce, Adam Perelman, Richard Selvey, Nancy Silbert, and Earl Wilson, Jr.

I learned much from people having special knowledge of the places where West and McKenney lived. In Bucks County: Karen and Boyce Budd, Lynn Greening, Fred Israel, John Langdon, Betty Orlemann, Leslie Pappas, Elise Pear, Allen Saalburg, Lester Sciss, Gloria Scoboria, and Bridget Wingert of the *Bucks County Herald*.

In Cleveland: Jim Doherty and Bill White of the DeJohn-Flynn-Mylott Funeral Homes; Susan Pardee of Cleveland Heights High School; Peggy Ottman; Eric J. Silverman of the Cleveland Heights

High School Alumni Foundation; Emma A. Taylor; and Carol Wilcox at the State Teachers Retirement System of Ohio.

In Los Angeles: Douglas Dutton, Yetive Moss, Howard Prouty, Frances Ring, Lore Sabersky, Carolyn See, and Victor and Nancy Sidhu.

Many others contributed valuable information of all kinds. With gratitude to: Dollie Banner, Alison Bond, Henry Bruck, Laurence B. Chase, members of the Cleveland Heights High School class of 1931, Brian Clifford, Prudence Crowther, Herb Dorfman, Jack Earley, Tom Field, April Franzino, Robert Gaye, Michael Granich, Kira Henehan, Ruth Beebe Hill, Louise Hirschfeld, Mike Ingster, Jennifer Josephy, Stephen King, Lynn Lane, Peter Lister, Leila Hadley Luce, Angela Masciarelli, Anthony Melchiorri, Ed Mikol, Bettye Musham, Deborah Paley, Robert Precht, Robert Rippner, Jo Ann Sayers, Victor Schmalzer, Anne Kaufman Schneider, Dieter Seelig, Joan Castle Sitwell, Joel Turner, Deborah Grace Winer, Marian Wood, Scott York, and Matt Yust.

I am blessed with supportive friends who listened to my theories year after year, and offered expert advice on subjects ranging from childhood learning disabilities to the correct translation of Yiddish expressions to the retail prices of 1930 Model A Fords. Thanks and appreciation to Erica Abeel, Anthony Adams, Myron Brenton, Gayle Feldman, Judith Hennessee, Christina Hensler, Diane Jacobs, Judith Rosenblatt, Marlene Sanders, Kendall Taylor, and Amanda Vaill. Lori Benton generously provided helpful technical assistance. The amazing Kevin Fitzpatrick designed the websites for www.lonelyheartsthebook.com, www.nathanaelwest.com, and www.eileenmckenney.com.

I am especially indebted to Susan Hirschman for reading early drafts and offering excellent suggestions.

Kudos to Andrea Schulz for her graceful and sensitive editing of the book and to her assistant, Lindsey Smith, for invaluable editorial help. Thanks also to Larry Cooper and Marian Ryan, the manuscript editors, and to Melissa Lotfy for her smart design.

I could not have undertaken this enterprise without the support of two inspirational individuals: Andre Bernard, whose enthusiasm led him to commission the project for Harcourt in 2004; and Lois Wallace, my agent of twenty-five years, a loyal friend, a terrific adviser, a patient companion on research excursions, and the first to believe that a misfit couple like *Miss Lonelyhearts* and *My Sister Eileen* could share a book.

PHOTO CREDITS

Nathan Weinstein, 1913: Brown University Library, used by permission of Harold Ober Associates. *Eileen and Ruth McKenney, 1915:* From *The Mc-Kenneys Carry On* dust jacket; author's archive. *Nat as a schoolboy:* Collection of Dorothy Herrmann. *Anna Weinstein with daughters:* Courtesy of Nancy Silbert. *Nat at Brown:* Brown University Library, used by permission of Harold Ober Associates. Eileen's yearbook picture: Author's archive. Gay Street (2 photos): Courtesy of Kevin C. Fitzpatrick. *Kenmore Hall Hotel:* Author's archive. *Sid and Laura Perelman:* Courtesy of Maxine R. Winokur. *Nat and John Sanford:* John Sanford Collection, Howard Gotlieb Archival Research Center at Boston University. *Alice Shepard:* Courtesy of Linda Seifert. *Josephine Herbst:* Courtesy of the Josephine Herbst Estate, from the Herbst Collection, Beinecke Rare Book and Manuscript Library, Yale University. *Nat in Erwinna:* Courtesy of the Josephine Herbst Estate, from the Herbst Collection, Beinecke Rare Book and Manuscript Library, Yale University. *Visiting Bucks County farm:* Copyright Lillian Hellman by special arrangement of the Estate of Lillian Hellman. *Ruth McKenney holding Tommy:* Courtesy of Jennifer E. Cazier. *Morris Jacobs with Tommy:* Courtesy of Jennifer E. Cazier. *St. Clair McKelway and friends:* © Bettmann/Corbis. *Katharine and E. B. White:* Photo by Esther Root Adams, August 1935, courtesy of Anthony Adams. *Parva-Sed-Apta:* Courtesy of Joel C. Turner. *Joseph Schrank:* Courtesy of Sarah Schrank Gold. *Nat and Sid Perelman in the Hollywood Hills:* Collection of Dorothy Herrmann. *Film clip from* The Day of the Locust: Paramount Pictures Corporation. *Eileen and her son:* Copyright Hillary R. B. Hillson. *Budd Schulberg:* Courtesy of Budd Schulberg. *Eileen in Hollywood:* Courtesy of Maxine R. Winokur. *Glamorous Eileen:* Courtesy of Maxine R. Winokur. *Nat fishing:* Collection of Dorothy Herrmann. *Eileen with dogs:* Brown University Library, used by permission of Harold Ober Associates. *Obituary clipping:* Courtesy of Maxine R. Winokur. My Sister Eileen *on Broadway:* Jay Parrino's The Mint–MMG Collectibles. *Grave stone:* Courtesy of Kevin C. Fitzpatrick.

INDEX